Overview

Contents

III JavaScript and LiveWire Pro

IV Java and Live Objects

V JavaScript in Practice

VI   JavaScript and Microsoft's Internet Explorer

Appendixes

Acknowledgments

Writing this book has been a process that has involved many people. I would like to thank the Sams.net staff who worked on the development of this book, in particular Kelly Murdock, Howard Jones, and Mark Taber, as well as all those others who contributed in so many ways.

Arman Danesh

About the Authors

Arman Danesh works as the Web Development Specialist at the Bahá'í World Centre in Haifa. He is also Editorial Director of Juxta Publishing Limited, based in Hong Kong. He received his Masters of Science in Mass Communication from Boston University in 1990. He has also worked as a technology journalist and is a regular contributor and Internet columnist for the *South China Morning Post* and *The Dataphile*. Arman lives with his wife, Tahirih, in Haifa, Israel.

Wes Tatters (wtatters@cnrstone.com) is a computer programmer, systems designer, and writer. He is the author of *Teach Yourself Netscape Web Publishing in a Week, Navigating the Internet with America Online*, and *Navigating the Internet with CompuServe* (all published by Sams.net).

Tell Us What You Think!

As a reader, you are the most important critic and commentator of our books. We value your opinion and want to know what we're doing right, what we could do better, what areas you'd like to see us publish in, and any other words of wisdom you're willing to pass our way. You can help us make strong books that meet your needs and give you the computer guidance you require.

Do you have access to CompuServe or the World Wide Web? Then check out our CompuServe forum by typing GO SAMS at any prompt. If you prefer the World Wide Web, check out our site at http://www.mcp.com.

> **NOTE**
>
> If you have a technical question about this book, call the technical support line at (800) 571-5840, ext. 3668.

As the team leader of the group that created this book, I welcome your comments. You can fax, e-mail, or write me directly to let me know what you did or didn't like about this book—as well as what we can do to make our books stronger. Here's the information:

FAX: 317/581-4669

E-mail: newtech_mgr@sams.mcp.com

Mail: Mark Taber
         Publishing Manager
         Sams.net Publishing
         201 W. 103rd Street
         Indianapolis, IN 46290

Introduction

Since Netscape introduced Navigator 2 in 1995, JavaScript has come to be accepted by many as a useful tool for adding interactivity to otherwise static Web pages.

In contrast to Java, which provides powerful capabilities but requires a strong programming background to manage, JavaScript offers a simple way to develop and deploy applications on a Web page.

Presently, JavaScript is the internal scripting language of Netscape's Navigator 3 and is one of two scripting languages available in Microsoft's Internet Explorer 3.0 Web browser. In addition, other vendors have indicated their interest in including JavaScript in their products in the future.

JavaScript has also moved from the client environment to be included as the scripting language in LiveWire, Netscape's client-server application development environment. LiveWire extends a server to support scripted client-server applications.

Given its integration into these leading browser and server products, JavaScript is an important tool for anyone developing sophisticated, interactive applications deployed using Web technology.

Goal of this Book

This book is designed to provide a firm understanding of JavaScript as it is presently deployed in Navigator, Internet Explorer, and LiveWire. After reading this book, you should be able to develop sophisticated client- and server-based applications using JavaScript embedded in HTML documents.

The book begins with a look at the basics of the JavaScript language, including its syntax, key objects and functions. and how to work with data and variables.

Part II examines the client JavaScript as it's implemented in Navigator 3. This includes coverage of the Navigator Object Tree, processing events triggered in the client, designing and producing interactive forms, maintaining client-side state information with cookies, and using JavaScript to work with multiple frames.

Part III moves to the server end and takes a look at the JavaScript implementation in the LiveWire and LiveWire Pro server extensions. Here you see how it's possible to produce server-based applications that can track individual clients using the application and generate dynamic content on the server before sending it to the client.

The fourth section looks at LiveConnect, Netscape's mechanism for connecting Java, plug-ins, and JavaScript in Navigator 3. Using LiveConnect, it's possible to call methods of Java applets from inside JavaScript, to do the same for plug-ins, and for Java applets to call JavaScript functions and methods. LiveConnect extends the functionality of all three beyond their own limitations allowing, for instance, JavaScript to produce Java graphical controls or for HTML buttons to be used to control a plug-in by using JavaScript as the middle layer.

Part V provides four examples of complete JavaScript-based applications:

- A language-switching interface
- JavaScript Solitaire
- A search engine interface
- A personalized home page using LiveWire

Finally, Part VI looks at Microsoft Internet Explorer. In addition to covering the JavaScript implementation in Internet Explorer and the Internet Explorer Object Model, Part VI also covers other additional features of Internet Explorer:

- VBScript—an alternative client-end scripting language
- ActiveX Controls
- HTML Layouts
- The Active Control Pad—a tool for developing Web pages, including ActiveX Controls, HTML Layouts, JavaScript and VBScript.

In addition, the appendixes provide a complete language reference, an HTML guide, a list of character entities and color names and values, an introduction to Navigator Gold—Netscape's integrated Web page editor and browser, and other useful resources.

Who Should Read This Book?

This book is designed as a developer's guide rather than a beginner's introduction to JavaScript. It is of interest to any Web developer looking to add interactivity to a Web site, and application developers who want to deploy network-oriented client-server applications on an intranet, or on the Internet, using Web technology to deliver applications to the desktop.

This book assumes that the reader has experience developing Web sites that use HTML, including forms, tables, and frames, and likely has experience using the Common Gateway Interface (CGI)—either on UNIX systems using PERL, C, or tcl, or on Windows or Mac systems.

It's helpful in grasping the programming concepts used in this book if you have previous programming experience in a structured programming language such as C, C++, Pascal, or Java. These concepts include arrays, procedures and functions, loops, variable scope, and logical operators.

Preparing to Begin

In order to take full advantage of this book, it is useful to have a copy of Navigator 3 to test the examples to experiment for yourself. Navigator 3 is available free of charge on all Windows platforms, for the MacOS, and for most major UNIX systems. You can download a copy from Netscape's Web page at http://home.netscape.com/, or from one of their numerous ftp servers and mirrors:

```
ftp://ftp.netscape.com/
ftp://ftp2.netscape.com/
ftp://ftp3.netscape.com/
ftp://ftp4.netscape.com/
ftp://ftp5.netscape.com/
ftp://ftp6.netscape.com/
ftp://ftp7.netscape.com/
ftp://ftp.leo.chuu.ac.jp/pub/WWW/netscape/ (Japan)
ftp://sunsite.ust.hk/pub/WWW/netscape/ (Hong Kong)
ftp://sunsite.huji.ac.il/Netscape/ (Israel)
ftp://ftp.adelaide.edu.au/pub/WWW/Netscape/ (Australia)
ftp://susnite.doc.ic.ac.uk/computing/information-systems/www/Netscape/ (United
Kingdom)
ftp://ftp.infomratik.rwth-aachen.de/pub/mirror/ftp.netscape.com/ (Germany)
ftp://wuarchive.wustl.edu/packages/www/Netscape/ (U.S.A.)
ftp://sunsite.unc.edu/pub/packages/infosystems/WWW/clients/Netscape/ (U.S.A.)
```

If you want to try Internet Explorer as an alternative browser, go to Microsoft's Internet Explorer Web page http://www.microsoft.com/ie.

Editing and Development Tools

In addition to a JavaScript-capable browser, it's important to find an editing tool with which you feel comfortable.

If you already do a lot of HTML coding, you probably have a favorite text editor which should be suitable for JavaScript programming. Basically, any text editor that produces ASCII text files can be used to editor JavaScript code.

You may also want to look at Netscape Navigator 3.0 Gold, available from the many Netscape ftp servers and mirrors, as an alternative to a plain text editor. Navigator Gold combines the Navigator browser with a WYSIWYG (what you see is what you get) editing environment for HTML and JavaScript.

The ActiveX Control Pad from Microsoft, discussed in Part VI, also provides a functional tool for adding scripts to Web pages based on a model of providing actions for events. It probably represents the first truly drag-and-drop development environment for JavaScript (as well as VBScript, an alternative scripting language in Internet Explorer 3).

I

JavaScript Basics

1

Introducing JavaScript

by Wes Tatters

As discussed in the Introduction, this book assumes that you already have a working knowledge of Netscape Web publishing techniques and the use of HTML. In addition, you also should have a basic understanding of the principals behind the use of JavaScript.

However, if this isn't the case, don't worry. The first section of this book is designed to provide you with all the basic JavaScript knowledge you need to understand the book's later sections.

> **NOTE**
>
> For additional information on HTML you should refer to Appendix B, "HTML Guide." Alternatively, *Teach Yourself Netscape Web Publishing in a Week*, also by Sams.net, provides a solid grounding in the many different aspects of Web publishing particular to the Netscape Navigator Web browser.

To get you started, this chapter examines the following topics:

- What is JavaScript?
- Why Would I Want to Use JavaScript?
- The <SCRIPT> and <SERVER> Tags
- The Development Environment

What Is JavaScript?

According to the press release made jointly by Netscape Communications and Sun Microsystems at JavaScript's launch, "JavaScript is an easy-to-use object scripting language designed for creating live online applications that link together objects and resources on both clients and servers. JavaScript is designed for use by HTML page authors and enterprise application developers to dynamically script the behavior of objects running on either a client or server."

OK, that's the official quote—what does it really mean?

The Basics

If you have ever had any contact with macros or scripting languages like Word Basic or Visual Basic for Applications—possibly in a word processor or a spreadsheet—then you already have a basic understanding of what JavaScript is all about.

In essence, JavaScript is a set of programming commands and instructions that can be used to enhance the way a Web page operates. By incorporating JavaScript commands into a Web page, you can programatically alter the way the page looks, insert or delete parts of a page's contents depending on system requirements, control the operation of a Web server, communicate with an online database, or perform any task previously associated with CGI communications. In addition, JavaScript has become the key to implementing many types of client-side interactivity, including dynamic forms that update in reaction to user input, page content programatically generated as a page loads, reacting to user events (such as clicking on links and submitting forms), and tracking user information between sessions. All of this would be impossible or extremely difficult using traditional CGI scripting.

> **NOTE**
>
> The Common Gateway Interface (CGI) is a mechanism that enables Web publishers to programatically control the operation of a Web server and manage exchanges between the server and a Web browser using scripting languages like PERL and Bourne shell scripts. The most common use for CGI is in the handling of data and requests submitted to a Web site with Forms.

Server JavaScript and Client JavaScript

To achieve such a high level of control over the appearance of a Web page, JavaScript actually comes in two different flavors—*Server-Side* JavaScript and *Client-Side* JavaScript.

> **NOTE**
>
> A server-side language is one that describes programs which run on a Web server, while a client-side language is one that describes programs which actually run on a Web browser.

Server-Side JavaScript

With the release of the Netscape FastTrack Web Server, LiveWire, and LiveWire Pro, the JavaScript language can be used as a server-side CGI replacement for the popular PERL and Bourne shell languages. Most Web publishers will already be familiar with both of these.

In the role of server-side scripting language, what makes JavaScript so different from other CGI languages like PERL is the fact that JavaScript was purposefully built to be a Web scripting language. (See Part III, "JavaScript and LiveWire Pro," for more information about FastTrack, LiveWire, and Server-Side JavaScript.)

While other languages, such as PERL and Bourne shell scripts, have been used for many years as the basis for many of the complex Web sites that currently exist on the Internet, learning to use, or simply coming to grips with their idiosyncrasies is—as many Web publishers discover—often a harrowing experience. Compared to such languages, writing code using Server JavaScript is a relatively straightforward task.

> **NOTE**
>
> Throughout this book, when you see the word JavaScript used on its own, you should treat the reference as one that relates to the JavaScript language in general. On the other hand, when a comment refers to a specific version of JavaScript, the term Client JavaScript or Server JavaScript is used.

Client-Side JavaScript

Apart from acting as a CGI replacement, JavaScript's biggest claim to fame is its ability to run on a Web browser.

When JavaScript first appeared in the early beta versions of Netscape Navigator 2.0 under the name LiveScript, very few people knew exactly what to make of this new capability. Today, many Web developers have begun to develop an appreciation of the advantages client-side programming can bring to a Web page.

The ability to actually generate the contents and appearance of a Web page on the fly (using a Web browser itself instead of relying on CGI programs and the sometimes limited resources available on a Web server) can lead to considerable performance benefits, as later chapters discuss in detail.

> **NOTE**
>
> It is important to understand early on that although the two versions of JavaScript, Client side and Server side, are syntactically the same, each is designed to perform different tasks. In recognition of these differences, each is dealt with in separate sections of the book. This section—Part I—examines the syntax and structure of the JavaScript language itself, then Part II, "JavaScript and Netscape Navigator," explores the unique elements of client side JavaScript. Part III examines the use of JavaScript in a server environment.

The JavaScript Language

The JavaScript language owes much of its heritage to the Java language developed by Sun Microsystems as a distributed Internet programming tool. In fact, much of the syntax and the command structure found in JavaScript is almost identical to that of Java. But unlike Java, which is a strongly typed language typical of the current trends in high-level compiled languages, JavaScript does not demand the same level of type declaration or type checking that Java requires.

In addition, JavaScript is—technically (more on this shortly)—not a compiled language. All compiled languages like Java, C, C++, Pascal, and earlier languages like FORTRAN and COBOL need to be run through a special program called—naturally enough—a compiler, before they can be executed. The compiler takes the English language-like commands that represent the code for a program and converts them into a form the computer can handle. This form is commonly know as a *binary* or *executable*.

NOTE

To learn more about Java and how it relates to JavaScript, refer to Part IV, "Java and Live Objects."

JavaScript, on the other hand, is an interpreted language. What this means is that there is no need for JavaScript programs to be precompiled. Instead, the commands are converted into an executable form at the time the program is run—or at *runtime*. From the Web publisher's point of view, the fact that JavaScript is an interpreted language makes it considerably easier to program, especially when compared to the complexities and idiosyncrasies of compiled languages.

WARNING

A note of caution is necessary—because JavaScript is interpreted, it's possible to generate scripts with errors and deploy them on a Web site, especially because no compiling is necessary before running the program. For this reason, it's important to thoroughly test your JavaScript applications before placing them on a publicly-accessible Web page. Otherwise, users may encounter annoying or troublesome error messages generated by Navigator in response to the errors in your scripts.

NOTE

The introduction of Server JavaScript has slightly muddied the definition of JavaScript as an interpreted language. This is because when server-side applications are created using JavaScript they are precompiled into what is called a bytecode format, which is not unlike a binary executable. For the moment, however, just keep in mind that the interpreted nature of JavaScript is what gives it much of its flexibility and ease of use, and this flexibility is not lost on Server JavaScript.

JavaScript Code Is Embedded

What makes JavaScript so different from other languages is the unique way that it integrates itself with the World Wide Web. Instead of being stored as a separate file—like a CGI script or a Java *applet*—JavaScript code is included as part of a standard HTML document, just like any other HTML tags and elements.

For this reason, JavaScript is effectively an extension of the HTML language all Web publishers are familiar with. To put this in real terms, by using JavaScript you can extend, modify, or manipulate the appearance of a Web page under program-based control.

Basically, JavaScript gives Web publishers the ability to create Web pages dynamically—technically the HTML code that defines how Web pages appear is written dynamically. For example, tasks such as adding the current time and date to a Web page, something which previously could only be accomplished by CGI scripts or server-side includes, can easily be performed using JavaScript at the time a Web page is displayed.

JavaScript Is Object-Oriented

JavaScript's Java heritage also brings with it one of the most powerful design principles present in the current crop of computer languages—*Object-oriented Programming (OOP)*.

Unlike traditional procedural languages such as Pascal and C, which define programs in terms of a top-down approach, object-oriented languages define programs in term of objects and how they interact. Objects consist basically of two things—state and behavior—or to put it in more common programming terms, variables or properties, and functions which in OOP terms are called *methods*. (See Chapter 3, "JavaScript and Object-Oriented Programming" for more information on the use of properties, methods and OOP.)

Why Would I Want to Use JavaScript?

The answer to this question depends, to a certain extent, on exactly what capabilities your Web site requires. If you currently have little or no need for CGI scripting at your site, you may find that on the surface, JavaScript seems to offer little or no benefit. Having said that, as you will soon discover, there are many ways that JavaScript can be used to enhance the capabilities of your Web site with very little effort.

If your site contains extensive CGI scripting, then what Client JavaScript enables you to do is move many simple (and not so simple) programming tasks at the Web browser (or client end) of the system, instead of relying on CGI scripts at the Web server end. In addition, Client JavaScript enables you to control with far greater efficiency the validation of information entered by users on forms and other data-entry screens, performing such task before they are ever transmitted back to a Web server. When integrated with frames, Client JavaScript brings a wide variety of new document presentation options to the Web publishing domain.

On the Server JavaScript side, there are also some benefits in moving from more traditional CGI languages to an integrated, purpose-designed, Web languages. There is a caveat here, however: you naturally need to have access to a Web server that supports Server JavaScript before such benefits can be obtained. Assuming that you do have access to such a Web server, the close association of Server JavaScript with the HTML pages that it relates to leads to a more streamlined approach to Web programming. (See Part III for more information.)

Increasing Server Efficiency

As more and more people begin to use the World Wide Web, many popular Web sites are rapidly being pushed to the limit of their current processing capabilities. As a result, Web operators are continually looking for ways to reduce the processing requirements for their systems—to ward off the need for expensive computer upgrades.

With the introduction of Client JavaScript, some exciting new performance options are now available to Web publishers. For example, say that you have created a form people use to enter their billing details for your online ordering system. When this form is submitted, the first thing your CGI script needs to do is validate the information provided and make sure that all the appropriate fields have been filled out correctly. You need to check that a name and address have been entered, that a billing method has been selected, that credit-card details have been completed—and the list goes on.

But what happens if your CGI script discovers that some information is missing? In this case, you need to alert the user that there are problems with the submission and then ask him to edit the details and resubmit the completed form. This entire process is very resource intensive. The Web server needs to allocate a dedicated resource to perform all the validation and checks. When there are errors, two additional data transmissions must be handled by the server—one to alert the user of errors, and one to receive the updated information.

By moving the initial validation and checking procedures to the Web browser—through the use of JavaScript—you remove the need for any additional transactions, because only one "valid" transaction is ever transmitted back to the server. This simple relocation of the validation process can amount to considerable performance savings when complex forms are being submitted on a regular basis.

CAUTION

Due to the insidious nature of some Web users, you still need to revalidate any data submitted with a JavaScript processed form at the server to protect against the transmission of corrupted data. Unfortunately, because JavaScript code is embedded in Web pages, it is more susceptible to corruption than scripts that run exclusively on your Web server.

JavaScript and Web Service Providers

With an increasing number of Web service providers severely limiting the availability of CGI script support for security reasons, JavaScript offers an excellent method of regaining much of the missing CGI functionality. It moves tasks that would previously have been performed by a server-side CGI script onto the Web browser.

Most Web service providers usually furnish some form of basic CGI script, which can take a form submitted by a user and perform basic processing operations, such as saving it to disk or mailing it to the site's owner. When it comes to more complex forms, however, in the past the only alternatives were to find another service provider or set up your own Web server. Today, with Client JavaScript, this no longer need be the case.

By using a Web service provider's basic form and processing CGI scripts with JavaScript routines buried in the Web page itself, there are very few form-based activities that cannot be duplicated on even the most restrictive and security-conscious Web service provider's site. In addition, by integrating Client and Server JavaScript together with some of the other features supported by Netscape's Web browsers, such as Java and plug-ins, you can do things on a Web page that would never have been considered possible before with even the most capable CGI script.

> **NOTE**
>
> Due to the secure nature of JavaScript, it is likely that in the future Web service providers may prefer to offer JavaScript CGI programming to their clients instead of access to more common languages like PERL.

Submitting Forms Without CGI

The `ACTION` attribute of the `<FORM>` tag has traditionally been associated with a CGI script located on a Web server. But, in fact, any URL can be assigned to the `ACTION` attribute. Doing so, however, has little value unless the resource associated with the URL can process the contents of the form in some way.

> **NOTE**
>
> Chapter 7, "Working with Forms," provides additional information about the `<FORM>` tag.

That having been said, there is one type of URL—apart from a CGI script—that can process the results of a form in a meaningful way—`mailto:`. For example, if you included the following `<FORM>` tag on a page, clicking the submit button would e-mail the contents of the form to my e-mail address:

```
<FORM METHOD="POST" ACTION="mailto:wtatters@world.net">
```

In the past, using such an `ACTION` could be relied upon only when the contents of the form were not vital, because there was no way to validate the information. By using JavaScript, you can now validate the data before it is e-mailed and even perform basic calculations or other processing.

> **NOTE**
>
> Using the `ACTION="mailto:email_address"` option relies on the fact that the Web user has properly configured his or her Web browser to send e-mail. If this has not been done, no e-mail message is transmitted.

Why Use JavaScript Instead of Java?

Unlike Java, JavaScript is designed for non-programmers. As such, it is relatively easy to use and is far less pedantic about details such as the declaration of variable types. In addition, as mentioned previously, you do not need to compile JavaScript code before it can be used—something which you need to do with most other languages, including Java. Both Java and JavaScript have their appropriate place in the realm of Internet programming.

Java is a very powerful language which can be used to create any manner of computer or Internet applications, ranging from simple Ticker Tape displays to complex data acquisition systems and even complete Web browsers. Basically, Java lets you incorporate or program new elements into a Web page. When it comes to working with the HTML contents of a Web page itself, the difficulty involved in doing so with Java basically makes the task impossible.

It is, however, the area of HTML control where JavaScript comes to the fore. JavaScript was designed as an HTML manipulation tool that integrates seamlessly with existing Web pages. On the other hand, if you wanted to build an Internet-based graphical Space Invaders game, JavaScript simply would not be appropriate to the task.

As a result, which language you use for a task in most cases comes down to the specifics of the task. If you want to control the appearance of a Web page or manage the input of data from a user, then JavaScript is the most likely choice. On the other hand, if you want to incorporate a new element or tool into a Web page, then Java is probably the tool for the job.

> **NOTE**
>
> Because JavaScript programs and Java applets can actually communicate with each other, the two languages should not be considered competitors, but complementary tools which can be used together. (See Chapter 15, "Communicating with Java Applets," for more information about how these two languages work together.)

The <SCRIPT> and <SERVER> Tags

As was mentioned previously, the code for JavaScript programs is embedded directly into Web pages. To accommodate the inclusion of JavaScript programs in a normal HTML document, Netscape has introduced two new tags, the <SCRIPT> tag for client-side code, and the <SERVER> tag for server-side code.

The <SCRIPT> Tag

By placing a <SCRIPT> tag in a document, you tell the Web browser to treat any lines of text following the tag as client-side script—program code that is to be executed by the Web browser—rather than as content for the Web page. This action then continues until a corresponding </SCRIPT> tag is encountered, at which point the Web browser reverts to its usual mode of operation, treating text as Web content.

The <SCRIPT> tag may also include a LANGUAGE attribute to declare the scripting language to be used. Currently, the two possible values for this attribute are LANGUAGE="LiveScript" and LANGUAGE="JavaScript". As a rule, however, you should always use the JavaScript option because LiveScript is included only for legacy scripts, and it is doubtful whether it will be supported in future Netscape Navigator releases.

> **TIP**
>
> As JavaScript evolves, the use of the LANGUAGE attribute is becoming less relevant. In fact, many Web publishers no longer bother about including it in their Web pages. However, as a matter of style it is still a good idea to include it so that people have some idea about what all this strange code is doing in your Web pages.

The <SERVER> Tag

Like the <SCRIPT> tag, by placing a <SERVER> tag in a document you indicate that any lines of text following the tag are to be treated as JavaScript source code. But in the case of the <SERVER>

tag the program code is to be executed by the Web server instead of the Web browser. As was the case for the <SCRIPT> tag, this action then continues until a corresponding </SERVER> tag is encountered.

> **NOTE**
>
> Because Server JavaScript code needs to be packaged into a Web application before it can be run, it is important to note that simply putting <SERVER> tags into a Web document doesn't automatically start any programs running on a Web server.

The Structure of a JavaScript Script

When you include any JavaScript code in an HTML document, apart from using the <SCRIPT> or <SERVER> tags, you should also follow a few other conventions:

- As a rule, <SCRIPT> and <SERVER> tags should be placed inside the <HEAD> and </HEAD> tags at the start of your document and not inside the <BODY> tags. This isn't a hard and fast requirement, but it is a standard that many Web publishers are adopting. Basically, because the code for your scripts is not to be displayed on the Web page itself, it should not be included in the <BODY> section, but in the <HEAD> section with all the other control and information tags, such as <TITLE> and <META>. The main exception to this rule is when you want to use JavaScript to generate dynamic HTML content to be displayed in the Web page.

- Because Web browsers that are not JavaScript-aware will attempt to treat your JavaScript code as part of the contents of your Web page, it is vitally important that you surround your entire JavaScript code with a <!-- comment tag -->. Doing this ensures that non-JavaScript-aware browsers can at least display your page correctly, if not make it work properly.

- Unlike HTML, which uses the <!-- comment tag -->, comments inside JavaScript code use the // symbol. Any line of JavaScript code that starts with this symbol is treated as a comment and ignored.

Taking these three points into consideration, the basic structure for including JavaScript code inside an HTML document looks something like the following:

```
<HEAD>
<TITLE>Test script</TITLE>
<SCRIPT LANGUAGE="JavaScript">
<!-- Use the start of a comment tag to hide the JavaScript code
  Your JavaScript code goes here
// close the comment tag on the line immediately before the </SCRIPT> tag --!>
</SCRIPT>
</HEAD>
```

```
<BODY>
    Your Web document goes here
</BODY>
</HTML>
```

The SRC Attribute

Besides the LANGUAGE attribute, the <SCRIPT> tag also can include a SRC attribute. Including an SRC attribute enables a JavaScript script stored in a separate file to be included as part of the current Web page. This is a handy option if you have several Web pages that all use the same JavaScript code and you don't want to type the scripts separately into each page.

When used like this, the <SCRIPT> tag takes the following form:

```
<SCRIPT LANGUAGE="JavaScript" SRC="http://script.js">
```

In this form, *script* can be any relative or absolute URL, and *.js* is the file extension for a JavaScript file.

One of the most important uses for the SRC attribute is the creation of what are called *Code libraries*. As you begin to work with JavaScript you will often find yourself including code in one page that needs to appear on others. By using the SRC attribute, you can write the code once and store it as a separate file. When you need access to the code, simply append it to the pages where you need it by using the SRC attribute.

The Development Environment

Because all JavaScript code is simply a part of an HTML document, you don't need to use any special tools to create your JavaScript programs. If you currently have a HTML editor or text editor (see Figure 1.1) that you are happy using, then for the most part you probably don't need any other tools.

Netscape GOLD

If, on the other hand, you are currently looking for a tool to assist you with your Web publishing needs, then the Netscape Navigator Gold program would be well worth a look. Apart from being a Web browser, Navigator Gold is also a HTML editor. (See Figure 1.2.)

By integrating the Web browsing capabilities of Netscape Navigator with an HTML editor, Netscape Communications has created a program that can assist greatly in the streamlining of your Web publishing tasks.

FIGURE 1.1.

Any text editor can be used to write JavaScript code.

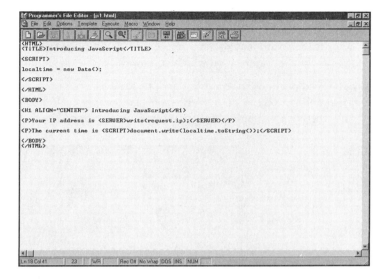

FIGURE 1.2.

Netscape Navigator Gold is both a Web browser and a HTML editor.

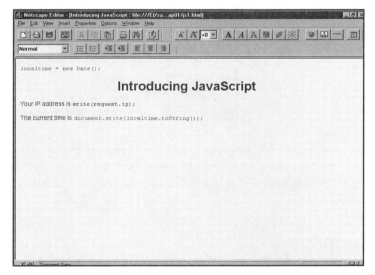

NOTE

To learn more about Netscape Navigator Gold refer to Appendix A, "Netscape Navigator and Netscape Gold."

LiveWire

For those readers who plan to make use of the capabilities provided by Server JavaScript, there is one additional program with which you need to become familiar.

As mentioned previously, Server JavaScript code needs to be precompiled into a Web application before it can be run on a Web server. To compile a Web application you need to have access to the Netscape Site Manager application shown in Figure 1.3.

FIGURE 1.3.

Netscape Site Manager lets you manage all aspects of your Web site.

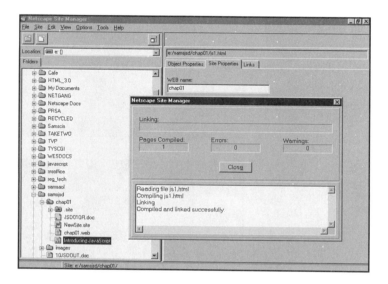

Site Manager, which is a part of the LiveWire server extensions, enables you to manage the layout and content of your Web site. It also includes the tools required to compile your Server JavaScript code into a Web application so that it can be executed correctly by a Netscape Web server.

Summary

JavaScript is an object-based scripting language designed by Netscape Communications specifically for manipulating and managing the contents of Web pages. JavaScript programs can be run either on a Web server or Web browser, depending upon your particular needs and requirements.

The most significant feature of JavaScript, and the one that separates it from other scripting languages, is the way that JavaScript code is physically embedded into a Web page instead of being stored in a stand-alone file. This integration, and JavaScript's ability to modify and manipulate the contents of a Web page dynamically, make it ideally suited to even the most complex Web publishing needs.

2

The JavaScript Language

by Wes Tatters

Before you delve into the specifics of JavaScript programming—whether on a Web server or a Web browser—it's important to understand the basic syntax of a JavaScript program.

To this end, this chapter examines the following topics, which are generic to both Server and Client JavaScript:

- Data types and variables
- Expressions and operators
- Programming commands

Data Types and Variables

Unlike most high-level languages, which expect you to define or declare all variables before they are used, JavaScript adopts a more flexible approach to variable management.

To explain how variables work in JavaScript, this section looks first at how variables are defined, and then at the data types that can be stored by a variable. And then, finally, it examines the literal values that can be assigned to a variable.

Variables

A *variable* is basically a user-defined container that can hold a value of some sort, be it a number, some text, or something else. But unlike most high-level languages that force you to limit the contents of each variable to a specific type, JavaScript variables are said to be loosely typed language. This means that you don't need to specify the type of information a variable contains when the variable is created. In fact, the same variable can be assigned to data of different types depending on your requirements.

To declare a variable in a JavaScript program, you would write the following:

```
var variablename;
```

In this form, *variablename* is any unique name you choose, provided that it meets the following requirements. Variable names can consist of any combination of the following:

- the letters A through Z
- the letters a through z
- the numbers 0 through 9 (but cannot start with a number)
- the underscore '_' symbol

In addition, variables are case sensitive. This means a variable named *Number* and a variable named *number* are treated as separate containers.

The only other limitation placed on variable names is that you cannot use what are called *reserved words* as variables. Table 2.1 lists the current reserved words for JavaScript. Many of these may already be familiar to you as JavaScript commands, while others will be recognizable by people familiar with Java.

Table 2.1. JavaScript reserved words.

abstract	continue	float	int	public	throws
boolean	default	for	interface	return	transient
break	do	function	long	short	true
byte	double	goto	native	static	try
case	else	if	new	super	var
catch	extends	implements	null	switch	void
char	false	import	package	synchronized	while
class	final	in	private	this	with
const	finally	instanceof	protected	throw	

Data Types

A variable in JavaScript can be assigned any type of value supported by the language definition. Currently, JavaScript recognizes five *data types*:

Numbers   A number can be any value, be it an integer (1, 25, -133) or floating point (0.299, 20.26, -100.908).

Strings   A string can represent any textual information such as: "Hello, my name is Wes Tatters."

Booleans   A Boolean can be either `true` or `false`.

> **NOTE**
>
> Unlike some other languages where Boolean values are represented by numbers such as 0 or 1, in JavaScript only `true` or `false` are acceptable.

Nulls	Null is a special statement that represents a null value. When you first declare a variable it is automatically assigned a value of null. (It is important to understand that a null value is different from a zero or an empty string.)
Objects	Objects are storage containers that hold both the value of a data element and any functions or methods that operate on that data. Chapter 3, "JavaScript and Object-Oriented Programming," explores the concept and use of objects in detail.

NOTE

To keep the JavaScript language simple and user friendly, there are no explicit `int`, `short`, `float`, `double`, `long`, or `char` data types. In addition, there is no mechanism for defining your own data types using `typedef`-like commands.

Literals

There are basically two ways that a variable can be assigned a value. It can be assigned at runtime based on some interaction by the user. (See Chapter 7, "Working with Forms," for more information.) Or it can be assigned by the programmer using what is called a *literal*.

In the most basic terms, a literal is a fixed value that can be assigned to a variable when a program is written. The following types of literals can be used in a JavaScript program.

- Integers
- Floating points
- Booleans
- Strings
- Escape characters

Integers

An *integer* is a whole number—such as 1, 2, 3, 4, 100—which can have either a positive or negative value. To assign an integer literal to a variable in a JavaScript program, you would write something like the following:

```
var variablename = integer_literal;
 or
variablename = integer_literal;
```

In the first form, a new variable is defined and assigned a integer value, while in the second form an existing variable is assigned an integer value.

> **TIP**
>
> The '=' sign placed between the `variable` and the `integer_literal` is called an assignment operator. See the "Expressions and Operators" topic later in the chapter for more detail.

In addition to the standard base 10 (Decimal) format, integer literals also can be written in either base 8 (Octal) or base 16 (Hex) format. Octal integers are indicated by placing a leading 0 in front of the number and Hex integers by placing a lead 0x in front of the number.

For example:

```
base10number = 10;
octalnumber = 012;
hexnumber = 0x0A;
```

Floating Points

A *floating point* literal can represent any number that is not considered a whole number or integer. That is, any number with a fractional component such as 1.2345 or -1.2345, or an exponential component like 12345E-4 or -12345E-4.

To assign a floating point literal to a variable in a JavaScript program you would write something like the following:

```
var variablename = float_literal;
 or
variblename = float_literal;
```

> **CAUTION**
>
> In the current implementation of JavaScript, on certain computer platforms, floating point literals sometimes suffer from what are called floating point errors.
>
> These errors sometimes result in a slight miscalculation of decimal values. This is, however, expected to be rectified before the release of Netscape Navigator 3.

Booleans

There are only two acceptable values for a Boolean literal. These are `true` or `false`. To assign a Boolean literal to a variable in a JavaScript program, you would write something like the following:

```
var variablename = true;
 or
variblename = false;
```

Strings

A *string* literal is simply a string of zero or more characters surrounded by either single (') or double (") quotes. To assign a string literal to a variable you would write something like the following:

```
var stringname = "some text";
var stringname = 'some text';
or
stringname = "some text";
stringname = 'some text';
```

> **NOTE**
>
> Be careful not to mix your single and double quotes when defining a string literal. If a literal starts with a double quote it must end with a double quote, and likewise for single quotes.

Escape Characters

When creating string literals, you may occasionally want to include characters in your string that have no physical representation. Such characters might include the backspace, tab, new line, or carriage return.

To represent these characters in a string literal, you first need to include a special character called the escape character. The escape character is represented by a backslash '\.' This tells JavaScript that the character following the backslash represents a special control character and not its actual value. Table 2.2 outlines the special characters currently supported by JavaScript.

Table 2.2. Escaped or special characters.

Escaped Character	*Description*
\'	Insert a quote.
\"	Insert a double quote.
\b	Insert a backspace.
\f	Insert a form feed.
\n	Insert a new line character.
\r	Insert a carriage return.
\t	Insert a tab character.

Expressions and Operators

Once you have defined a variable, you can assign new values to the variable, or work with the existing value using what are called *operators* and *expressions*.

This section examines what an expression is and explains the wide variety of operators provided by JavaScript.

What Are Expressions?

To quote from Netscape Communications' online JavaScript guide, "An expression is any valid set of literals, variables, operators, and expressions that evaluates to a single value."

Think back to first grade math and the question, "What is 1 + 1?" The statement 1 + 1 represents an expression. It describes a set of information that evaluates to a single value, which in this case is 2.

1 + 1 represents the most simple form of expression. It contains two integer literals that are added together using the *arithmetic operator* plus "+" (discussed in more detail later). This basic expression forms the basis of all other types of expression.

Assigned Expressions

To take this example one step further, look at the statement

```
result = 1 + 1;
```

This is also an expression. However, this time the result of the expression is explicitly assigned to the variable `result` using the assignment operator equals "=."

Expression Types

By using the various operators described later in this section, you can create three different types of expressions in JavaScript. These types are as follows:

Arithmetic Expressions	Any expression that evaluates to a number is considered an arithmetic expression.
Logical Expressions	These are a special group of expressions that evaluate to either a true or false result.
String Expressions	A string expression can be used to add strings together. It evaluates to a new string.

Conditional Expressions

There is a special type of expression provided by JavaScript called a *conditional expression*. A conditional expression is one that can evaluate to one of two different results depending on a user-defined condition. A conditional expression takes the following form:

```
condition ? expression1 : expression2
```

`condition` is a logical expression that must evaluate to either `true` or `false`. If the condition evaluates to true then the entire expression evaluates to *expression1*. If the `condition` evaluates to `false` then the entire expression evaluates to *expression2*.

Supported Operators

In their most basic state, all expressions take the same general form:

```
left_operand operator right_operand
```

Each *operand* can be either a variable or literal value, depending on the type of expression and the type of *operator* that controls the expression.

Table 2.3 outlines all of the operators that can be used in JavaScript expressions. In this table the operators are grouped by the following types:

Arithmetic Operators	Arithmetic operators take numeric literals or numeric variables as their operands and return a numerical value.
Bitwise Operators	Bitwise operators treat their operands as a set of binary bits (zeros and ones). They perform operations on this binary representation, then return the result as a numeric values.
Logical Operators	Logical operators work with Boolean (logical) values and they return a Boolean value. (Booleans use only `true` and `false` values.)
Comparison Operators	Comparison operators compare the values of their operands and return a Boolean value. This Boolean value indicates if the result of the comparison was `true` or not `true` (`false`).
String Operators	String operators take string values in their operands and return a string value as the result.
Assignment Operator	Assignment operators assign a new value to their left operand based on the value of their right operand. The only limitation placed on this type of expression is that the left operand cannot be literal.

Table 2.3. Summary of JavaScript operators.

Name of Operator	Syntax	Result
Arithmetic Operators		
Addition	x + y	Adds x and y.
Subtraction	x - y	Subtracts y from x.
Multiplication	x * y	Multiplies x by y.
Division	x / y	Divides x by y.
Modulus	x % y	Evaluates to the remainder when dividing x by y.
Preincrement	++x	Adds 1 to x.
Postincrement	x++	Evaluates to x then adds 1 to the value of x.
Predecrement	- -x	Subtracts 1 from x.
Postdecrement	x- -	Evaluates to x then subtracts 1 from the value of x.
Unary negation	-x	Negates the value of x.
Bitwise Operators		
Bitwise AND	x & y	AND's the binary representation of x and y.
Bitwise OR	x ¦ y	OR's the binary representation of x and y.
Bitwise XOR	x ^ y	Exclusive OR's the binary representation of x and y.
Left Shift	x << y	Shifts bits in the binary representation of x, y positions to the left. Zero value bits are shifted in from the right.
Sign-propagating Right Shift	x >> y	Shifts bits in the binary. representation of x, y positions to the right. Value of left-most bit is shifted in from the left.

continues

Table 2.3. continued

Name of Operator	Syntax	Result
Zero-fill Right Shift	x >>> y	Shifts bits in the binary representation of x, y positions to the right. Zero value bits are shifted in from the left.

Logical Operators

And	exp1 && exp2	Evaluates to true if *exp1* and *exp2* both evaluate to true.
Or	exp1 ¦¦ exp2	Evaluates to true if either *exp1* or *exp2* evaluate to true.
Not	!exp1	Evaluates to true if *exp1* is not true.

Comparison Operators

Equals	x == y	Returns true if x is equal to y.
Not equal	x != y	Returns true if x is not equal to y.
Less than	x < y	Returns true if x is less than y.
Less than or equal to	x <= y	Returns true if x is less than or equal to y.
Greater than	x > y	Returns true if x is greater than y.
Greater than or equal to	x >= y	Returns true if x is greater than or equal to y.

String Operators

Concatenation	x + y	Concatenates string x and string y together.

Assignment Operators

Equal	x = y	Assigns the value of y to x.
Compound Arithmetic	x += y	Adds y to x and assigns the result to x.
	x -= y	Subtracts y from x and assigns the result to x.

Name of Operator	Syntax	Result
	x *= y	Multiplies x by y and assigns the result to x.
	x /= y	Divides x by y and assigns the result to x.
	x %= y	Takes the modulus of x and y and assigns the result to x.
Compound Bitwise	x &= y	AND is the binary representation of x and y and assigns the result to x.
	x ¦= y	OR is the binary representation of x and y and assigns the result to x.
	x ^= y	Exclusive OR is the binary representation of x and y and assigns the result to x.
	x <<= y	Shifts bits in the binary representation of x, y positions to the left. Zero value bits are shifted in from the right and the result is assigned to x.
	x >>= y	Shifts bits in the binary representation of x, y positions to the right. Value of left-most bit is shifted in from the left and the result is assigned to x.
	x >>>= y	Shifts bits in the binary representation of x, y positions to the right. Zero value bits are shifted in from the left and the result is assigned to x.

Operator Precedence

When you combine more than one operator in an expression, the precedence of operators determines the order in which they are applied when evaluating an expression.

The precedence of operators for JavaScript, from highest to lowest, is as follows:

call, member	`() []`
negation/increment	`! ~ - ++ --`
multiply/divide	`* / %`
addition/subtraction	`+ -`
Bitwise shift	`<< >> >>>`
relational	`< <= > >=`
equality	`== !=`
bitwise-and	`&`
bitwise-xor	`^`
bitwise-or	`¦`
logical-and	`&&`
logical-or	`¦¦`
conditional	`?:`
assignment	`= += -= *= /= %= <<= >>= >>>= &= ^= ¦=`
comma	`,`

When calculating the value of an expression, any operators higher up the precedence list are evaluated before those lower on the list. In most situations this order is acceptable, however, you can override the order using parentheses when needed.

For example, `'10 + 10 * 10 + 10'` evaluates to 120 using the normal order of precedence rules because `'10 * 10'` is evaluated first. But by using parentheses, as in `'( 10 + 10 ) * ( 10 + 10 )'` the result is 400 because the two `'10 + 10'` expressions are forced to evaluate first.

Programming Commands

Regardless of what language you use, a program is simply a set of instructions that describe to a computer some action, or group of actions, you want it to perform. In the most basic case, this set of instructions starts at the beginning of a list of code and works through each instruction in the list one at a time until it reaches the end:

```
<SCRIPT LANGUAGE="JavaScript">
// start of program - NOTE: lines that start with '//' are treated as comments
document.write( "step one") ;
```

```
document.write( "step two") ;
// end of program
</SCRIPT>
```

> **NOTE**
>
> `document.write()` is a method associated with the document object in Client
> JavaScript. It is used to send text to a Web page. Chapter 5, "The Netscape Navigator
> Object Tree," discusses its use and syntax in detail.

You will rarely want a program to proceed straight through a list of steps—especially in JavaScript—because it would be easier to write the messages on the screen using HTML than to code them by using JavaScript. For this reason, most programming languages include a basic set of instructions that enable you to control the flow of the instructions.

The final section of this chapter examines each of the basic commands and statements included in the JavaScript language and discusses the reasons from their use.

Comments

The first command is not so much a programming command as the lack of one. Comments are used in a JavaScript program to insert messages and other information that you don't actually want to be executed.

By placing // before any text on a line of JavaScript code you indicate that any text following it should be treated as comments. Alternatively, if you want to enter a number of lines of comments, simply surround the lot with /* *your comments go here* */.

```
/* This comment can be spread
 over a number of lines */

// This is a comment on a single line

var number = 1; // this is also a comment
```

Statement Blocks

A statement block is a group of statements or programming commands that have been surrounded by a pair of braces {...}. You can use a statement block anywhere in your JavaScript program that a single command would normally be placed, as shown here:

```
{
 Place as many lines of code ;
 as you need inside the statement block ;
}
```

For the most part, you only used statement blocks in combination with other commands that are discussed later in the chapter.

The Semicolon

In JavaScript, the semicolon ';' has a special purpose. It is used as a separator between program statements. By using a semicolon the following line of code is totally acceptable:

```
var num1 = 1 ; var num2 = 3 ; var num3 = num1 + num2 ;
```

When JavaScript encounters this line, it uses the semicolons to indicate where each new statement starts and the old one ends. In fact, as far as JavaScript is concerned, the previous line of code is no different from the following:

```
var num1 = 1 ;
var num2 = 3 ;
var num3 = num1 + num2 ;
```

> **NOTE**
>
> The current version of Client JavaScript does not require a semicolon after each statement if they are placed on separate lines. For consistency's sake, however, it is good practice to include them.

var **Revisited**

The var statement was introduced during the discussion of variable declarations earlier in this chapter. The purpose of the var statement is to indicate the declaration of a new variable. See the following example:

```
var somevariable = "some value";
```

This declares a new variable and stores the string literal "some value" inside it.

> **NOTE**
>
> The current version of JavaScript does not actually require the use of the var statement at all. In fact, if you use a variable name that has not been declared previously, JavaScript automatically declares it. However, this may change in the future, so it is a good idea to use the var statement for all new variable declarations.

Conditional Tests

One of the most common actions performed by most computer programs is the conditional execution of program code depending on the prevailing situation when the program is run.

By using conditional commands you can control if and when commands or blocks of commands are executed.

The `if` Statement

The first instruction used for this purpose is called the `if` statement. It enables you to perform tests inside program code to determine which parts of the program should be run under any given situation. The basic syntax of the if statement is

```
if ( logical expression ) statement;
```

For example, assume that you have a Web site that asks whether a person is male or female. In such cases, you might want to respond to the person using a gender-specific response, based on the indicated sex:

```
if ( Sex == "male" ) document.write("Thank you for your response, Sir" ) ;
if ( Sex == "female" ) document.write("Thank you for your response, Madam" ) ;
```

If this piece of code were run and the variable `Sex` had been assigned a value of `"male"`, the first `document.write()` method would be called. If it had been assigned a value of `"female"`, the second statement would be displayed.

The logical expression next to the `if` statement performs a comparison between the variable `Sex` and the word `"male"`. This comparison is controlled by what are called comparison operators. In this case, a test for equivalence was performed as signified by the == symbol. Table 2.3, discussed previously, lists the comparison operators currently recognized by JavaScript.

The previous code also could have been written using the statement block parentheses discussed earlier in this chapter. In such a case the *statement* section of the `if` command would be replaced by a statement block as shown here:

```
if ( Sex == "male" ) {
 document.write("Thank you for your response, Sir" ) ;
}
if ( Sex == "female" ) {
 document.write("Thank you for your response, Madam" ) ;
}
```

`if…else`

The preceding example also could have been written in a slightly different way, by using a different version of the `if` statement that incorporates an `else` statement:

```
if ( Sex == "male" ) {
 document.write("Thank you for your response, Sir" ) ;
} else {
 document.write("Thank you for your response, Madam" ) ;
}
```

In this example, because there is no need for a second `if` test—because a person can be only male or female—the `else` statement was used to tell the program to display the second message if the first test failed.

NOTE

In both of the preceding examples, any number of statements could be assigned to each outcome by including each statement inside the appropriate set of braces.

Looping Statements

On occasion, you will want a group of statements to run multiple times rather than just once. Two looping statements are supported by JavaScript to carry out this task. The first kind of statement, called a `for` loop, is ideal for situations in which you want a group of instructions to occur a specified number of times. And the second kind, the `while` loop, is better suited to situations in which the number of loops required is to be determined by an outside source.

`for` Loops

The basic structure of a `for` loop looks like this:

```
for (var count = 1; count <= 10; ++count ) {
 your statements go here ;
}
```

In this example, a variable called `count` is declared and set to a value of 1. Then a test is made to see whether the value of `count` is less than or equal to 10. If it is, all the statements inside the braces, `{}`, following the `for` statement, are executed once. Then, the value of `count` is incremented by 1 by the statement `++count`, and the `count <= 10` test is performed again. If the result is still true, all the instructions inside the braces are executed again. This process then proceeds until the value of `count` is greater than 10, at which point the `for` loop ends.

`while` Loops

The basic structure of a `while` loop looks like the following:

```
while ( logical expression ) {
 your statements go here ;
}
```

Unlike the `for` loop, which has a built-in increment mechanism, the only test required for a `while` loop is a true result from the logical expression or condition test following the `while` statement. This test could be an equivalence test, as in `a == b`, or any of the other tests mentioned previously in the `if` statement.

As long as this condition tests true, the statements inside the braces following the `while` loop continue to run forever—or at least until you close your Web browser.

> **CAUTION**
>
> When using `while` loops, you need to avoid creating loops that never end. (Such a loop is known as an infinite loop.) If you do manage to create an endless loop, about the only option you have to halt the loop is to shut down the Web browser or Web server.

break

When working with `for` and `while` loops, you will sometimes encounter situations where you need to terminate the loop prematurely. The easiest way to do this is by using the `break` statement, as shown here:

```
while ( true ) {
 Some code;
 if ( sometest ) break;
 Some other code;
}
```

When a program encounters a `break` statement while executing a `for` or `while` loop, the loop is terminated immediately and program execution moves to the first command following the loop.

continue

The `continue` statement works similarly to the `break` statement. Instead of terminating the loop entirely, the `continue` statement terminates the current iteration of the loop:

```
for ( var count = 1; count < 100 ; count++ ) {
 Some code ;
 if ( sometest ) continue ;
 Some other code ;
}
```

When a program encounters a `continue` statement while executing a `for` or `while` loop, the current pass through the loop is terminated, ignoring additional commands. Program execution moves back to the first statement of the loop.

Functions

The final programming element for this chapter is that of functions. In many programming languages, including JavaScript, functions—and their object-oriented relative, the method—represent the basic building block for expanding the functionality of the language.

Basically, functions are small blocks of program code that can be called by other parts of a program. There are two types of functions supported in JavaScript—pre-defined functions and user-defined functions.

Pre-defined functions have been built in the JavaScript language, while user-defined functions are created by JavaScript programmers like yourself.

Defining a Function

To define a function for a JavaScript program, you write something like the following:

```
<SCRIPT LANGUAGE="JavaScript">

function functionName( operands ) {
 The actions to be performed by your function go here ;
}
</SCRIPT>
```

functionName is any unique name you choose, and *operands* is a list of any values or variables you want to hand to the function. Following the function definition and inside the set of braces, { }, you include the list of instructions you want the function to perform. These could be a set of calculations, validation tests for a form, or just about anything else you can think of.

> **NOTE**
>
> JavaScript also includes a set of built-in objects and functions that enable you to perform mathematical operations, string manipulation, and date and time calculations. Many of these functions are examined in Chapter 4, "General Objects and Functions."

The `return` Statement

The `return` statement is used in conjunction with a function definition to stop the execution of the function and return program control to the program code that called the function in the first place. The syntax for the `return` statement follows:

```
return expression;
```

expression can be any value. The contents of *expression* are returned to the calling program as the value of the function.

Using Functions

Once a function has been defined for a JavaScript program, it can then be called from anywhere else in the program, in the same way that you use JavaScript's built-in commands. Take for example the following function definition:

```
function add( op1, op2 ) {
 return ( op1 + op2 );
}
```

In this code a function called `add()` is defined with two operands called `op1` and `op2`. These are the variables that receive values sent from some calling program code. In the `add()` function, the contents of the `op1` and `op2` variables are added together. The result is handed back from the function to the called program using the return statement.

By including the add() function definition as a part of a JavaScript program you make it available for use anywhere within the current Web page. Take for example the following program:

```
<SCRIPT LANGUAGE="JavaScript">

//The function definition starts here
function add( op1, op2 ) {
 return ( op1 + op2 );
}

//The JavaScript program code starts here
var num1 = 50;
var num2 = 25;
var answer = 0;

answer = add( num1, num2 ); // this line calls the function add()

document.write( answer );
</SCRIPT>
```

With the add() function defined at the top of the program, it can simply be used as though it was an expression, because it evaluates to a result.

> **NOTE**
>
> Unlike some other languages, there is no physical requirement covering where in your program code function definitions should be placed. However, many programmers find that declaring all their JavaScript functions at the top of a Web page makes for easier code management.

Variable Scope

When you begin to deal with functions, you need to be aware of a new facet to variables.

As a rule, any variables that you declare inside a JavaScript program are automatically available throughout the entire program. Such variables are said to be *global variables*. However, when you declare a variable inside a function, that variable is only available inside the function itself. Such a variable is said to be a *local variable*.

Summary

Despite the fact that JavaScript is a relatively simple language in both syntax and variable definition, it provides enough powerful capabilities to handle all but the most complex of Web publishing needs.

Its true power, does not, however, lie in its seemingly limited command set or data types, but in the object-based framework that surrounds it. The principles behind this object-based structure are examined in Chapter 3.

3

JavaScript and Object-Oriented Programming

by Arman Danesh

To effectively use JavaScript, it's important to understand the underlying concepts of object-oriented programming and how they relate to JavaScript.

Although JavaScript is object-based, it doesn't offer the full power of object-oriented languages, such as Java and C++. Still, without understanding objects, properties, and methods and how they all work, it isn't possible to leverage all the potential of JavaScript.

This understanding of objects and how they work is especially important for programmers who have no previous experience with object-oriented languages and have used only procedural programming languages, such as C and Pascal.

This chapter briefly examines object-oriented programming and then moves on to look at the following:

■ The JavaScript object model
■ The Navigator object tree
■ User-defined objects
■ Arrays

Object-Oriented Programming

Describing objects, as used in programming, requires an analogy. In her popular book, *Teach Yourself Java*, well-known Web author Laura Lemay uses Lego pieces as an example. These small plastic building blocks—which take many different shapes and sizes—can be put together to create any number of different objects, from a car to an airplane to a city.

These individual pieces are *objects*, and the combined result is an *application* or a *program*. By piecing together many objects, a complete program is built. Each object is self-contained; it has a specific role to play and pre-defined ways of talking to other objects.

Beyond this example, another analogy can be used to describe objects themselves. Individual objects are made up of related information and methods for dealing with that information. For example, a car has many pieces of information, including its year of manufacture, its manufacturer, its model, its color, and its owner. This information can be used to print a specification of the car, to change its owner, or to paint it a new color, among other things.

In object-oriented programming terms, these pieces of data are known as *properties* of an object; the different actions you can take based on that data are called *methods*.

For instance, the car object could have the following properties:

■ year
■ make
■ model

- color
- owner

It also could have these methods:

- `printInfo`
- `newOwner`
- `rePaint`

Classes

The `car` object just defined is really more of a template for multiple objects with similar properties and methods, which are collectively called a *class*. A class defines all the properties and methods of a particular set of objects.

Rather than defining individual objects, object-oriented programming works by defining classes, or abstract models, for the different objects a program needs to work with.

Instances

Once a class has been defined for a general category of objects, you need to create specific instances of it for each particular case to which the object applies. For instance, you could take the `car` class defined earlier and create instances of it for Joe's red 1990 Ford Mustang and Sue's green 1994 Honda Accord. The year property of the first instance would be 1990, and the color property of the second instance would be green.

Each of these would be an *instance* of the car class. This instance is an actual object, and although the class is general, the instance is a specific concrete representation of the class.

Inheritance

Classes are grouped together into hierarchies, which makes it possible for classes to inherit properties and methods from an existing class and then add or change properties and methods for a specific purpose. This is called *inheritance*—when a new class inherits the properties and methods of an existing class.

As an example, you could create a new class called `foreignCar` that's a subclass (one layer lower in the hierarchy) of the `car` class defined earlier. This new class will inherit all the properties and methods of the `car` class, but you could extend it by adding a new property—`country`— to indicate the country of manufacture and redefine the `printInfo` method to also print the country of manufacture.

The JavaScript Object Model

With this basic understanding of object-oriented programming, you can see what aspects of it are applied in JavaScript. JavaScript is not a true object-oriented programming language. Instead, it uses objects and instances but abandons some of the larger, and more complex, mechanisms, such as classes and inheritance. For this reason, JavaScript is often referred to as being *object-based* rather than object-oriented.

JavaScript offers a compact set of data types, functions, and keywords, along with sets of client and server objects that are enough for most scripting needs.

The Navigator Object Hierarchy

The set of built-in objects in client JavaScript offers information about the currently loaded Web page, as well as the environment in which that page exists. These objects are organized in the Navigator Object Hierarchy, which takes the following form:

```
navigator
    window
    frame
    location
    history
    document
            forms
            anchors
            links
```

These objects, and other subobjects, make up the key objects available in client JavaScript. They are outlined in Table 3.1.

Table 3.1. The Navigator Object Hierarchy.

Object	Description
navigator	Provides information about the client browser.
window	Provides methods and properties for dealing with an actual Navigator window. Each window is a separate object.
frame	Provides properties and methods for dealing with a frame. Each frame is a separate object.
location	Provides methods and properties for working with the URL loaded in the window.
history	Is used for working with the window's history list.

Object	Description
document	Provides properties and methods for working with a document, creating output in the document window, and performing other document-related tasks.
forms	Provides properties and methods for working with a form and its elements. Each form is a separate form object.
anchors	Provides mechanisms for handling anchors. Each anchor is a separate anchor object.
links	Provides mechanisms for handling links. Each link is a separate link object.

These objects are available only in client JavaScript. The objects specific to server JavaScript are discussed in Chapter 12, "The LiveWire Object Tree."

Other Objects

In addition to the objects available in the Navigator Object Hierarchy, JavaScript offers some other objects that have more general applications; they are listed in Table 3.2.

Table 3.2. Other JavaScript objects.

Object	Description
string	Allows programs to work with string data. Each string variable in JavaScript is actually an instance of this object.
Math	Provides methods and properties to perform mathematical calculations ranging from trigonometry to square roots.
Date	Provides methods and functions for tracking and manipulating dates.

User-Defined Objects

Users can define their own objects and then create instances of them in JavaScript by creating a constructor function. A *constructor function* defines the properties and methods that make up an object—much as a class does in object-oriented programming. Using a constructor function, you can define multiple instances of the object.

In general, this is the syntax for the constructor function:

```
function functionName(parameters) {
   Object Definition
}
```

For example, you could create a simple version of the car object with a single property for the owner and nothing else:

```
function car() {
   this.owner = "";
}
```

Here, you define a constructor function for the car object that takes no parameters. In the function, you define a single property called owner and assign an empty string to the property. There are two important points to remember:

- The keyword this refers to the current object being created by the constructor function.

- Properties are referred to in the form *objectName.propertyName*—that's why you can use *this.propertyName* in a constructor function.

In the previous example, you don't pass any parameters to the constructor function or assign an initial value to the owner property (other than the empty string, of course).

To use the object, you need to create an instance of it. For example, you could create an instance called car1 using the new keyword:

```
var car1 = new car();
```

Once this is done, you can refer to the owner property as car1.owner and assign a name to it:

```
car1.owner = "Owner's Name";
```

Parameters can be passed to the function so that values are assigned to the properties when you instantiate an object. For instance, if you create a name parameter in the constructor definition,

```
function car(name) {
   this.owner = name;
}
```

then you can create an instance of the car object and assign a value to the owner property with one command:

```
var car1 = new car("Owner's Name");
```

Now that you see how this basic framework operates, you can extend the constructor function to define all the properties of the car object:

```
function car(name) {
   this.owner = name;
   this.maker = "Does not own a car";
   this.model = "Does not own a car";
```

```
        this.color = "Does not own a car";
        this.year = "Does not own a car";
}
```

Next, you could define a instance of the object for a particular owner; once he or she buys a car, you could then assign values to the other four properties (other than `owner`):

```
var car1 = new car("Owner's name");
car1.maker = "Ford";
car1.model = "Mustang";
car1.color = "red";
car1.year = "1990";
```

Now you need to add methods to the function. This is a two-step process: first, create a function that defines the method, and second, add the method to the constructor function.

For instance, if you want to define the `printInfo` method, then create a function that specifies how the method works:

```
function doPrintInfo() {
    writeln("Owner's Name:" + this.name);
    writeln("Manufacturer:" + this.maker);
    writeln("Model       :" + this.model);
    writeln("Color       :" + this.color);
    writeln("Year:       :" + this.year);
}
```

Note that this function uses the `this` keyword again to refer to the particular object the function is associated with.

> **NOTE**
>
> This function uses the `writeln()` method of the document object, which is discussed in more detail in Chapter 4, "General Objects and Functions." The `writeln()` method allows a script creating HTML output to be displayed in the document window.

The next step is to associate the function as a method of the `car` object by adding this line to the constructor function for the object:

```
this.printInfo = doPrintInfo;
```

This statement indicates that the `printInfo` method is defined by the `doPrintInfo` function.

Extending this, you can create the `newOwner` and `rePaint` methods by first writing functions to define the methods

```
function doNewOwner() {
    this.owner = prompt("Enter the new owner's name:","Name");
}

function doRePaint() {
    this.color = prompt("Enter the new color:","Color");
}
```

and then adding them to the constructor function:

```
function car(name) {
   this.owner = name;
   this.maker = "Does not own a car";
   this.model = "Does not own a car";
   this.color = "Does not own a car";
   this.year = "Does not own a car";
   this.printInfo = doPrintInfo;
   this.newOwner = doNewOwner;
   this.rePaint = doRePaint;
}
```

You could then define an instance of the car object, assign values to its properties, and print the information out with the following commands:

```
var car1 = new car("John");
car1.maker = "Honda";
car1.model = "Accord";
car1.color = "White";
car1.year = "1994";
car1.printInfo();
```

Those statements would produce text like this:

```
Owner's Name : John
Manufacturer : Honda
Model        : Accord
Color        : White
Year         : 1994
```

Objects as Properties of Objects

Beyond assigning simple properties to objects, you also can use objects as properties of another object. For instance, if you were to create an engine object with two properties,

```
function engine() {
   this.cylinders = 0;
   this.horsepower = 0;
}
```

you could add it to your definition of the car object:

```
function car(name) {
   this.owner = name;
   this.maker = "Does not own a car";
   this.model = "Does not own a car";
   this.color = "Does not own a car";
   this.year = "Does not own a car";
   this.printInfo = doPrintInfo;
   this.newOwner = doNewOwner;
   this.rePaint = doRePaint;
   this.engine = new engine();
}
```

Notice that the property is defined in the same way that an instance of the car object was created earlier by using the new keyword.

If you create an instance of the car object called car1, you can refer to the properties of the engine property as car1.engine.cylinders and car1.engine.horsepower.

Adding Properties to an Object

Once an object has been defined with a constructor function and instances have been created, you might need to extend it by adding properties to either a particular instance or all instances of the object.

Adding a Property to a Specific Object Instance

It's easy to add a property to a specific instance of an object. For example, if you have two instances of the car object—car1 and car2—you can add an accident property to car2 simply by assigning a value to it:

```
car2.accident = true;
```

This would not add the property to car1, however, and future instances of the car object wouldn't have the accident property unless it was explicitly created for them in the same way.

Adding a Property to All Instances of an Object

You also can add a property or method to all instances of an object, as well as future instances of an object, by using the prototype property of all constructor functions. The syntax for this property can be one of the following two:

```
constructorFunctionName.prototype.newPropertyName = value;
```

```
constructorFunctionName.prototype.newMethodName = methodDefinitionName;
```

For instance, if after creating the two car instances in the previous example, you wanted to add an accident property to both instances as well as to the constructor function, then you could use the following:

```
car.prototype.accident = false;
```

This statement would add the properties to all instances of the object and to the constructor and would set the initial value to false. If you then created a new instance called car3, it would automatically include an accident property with a false value.

> **NOTE**
>
> The prototype property isn't available in Navigator 2 and works only with Navigator 3. If you need to ensure full compatibility with Navigator 2 users, it's best to avoid this feature of JavaScript.

Arrays in JavaScript

In JavaScript, *arrays* are actually a type of object; each array entry is, in fact, a property of an instance of the `Array` object. Arrays are created by creating instances of the `Array()` constructor function using the following form:

```
var arrayName = new Array();
```

Individual array elements are referred to with *arrayName[index]* and all arrays start at index zero.

Array lengths in JavaScript aren't fixed but can be increased dynamically by simply assigning values to new array entries, in much the same way that you dynamically added properties to an instance of an object earlier in this chapter.

For example, the following lines would create an array named `testArray` and set its size to 100 elements (from zero to 99) by assigning an empty string to the element with index 99:

```
var testArray = new Array();
testArray[99] = "";
```

Next, you could extend the array's length again by assigning a value to an even larger index.

You also can set an initial size for an array by passing the number of elements to the `Array()` constructor function as an argument:

```
var testArray = new Array(100);
```

It's also possible to create an array and assign values to all its initial elements at the time the array is created. This is done by passing the values for the elements to the `Array()` function as arguments:

```
var anotherArray = new Array("One element",2,false);
```

This statement would create a three-element array with the values `"One element"`, 2, and `false` assigned to the array.

> **NOTE**
>
> Unlike some structured programming languages, JavaScript doesn't require all entries in an array to share the same data type. In the previous example, for instance, you created a three-element array of a string, an integer, and a Boolean value, respectively.

Because arrays are objects, they also have some methods and properties:

- `join()`—Returns all elements of the array joined together as a single string. Takes one argument—a string used as the separator between each element of the array in the final string. If the argument is omitted, `join()` uses a comma as the separator.
- `reverse()`—Reverses the order of elements in the array.
- `length`—Indicates the number of elements in the array (the index of the last element in the array would be one less than the value of the `length` property).

Summary

In this chapter, you took a close look at objects, the building blocks on which JavaScript is built. Sets of pre-defined objects are what give both client and server JavaScript their capabilities.

Objects define groups of information and methods for working with that information. As a programmer, you can extend JavaScript by creating objects with their own properties and methods.

You also looked at the Navigator Object Hierarchy—that set of objects that makes up the core of client JavaScript—and learned about some other objects found in JavaScript, such as the `string` and `Date` objects.

Finally, you learned about arrays and their relationship with the JavaScript object model. As a unique type of object, arrays share many of the features of objects and have a flexibility not found in many other languages.

In the next chapter, you'll move on to explore the main objects and functions of client JavaScript.

4

General Objects and Functions

by Wes Tatters

The separation of language capabilities into those provided by Server JavaScript and those provided by Client JavaScript through the use of Objects means that the size of each runtime system can be kept down to a minimum. Only those objects and methods that are actually supported by either version need to be included.

There are, however, some objects and stand-alone functions that need to be made available in both Server and Client JavaScript. In this chapter each of these objects and the properties and methods they contain are examined in detail. The topics to be discussed include the following:

- The `String` Object
- The `Math` Object
- The `Date` Object
- Pre-defined Functions

The `String` Object

It's easy to consider variables that contain strings as just that, variables. In actual fact, all strings are stored internally in a *String object*.

NOTE

Brendan Eich—the Netscape developer largely responsibly for the development of JavaScript—describes objects like the String object as *First Class* objects.

The String object is basically the same as all of the objects you have encountered previously—it contains properties and methods. But unlike objects you create yourself, which require a call to the new operator to instantiate them, new String objects are created automatically by JavaScript whenever they are needed. Take the following as an example:

```
var aString = "This is a string" ;
```

This statement actually creates a new variable called *aString* and assigns a String object to it that contains the value "This is a string." (It should also be noted that the string literal "This is a string" is treated internally by JavaScript as a String object.)

In addition, by taking advantage of the new operator, a string also can be defined using the statement

```
var aString = new String("This is a string");
```

Properties

The String object makes only one of its properties publicly accessible. This is the `.length` property.

string.length

The length property reflects the number of characters, or the length, of a string object. In addition, it is a read-only property. This means that the value of the property cannot be manually altered by the programmer.

To use the length property in a program, simply append `.length` to any string variable:

```
var aString = "This is a string" ;
document.write( aString.length );
```

This example causes the number "16" to be displayed on the Web page.

String Literals as Objects

Because JavaScript treats string literals as true `String` objects, you can actually use a string literal wherever you would normally use a string variable. For example, the following code

```
var aString = "This is a string" ;
var aStringLength = aString.length ;
```

can be written as

```
var aStringLength = "This is a string".length ;
```

The same is true for all of the methods listed in the following sections, although exactly why you would want to use this feature is best left up to the imagination.

Methods

The methods supported by the `String` object fall into one of two categories:

■ Methods that work with the string contents.
■ Methods that return HTML formatted text.

String Contents Methods

The first set of methods supported by the `String` object all perform functions related to the contents of the string. By using these methods you can locate specific characters in a string, obtain a subsection of the string, or alter its case.

string.charAt()

The `charAt()` method returns the value of a character located at a specific position in a `String` object. The syntax for the `charAt()` method is as follows:

```
stringname.charAt( index )
```

Index is an integer literal or a variable between 0 and `string.length-1`. All strings in JavaScript are indexed from left to right, with the first character in the string located in index position 0, the second in index position 1, the third in index position 2, and so on. As a result, the index position of the last character in the string is located in index position `string.length` minus one and not `string.length`.

To print out the third character in a string you would write something like the following:

```
var aString = "This is a string" ;
var character = aString.charAt( 2 ) ;
document.write( character );
```

> **NOTE**
>
> If you set an *index* value that is larger than the length of the string, JavaScript returns an empty string.

string.indexOf()

The `indexOf()` method returns the position of a specific character within a string. The syntax for the `indexOf()` method is

```
stringname.indexOf( character, [starting_index])
```

Character can be either a string literal or a string variable that represents the character for which you want to search. Take the following as an example:

```
var aString = "This is a string" ;
var number = aString.indexOf( 'a' );
document.write( number );
```

The statement `aString.indexOf( 'a' )` is used to search the content of `aString` for the first occurrence of the letter 'a'. The index value returned to `number`—8 in this example—remembering that the index position of the first character is 0.

> **NOTE**
>
> If `indexOf()` cannot find the character in the string, a value of -1 is returned.

The indexOf() method also supports a second format that makes use of the optional *starting_index* parameter. By default, indexOf() starts searching at the first character in the string. However, if you include a *starting_index* value, the search commences at the character in the position indicated by *starting_index*:

```
var aString = "This is a string" ;
var number = aString.indexOf( 's' , 8 );
document.write( number );
```

The value assigned to number is 10 because that is the index position of the first 's' located after the character in index position 8, which you already know is an 'a'.

string.lastIndexOf()

The lastIndexOf() method returns the position of a specific character within a string, but instead of searching the string from left to right, as was the case for indexOf(), lastIndexOf() searches the string from right to left. The syntax for the lastIndexOf() method is

```
stringname.lastIndexOf( character, [starting_index])
```

Character can be either a string literal or a string variable that represents the character you want to search for. Take the following as an example:

```
var aString = "This is a string" ;
var number = aString.lastIndexOf( 's' );
document.write( number );
```

This time, the statement aString.lastIndexOf('s') is used to search the content of aString for the last occurrence of the letter 's', by searching the string from right to left. The index value returned to number in this example is 10.

NOTE

Like indexOf(), if lastIndexOf() cannot find the character in the string, a value of -1 is returned.

By using the optional *starting_index* parameter of the lastIndexOf() method, you can search the string from a specific starting point. By default, lastIndexOf() starts searching at the index location represented by string.length-1. However, if you include a *starting_index* value, the search commences at the character in the position indicated by *starting_index* and continues searching to the right of this character until it reaches the beginning of the string:

```
var aString = "This is a string" ;
var number = aString.indexOf( 's' , 8 );
document.write( number );
```

The value assigned to number is 6 because that is the index position of the first 's' located to the right of index position 8.

string.substring()

The substring() method is used to return a subsection of a string. The syntax for substring() follows:

```
stringname.substring( indexA, indexB )
```

indexA and *indexB* represent index positions within the string. JavaScript uses these two values to determine which part of the string you want returned.

If the value of *indexA* is less than *indexB*, then a string starting with the character at position *indexA* and ending with the character prior to position *indexB* is returned. On the other hand, if *indexA* is greater than *indexB*, then the a string starting with the character at position *indexB* and ending with the character prior to position *indexA* is returned. Finally, if *indexA* and *indexB* are equal, an empty string is returned.

As a result, to select just the word "string" from the string aString, you could write either of the following:

```
var newString = aString.substring( 10 , 16 ) ;
var newString = aString.substring( 16 , 10 ) ;
```

There is also a special version of the substring() method that takes only one parameter. In this case, the section of the string starting at the index position indicated by the parameter and finishing at the end of the string is returned.

For this reason, because the word "string" in aString is at the very end of the string, you also could use the following format:

```
var newString = aString.substring( 10 ) ;
```

string.toLowerCase()

The toLowerCase() method is used to return a new string with all the letters in the existing string converted to lower case. The syntax for the toLowerCase() method is

```
stringname.toLowerCase()
```

Take for example

```
var sometext = "THIS IS SOME TEXT";
document.write(sometext.toLowerCase() )
```

This prints out "this is some text" on the Web page.

string.toUpperCase()

The `toUpperCase()` method is used to return a new string with all the letters in the existing string converted to upper case. The syntax for the `toUpperCase()` method is:

stringname`.toUpperCase()`

The `toUpperCase()` method basically performs the reverse operation to that of the `toLowerCase()` method:

```
var sometext = "this is some text";
document.write(sometext.toUpperCase() )
```

This prints out "THIS IS SOME TEXT" on the Web page.

HTML Text Formatting Methods

One of the most common uses of JavaScript is for dynamic HTML creation, or in other words, building Web pages on the fly. To assist with this task, the String object includes a collection of methods that build the HTML code for many of the standard HTML tags.

string.anchor()

The `anchor()` method returns the HTML code needed to insert an anchor into a Web page. The syntax for `anchor()` follows:

stringname`.anchor(` *anchorname* `)`

Anchorname is the text associated with the NAME property in the `<A>` tag. To understand what is going on here, look at the following example:

```
var someText = "The top of a page";
var anAnchor = someText.anchor( "Heading" );
document.write( anAnchor );
```

The second line of code in this example creates a new string called `anAnchor` containing the following text:

```
<A NAME="Heading">The top of a page</A>
```

This text represents the code needed to define an anchor using HTML. Once created, to include this anchor code into your Web page all you need to do is write it out using the `document.write()` or `document.writeln()` methods in Client JavaScript, or the `write()` function in Server JavaScript.

> **NOTE**
>
> Refer to Appendix B, "HTML Guide," for more information about the meaning of the HTML tags themselves.

string.fontcolor()

The fontcolor() method returns the HTML code needed to change the color of a block of text on a Web page. The syntax for fontcolor() is as follows:

```
stringname.fontcolor( fontcolor )
```

The contents of variable *stringname* represent the text you want displayed and *fontcolor* represent the new color as either a hexadecimal RGB triplet or a color string literal. (Appendix E, "Colors by Name and Hex Value," contains a list of valid color string literals and their corresponding RGB hexadecimal triplet values.)

The HTML code returned by the *fontcolor()* method looks like

```
<FONT COLOR=fontcolor>contents of stringname</FONT>
```

string.fontsize()

The fontsize() method returns the HTML code needed to change the size of a block of text on a Web page. The syntax for fontsize() is as follows:

```
stringname.fontsize( fontsize )
```

The contents of variable *stringname* represents the text to be displayed, and *fontsize* is the size of the text. There are currently seven font sizes recognized by JavaScript—1 being the smallest and 7 the largest. In addition, relative font sizes are also supported by using positive or negative numbers such as -2 or +1.

The HTML code returned by the *fontsize()* method takes the following form:

```
<FONT SIZE=fontsize>contents of stringname</FONT>
```

string.link()

The link() method returns the HTML code needed to include a hyperlink on a Web page. The syntax for link() follows:

```
stringname.link( href )
```

The contents of *stringname* are used as the link text and the contents of *href* as the destination for the hyperlink.

The HTML code returned by the *link()* method takes the following form:

```
<A HREF=href>contents of stringname</A>
```

Character Formatting

The remaining HTML text formatting methods all create HTML tag code that falls into the category of character formatting. Table 4.1 lists each of these methods and describes the nature of the HTML code created by them.

Table 4.1. Character formatting methods for the `String` object.

String Method	HTML Code Created
stringname.big()	<BIG>contents of stringname </BIG>
stringname.blink()	<BLINK>contents of stringname </BLINK>
stringname.bold()	<B>contents of stringname </B>
stringname.fixed()	<FIXED>contents of stringname </FIXED>
stringname.italics()	<I>contents of stringname </I>
stringname.small()	<SMALL>contents of stringname </SMALL>
stringname.strike()	<STRIKE>contents of stringname </STRIKE>

The Math Object

The `Math` object provides a set of constant mathematical values and a collection of methods that perform most of the common mathematical operations found in programming language today.

To use any of the properties or methods of the `Math` object in your JavaScript code, simply treat the object as you would any other:

```
var number = 9;
var newnumber = Math.sqrt( number );
```

This code creates a variable called `number` and assigns a value of 9 to it. On the second line, another variable called `newnumber` is created. `newnumber` is assigned the value returned by calling the square root method of the `Math` object with `number` as an argument.

Properties

Table 4.2 list all of the public properties that can be accessed using the `Math` object. Note that all of these properties are read-only because they fall into the category of constants.

Table 4.2. Properties of the `Math` object.

Math Property	Approximate Value	Description
Math.E	2.718	Euler's constant E—the base for natural logarithms.
Math.LN2	0.693	The natural logarithm of 2.
Math.LN10	2.302	The natural logarithm of 10.

continues

Table 4.2. continued

Math Property	Approximate Value	Description
Math.LOG2E	1.442	The base 2 logarithm of E.
Math.LOG10E	0.434	The base 10 logarithm of E.
Math.PI	3.14159	The ratio of the circumference of a circle to its diameter.
Math.SQRT1_2	0.707	The square root of 0.5.
Math.SQRT2	1.414	The square root of 2.

NOTE

Because of the problems associated with floating point numbers, you should always use the constants provided by the Math object wherever it is appropriate to do so.

Methods

Table 4.3 lists all of the methods currently supported by the Math object. For each method, the table lists the syntax and a short description of its use.

Table 4.3. Methods provided by the Math object.

Math Method	Description
Math.abs(*num*)	Returns the absolute value of *num*.
Math.acos(*num*)	Returns the arc cosine of *num* in radians.
Math.asin(*num*)	Returns the arc sine of *num* in radians.
Math.atan(*num*)	Returns the arc tangent of *num* in radians.
Math.atan2(*x,y*)	Returns the angle of the polar coordinate corresponding to the cartesian coordinate *x,y*.
Math.ceil(*num*)	Returns the lowest integer that is greater than or equal to *num*.
Math.cos(*num*)	Returns the cosine of *num* in radians.
Math.exp(*num*)	Returns E—Euler's constant—raised to the power of *num*.
Math.floor(*num*)	Returns the largest integer that is less than or equal to *num*.

Math Method	Description
Math.log(*num*)	Returns the natural logarithm—base E—of *num*.
Math.max(*num1, num2*)	Returns the larger of the two numbers.
Math.min(*num1, num2*)	Returns the smallest of the two numbers.
Math.pow(base, exponent)	Returns *base* raised to the *exponent* power.
Math.random()	Returns a random number. (This function is not currently supported on all platforms.)
Math.round(*num*)	Return *num* rounded to the nearest integer.
Math.sin(*num*)	Returns the sine of *num* in radians.
Math.sqrt(*num*)	Returns the square root of *num*.
Math.tan(*num*)	Returns the tangent of *num*.

The Date Object

Unlike most other languages that include a built-in date data type, in JavaScript there is no explicit date data type. JavaScript does provide a Date object that not only removes the need for a date data type but also introduces a valuable collection of methods enabling you to manipulate the contents of Date objects.

To use the Date object in JavaScript, you first need to create a new Date object using the new statement and the special built-in Date() constructor function. The Date() constructor takes one of the following forms:

```
dateObjectName = new Date();
dateObjectName = new Date("month day, year hours:minutes:seconds")
dateObjectName = new Date(year, month, day);
dateObjectName = new Date(year, month, day, hours, minutes, sec );
```

If you use the first form new Date(), a new Date object containing the current time and date is created. The second form takes a string or string literal like "January 1, 1996 08:30:00". The third form takes three integers or integer literals and only sets the date components of the Date object. And finally, the fourth form also uses integers, but sets both the time and date components.

In the third and fourth form, the value of the *year* integer is calculated by subtracting 1900 from the year, so that for 1996 you need to set *year* to 96 and the *month* value to an integer between 0 and 11. January = 0, February = 1, March = 2, and so on. For example,

```
1Date = new Date(96,9,22);
```

would create an instance of the Date object called aDate set to October 22, 1996.

> **NOTE**
>
> Internally, JavaScript stores all dates as an integer number representing the number of milliseconds since January 1, 1970 00:00:00. This basically means that you cannot use the Date object to hold any date earlier that January 1, 1970.

Methods

There are no public properties associated with a Date object. Instead, to access or alter the contents of a Date object, you need to use one of the many built-in date methods. For example, to create a Date object that holds a date exactly one year from the present time you could write the following:

```
var currentdate = new date();
var currentyear = currentdate.getYear();
var nextyear = currentyear + 1;
currentdate.setYear( nextyear );
```

After creating a new Date object and setting it to the current date, the getYear() function is called to obtain an integer representation of the year. One is added to this currentyear integer and then the resulting value nextyear is used to set the year component of currentdate to the following year.

Set and Get Methods

The Date object contains methods to set and get the values assigned to each different component of a date. Table 4.4 lists all of the set and get methods, including their syntax and a brief description of each one's use.

Table 4.4. Set and Get methods provided by the Date object.

Date Method	Description
datename.getDate()	Returns the day of the month from object datename as an integer, where 1 is the first day of the month.
datename.getDay()	Returns the day of the week from object datename as an integer, where 0 = Sunday, 1 = Monday, 2 = Tuesday, 3 = Wednesday, 4 = Thursday, 5 = Friday and 6 = Saturday.
datename.getHours()	Returns the hour of the day from object datename as an integer between 0 and 23.

Date Method	*Description*
`datename.getMinutes()`	Returns the minute value from object `datename` as an integer between 0 and 59.
`datename.getMonth()`	Returns the month value from object `datename` as an integer between 0 and 11. January = 0, February = 1, March = 2 and so on.
`datename.getSeconds()`	Returns the seconds value from object `datename` as an integer between 0 and 59.
`datename.getTime()`	Returns a numeric value corresponding to the time represented by object `datename`. The number returned equals the number of milliseconds since January 1970 00:00:00.
`datename.getTimeZoneoffset()`	Returns the difference between local time and GMT in minutes.
`datename.getYear()`	Returns the year value from object `datename` as an integer. The value is calculated by subtracting 1900 from the year, so that 1996 returns a value of 96.
`datename.setDate( dayvalue )`	Sets the day of the month value for object `datename` as an integer, where `dayvalue` is a number between 1 and 31.
`datename.setHours( hour )`	Sets the hour of the day for object `datename`. `Hour` is an integer between 0 and 23.
`datename.setMinutes( min )`	Sets the minutes value of object `datename`. `Min` is an integer between 0 and 59.
`datename.setMonth( month )`	Sets the month value of object `datename`. `Month` is an integer between 0 and 11.
`datename.setSeconds( secs )`	Sets the seconds value of object `datename`. `Secs` is an integer between 0 and 59.
`datename.setTime( date )`	Sets the value of object `datename`. `Date` is a date expressed as the number of milliseconds since January 1970 00:00:00.
`datename.setYear( year )`	Sets the year value of object `datename` as an integer. The value of `year` is calculated by subtracting 1900 from the actual year.

String Values

There are currently three methods in the `Date` object that can be used to convert the contents of a `Date` object to a string. Table 4.5 outlines the use of these three methods.

Table 4.5. Methods used to convert a `Date` object to a string.

Date Method	*Description*
`datename.toGMTString()`	Returns the date represented by object `datename` as a string. The value of the string is formatted based on GMT. Because my location is 10 hours ahead of GMT, a string like `"Sun, 31 Dec 1995 22:30:00 GMT"` is returned.
`datename.toLocaleString()`	Returns the date represented by object `datename` as a string. The value of the string is formatted based on local time. The format of this string is controlled by your computer platform and its date preferences. On my system, a string like `"01/01/96 08:30:00"` is returned.
`datename.toString()`	Returns a string value in a form similar to `"Mon Jan 01 08:30:00 EAS 1996"`. Again this format may vary somewhat from computer system to computer system.

NOTE

As a rule you shouldn't use the `toString()` method in your own code, because it is technically an internal method automatically called by JavaScript when needed. For example, the use of

```
document.write( datename );
```

is preferable to

```
document.write( datename.toString() );
```

which actually gives the same result.

Date to Integer Conversion

There are two special methods which have not yet been discussed. These methods are used to convert a date represented either as a string or a set of integers into a single integer value representing the number of milliseconds since January 1970 00:00:00.

> **NOTE**
>
> The `parse()` and `UTC()` methods outlined in this section are both called static methods. Basically this means that you call them using the base object `Date` instead of an individual `Date` object. For example, to call `parse()` you need to use
>
> `Date.parse()`
>
> and not
>
> `dateobjectname.parse()`.

Date.parse()

The `parse()` method takes a string date and returns an integer representing the number of milliseconds since January 1970 00:00:00. The syntax of the `parse()` method is

`Date.parse( datestring )`

Datestring is a string of the form "Mon, 1 Jan 1996 08:80:00". The `parse()` method also can recognize a variety of other date formats including the following:

```
var number = Date.parse( "1 Jan 1996 08:80:00" );
var number = Date.parse( "1 Jan 1996" );
var number = Date.parse( "Jan 1, 1996" );
var number = Date.parse( "01/01/1996" );
var number = Date.parse( "01/01/96" );
```

In all of the preceding examples, JavaScript assumes you are referring to local time. The `parse()` method also can be used to calculate dates and times based on Universal Coordinated Time or GMT. The following examples demonstrate some of the formats recognized when using UTC coding:

```
var number = Date.parse( "Sun, 31 Dec 1995 22:30:00 GMT" );
var number = Date.parse( "31 Dec 1995 22:30:00 GMT" );
var number = Date.parse( "12/31/1995 22:30:00 GMT" );
var number = Date.parse( "31 Dec 1995 22:30:00 GMT +1000" );
var number = Date.parse( "12/31/1995 22:30:00 GMT +1000" );
```

Date.UTC()

The `UTC()` method returns the number of milliseconds in a date since January 1, 1970 00:00:00 GMT as opposed to local time. The syntax of the `UTC()` method is as follows:

`Date.UTC( year, month, day, [hrs], [min], [sec])`

Year, month, day, hrs, min, and *sec* are all integers that abide by the following rules:

- ■ *year* is a year after 1970 which is shown as 70.
- ■ *month* is a month between 0-11.
- ■ *date* is a day of the month between 1-31.

- *hrs* is hours between 0-23. (Optional)
- *min* is minutes between 0-59. (Optional)
- *sec* is seconds between 0-59. (Optional)

The main reason for the existence of the UTC() method is so the value of new Date objects can be defined using GMT time instead of local time. The following example demonstrates how this is done:

```
gmtDate = new Date( Date.UTC(95, 12, 31, 23, 30, 0) );
```

Pre-Defined Functions

Apart from built-in objects and methods, JavaScript also includes a small set of redefined functions that are not directly associated with any specific objects. These functions are:

- The eval() function
- The parseInt() function
- The parseFloat() function
- The isNaN() function

> **NOTE**
>
> Netscape refers to these functions as *Top Level* functions.

The eval() Function

The eval() function takes a string and processes it as though it was an expression or a block of JavaScript commands. Its syntax is as follows:

```
returnvalue = eval( evalstring );
```

If the contents of *evalstring* evaluate to an expression, then the result of the expression is stored in *returnvalue*. Alternatively, if the string contains JavaScript commands, they are executed as though they were a part of the JavaScript program.

The following example demonstrates how eval() can be used:

```
var somestring = "1 + 1";
display.write( somestring );
display.write( " = " );
display.write( eval( somestring ) );
```

If this code was run on a Web page, the result would be a line of text that said:

```
1 + 1 = 2
```

The `eval( somestring )` statement in the last line of code is used to evaluate the contents of `somestring`, which in this case contains an expression. Once evaluated, the result of this expression, '2', is returned to the `document.write()` statement so that it can be displayed on the Web page.

The `parseFloat()` Function

The `parseFloat()` function examines the contents of a string. If it encounters a valid string, it is converted into a floating point value. This value is returned as the function result. The syntax of `parseFloat()` is as follows:

```
returnfloat = parseFloat( stringfloat );
```

Stringfloat is a string containing a number stored in string format that adheres to the following rules:

1. If the function encounters any character other than a sign (+ or -), numeral (0-9), a decimal point, or an exponent in stringfloat, then it returns the value up to that point and ignores the invalid character and all remaining characters.

2. If the first character cannot be converted to a number, parseFloat() returns one of the following values:

    ■ 0 on Windows platforms.

    ■ "NaN" on any other platform, indicating that the value is not a number. (See the `isNaN()` function later for more information.)

The `parseInt()` Function

The `parseInt()` function examines the contents of a string. If it encounters a valid number, the number is converted into an integer value. This value is then returned as the function result. The syntax of `parseInt()` follows:

```
returnint = parseInt( stringint, [ radix ] );
```

Stringint is a string containing a number stored in string format and *radix* is an optional parameter that indicates the base of the number stored in the string. A radix of 10 indicates that the number is a decimal, a radix of 8 indicates that the number is Octal, and a radix of 16 indicates that the number is Hexadecimal.

Only strings that comply with the following rules are converted to an integer value:

If the function encounters any character other than a sign (+ or -), the numerals (0-9), or the appropriate alphabetical characters for a radix to about 10, then it returns the value up to that point and ignores the invalid character and all remaining characters. (When the radix is set to 16 the letters A through F are used to indicate units about '9'.)

If the first character cannot be converted to a number, parseInt() returns one of the following values:

- 0 on Windows platforms.
- "NaN" on any other platform, indicating that the value is not a number. (See the inNaN() function later for more information.)

The following example outlines some of the possible valid string formats for the parseInt() function.

```
var somenumber = parseInt("1010", 2) ;
var somenumber = parseInt("217", 8) ;
var somenumber = parseInt("15", 10) ;
var somenumber = parseInt("FA00", 16) ;
var somestring = "1234" ;
var somenumber = parseInt( somestring ) ;
```

The isNaN() Function

When JavaScript encounters a string that cannot be converted to a number using either parseInt() or parseFloat(), it returns one of two possible values depending on the computer platform.

If you are on a Windows based system a zero value is returned, but on all other systems a special result called a NaN (Not a Number) is returned.

On UNIX systems you can test whether the result was a NaN using the isNaN() function. The format of the isNaN() function follows:

```
var boolvalue = isNaN( somenumber );
```

somenumber is the result returned from either a parseInt() or parseFloat() function. If the content of somenumber is a NaN, then the value true is assigned to boolvalue; otherwise it is assigned a value of false.

Summary

To incorporate basic string formatting, date management, and mathematical functions into JavaScript, a group of special stand-alone objects and methods have been created. These objects exist in both Client and Server JavaScript.

In addition, JavaScript also includes a small number of Top Level functions as a part of the basic language. These functions enable you to evaluate and parse strings containing expressions, JavaScript commands, and integer or floating point values.

II

JavaScript and Netscape Navigator

5

The Netscape Navigator Object Tree

by Arman Danesh

The Navigator Object Tree is at the core of client JavaScript. It is a hierarchical collection of core objects for scripting client-side applications using JavaScript.

The objects in the Navigator Object Tree provide methods and properties for working with windows, frames, URLs, documents, and the Navigator history list.

The five objects in the Navigator Object Tree are covered in this chapter:

- The navigator Object
- The window Object
- The location Object
- The history Object
- The document Object

The Navigator Object Tree

The Navigator Object Tree provides the core objects—with associated properties and methods—for working with the client Navigator environment in JavaScript. These objects can be used for a variety of tasks including working with Navigator itself, manipulating client windows and their loaded documents, as well as manipulating URLs and Navigator's history list.

The Navigator Object Tree is organized into a hierarchy with two top-level objects: navigator and window. The structure of the tree and its objects is outlined in Figure 5.1.

The objects in the Navigator Object Tree are described in Table 5.1.

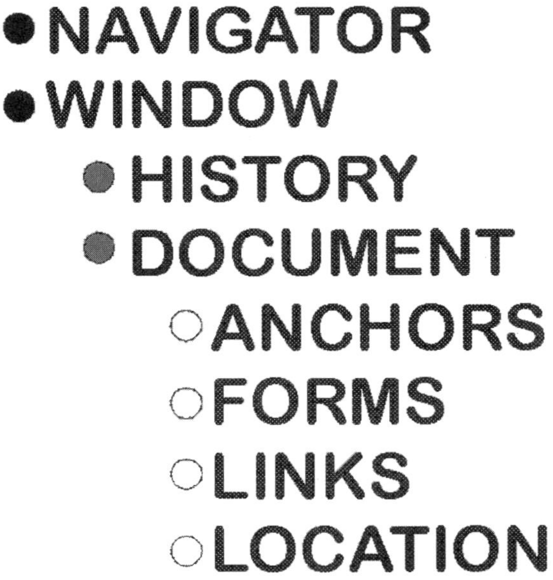

FIGURE 5.1.
The Navigator Object Tree.

- **NAVIGATOR**
- **WINDOW**
  - **HISTORY**
  - **DOCUMENT**
    - ○ **ANCHORS**
    - ○ **FORMS**
    - ○ **LINKS**
    - ○ **LOCATION**

Table 5.1. The objects in the Navigator Object Tree.

Object	Description
navigator	Provides information about the current version of Navigator.
window	Provides methods and properties for dealing with the windows and frames.
history	Provides limited access to the history list for a given window or frame.
document	Provides properties and methods for working with documents and elements of a document.
forms	Provides the properties and methods needed to work with forms and create interactive forms.
anchor	Provides the tools needed for scripts to work with anchors.
location	Provides methods and properties for working with URLs, including the currently loaded URL.
link	Provides mechanism for manipulating links in JavaScript.

The navigator Object

The navigator object provides six properties and one method, which provide information about the overall Navigator environment:

- appName—Reflects the name of the browser represented as a string. In the case of Navigator, appName takes the value "Netscape".

- appVersion—Reflects the version number of the browser represented as a string in the form *VersionNumber (Platform; Version)* where *VersionNumber* is the version number of the browser, *Platform* represents the operating system the browser runs under, and *Version* indicates whether the browser is the international or domestic version. For instance, in the international release version of Navigator 2.0 for Windows 3.1, navigator.appVersion has the value "2.0 (Win16; I)".

- appCodeName—Reflects the code name of the current browser represented as a string. For all versions of Navigator, navigator.appCodeName takes the value "Mozilla".

- javaEnabled()—Returns a Boolean value indicating if Java is enabled in the client browser.

- userAgent—Reflects the complete user agent identification of the browser as a string combining appName, appVersion, and appCodeName (that is, "Mozilla/2.0 (Win16; I)").

- ■ mimeTypes—Reflects the mime types available in Navigator in an array of mimeType objects.
- ■ plugins—Reflects the plug-ins available in Navigator in an array of plugin objects.

The plugins and mimeTypes properties are discussed in more detail in Chapter 16, "Navigator Plug-ins."

One of the more popular uses of the properties of the navigator object is to reflect the users back to them in a Web page. Many Web pages enable users to know what browser they are using to visit a site. This can be done with CGI-BIN scripts, but JavaScript enables it to happen entirely at the client end.

In addition, the navigator object can be used to customize content based on the version of the browser the user is using. For instance, Navigator 3 supports additional features, such as background colors in individual table cells. If incorrectly used, users of browsers that don't support cell background may be faced with unreadable text.

The following HTML document displays its title in a single table cell. On Navigator 3, the background of the cell is black with white text but on Navigator 2.0, the text should be the default color for the document with the default background color.

This is done using the appVersion property of the navigator object:

```
<HTML>

<HEAD>
<TITLE>navigator Example</TITLE>
</HEAD>

<BODY>
<DIV ALIGN=CENTER>
<TABLE WIDTH=50% BGCOLOR="black" BORDER=1 ALIGN=CENTER>
<TR>
<TD>

<SCRIPT LANGUAGE="JavaScript">
if (navigator.appVersion.charAt(0) == "3")
  document.writeln('<FONT COLOR="white">');
</SCRIPT>

<DIV ALIGN=CENTER>
<H1>WELCOME</H1>
</CENTER>

<SCRIPT LANGUAGE="JavaScript">
if (navigator.appVersion.charAt(0) == "3")
  document.writeln('</FONT>');
</SCRIPT>

</TD>
</TR>
</TABLE>
```

```
This page is customized to your browser using JavaScript.
</DIV>

</BODY>

</HTML>
```

The results of this script look like Figure 5.2.

In this example, checking the first character of the `navigator.appVersion` string using the `charAt()` method of the `string` object enables the script to determine if Navigator 3 is being used. If so, then the `<FONT>` tag is used to change the color of the title text to white.

FIGURE 5.2.

Using JavaScript's `navigator` *object, it is possible to customize content based on the version of Navigator being used.*

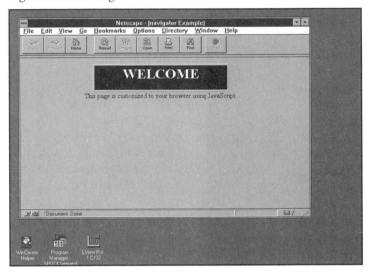

The `window` Object

The `window` object is the parent object for each open Navigator window and its loaded document, `location` object, and history list.

Generally, the `window` object is not referred to explicitly because it is the assumed parent for any object, property, or method reference. For instance, the `document` object can be referred to as `document` rather than `window.document` and the `confirm()` method as `confirm()` rather than `window.confirm()`.

It is possible to use the special keyword `self` to refer to the current window. For instance, `self.location` refers to the `location` object for the current window.

Table 5.2 outlines the properties and methods of the `window` object.

Table 5.2. Properties and methods of the `window` object.

Name	Description
frames	An array of `frame` objects for each child frame in a window. Frames are discussed in detail in Chapter 8, "Frames and JavaScript."
opener	The name of the window that holds the calling document when opened with `window.open()`.
status	A string containing the text displayed in the status bar of a window. Can be used to display messages to the user.
defaultStatus	A string reflecting the default value displayed in the status bar of a window.
alert()	Displays a message in a dialog box with an OK button. Takes a single string argument to display in the dialog box.
blur()	Removes focus from the current window. In most operating systems this sends the window to the back.
confirm()	Displays a message in a dialog box with an OK button and a Cancel button. Returns true when the user clicks on OK, and false otherwise. Takes a single string argument to display in the dialog box.
close()	Closes the current window.
focus()	Gives focus to the current window. In most operating systems this brings the window to the front.
open()	Opens a new window with a specified document or opens a specified document in an existing named window. Takes three arguments: the document URL or name, the window name, and a string of parameters defining the appearance of the new window.
prompt()	Displays a message in a dialog box along with a text entry field and an OK button. The value in the text entry field is returned by the `prompt()` method when the user clicks the OK button. Takes two string arguments: a message to display to the user, and default initial content for the text entry field.

Name	Description
`Scroll()`	Scrolls the window to a specified x,y coordinate passed to the method as arguments.
`setTimeout()`	Sets a timer for a specified number of milliseconds and then evaluates an expression when the timer has finished counting. Program operation continues while the timer is counting down. Takes two arguments—a string to evaluate and an integer specifying the delay in milliseconds. Timeouts are discussed in more detail in Chapter 8.
`clearTimeout()`	Cancels a previously set timeout.

Some of these properties and methods deserve a more detailed discussion.

The `status` Property

The status bar at the bottom of Navigator windows can be used by script authors for many purposes, including the display of welcome messages, displaying descriptions of links, and presenting scrolling text messages.

The status bar can be dynamically updated by assigning a new value to `window.status`. The following script demonstrates how `window.status` can be used to display descriptions of links when the user points at a link:

```
<HTML>

<HEAD>
<TITLE>status Example</TITLE>
</HEAD>

<BODY>
Point at these links and look at the status bar:
<A HREF="home.html"
 onMouseover="self.status='Go back home ...'; return true">Home</A><BR>
<A HREF="next.html"
 onMouseover="self.status='Go to the next page'; return true">Next</A>
</BODY>

</HTML>
```

Here, the `onMouseover` event handler is used to update the `status` property (as shown in Figure 5.3). Event handlers are discussed in more detail in Chapter 6, "Event Processing." Notice the use of the `self` keyword to refer to the window object for the current window.

FIGURE 5.3.

Using the status *property, it's possible to display custom text in the status bar.*

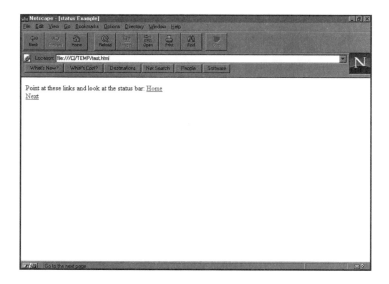

Working with Dialog Boxes

As indicated in Table 5.2, there are three methods for producing dialog boxes:

- `alert()`
- `confirm()`
- `prompt()`

Each of these produces different results.

The `alert()` method is generally used to display just that—an alert message—to the user. It takes a single string argument:

```
window.alert("This is a test");
```

and produces results similar to those shown in Figure 5.4.

Here the user can press the OK button and has no other choices.

The `confirm()` method adds one feature to the dialog box—a Cancel button, producing results similar to those shown in Figure 5.5:

```
window.confirm("Continue?");
```

Because the `confirm()` dialog box returns a Boolean value based on the user's selection, it can be used to interact with the user. For instance, the following code segment executes only if the user clicks OK in the confirm dialog box:

```
if (confirm(message)) {
    JavaScript Code
}
```

FIGURE 5.4.

An Alert dialog box.

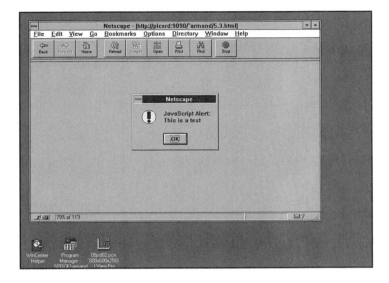

FIGURE 5.5.

A Confirm dialog box.

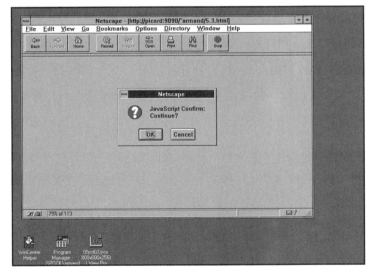

The prompt() method takes dialog box interaction a step further: it offers the user the opportunity to enter information. The prompt() method takes two arguments—a message and default text for the text entry field:

```
prompt("Enter a color:","Blue");
```

which produces results similar to those shown in Figure 5.6.

FIGURE 5.6.
A Prompt dialog box.

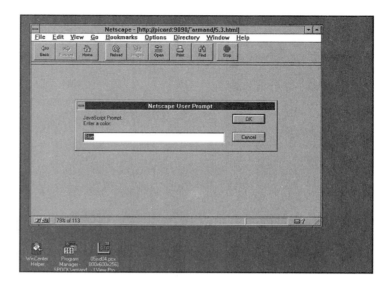

Here, the value in the text field is returned by the prompt() method if the user clicks OK. If the user clicks Cancel, then the null value is returned.

Opening and Closing Windows

The open() and close() methods provide the capability to open and close windows.

The open() method takes three arguments—two required arguments and one optional argument:

```
open("URL","windowName","parameterList");
```

parameterList is a comma-separated list of entries that specify the size and appearance of the new Navigator window. The possible entries in the parameter list follow:

- ■ toolbar—specifies if the standard tool bar should appear
- ■ location—specifies if the location field should be displayed
- ■ directories—specifies if the directory buttons should be displayed
- ■ status—specifies if the status bar appears
- ■ menubar—indicates if the menu bar should be presented
- ■ scrollbars—indicates if scroll bars should be used when the document is larger than the window
- ■ resizable—specifies if the user should be allowed to resize the window
- ■ width—specifies the width of the window in pixels
- ■ height—indicates the height of the window in pixels

With the exception of width and height, which take integer values, these parameters can be set with a value of 1 or yes, or turned off with a value of 0 or no.

For instance, the command

```
window.open("new.html","newWindow","toolbar=no,location=yes,directories=no,
➥status=no,menubar=no,scrollbars=no,resizable=0,width=200,height=300");
```

produces a 200 × 300 pixel window with a visible location field, no toolbar, no directory buttons, no status bar, and no scrollbars. The window is not resizable by the user. This window would look like Figure 5.7.

FIGURE 5.7.

Using the open() *method, new windows can be customized.*

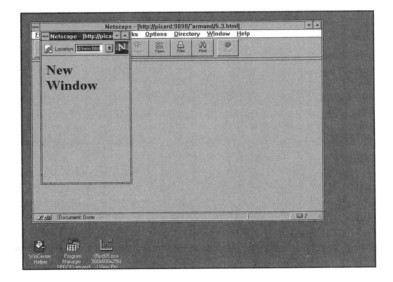

The close() method takes no arguments and can be used to close a window opened by the script or the window containing the script. To close the current window, simply use

```
self.close();
```

Closing a window opened by the script requires that a reference to the new window be created when it is first opened. This is accomplished by assigning the window object for the new window to a variable and then using the pointer to the window object to call the close() method for the new window:

```
windowPointer = window.open("URL","windowName");
windowPointer.close();
```

Window Focus

By using the focus() and blur() methods it is possible to control which window is in the front and to arbitrarily send a window to the back.

The following page provides two simple buttons: one creates a new window and the other brings it to the front, as shown in Figure 5.8:

```
<HTML>

<HEAD>
<TITLE>focus Example</TITLE>

<SCRIPT LANGUAGE="JavaScript">
var pointer;
</SCRIPT>
</HEAD>

<BODY>
<FORM>
<INPUT TYPE=button VALUE="Create Window"
 onClick="pointer = self.open('new.html','newWindow');"><BR>
<INPUT TYPE=button VALUE="Bring Window to Front"
 onClick="pointer.focus()">
</FORM>
</BODY>

</HTML>
```

FIGURE 5.8.

The focus() *method brings a window to the top.*

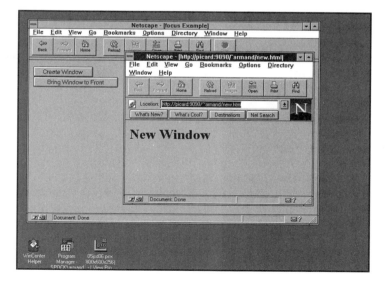

The `history` Object

The `history` object provides the properties and methods needed to work with the history list of a window or frame.

The `history` object does not actually make the content of the list available to the script for security. This is done to prevent scripts from obtaining information about the browsing habits of users and returning it to a server. In addition, some URLs actually encode passwords and other information into the URL, and this needs to be protected from malicious scripts.

Instead, the methods and properties of the `history` object are designed to allow for navigation of the history list:

- `length`—An integer reflecting the length of the history list
- `back()`—Loads the previous URL in the history list
- `forward()`—Loads the next URL in the history list
- `go()`—Loads the URL indicated by an offset from the current place in the list

For instance, `history.back()` jumps back to the previous document while `history.go(2)` jumps forward two documents in the history list.

A string argument also can be passed to the `go()` method. This loads the nearest document in the list that contains the string passed as an argument. This string matching is case insensitive.

The `document` Object

The `document` object is the primary top-level object inside each window or frame. It provides the necessary properties and methods to interact with most of the elements inside a Web document.

The properties and methods of the `document` object are outlined in Table 5.3.

Table 5.3. Methods and properties of the `document` object.

Name	Description
`alinkColor`	The RGB value for the color of activated links.
`applets`	An array reflecting the applets in a document.
`anchors`	An array of anchor objects representing each named anchor in a document.
`bgColor`	The RGB value for the background color of a document.
`cookie`	A string reflecting all cookies for a document. Cookies are discussed in detail in Chapter 9, "Using Cookies."

continues

Table 5.3. continued

Name	Description
Embeds	An array reflecting the plug-ins in a document.
fgColor	The RGB value for the foreground color of a document.
forms	An array of form objects representing each form in a document. Forms are discussed in detail in Chapter 7, "Working with Forms."
images	An array of image objects representing each in-line image in a document.
lastModified	A string reflecting the last date the document was modified.
linkColor	The RGB value for the color of links.
location	An object defining the full URL of a document.
referrer	Reflects the URL of the document that called the current document.
title	A string representing a document title.
vlinkColor	The RGB value of the color of followed links.
open()	Opens a stream of a particular MIME type in the current window. Takes a single string representing the MIME type as an argument.
close()	Closes an output stream opened with document.open().
clear()	Clears the content of a document window after the stream has been closed with document.close().
write()	Outputs text in the stream of the current file. Takes a string as an argument.
writeln()	Output text followed by a new line in the stream of the current file. Takes a string as an argument.

Writing Text to the Current Document Stream

The write() and writeln() methods can be used to output text in the current HTML as it is being rendered.

A basic example of this follows, producing results like those shown in Figure 5.9:

```
<BODY>

<H1>
```

```
<SCRIPT LANGUAGE="JavaScript">
document.writeln("Output by JavaScript");
</SCRIPT>

</H1>

</BODY>
```

FIGURE 5.9.

The writeln() *method can produce HTML output in the current document.*

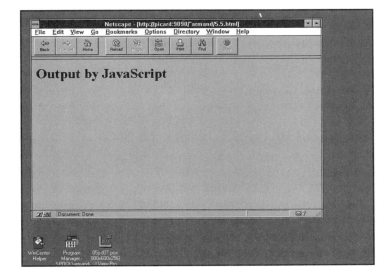

Working with Document Colors

The color properties—alinkColor, bgColor, fgColor, linkColor, vlinkColor—reflect the various color attributes set in the <BODY> tag, such as BGCOLOR, LINK, and VLINK.

These colors are generally specified as hexadecimal triplets. Netscape also supports a list of color names, which are outlined in Appendix E, "Colors by Name and Hex Value."

More than just reflecting the settings in a document, these color properties can be used to dynamically change colors. This is done by assigning new values to the properties.

The following page provides a simple form to change background color dynamically:

```
<HTML>

<HEAD>
<TITLE>Color Example</TITLE>
</HEAD>

<BODY BGCOLOR="#FFFFFF">
<H1>Color Example</H1>
Use the following form to change the background color:
<BR>
```

```
<FORM>
<INPUT TYPE=text NAME="color">
<BR>
<INPUT TYPE=button VALUE="Change Color"
 onClick="document.bgColor=this.form.color.value">
</FORM>
</BODY>

</HTML>
```

This example produces results like those shown in Figure 5.10. This example uses event handlers and forms, which are described in Chapters 6 and 7 respectively.

FIGURE 5.10.

Document colors can be updated dynamically.

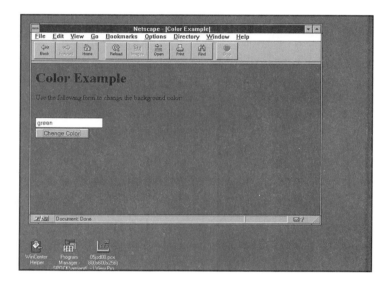

The anchors Array

Anchors in HTML are created using the `<A>` tag in the form

```
<A NAME="name">
```

These anchors can be referenced internally within a document by linking to `<A HREF="#name">` or from another document by linking to `<A HREF="URL#name">`.

These anchors are exposed in JavaScript through the anchors array. Each entry in the array is a single anchor object. Anchors appear in the array in the order of their appearance in the HTML source code, starting with an index of 0.

The anchors array has a single property: length. The actual names of anchors are not reflected in the anchor object. Rather, the array can be used to verify if anchors exist.

The `links` Array

Links are defined in HTML using the `<A>` tag of the form

```
<A HREF="URL">
```

These links are reflected into an array of `link` objects and `Area` objects called `links`. As with the anchors array, links are reflected into the array in the order of their appearance in the HTML code and the array has a single property: `length`.

The `link` and `Area` objects have several properties:

- `hash`—A string reflecting the anchor portion of the link URL (after the "#")
- `host`—A string reflecting the `hostname:port` portion of the link URL
- `hostname`—A string reflecting the host and domain name of the link URL
- `href`—Reflects the entire link URL
- `pathname`—A string reflecting the path portion of the link URL
- `port`—A string reflecting the port number from the link URL
- `protocol`—A string reflecting the protocol of the link URL (before the ":")
- `search`—A string reflecting the query portion of the link URL (after the "?")
- `target`—A string reflecting the `TARGET` attribute of the `<A>` tag

These properties can be updated dynamically by assigning new values to them.

The `location` Object

The `location` object is similar to the `link` object except that it reflects the URL of the current document rather than the URL of a link. It has the same properties as the `link` object—with the exception of the `target` property—and adds several methods:

- `reload()`—Reloads the current document.
- `replace()`—Replaces the current document in the history list. Takes a string argument indicating the URL to load into the current place in the history list.

Opening and Closing Documents

The `open()` method allows an existing window to be opened for writing a new document of a specified MIME type. For instance, the following prepares the existing window referenced by `windowPointer` for receiving HTML.

```
windowPointer.document.open("text/html");
```

Once this stream has been opened, `document.write()` and `document.writeln()` can be used to output the data to be displayed. This stream of data continues until `document.close()` is issued, closing the document stream. Subsequent `document.write()` statements can't write to the document.

For example,

```
<SCRIPT LANGUAGE="JavaScript">

newWindow = window.open("","anotherWindow");
newWindow.document.open("text/html");
newWindow.document.writeln("<H1>Hello in another window!</H1>");
newWindow.document.close();

</SCRIPT>
```

opens a new window called `anotherWindow`, opens a document stream for HTML output, writes out a message, and closes the document.

The `clear()` method can be used after the `close()` method to clear a document window.

Summary

The Navigator Object Tree provides the core of client JavaScript. It includes objects for working with the navigator environment, windows, documents, history lists, and URLs.

In the later chapters, some of the features of the Navigator Object Tree are examined more closely, including the `form` object and Frames.

Chapter 6 covers events processing, which is the key to creating interactive Web applications and dynamic forms.

6

Event Processing

by Wes Tatters

To take full advantage of the powerful capabilities provided by client JavaScript, you need to understand how Netscape Navigator handles *events*.

Events are basically special signals, or messages, which *"occur"* when certain pre-defined actions take place within a Web browser, or when a user interacts with a Web page.

This chapter examines the types of events that exist in client JavaScript and also looks at how *event handlers* can programmatically intercept these event messages. The topics to be discussed include the following:

- The Netscape Navigator event model
- Document-based Events
- Form-based events
- Anchor-based events
- Image-based events
- Window-based events
- Advanced event-processing options

The Netscape Navigator Event Model

Unlike procedural programming languages, which execute their instructions in a predetermined order—traditionally starting with the first instruction and working through to the last—languages like JavaScript have been designed so that they don't need a pre-defined starting or ending point.

Through the use of messaging systems, (or events, in the case of JavaScript) such languages can be made to execute sets of instructions that react to user requests and actions that have no pre-determined order or flow.

For example, when a new document is loaded into Netscape Navigator a *load event* message is triggered by JavaScript, indicating when the Web page has been completely loaded. This message can then be intercepted by a JavaScript program with an event handler, which can be programmed to react to the loading of the new page in some way.

Event Types

The types of events currently recognized by JavaScript fall into one of five basic categories. The following list briefly outlines what each of the categories are. Later in the chapter each of the specific events and their handlers are examined in more detail.

Document-based events	These events are triggered whenever a new page is loaded or an old page is exited. They include the load event and the unload event.
Form-based events	These events are triggered when a user interacts with a form on a Web page. They include the focus, blur, change select, and submit events.
Anchor-based events	Whenever a user clicks on a hyperlink in a Web page, an anchor-based event is triggered. Anchor-based events include the click and mouseover events.
Element-based events	These events communicate the status of images associated with a Web page. They include the load, error, and abort events.
Window-based events	Whenever more than one window is displayed by Netscape Navigator, window-based events are used to indicate which window is currently active. They include the blur and focus event.

Event Handlers

Once an event message has been triggered, you need a way to intercept the message and react to it. This is achieved in JavaScript through the use of *event handlers*.

Event handlers are a block of JavaScript commands that have been directly associated with an HTML tag that relates to the particular type of event you want to intercept. The basic syntax for an event handler follows:

```
<TAG ATTRIBUTES onEventHandler="JavaScript commands">
```

The TAG represents an HTML tag supporting a particular category of events, and onEventHandler is the name of the event you want to intercept. The JavaScript commands that you want to execute when this event message is activated are placed inside the quotes following the equal sign.

For example, to intercept the document load event and display an alert message indicating when a Web page has loaded, you would write

```
<BODY onLoad="window.alert('Page Loaded');">
  Your Web page contents go here.
</BODY>
```

In this example, the <BODY> document tag includes an onLoad event handler to intercept the document load event message. When this message is triggered, the JavaScript statement window.alert ('Page Loaded') is executed, causing an alert box like the one shown in Figure 6.1 to be displayed.

FIGURE 6.1.

The onLoad *event handler can trigger an alert message to tell you when a Web page is completely loaded.*

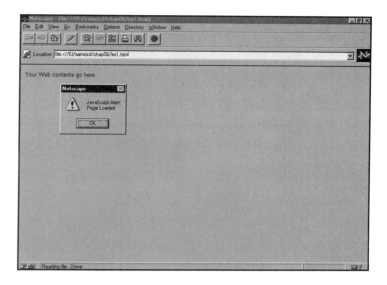

If you want an event handler to execute more than one command, you can include all the commands inside the quotes, separating each instruction with a semicolon:

```
<BODY onLoad="window.alert('Page Loaded'); count = count + 1; ">
```

An alternative method is to call your own pre-defined functions or methods:

```
<BODY onLoad="myFunction();">
```

this keyword

The this keyword—mentioned in previous chapters—takes on a special significance when it is associated with events and event handlers. Take for example the following statement:

```
<BODY onLoad="myFunction( this );">
```

When the term this is used inside an event handler, it represents an alias or pointer to the object directly associated with the current tag. In this case, this points to the window object for the current document.

Document-Based Events

As you have already read, document-based events are sent whenever a new Web page is loaded or when an old Web page is exited. Specifically, the two events that are generated for documents are the load event, which occurs whenever a new page is loaded, and the unload event, which occurs whenever a page is exited.

There are two HTML tags that can be associated with document-based events. These are the `<BODY>` tag and the `<FRAMESET>` tag. (A detailed discussion of the `<FRAMESET>` tag can be found in Chapter 8, "Frames and JavaScript.")

onLoad **Event Handler**

When attached to a `<BODY>` tag, the onLoad event handler is called once a Web page has been completely loaded. To include an onLoad event handler in a `<BODY>` tag, you would write something like the following:

```
<BODY onLoad="window.alert("Welcome to the World's best Web page");">
```

Alternatively, when attached to a `<FRAMESET>` tag, the onLoad event handler is called once the entire frameset has been completely loaded. When included in a `<FRAMESET>` tag, the onLoad event handler takes the following form:

```
<FRAMESET ROWS="*,*" onLoad="myFunct("frameset loaded");">
    <FRAME …>
    <FRAME …>
</FRAMESET>
```

NOTE

It is important to understand that the load event is not triggered when the Web page is first displayed, but instead when all elements (including images, applets, and plug-ins) are fully loaded and displayed.

onUnload **Event Handler**

When attached to a `<BODY>` tag, the onUnload event handler is called as a Web page is exited, either by loading a new Web page or by closing the Navigator program. The onUnload event handler is included in the `<BODY>` tag in much the same way as the onLoad event handler:

```
<BODY onLoad="window.alert('welcome');" onUnload="window.alert('bye');">
```

This example also demonstrates that a document can have both an onLoad and an onUnload event handler associated with it at the same time.

Like the onLoad event handler, the onUnload event handler can be associated with a `<FRAMESET>` tag, in which case the onUnload event handler is only called when the entire frameset is exited.

Form-Based Events

One of the most useful functions associated with events in client JavaScript is the ability to intercept actions taken by a user as he or she fills out information on a form.

Most of the HTML elements associated with forms support one or more event handlers, depending on the purpose of the element. Table 6.1 outlines each of the form elements and the event handlers they support. The following pages then examine the use of each event handler.

Table 6.1. Form-based event handlers in client JavaScript.

Form Element	Event Handlers Recognized
Button element	onClick
Checkbox	onClick
Radio button	onClick
Selection list	onBlur, onChange, onFocus
Text element	onBlur, onChange, onFocus, onSelect
Textarea element	onBlur, onChange, onFocus, onSelect
Reset button	onClick
Submit button	onClick
Form	onSubmit

> **NOTE**
>
> The following pages discuss the events that can be associated with the form tag and form fields but do not examine the process of programming forms in detail. This discussion is left to Chapter 7, "Working with Forms."

onFocus **Event Handler**

Consider the form shown in Figure 6.2, which contains a number of separate fields where a user can enter information. When the user places the cursor into one of these fields, that field is said to be *given focus*. Once a field has focus, a user can type information into it.

When one field has the focus, all other fields on the form are said to be *out of focus*, or *blurred*.

To help programmers keep track of which field is currently in focus, a focus event message is generated by JavaScript whenever a user enters a select, text, or textarea field. This focus event can be intercepted by including an onFocus event handler in any <INPUT> tag of type TEXT, in any <SELECT> tag, or any <TEXTAREA> tag. (See Chapter 7 for a full discussion of these tags.)

You declare an onFocus event handler for a text input field by writing the following:

```
<INPUT TYPE="TEXT" SIZE="2" NAME="Country" onFocus="SetCountry( this )">
```

In this example, whenever a user clicks on the Country field or attempts to enter it by any other means, the function SetCountry(this) is automatically called. (In this case, this points to a text object that represents the Country field.) See Chapter 7 for more details on developing interactive forms using JavaScript.

FIGURE 6.2.

A simple data entry form with focus on the Given Names field.

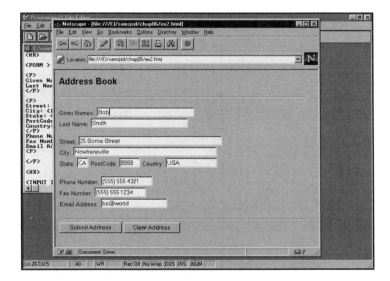

onBlur **Event Handler**

The blur event indicates the opposite action to that of a focus event. Whenever a user exits a select, text, or textarea field, a blur event is triggered. To intercept the blur event, an onBlur event handler can be associated with any <INPUT> tag of type TEXT, any <SELECT> tag, or <TEXTAREA> tag.

One of the main uses of the onBlur event handler is for validating the contents of a field once it has been entered. In the following example, a function called valid() is executed when the user exits the e-mail field. The function is passed the value of the e-mail field by using the statement this.value:

```
<INPUT TYPE="TEXT" SIZE="20" NAME="Email" onBlur="valid( this.value )">
```

onChange **Event Handler**

Whenever a user exits a select, text, or textarea field where the contents of the field have been altered, a change event is triggered. To intercept the change event, an onChange event handler can be associated with any <INPUT> tag of type TEXT, any <SELECT> tag, or any <TEXTAREA> tag.

Like the onBlur event handler, the main use of the onChange event handler is for validating the contents of a field once it has been entered. In the following example, a function called valid() is executed whenever the user exits the e-mail field and the contents of the field have been altered:

```
<INPUT TYPE="TEXT" SIZE="20" NAME="Email"
➥onChange="if (this.value == '') { alert('Please Enter a Value') }">
```

This event handler would produce results like those shown in Figure 6.3 if the user removes focus from the field without entering a value.

FIGURE 6.3.

Using the onBlur *event handler, it is possible to perform basic validation on form data.*

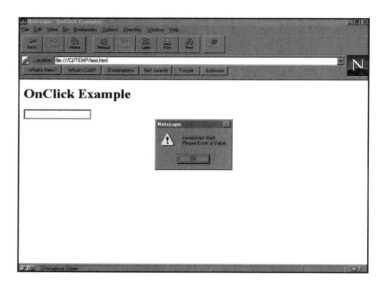

onClick **Event Handler**

Whenever a checkbox, radio button, submit or reset button, or a form button is clicked by the user, a click event is triggered. To intercept these click events, an onClick event handler can be associated with any <INPUT> tag of type BUTTON, CHECKBOX, RADIO, RESET, or SUBMIT.

For example, to detect when a user has clicked on the submit button of a form, you would write something like the following:

```
<INPUT TYPE="SUBMIT" VALUE="Submit Address" onClick="validate( this.form );">
```

In this example, the function validate() is executed whenever a user clicks on the Submit Address button. Also, the special alias this.form has been used to pass the current form object to the validate() function instead of passing the submit object, which would have been the case if validate(this) had been used.

> **NOTE**
>
> By returning a value of false to an onClick handler, the action associated with a button can be canceled. For example, if the event handler code in the previous example had been written as onClick="return validate(this.form)" and the function validate() returned a value of false, the form submission would be canceled.

onSelect **Event Handler**

A select event occurs when a user selects or highlights any of the text within a text or textarea field. To intercept a select event, place an onSelect event handler in the appropriate TEXT type <INPUT> tag or <TEXTAREA> tag.

To incorporate an onSelect event handler into a <TEXTAREA> tag, you would write the following:

```
<TEXTAREA NAME="TextItem" ROWS=6 COLS=55 onSelect="selectText()">
Selecting any of the text in this field
will cause a select event to be triggered.
</TEXTAREA>
```

Whenever a user selects any of the text in the TextItem field, the selectText() function indicated by the onSelect event handler is called.

> **NOTE**
>
> The implementation of onSelect is currently unstable as of Navigator 3.0b3 and does not work as advertised on the Windows platform.

onSubmit **Event Handler**

Unlike all of the other form-based events that interact with specific fields on a form, the submit event is only available from within the <FORM> tag itself. When a user attempts to submit a form, a click event is first generated for the appropriate submit button. Once this event has been processed, a submit event is triggered.

To intercept a submit event, place an onSubmit event handler within the forms <FORM> tag, as shown in the following example:

```
<FORM METHOD="POST" NAME="myForm"
     ACTION="../cgi-bin/form"
     onSubmit="return valid( this );" >
```

In this example, a function called valid() is executed when a user attempts to submit the form. The function performs some processing to verify that the user has entered the correct information. If any information is wrong, valid() returns a result of false; otherwise it returns a true result. When a false result is returned by the onSubmit event handler, the submission process is aborted.

> **NOTE**
>
> When this is used inside a <FORM> tag, it refers to the form object itself and not to any single element, as was the case in previous examples.

Anchor-Based Events

Anchor-based events are caused by the user either clicking on a hyperlink within a Web page or by moving the mouse cursor over the top of a hyperlink. Hyperlinks are defined using the <A> tag in HTML.

onClick **Event Handler**

Whenever a user clicks on a hyperlink within a Web page, a click event is triggered within JavaScript. To intercept this click event, you place an onClick event handler within the link tag:

```
<A HREF="some URL" onClick="someFunction();">This is a link</A>
```

One of the most common reasons for using an onClick handler with a hyperlink is to dynamically alter the destination of the link.

This can be easily achieved in JavaScript using a link like the following:

```
<A HREF="some URL" onClick="this.href = randomLink();">This is a link</A>
```

In this example, whenever the user clicks on the link, a function called `randomLink()` is executed. This function returns a URL which is then assigned to `this.href`—a property of the link object. Once `this.href` is set, the new link is opened, replacing the old Web page.

As was the case in the earlier discussion of `onClick` handlers for form-based events, the click event for a hyperlink can also be canceled by returning a value of `false` to the `onClick` handler:

```
<A HREF="some URL" onClick="return someFunction();">This is a link</A>
```

If the function `someFunction()` returns a `false` value, then the click event is canceled, and no new page loaded.

onMouseOver **Event Handler**

When a user moves the mouse cursor over a hyperlink, a mouseover event is triggered. To intercept a mouseover event, you place an `onMouseOver` event handler within the link tag:

```
<A HREF="some URL" onMouseOver="someFunction();">This is a link</A>
```

One of the most common reasons for using an `onMouseOver` handler with a hyperlink is to display a message or description in the status line indicating the action performed by the link. To do this, you write the following:

```
<A HREF="some URL"
   onMouseOver="window.status='Click to load a new page'; return true;">
New Page</A>
```

In this example, whenever the user moves the mouse cursor over the top of the New Page link, the message "Click to load a new page" is displayed in the status bar.

> **NOTE**
>
> You must return a value of `true` to the `onMouseOver` event handler before any message can be displayed in the status bar. This is achieved by placing the statement `return true;` as the last command the event handler executes.

onMouseOut **Event Handler**

The mouseout event represents the opposite of the mouseover event. Whereas a mouseover event is triggered when a user moves the mouse cursor over a hyperlink, the mouseout event is triggered when the user moves the mouse cursor off the link again.

To intercept a mouseout event, you place an `onMouseOut` event handler within the link tag:

```
<A HREF="some URL" onMouseOut="someFunction();">This is a link</A>
```

The most common reason for using an `onMouseOut` handler with a hyperlink is to remove a message or description from the status line that was put there by an `onMouseOver` event. To do this, you write the following:

```
<A HREF="some URL"
   onMouseOver ="window.status='Click to load a new page'; return true;"
   onMouseOut  ="window.status=''; return true;" >
New Page</A>
```

In this example, whenever the user moves the mouse cursor over the top of the New Page link, the message "Click to load a new page" is displayed in the status bar. When the cursor is moved away from the hyperlink, the `onMouseOut` event handler is triggered to remove the message from the status bar. These results look like those shown in Figures 6.4 and 6.5.

> **NOTE**
>
> Like the `onMouseOver` event handler, you must return a value of `true` to the `onMouseOut` event handler before any message can be displayed in the status bar. This is achieved by placing the statement `return true;` as the last command the event handler executes.

FIGURE 6.4.

The onMouseOver *event handler can be used to display text in the status bar when the mouse pointer moves over a link.*

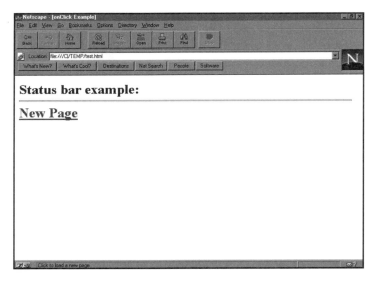

FIGURE 6.5.

The onMouseOut *event is used to react to the user moving the mouse pointer off of a link.*

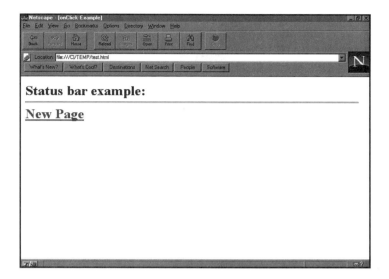

Element-Based Events

Any information displayed on a Web page other than text is treated by Netscape Navigator as a separate page element. In the current Navigator version, these elements fall into one of three categories:

■ Images

■ Java applets

■ Plug-in objects

Because these elements are treated as separate entities from the rest of a Web page, it is often useful to know when each has completed loading. For this reason JavaScript includes a small set of element-based event handlers that can be used to intercept element load events, load error events, and load abort events.

Presently, Navigator 3 supports these events for images.

onLoad **Event Handler**

Like the document load event that is triggered when an entire Web page is loaded, an element load event is triggered when the element it is associated with is fully loaded. To intercept the element load event for an image, you place an onLoad event handler in the element tag associated with the item you are interested in.

For example, to attach an onLoad event to an image you would write the following:

```
<IMG SRC="someimage.gif" HEIGHT="50" WIDTH="50" onLoad="someFunction();">
```

In this example, the function someFunction() is called once the image has been completely loaded.

onError **Event Handler**

An error event is triggered for an image if any problems occur while the image is being loaded. This could include not being able to access the required file, some software related difficulty, or possibly some form of version incompatibilities.

To intercept the error event for an image, place an onError event handler in the element tag associated with the item you are interested in.

For example, to attach an onError event to an image you would write the following:

```
<IMG SRC="someimage.gif" HEIGHT="50" WIDTH="50" onError="someFunction();">
```

In this example the function someFunction() is called only if there is an error while loading the image, which results in the image not being able to load completely.

onAbort **Event Handler**

Because Netscape navigator normally loads and displays the text contents of a Web page before any other elements are displayed, you sometimes encounter situations where other elements are never completely loaded, either because the user has clicked on the stop button or because a new hyperlink has been selected. In such cases an abort event is triggered for each image.

To intercept the image abort event, place an onAbort event handler in the tag associated with the image you are interested in.

For example, to attach an onAbort event to an image, you would write the following:

```
<IMG SRC="someimage.gif" HEIGHT="50" WIDTH="50" onAbort="someFunction();">
```

In this example, the function someFunction() is called only if the loading of the specified image is stopped, by the user either clicking on the stop button or selecting a new Webpage.

Window-Based Events

Because Netscape Navigator enables you to open more than one window at once, it is often very useful to know exactly which window is currently active, or, in other words, which window has focus. The two window-based events discussed in this section enable you to keep track of when a window gains focus and when it loses it.

onFocus **Event Handler**

Whenever a window is activated or brought into focus, a window focus event is triggered by JavaScript. This event can be intercepted by placing a window onFocus event handler in either the <BODY> tag of a single frame window or the <FRAMESET> tag of a frameset window.

For example, to assign the function myFunction() to the window onFocus event handler of the current browser window, you would write

```
<BODY onFocus=" myFunction();" >
```

Whenever the window containing this document gains focus, the function myFunction() is automatically called.

onBlur **Event Handler**

When a window loses focus, a window blur event is triggered by JavaScript. This event can be intercepted by using a window onBlur event handler. To intercept a window blur event you place an onBlur event handler in either the <BODY> tag of a single frame window or the <FRAMESET> tag of a frameset window.

For example, to attach an onBlur event handler to a frameset you would write the following:

```
<FRAMESET ROWS="*,*" onBlur="myFunction();" >
    <FRAME …>
    <FRAME …>
</FRAMESET>
```

This command assigns the function myFunction() to the window onBlur event handler of the current browser window. Once set, whenever this window loses focus, myFunction() is called automatically.

Advanced Event Processing Options

In addition to defining event handlers by coding them into your HTML code, many handlers also can be maintained programmatically. This section examines the process of defining event handlers in JavaScript code and looks at how event messages can be triggered by JavaScript commands.

Assigning Events by Code

Whenever you assign an event handler to a tag, what actually happens internally in the Web browser is that an event property of the object associated with the tag is set to contain the JavaScript code you defined in the event handler. See the following example:

```
<BODY onFocus="myFocusFunction();" onBlur="myBlurFunction();" >
```

Internally two properties of the window object are set, because window events are associated with the window object. In this case, `window.onfocus` is set equal to `"myFocusFunct();"`, and `window.onblur` is set equal to `"myBlurFunction();"`.

The fact that these properties exist means that you can set their contents using JavaScript code. For this reason, the event handlers in the previous `<BODY>` statement also could have been defined using the following JavaScript code:

```
<SCRIPT>
window.onfocus = myFocusFunction ;
window.onblur = myBlurFunction ;
</SCRIPT>
```

There are a few items to which you need to pay close attention. First, the name of the property is written in all lowercase, so `onFocus` becomes `onfocus`. HTML code in not case-specific, remember.

Second, when indicating which function should be called, you only write the function name and not the trailing parentheses. You need to do this so that the actual function is assigned to the event handler and not the result of a call to the function.

Objects Associated with Event Handlers

Table 6.2 lists all of the event handlers that can be set programmatically. It also lists the corresponding objects of the event handlers.

> **NOTE**
>
> Some of these handlers are still under development as of Navigator 3b3, but most are expected in the final Navigator 3 release.

Table 6.2. Objects associated with event handlers.

Event Type	Handler	Object	Example
Document	onLoad	document	document.onload =
	onUnload	document	document.onunload =
Form	onSubmit	form	document.myform.onsubmit =
	onBlur	text	document.myform.textname.onblur =
	onBlur	textarea	document.myform.textaname.onblur =
	onBlur	select	document.myform.selectname.onblur =
	onChange	text	document.myform.textname.onchange =
	onChange	textarea	document.myform.textaname.onchange =

Event Type	Handler	Object	Example
	onChange	select	document.myform.selectname.onchange =
	onClick	button	document.myform.buttonname.onfocus =
	onClick	checkbox	document.myform.checkname.onfocus =
	onClick	radio	document.myform.radioname.onfocus =
	onClick	reset	document.myform.resetname.onfocus =
	onClick	submit	document.myform.submitname.onfocus =
	onFocus	text	document.myform.textname.onfocus =
	onFocus	textarea	document.myform.textaname.onfocus =
	onFocus	select	document.myform.selectname.onfocus =
	onSelect	text	document.myform.textname.onselect =
	onSelect	textarea	document.myform.textaname.onselect =
Anchor	onClick	link	document.links[0].onclick =
	onMouseOver	link	document.links[0].onmouseover =
	onMouseOut	link	document.links[0].onmouseout =
Element	onAbort	image	document.images[0].onabort =
	onAbort	applet	document.applets[0].onabort =
	onAbort	plugin	navigator.plugins[0].onabort =
	onError	image	document.images[0].onerror =
	onError	applet	document.applets[0].onerror =
	onError	plugin	navigator.plugins[0].onerror =
	onLoad	image	document.images[0].onload =
	onLoad	applet	document.applets[0].onload =
	onLoad	plugin	navigator.plugins[0].onload =
Window	onBlur	window	window.onblur =
	onFocus	window	window.onfocus =

NOTE

Refer to the online JavaScript guide provided by Netscape for the most up-to-date information on supported element handlers.

Triggering Events by Code

So far in this chapter, all of the discussions dealing with the triggering of events have indicated that the events were triggered by some user driven action, be it interaction with a form, selecting a link, or loading a new Web page. Most events are triggered by user-driven action, but there is a way to trigger some of the events discussed in this chapter by using JavaScript program calls.

Take for example the blur and focus window events. Traditionally, these events are triggered when the user brings a new window into focus by clicking on a window. With the introduction of the window.blur() and window.focus() methods to the window object, it is now possible to force a window into or out of focus using program calls.

If the method window.blur() is called from anywhere within a JavaScript program, the window associated with the object is forced out of focus, sending it to the back of the screen on most platforms. Likewise, the window.focus() method can be called to force a window back into focus, or to put it in different terms, back to being the top window on the screen.

The following list outlines the various methods that can be used to programmatically cause events to take place.

blur()   The blur() method can be used with window, text, textarea, select, and password objects to force the given element out of focus.

focus()   The focus() method can be used with window, text, textarea, select, and password objects to force the given element into focus.

select()   When used with either a text, textarea, select, or password object, the select() method causes all the text in the chosen field to be selected or highlighted.

The focus() and select() methods are often used together to programmatically select a field on a form and highlight its contents.

For example, if a field in a form has an onBlur event handler associated with it that calls a function validate(this), the field can be forced back into focus and highlighted by using code like the following:

```
function validate( field ) {
    if ( field == "" ) {
        alert("You must complete the name field.")
        field.focus()
        field.select()
    }
}
```

click()   The click() method enables you to simulate the clicking of a radio button, checkbox, form button, or the submit and reset buttons.

If `click()` is used with a radio button, the chosen radio button becomes the selected radio button. For checkboxes, the checkbox is toggled on and off. For buttons on a form, any action associated with the button is activated as though the user had selected it herself.

As an example of using events programmatically, the following code uses a hypertext link to submit the form name `testForm`:

```
<FORM NAME="testForm" METHOD="POST" ACTION="someURL">
<INPUT TYPE=text NAME="testField">
</FORM>
<A HREF="javascript:document.testForm.submit()">Submit Form</A>
```

Summary

Events and their corresponding event handlers form the basis of much of the interaction with a Web page that JavaScript makes possible. These events can be categorized into one of five categories: document-based events, form-based events, anchor-based events, element-based events and window-based events.

To interact with any of the events in these five categories, you use what are called event handlers. Event handlers are blocks of JavaScript code that tell a JavaScript program how to react to events.

Now that you have an understanding of how events and event handlers work in JavaScript, you are better ready to understand the intricacies of work with forms. This topic is discussed in the next chapter.

7

Working with Forms

by Arman Danesh

HTML provides for basic interactivity with forms. Forms enable page authors to request user input with a variety of interface tools, including text fields, checkboxes, and drop-down lists. However, the degree of interaction with the user is limited because the data from the forms must be submitted to the server for processing.

Client JavaScript extends this model to enable interactivity in forms without requiring the form's content to be sent to the server. Forms are defined in JavaScript with the Form object and each form element, such as text input fields and radio buttons, is further defined by objects. This chapter examines these objects and their properties, methods, and events. The topics to be discussed include the following:

■ The <FORM> Tag
■ The Form Object
■ Form Element Objects
■ Form Validation

The <FORM> Tag

Forms in HTML are defined using the <FORM> tag. Using the <FORM> tag, the global properties of a form are defined, including how the document should be processed, the name of the form, and an event handler for when a form is submitted.

The <FORM> tag takes five possible attributes—METHOD, ACTION, TARGET, NAME, and ENCTYPE—in addition to the onSubmit event handler.

The METHOD Attribute

The METHOD attribute can take two values: GET or POST. These indicate how the form data should be submitted to the server for CGI processing. The GET method attaches all the contents of the form elements to the URL specified in the ACTION attribute.

The GET Method

GET-type submissions look like:

```
Script_URL?element_name_1=element_value_1&element_name_2=element_value_2
```

The Script_URL is specified with the ACTION attribute, which is discussed in a following section. This is followed by a question mark and then name=value pairs for each form element. Each pair is separated by an ampersand.

The POST Method

Unlike the GET method, the POST method transfers the form content to the server through the standard-input, which is accessible to CGI scripts or programs.

The ACTION Attribute

The ACTION attribute is used to specify the URL of a CGI script or a LiveWire application that will process the contents of the form. ACTION URLs also can take the form mailto:*email@host.name* if the contents of the form are simply to be e-mailed to someone.

For instance, to direct the contents of the form to a CGI script called processform using the POST method, the FORM tag would look like

```
<FORM METHOD=POST ACTION="/cgi-bin/processform">
```

The TARGET Attribute

The TARGET attribute is used to indicate the window or frame where the results of processing the form contents should be displayed. Anything returned from the CGI script or LiveWire application specified in the ACTION attribute is displayed in the named frame or window.

In addition to specifying existing windows or frames, new windows can be created to display the returned content simply by specifying a new name in the TARGET attribute.

In addition, the four special window names—_top, _parent, _self, and _blank—can be used in the TARGET attribute. These are discussed in more detail in Chapter 8, "Frames and JavaScript."

The NAME Attribute

The NAME attribute enables each form to be named. This is useful in scripts in which more than one form needs to be worked with. You see how named forms are used later in this chapter.

> **NOTE**
>
> Names of forms, like names of windows and frames, cannot contain any spaces.

The ENCTYPE Attribute

The ENCTYPE attribute specifies the MIME type of the data being sent from the form to the script on the server. The default mime type is application/x-www-form-urlencoded.

The form Object

Each form in an HTML document is defined by its own object in JavaScript. As you learned in Chapter 5 when you looked at the Navigator Object Tree, the form object is a property of the document object.

The `forms` Array

All the forms in an HTML document are stored in an array called `forms`, so it's possible to access a specific form, and its properties or methods, using an index number. Indexes for each form are numbered sequentially as they are defined in the HTML document and start at zero— the default initial index for all JavaScript arrays. For instance, you can refer to

```
document.forms[index].propertyName
```

or

```
document.forms[index].methodName()
```

At the same time, forms can be referred to by the name specified in the NAME attribute of the `<FORM>` tag. For instance, `document.formName.propertyName` refers to a property of the form with the name `formName`.

Properties of the `form` Object

The `form` object has six properties—`action`, `elements`, `encoding`, `length`, `method`, and `target`. In addition, objects for each form element are properties of the `form` object.

The `action` Property

The `action` property is a string that reflects the ACTION attribute of the `<FORM>` tag. The action property can be dynamically changed at any time by assigning a new string to the property. This effectively overrides any ACTION value specified in the `<FORM>` tag.

For instance, if the ACTION attribute of a form named `formName` has been defined as `Script_URL` in the `<FORM>` tag, then

```
document.formName.action = "New_Script_URL";
```

would change the value to `New_Script_URL` and any subsequent attempt to submit the form's contents would direct the submission to `New_Script_URL` instead of `Script_URL`.

The `elements` Array

The `elements` array is an array of objects for each element in the form. The elements appear in the array in the order in which they appear in the HTML source code.

The elements array can be used to reference specific form elements. For instance,

```
document.formName.elements[0]
```

refers to the first element in the form named `formName`, and

```
document.forms[1].elements[2]
```

refers to the third element in the second form in a document.

Like the `forms` array, an alternate method of referring to form elements is by their names. As you will see later in this chapter when individual form elements are discussed, these elements can have names.

For instance, you could refer to a text field named *fieldName* in a form named *formName* as

`document.`*formName*`.`*fieldName*

The length of the elements array is specified by the `length` property:

`document.`*formName*`.elements.length`

The encoding Property

The encoding property is a string that reflects the value of the ENCTYPE attribute in the <FORM> tag. It specifies the MIME type of the data being submitted to the server for processing.

Like the `action` property, a new value can be assigned to the `encoding` property at any time, effectively overriding the value specified in the ENCTYPE attribute.

The length Property

Like the `length` property of the `elements` array, the number of elements in a form is also reflected in the `length` property of the `form` object. Just as

`document.`*formName*`.elements.length`

reflects the number of elements in a form, so does

`document.`*formName*`.length`

The method Property

The `method` property is a string that reflects the value of the METHOD attribute of the <FORM> tag. Its value should be either `get` or `post`.

Like the `action` and `encoding` properties, a new value can be assigned to the `method` property, effectively overriding the value specified in the METHOD attribute.

The target Property

The `target` property is a string that reflects the value of the TARGET attribute of the <FORM> tag. Its value is the name of the frame or window that receives the result of submitting the form.

Again, the `target` property can be assigned a new value, overriding the original value in the <FORM> tag. The value assigned to the target property can't be an expression or variable.

Method of the `form` Object

The `form` object has one method—the `submit()` method.

The `submit()` Method

The `submit()` method submits the form as if the user had clicked on the submit button. The `submit()` also triggers the `onSubmit` event handler for the given form.

> **NOTE**
>
> Event methods such as `submit()` trigger their corresponding event handlers. It's important to be aware of this and ensure that you avoid circular loops in which event handlers call their corresponding event methods, in turn triggering the event handler again.

Event Handler of the `form` Object

The `form` object has one event handler—the `onSubmit` event handler.

The `onSubmit` Event Handler

The `onSubmit` event handler is specified in the `<FORM>` tag:

```
<FORM METHOD="method" ACTION="action" onSubmit="JavaScript_Code">
```

The code executed by the `onSubmit` event handler can be used to prevent the form from being submitted. If the code uses a `return` statement to return a value of `false`, then the form isn't submitted. Otherwise, the form is submitted.

Field-Based Objects

HTML forms can contain seven different types of input fields: text fields, `textarea` fields, radio buttons, checkbox buttons, hidden fields, password fields, and select menus.

Each of these fields is reflected by an object that is also a property of the form object.

The `<INPUT>` tag is used to define many of these fields in a form. The `<INPUT>` tag takes four attributes: `TYPE`, `NAME`, `VALUE`, and `SIZE`. The `<INPUT>` tag is used to define five of the input fields—text fields, radio buttons, checkbox buttons, hidden fields, and password fields—as well as the button elements discussed later in this chapter.

The `TYPE` attribute specifies the type of form element being defined with the `<INPUT>` tag. It takes the following possible values: `text`, `radio`, `checkbox`, `hidden`, `password`, `button`, `reset`, or `submit`.

The NAME attribute is a string specifying the name of the field, and the VALUE attribute is a string specifying the initial value of a text field or the name of a button or checkbox.

The SIZE attribute specifies the number of characters a text field can display before it has to scroll the text in the field. The value of SIZE is an integer.

The text Object

The text object reflects text fields in forms. Text fields are single-line fields where the user can enter text in the form. They are defined using the <INPUT> tag. For instance,

```
<INPUT TYPE="text" NAME="fieldName" VALUE="initialValue" SIZE="size">
```

defines a text field with the name fieldName, an initial value of initialValue, and a size of size characters.

The text object has three properties, three methods, and four event handlers.

The defaultValue Property

The defaultValue property reflects the initial value of a text field as defined by the VALUE attribute of the INPUT tag. It is a string.

The value of defaultValue can be changed but doesn't cause the displayed value of the field to be updated. Rather, the next time the defaultValue property is evaluated, it returns the new value. For instance, the following code segment changes the defaultValue of the text field named firstName in the form named testForm:

```
document.testForm.firstName.defaultValue = "A New Value";
```

Subsequent references to document.testForm.firstName.defaultValue return "A New Value."

The name Property

The name property is a string containing the value of the NAME attribute in the INPUT tag. The name property can be changed to override the value in the NAME attribute.

The following for loop searches through all the elements of a form named thisForm and when it finds a field named testField, it changes the name to newTestField:

```
for (i = 0; i < document.thisForm.elements.length; i++) {
    if (document.thisForm.elements[i].name == "testField")
    document.thisForm.elements[i].name = "newTestField";
}
```

The value Property

The value property is a string value reflecting the current value in the text field. Changing the value of the value property causes the actual text displayed in the text field to be updated to the new value of the property.

The `focus()` Method

The `focus()` method causes input focus to be directed to the text object. This then enables the user to enter text into the field or the data in the field to be changed by the script.

Consider the following example:

```
<FORM METHOD=POST ACTION="SomeURL" NAME="testForm"
➡onSubmit="if (document.testForm.nameField.value == "") {
   alert ("Please enter a name");
   document.testForm.nameField.focus();
   return false;
}">
<INPUT TYPE="text" NAME="nameField" VALUE="" SIZE=30>
<INPUT TYPE="submit">
</FORM>
```

The `focus()` method is used in the `onSubmit` event handler. If the field `nameField` is blank, focus is returned to the field and the `submit` event is canceled by returning a `false` value.

The `blur()` Method

Focus is removed from a text field using the `blur()` method.

For instance, in the following code segment, the field `displayField` is used by the script to display output but should not be alterable by the user. The `blur()` method in the `onFocus` event handler ensures that focus can never be given to the field:

```
<INPUT TYPE="text" NAME="displayField" VALUE="Initial Value"
onFocus="this.blur()">
```

Notice the use of the `this` keyword to refer to the current `text` object.

The `select()` Method

The `select()` method is used to select and highlight the content of the text field. This does not, by default, force input focus into the field, however.

The following code segment gives input focus to the field `nameField` in the form `testForm` and then highlights the text in the field.

```
document.testForm.nameField.focus();
document.testForm.nameField.select();
```

Event Handlers of the `text` Object

The `text` object has four event handlers: `onFocus`, `onBlur`, `onChange`, and `onSelect`.

`onFocus` and `onBlur` specify JavaScript code to execute when input focus is given to, or removed from, the text field. `onChange` is triggered when the user changes the value of a text field and then removes focus from the field. The `onSelect` event handler specifies actions to occur when the user selects (or highlights) some or all of the text in the field.

The textarea Object

A textarea in a form is similar to a text field in that it enables the user to enter text. Unlike the text field, the textarea field supports multi-line text entry.

The textarea field is defined in a form using the <TEXTAREA> tag. The <TEXTAREA> tag takes four attributes: NAME, ROWS, COLS, and WRAP.

NAME is a string specifying the name of the text field. ROWS and COLS are integers defining the size of the viewable area of the textarea field in characters. Scrollbars enable text blocks larger than the field to be entered and viewed.

The WRAP attribute specifies how to handle text wrapping when the user enters text into the field. It takes three possible values: off, virtual, and physical. With WRAP set to off, no text wrapping occurs—the user must hit return to wrap to the next line. The virtual value causes text to be wrapped in the display, but the value sent to the server for processing doesn't include the line breaks generated by line wrapping. The physical value causes text wrapping to be displayed and the resulting line breaks to be sent to the server when the form is submitted.

Initial text to be displayed in the textarea field is contained between the <TEXTAREA> and </TEXTAREA> tags.

For instance,

```
<TEXTAREA NAME="testField" ROWS=15 COLS=40 WRAP=physical> Initial Text </TEXTAREA>
```

Defines a 40 column by 15 row textarea field with physical wrapping named testField and an initial value of "Initial Text".

The textarea object has three properties, three methods, and four event handlers.

FIGURE 7.1.
The textarea field is a multi-line text entry field that can contain an initial value.

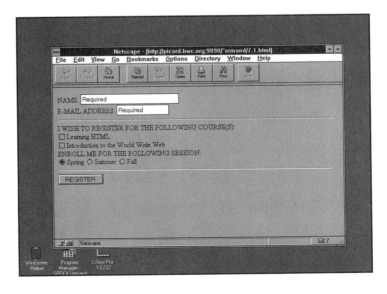

The `defaultValue` Property

The `defaultValue` property reflects the initial value of a `textarea` field as defined by the text between the `<TEXTAREA>` and `</TEXTAREA>` tags.

The value of `defaultValue` can be changed but doesn't cause the displayed value of the field to be updated. Rather, the next time the `defaultValue` property is evaluated, it returns the new value.

The `name` Property

The `name` property is a string containing the value of the NAME attribute in the TEXTAREA tag. The `name` property can be changed to override the value in the NAME attribute.

The `value` Property

The `value` property is a string value reflecting the current value in the `textarea` field. Changing the value of the `value` property causes the actual text displayed in the `textarea` field to be updated to the new value of the property.

The `focus()` Method

The `focus()` method causes focus to be directed to the `textarea` object. This then enables the user to enter text into the field or the data in the field to be changed by the script.

The `blur()` Method

Focus is removed from a `textarea` field using the `blur()` method.

The `select()` Method

The `select()` method is used to select and highlight the content of the `text` field. This does not, by default, force input focus into the field, however.

Event Handlers of the `textarea` Object

The `textarea` object has four event handlers: `onFocus`, `onBlur`, `onChange`, and `onSelect`.

`onFocus` and `onBlur` specify JavaScript code to execute when input focus is given to, or removed from, the `textarea` field. `onChange` is triggered when the user changes the value of a `textarea` field and then removes focus from the field. The `onSelect` event handler specifies actions to occur when the user selects (or highlights) some or all of the text in the field.

The `radio` Object

Radio buttons are a set of clickable buttons on an HTML form in which only one button can be selected at any one time.

They are defined by multiple <INPUT> tags, all with TYPE set to radio and the same NAME. The VALUE attribute of each <INPUT> tag specifies the value sent to the server when the form is submitted. A special attribute, CHECKED, enables the initial selection to be specified.

The text to be displayed next to each radio button is placed outside the <INPUT> tags.

For instance, the HTML code

```
<INPUT TYPE=radio NAME=testRadio VALUE="One">Choice One<BR>
<INPUT TYPE=radio NAME=testRadio VALUE="Two" CHECKED>Choice Two<BR>
<INPUT TYPE=radio NAME=testRadio VALUE="Three">Choice Three
```

produces results similar to those shown in Figure 7.2.

FIGURE 7.2.
Radio buttons enable users to select one of many options.

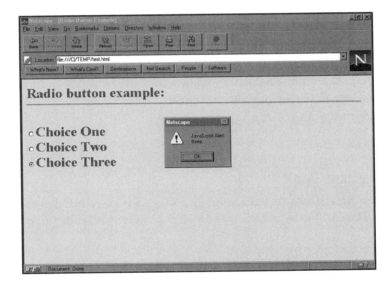

Individual radio buttons within the set of radio buttons are referenced by index numbers. For instance, the third of the preceding choices above would be referred to by document.formName.testRadio[2] and its properties would be referred to as document.formName.testRadio[2].*propertyName*.

Radio buttons have five properties, one method, and one event handler.

The checked **Property**

The checked property is a Boolean indicating if a given radio button is checked or unchecked. It evaluates to true if the button is checked. The value of checked can be set at any time to force a new button to be selected.

For instance, in the preceding radio button example, the initial value of `document.formName.testRadio[1].checked` is `true` and both `document.formName.testRadio[0].checked` and `document.formName.testRadio[2].checked` are `false`. By setting

```
document.formName.testRadio[2].checked = true;
```

the third button becomes selected and the second button is deselected.

The `defaultChecked` Property

The `defaultChecked` property reflects whether the CHECKED attribute appears in the `<INPUT>` tag for a given button. It is a Boolean value that can be overridden by setting the value of the `defaultChecked` property.

The `length` Property

The `length` property is an integer value indicating the number of buttons in a radio button object. Because it's not specific to a particular button in a group, the use of an index isn't needed. For instance, in the preceding example,

```
document.formName.testRadio.length
```

has a value of 3.

The `name` Property

The value of the NAME attribute in the `<INPUT>` tag is reflected in the `name` property. The value can be changed by assigning a new value to `name`, overriding the value in the NAME attribute.

The `value` Property

The `value` property reflects the value of the VALUE attribute for a particular button. This should not be confused with the selection state of a specific button or the text displayed to the user.

The value of the `value` property can be changed to override the VALUE attribute.

The `click()` Method

The `click()` method is used to cause a radio button to be selected. The `click()` method simulates a mouse click on the button. Similar results can be achieved by setting the `checked` property manually.

For instance, in the preceding example, where the selected radio button was changed to the third button, it is also possible to use

```
document.formName.testRadio[2].click()
```

The `onClick` Event Handler

The `onClick` event handler specifies actions to take when a specific button is selected. Each button in a radio object can have a different `onClick` event handler:

```
<INPUT TYPE=radio NAME=testRadio VALUE="One" onClick="alert('one')">Choice One<BR>
<INPUT TYPE=radio NAME=testRadio VALUE="Two" CHECKED onClick="alert('two')">Choice
Two<BR>
<INPUT TYPE=radio NAME=testRadio VALUE="Three" onClick="alert('three')">Choice
Three
```

The `checkbox` Object

Checkboxes are on-off toggle switches. Unlike radio buttons, which function in groups, checkboxes are individual toggle switches. (See Figure 7.3.)

The `<INPUT>` tag is used to create a checkbox. The `TYPE` attribute needs to be set to checkbox. The `VALUE` attribute is used to specify the value sent to the server when the form is submitted. The `CHECKED` attribute can be used to cause the checkbox to be checked when it first displays.

Like radio buttons, the text to be displayed is placed outside the `<INPUT>` tag:

```
<INPUT TYPE="checkbox" NAME="testCheck" VALUE="testValue" CHECKED>Checkbox
```

FIGURE 7.3.

Checkboxes are toggle switches that can be selected or deselected by the user.

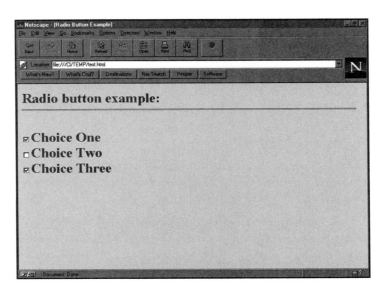

The `checkbox` object reflects checkboxes from HTML forms. It has four properties and, like radio buttons, one method and one event handler.

The checked Property

The checked property is a Boolean indicating if a given checkbox is checked or unchecked. It evaluates to true if the button is checked. The value of checked can be set at any time to force a new button to be selected.

For instance, in the preceding checkbox button example, the initial value of document.formName.testCheck.checked is true. By setting

```
document.formName.testCheck.checked = false;
```

the display is updated so that the checkbox is unchecked.

The defaultChecked Property

The defaultChecked property reflects whether the CHECKED attribute appears in the <INPUT> tag for the checkbox. It is a Boolean value that can be overridden by setting the value of the defaultChecked property.

The name Property

The value of the NAME attribute in the <INPUT> tag is reflected in the name property. The value can be changed by assigning a new value to name, overriding the value in the NAME attribute.

The value Property

The value property reflects the value of the VALUE attribute for a particular button. This should not be confused with the selection state of a specific button or the text displayed to the user.

The value of the value property can be changed to override the VALUE attribute.

The click() Method

The click() method is used to cause a checkbox to be selected. The click() method simulates a mouse click on the button. Similar results can be achieved by setting the checked property manually.

For instance, in the preceding example where the box was checked using the checked property, it is also possible to use

```
document.formName.testCheck.click()
```

The onClick Event Handler

The onClick event handler specifies action to take when a specific button is selected.

The hidden **Object**

hidden objects are text fields that aren't displayed in forms. They can be used to pass values to a CGI script that isn't intended for display to the user.

Hidden fields are defined using the <INPUT> tag with a TYPE attribute set to hidden. The NAME and VALUE attributes can be used.

Properties of the hidden **Object**

The hidden object has two properties that function like the corresponding ones in the text object: name and value. Both are string values reflecting the corresponding attributes from the <INPUT> tag. They can be assigned new values to override the values in the <INPUT> tag.

There are no methods or event handlers for the hidden object.

The password **Object**

Password fields are special cases of the text field that display each character entered as an asterisk (*).

The password object is defined using the <INPUT> tag with the TYPE attribute set to password. Like a text field, it can take the NAME, VALUE, and SIZE attributes.

There are three properties and methods associated with the password object. The password object has no event handlers.

The defaultValue **Property**

The defaultValue property of the password object is somewhat different from the corresponding property of the text object. Rather than taking on the initial value of the VALUE attribute, for security reasons, the defaultValue property is set to the null value.

As with the text object, you can change the value of the defaultValue property, overriding its initial value. When this is done, defaultValue evaluates to its new value rather than the null value.

The name **Property**

As with the text object, the name property is a string containing the value of the NAME attribute in the INPUT tag. The name property can be changed to override the value in the NAME attribute.

The value **Property**

Like the defaultValue property, the value property functions differently than the text object's value property.

The initial value of the value property is the value set in the VALUE attribute of the <INPUT> tag. Scripts can change the value of the property by assigning new string values to it. If this is done, evaluating the value property subsequently returns the new value.

However, if the user changes the content of the password field in the form, then evaluating the value property returns the null value for security reasons.

The focus() Method

The focus() method causes focus to be directed to the password object. This then enables the user to enter text into the field or the data in the field to be changed by the script.

The blur() Method

Focus is removed from a password field using the blur() method.

The select() Method

The select() method is used to select and highlight the content of the password field. This does not, by default, force input focus into the field, however.

The select Object

The select object is different from the other form fields you have seen so far. The select object takes the shape of drop-down or scrolling menus in a form.

In the form of a drop-down menu, a single item can be selected. A scrolling list can be used to select one or more options.

Select menus are built using two tags: <SELECT> and <OPTION>.

The <SELECT> tag defines the overall menu structure and properties. It takes three attributes: NAME, SIZE, and MULTIPLE.

NAME takes a string value that specifies the name of the selection object. SIZE is an integer that indicates the number of visible items at one time. If this value is greater than one, then the list is a scrolling menu; otherwise, it's a drop-down menu. MULTIPLE is used to indicate if the user should be able to select more than one item on the list. The use of the MULTIPLE attribute forces the list to be a scrolling menu even if the SIZE attribute is set to one.

For instance, the HTML code

```
<SELECT NAME="testSelect" SIZE=1>
Select Definition
</SELECT>
```

defines a drop-down menu while

```
<SELECT NAME="testSelect2" SIZE=4 MULTIPLE>
Select Definition
</SELECT>
```

defines a scrolling list with four visible items in which the user can choose more than one option.

The content of the list itself is defined using the `<OPTION>` tag. This tag takes two attributes: VALUE—a string specifying the value to send to the server if the option is selected when the form is submitted to the server, and SELECTED, which indicates that the option should be selected by default.

Using the `<OPTION>` tag, the two preceding examples could be extended to become

```
<SELECT NAME="testSelect" SIZE=1>
<OPTION VALUE="one" SELECTED>One
<OPTION VALUE="two">Two
<OPTION VALUE="three">Three
</SELECT>
```

and

```
<SELECT NAME="testSelect2" SIZE=4 MULTIPLE>
<OPTION VALUE="a">A
<OPTION VALUE="b" SELECTED>B
<OPTION VALUE="c">C
<OPTION VALUE="d" SELECTED>D
<OPTION VALUE="e">E
</SELECT>
```

FIGURE 7.4.

Drop-down menus and scrolling menus with multiple selections are made possible with the select object.

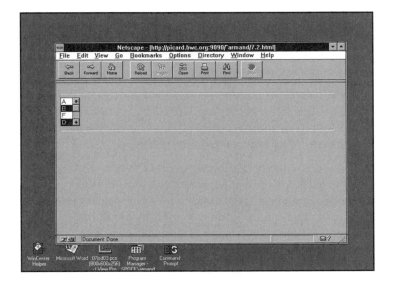

The `select` object has four properties, two methods, and three event handlers. One of the properties of the `select` object, the `options` array, provides access to each of the options in the select list. The `options` array itself has eight properties.

Properties of the `select` Object

In addition to the `options` array, the `select` object has three other properties: `length`, `name`, and `selectedIndex`.

The `length` property indicates the number of options in the `select` object. The name property is a string reflecting the NAME attribute of the `<SELECT>` tag. The name of the object can be changed by assigning a new value to the `name` property.

The `selectedIndex` property is an integer reflecting the index (in the `options` array) of currently selected options. It can be set to a new value which will dynamically update the menu's display.

However, the `selectedIndex` property is less useful with lists that have the MULTIPLE attribute. In these cases, the `selectedIndex` property evaluates to the index of the first selected option. If a new value is assigned to the property, then all selected options are cleared and the one new option is selected.

The `options` Array

The `options` array reflects the options in the select list in the order in which they are defined in the HTML source code. The `options` array itself has eight properties: `defaultSelected`, `index`, `length`, `name`, `selected`, `selectedIndex`, `text`, and `value`.

The `length` property is an integer reflecting the number of options in the select list—it is the same value as the `length` property of the `select` object.

The `defaultSelected` property is a Boolean value that indicates if the SELECTED attribute is used in the given option's `<OPTION>` tag. The value of the `defaultSelected` property can be changed, effectively overriding the SELECTED attribute. Changing the `defaultSelected` property doesn't cause the select list's appearance to be updated.

The `selected` property is a Boolean value reflecting the current selection state of any single option—in lists with or without the MUTLIPLE attribute set. Changing the value of the `selected` property dynamically changes the select list's display to reflect the new values. The `selectedIndex` property functions in the same way as the `selectedIndex` property of the `select` object. Because `selectedIndex` is not unique for any particular option, it isn't necessary to specify an index when referring to the property:

```
selectListName.options.selectedIndex
```

The `name` property is a string reflecting the name of the `select` options. Like `selectedIndex`, it doesn't refer to a specific option and can be referred to without an index number: `selectListName.options.name`.

The text property contains a string reflecting the text displayed in the select list for a given option. Similarly, the value property reflects the value of the VALUE attribute of the <OPTION> tag. Both values can be changed, effectively overriding their original values.

The index property is an integer reflecting the index of the option in question.

Dynamically Updating Select Lists

With the release of Navigator 3, it's now possible to dynamically modify the options in a select list.

By changing the value of the text property and the value property of an option, its value and the text displayed in the menu are dynamically updated to reflect the new values. In Navigator 2, changes to the text property were not reflected in the displayed menu, which retained its original appearance regardless of the value of the text property.

For instance, if you have a select list in the form formName defined as the following,

```
<SELECT NAME="testSelect2" SIZE=4 MULTIPLE>
<OPTION VALUE="a">A
<OPTION VALUE="b" SELECTED>B
<OPTION VALUE="c">C
<OPTION VALUE="d" SELECTED>D
<OPTION VALUE="e">E
</SELECT>
```

then the displayed text of the third option (and the value returned to the server) can be changed:

```
document.formName.testSelect.options[2].text = "F";
document.formName.testSelect.options[2].value = "f";
```

FIGURE 7.5.

In Navigator 3, text displayed in select lists can be dynamically changed.

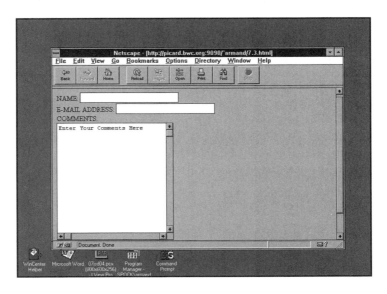

Methods and Event Handlers of the `select` Object

The `select` object has two methods: `blur()` and `focus()`. Like these methods in other objects, the `blur()` method removes input focus from the select list and the `focus()` method gives input focus to the list.

Corresponding to the `focus()` and `blur()` methods are the `onFocus` and `onBlur` event handlers, which are used in the `<SELECT>` tag to specify code to be executed when focus is given or removed from the select list.

A third event handler, `onChange`, is triggered when the currently selected option or options change. The `onChange` event handler should be placed in the `<SELECT>` tag:

```
<SELECT NAME="selectName" SIZE=size onChange="JavaScript Code">
```

Button-Based Objects

HTML forms can contain three types of buttons: reset buttons, submit buttons, and generic buttons.

Reset buttons and submit buttons have specific purposes—reset buttons clear the contents of form fields to their default values and submit buttons submit the forms to the URL specified in the `ACTION` attribute of the `<FORM>` tag. Generic buttons, on the other hand, have no specific function attached to them.

All three types of buttons have JavaScript objects associated with them.

Generic Buttons

Generic buttons are defined in HTML using the `<INPUT>` tag with the `TYPE` attribute set to `button`. The `<INPUT>` tag also can take a `NAME` and `VALUE` attribute. The `VALUE` attribute is displayed as the text of the button in the form.

Buttons are reflected into JavaScript through the `button` object. The `button` object has two properties—`name` and `value`—that reflect the corresponding attributes from the `<INPUT>` tag. These properties can be changed to override their original values. Changing the `value` property, however, doesn't change the text that appears in the button.

The `button` object also has a `click()` method that simulates a user clicking the button, and an `onClick` event handler, which specifies code to execute when the button is clicked.

The `reset` Object

Reset buttons are defined using the `<INPUT>` tag with the `TYPE` attribute set to `reset`. `NAME` and `VALUE` attributes also can be used. The value of the `VALUE` attribute is displayed as the text of the button in the form.

The reset object has two properties, name and value, which can reflect the NAME and VALUE attributes in the <INPUT> tag. These properties can be changed to override their original values, but changing the value doesn't change the text displayed in the button.

Like the generic button object, the reset object has a click() method and an onClick event handler.

The submit Object

Like the generic and reset buttons, the submit button is defined with the <INPUT> tag, except that its TYPE attribute is set to submit. NAME and VALUE attributes can be used and the value of the VALUE attribute is displayed as the text of the button in the form.

The submit object has the same properties, methods, and event handlers as the reset and button objects: name and value properties, the click() method, and the onClick event handler.

Form Validation

One of the strengths of being able to work with forms in JavaScript is that it is possible to perform form validation before sending the form to the server.

With traditional CGI processing of forms, it is necessary to send a form to the server to determine if it has been correctly, and completely, filled out. If the user has incorrectly filled out the form or not provided required data, then the new form has to be returned to the user requesting the corrected or additional data.

With JavaScript these extra transactions with the server can be avoided.

By way of example, the following shows form validation on a simple comments form:

```
<FORM METHOD=POST ACTION="/cgi-bin/comment" NAME="commentForm"
➥onSubmit="if (this.name.value == "") {
   alert("Please enter your name.");
   return false;
} else if (this.email.value == "")
   alert("Please enter your e-mail address.");
   return false;
}">
NAME: <INPUT TYPE="text" NAME="name" SIZE=30><BR>
E-MAIL ADDRESS: <INPUT TYPE="text" NAME="email" SIZE=30><BR>
COMMENTS:<BR>
<TEXTAREA ROWS=15 COLS=30 NAME="comments">
Enter Your Comments Here
</TEXTAREA>
```

This form is submitted by the post method to the script /cgi-bin/comment. The form has three fields: two text fields and one textarea field. (See Figure 7.6.)

FIGURE 7.6.
JavaScript can be used to validate forms like this comment form.

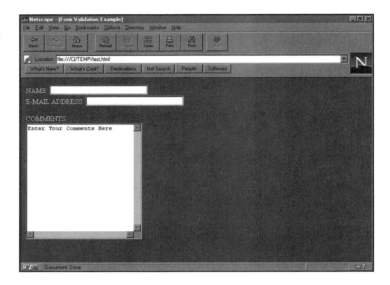

The validation of the form takes place in the onSubmit event handler before the data is submitted to the server. Two checks are made on the form's fields. First the name field is checked to see if it is blank. If it is, the user is asked for his or her name and a false value is returned to prevent submission of the form.

Next, the email field is checked to see if it blank. Again, if it is, the user is alerted and a false value is returned.

Using methods of the string object, it's possible to perform more sophisticated validation on the email field, such as checking if the email address contains an @ symbol:

```
<FORM METHOD=POST ACTION="/cgi-bin/comment" NAME="commentForm"
➥onSubmit="if (this.name.value == "") {
   alert("Please enter your name.");
   return false;
} else if (this.email.value == "") {
   alert("Please enter your e-mail address.");
   return false;
} else if (this.email.value.indexOf('@',0) < 0) {
   alert("Please enter a valid e-mail address.");
   return false;
}">
NAME: <INPUT TYPE="text" NAME="name" SIZE=30><BR>
E-MAIL ADDRESS: <INPUT TYPE="text" NAME="email" SIZE=30><BR>
COMMENTS:<BR>
<TEXTAREA ROWS=15 COLS=30 NAME="comments">
Enter Your Comments Here
</TEXTAREA>
```

By using the indexOf() method of the string object, it's possible to confirm if the e-mail address has an @ symbol in it.

Summary

HTML forms provide a basic level of interactivity with Web pages. However, all this interactivity has traditionally relied on the server for processing and reacting to user input.

JavaScript makes it possible to add dynamic, client-side interactivity to HTML forms. With JavaScript, you can now react to user input, generate content for form fields, and react to user mouse-clicks in forms. Because there are so many properties, methods, and event handlers, Table 7.1 outlines the properties, methods, and event handlers of the various form element objects.

Table 7.1. Form element objects and their properties, methods, and event handlers.

Object	Properties	Methods	Event Handlers
button	name value	click()	onClick()
checkbox	checked defaultChecked name value	click()	onClick
hidden	name value		
password	defaultValue name value	focus() blur()	
radio	checked defaultChecked length name value	click()	onClick
reset	name value	click()	onClick
select	length name selectedIndex options (array) - defaultSelected - index - length - name	blur() focus()	onBlur onFocus onChange

continues

Table 7.1. continued

Object	Properties	Methods	Event Handlers
	- selected		
	- selectedIndex		
	- text		
	- value		
submit	name	click()	onClick
	value		
text	defaultValue	blur()	onBlur
	name	focus()	onFocus
	value	select()	onSelect
			onChange
textarea	defaultValue	blur()	onBlur
	name	focus()	onFocus
	value	select()	onSelect
			onChange

The next chapter examines frames, which enable windows to be divided into separate sections that each displays different HTML documents. JavaScript objects and properties for working with frames will be discussed as well.

8

Frames and JavaScript

by Arman Danesh

Traditionally, Web browsers have been limited to displaying a single HTML document in a single document window.

It simply wasn't possible for Web authors to create sophisticated interfaces involving fixed toolbars, menus, and work areas. Instead, any time the user requested new information, the complete browser window had to be cleared and updated with a new document.

Starting with Navigator 2, Netscape introduced an extension for HTML known as frames. Frames allow a browser window to be divided into multiple rectangular spaces, or frames, each of which contains separate documents.

Combining frames with JavaScript provides a powerful mechanism for creating sophisticated Web-based interfaces and applications. This chapter shows you how to take advantage of frames and how to work with frames in JavaScript. Specifically, it looks at the following topics:

- Frame Basics
- The `frame` Object
- Managing Cross-Frame Communication

Frame Basics

Frames enable a browser window to be divided into multiple rectangular panes, each containing its own documents. Links in one document can be made to appear in another frame without requiring a complete update or refresh of all the frames in the window.

> **NOTE**
>
> Making links display in a different frame is known as targeting. Different links in the same document can be targeted at different frames as well as at new browser windows.

Using cross-frame links, it's possible to create fixed, permanent mastheads, menu or tool bars, or search forms. Frames also can reduce bandwidth demands by requiring common components such as menus and logos to be loaded once in their own frame (instead of repeatedly with each document request by the user).

FIGURE 8.1.

Frames can be used to create fixed menus and logos, as shown in this example from Landegg Academy in Switzerland (http://www.landegg.org/landegg/).

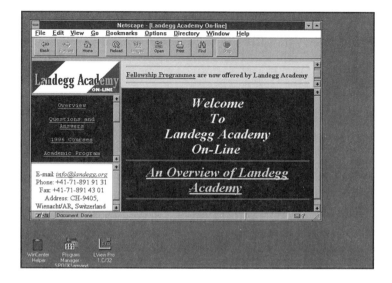

Tags for Creating Frames

Frames are defined using two new HTML tags: <FRAMESET> and <FRAMES>.

<FRAMESET> is defined in the parent document—the document originally accessed by the user. The <FRAMESET> tag defines how a window should be divided into frames. It can be used to specify rows and columns and their sizes.

The <FRAME> tag is used to indicate which document should be displayed in each of the frames defined in the <FRAMESET> tag.

A third tag, <NOFRAMES>, provides a mechanism for providing text or HTML for users of non-frames capable browsers.

NOTE

Frameset documents are not restricted to loading into complete windows. The document loaded into an individual frame of a frameset document can be another frameset, which then divides the individual frame according to the specifications of the <FRAMESET> tag. This is explained in more detail later in this chapter, in the section on "Embedded Frames."

The <FRAMESET> Tag

The <FRAMESET> tag defines how to split a window into rows or columns. It takes two possible attributes: ROWS and COLS.

ROWS defines the number of rows into which you may divide the window, and COLS specifies the number of columns into which you can divide the window. The value assigned to rows or columns can either be in pixels or a percentage of the window size into which the frameset is loaded. For instance,

```
<FRAMESET ROWS="100,*">
```

creates two frames in rows—the top frame is 100 pixels deep and the second row fills the remainder of the available space. The asterisk is used to indicate the remaining space. If the user resizes the window, the 100 pixel-deep frame retains the same depth, and the size of the lower frame changes to accommodate the new window dimensions.

Relative frame sizes are specified with percentages:

```
<FRAMESET COLS="25%,*,25%">
```

This <FRAMESET> tag creates three frames in columns. The outer columns are each 25 percent of the width of the available space and the center frame fills the remaining space.

The ROWS and COLUMNS attributes can be used together to create a grid of rows and columns. For instance, the frameset tag

```
<FRAMESET ROWS="25%,*" COLS="10%,35%,*">
```

creates results like those shown in Figure 8.2.

FIGURE 8.2.

Combining ROWS *and* COLS *produces grids.*

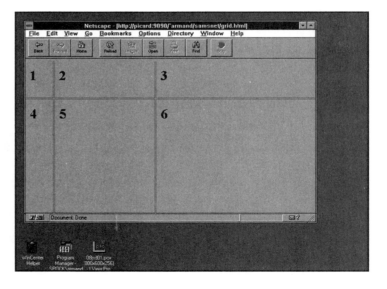

When combining ROWS and COLS in a `<FRAMESET>` tag, the order of frames proceeds from the top-left frame to the bottom-right frame, counting across rows and then down columns.

The `<FRAME>` Tag

The `<FRAME>` tag is used to specify which documents are loaded in each frame of the frameset.

The `<FRAME>` tag takes six possible attributes, as outlined in Table 8.1.

Table 8.1. Attributes of the `<FRAME>` tag.

Attribute	Description
SRC	Specifies the URL of the HTML file to be displayed in a frame.
NAME	Specifies the name of a frame for use in targeting and in JavaScript.
NORESIZE	Indicates that a frame cannot be resized by the user.
SCROLLING	Specifies if scroll bars should be displayed. Possible values are YES, NO, and AUTO.
MARGINHEIGHT	Indicates the width of the top and bottom margins in pixels.
MARGINWIDTH	Indicates the width of the left and right margins in pixels.

For instance, the following code loads `document1.html` in `frame1` and `document2.html` in `frame2`.

```
<FRAMESET ROWS="150,*">
   <FRAME SRC="document1.html" NAME="frame1" SCROLLING="NO">
   <FRAME SRC="document2.html" NAME="frame2" NORESIZE>
</FRAMESET>
```

The NORESIZE tag indicates that the size of the frames is fixed and, because there are only two frames, both frames are effectively of fixed size. The SCROLLING="NO" attribute means the top frame won't have scrollbars even if the document doesn't fit in the frame. The AUTO value of the SCROLLING attribute places scrollbars in a frame only if the document doesn't fit. By default, scrollbars appear when necessary.

The `<NOFRAMES>` Tag

The `<NOFRAMES>` tag is a mechanism for providing non-frame content to browsers that don't support Netscape's frame extensions.

Any content between `<NOFRAMES>` and `</NOFRAMES>` is ignored by Navigator and other frames-capable browsers, but is evaluated and displayed by other browsers.

For example, in the following HTML code, users with other browsers are told they need to use Navigator to view the site.

```
<FRAMESET ROWS="25%,*">
   <FRAME SRC="document1.html">
   <FRAME SRC="document2.html">
</FRAMESET>

<NOFRAMES>
   This site uses frames. Please download
   Netscape Navigator 2 or 3 or another
   frames-capable browser.
</NOFRAMES>
```

This produces results like those shown in Figure 8.3.

FIGURE 8.3.
Using `<NOFRAMES>`, *special content for users of other browsers can be displayed.*

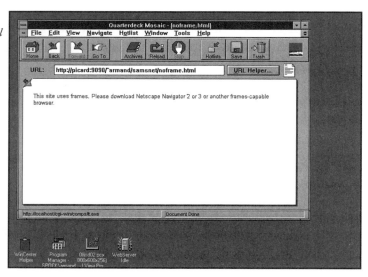

Embedded Framesets

With simple frameset structures, frame layouts are limited to rows, columns, or simple grids. However, many sites use more complicated page layouts, like the ones shown in Figure 8.4.

Complex embedded framesets are achieved by using embedded framesets. The principle behind embedding framesets is that it is possible for a document loaded into any frame to be a frameset document. This embedded frameset then uses the space available to it in its assigned frame to display the layout defined in its `<FRAMESET>` tag.

FIGURE 8.4.
Embedded framesets can be used to create complex frame layouts.

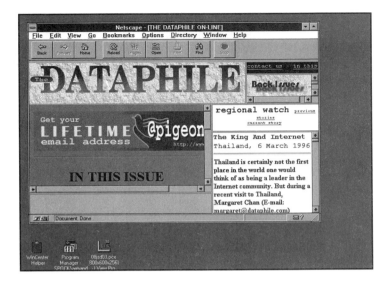

Embedded framesets can either be loaded from separate HTML files using the <FRAME> tag in the parent frameset document, or the child <FRAMESET> definition can actually be in the same document as the parent <FRAMESET>.

For instance, if you have a parent frameset document

```
<FRAMESET ROWS="50%,*">
    <FRAME SRC="document1.html">
    <FRAME SRC="document2.html" NAME="frame2">
</FRAMESET>
```

where document1.html contains another frameset

```
<FRAMESET COLS="50%,*">
    <FRAME SRC="document3.html" NAME="frame3">
    <FRAME SRC="document4.html" NAME="frame4">
</FRAMESET>
```

then the result would be two rows where the top frame is further divided into two columns, as shown in Figure 8.5.

The embedded framesets created above with two files also can be created in one frameset file by replacing the first <FRAME> tag with the embedded frameset

```
<FRAMESET ROWS="50%,*">
    <FRAMESET COLS="50%,*">
        <FRAME SRC="document3.html" NAME="frame3">
        <FRAME SRC="document4.html" NAME="frame4">
    </FRAMESET>
    <FRAME SRC="document2.html" NAME="frame2">
</FRAMESET>
```

FIGURE 8.5.

Embedded framesets can be created in multiple files or a single file.

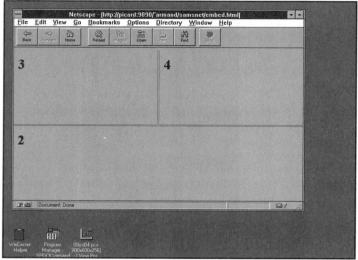

Targeting Frames

One main purpose behind naming frames with the NAME attribute of the <FRAME> tag is to target links.

For instance, in the preceding example, links in document2.html could be targeted at frame 4 by adding the attribute TARGET to the <A> tag:

```
<A HREF="link1.html" TARGET="frame4">
```

As mentioned in Chapter 7, "Working with Forms," when the <FORM> tag was discussed, the TARGET attribute can be used in the <FORM> tag to target the results of a form submission to another frame:

```
<FORM METHOD=method ACTIOn="Script_URL" TARGET="frame4">
```

For documents with numerous links all targeted at the same frame, the <BASE> tag can be used to set a global target for a whole document. The <BASE> tag usually appears in the header of an HTML document and takes the form

```
<BASE TARGET="targetName">
```

The global target defined in the <BASE> tag can be overridden by a TARGET attribute in an <A> or a <FROM> tag elsewhere in the same document.

Targeting is not limited to named frames. Netscape provides four special names that can be used as targets: _blank, _self, _parent, and _top.

`_blank` causes the link or form submission result to open in a new, unnamed window. `_self` causes links to load in the same frame in which the link was clicked, `_parent` causes links or form results to appear in the immediate parent frameset, and `_top` causes links to load in the full browser window.

The `frame` Object

The `frame` object in JavaScript reflects frames defined in an HTML file. Frame objects are stored in the `frames` array, which is a property of the `window` object. In this way, each frame in a window is accessible by an index number in the array. Index numbers start at zero. Objects are stored in the array in the order of their specification in the frameset document.

By using the special keyword `parent`, it is possible to reference any other frame in a window, using the frame's index number. For instance, in the frameset

```
<FRAMESET ROWS="50%,*">
    <FRAME SRC="document1.html">
    <FRAME SRC="document2.html" NAME="frame2">
</FRAMESET>
```

a script in `document1.html` could refer to `frame2` with

```
parent.frames[1]
```

Similarly, the first frame is

```
parent.frames[0].
```

Frame names also can be used to refer to the specific named frames. In this example, the second frame could be referenced with

```
parent.frame2
```

In the case of embedded framesets, things are a little more complicated. In the preceding four-document example, where the first frameset document looked like

```
<FRAMESET ROWS="50%,*">
    <FRAME SRC="document1.html">
    <FRAME SRC="document2.html" NAME="frame2">
</FRAMESET>
```

and `document1.html` was another frameset defined by

```
<FRAMESET COLS="50%,*">
    <FRAME SRC="document3.html" NAME="frame3">
    <FRAME SRC="document4.html" NAME="frame4">
</FRAMESET>
```

the simple use of `parent.frameName` or `parent.frames[index]` can't always be maintained.

For instance, for a script in `frame4` to access `frame2` it is not sufficient to simply use `parent.frames[1]`, because the immediate parent frameset of `frame4` is `frame1` and within that frameset `frames[1]` refers to `frame4`. Instead, the following for,

```
parent.parent.frames[1]
```

would be used to refer to the second frame in the parent of the immediate parent frameset.

> **NOTE**
>
> In some cases it is possible to eliminate the use of multiple parent references to get to the desired object. Using the special keyword top, it is possible to refer to the top frameset in the current window. In this way, the preceding example could use `top.frames[1]` to refer to `frame2`.

The `frames` array has one property—`length`—which is an integer indicating the number of `frame` objects stored in the `frames` array. Effectively, this number is the number of child frames within a frameset.

Properties of the `frame` Object

The `frame` object has a number of properties available for working directly with the frame itself in relation to the frameset. This is different from working with documents in the frame or the frame's history list.

The properties of the `frame` object follow:

- ■ `frames`: An array reflecting all of the current frame
- ■ `name`: A string reflecting the value of the NAME attribute in the <FRAME> tag
- ■ `length`: An integer reflecting the number of child frames in the frame

For instance, in the preceding embedded frameset example, a script in `frame1` could use `self.length` to return a value of zero and `parent.frames[1].name` to return the string "frame2."

In addition, each `frame` object has a `document` object, a `location` object, and a `history` object as properties. This is tied to the fact that each frame has a document loaded into it, and a separate history list distinct from the history list for the window.

Methods of the `frame` Object

The `frame` object has two methods: `clearTimeout()` and `setTimeout()`.

Both of these methods are related to the timing of events. Together they provide a simple method for scheduling actions and, if necessary, canceling those actions before they occur.

The `setTimeout()` method enables an expression to be evaluated after a specified delay in milliseconds. The basic syntax of a `setTimeout()` command is

```
timeOut = setTimeout("expression",delay);
```

While *timeOut* is a name assigned to the specific scheduled event, *expression* is a string or property to be evaluated, and *delay* is an integer indicating the number of milliseconds to wait before evaluating the expression.

For instance, the following code would wait two seconds (2,000 milliseconds) before executing the `alert()` method specified in the expression portion of the command.

```
delayAlert = setTimeout("alert('You made it')",2000);
```

Being able to name each time-out means it is possible to use the `clearTimeout()` method to cancel a scheduled time-out before its expression is evaluated. Using the syntax

```
clearTimeout(timeOut);
```

where *timeOut* is the name of the *timeOut* (such as `delayAlert` in the `alert()` preceding example), it is possible to cancel a time-out that hasn't occurred.

NOTE

Specifying a name for a time-out is not required. It is optional. If no name is specified, it isn't possible to clear the time-out with `clearTimeout()`.

To illustrate the use of the `setTimeout()` method, the following document can be used to load a random string into a frame which is at a set interval:

```
<HEAD>
<TITLE>setTimeout() Example</TITLE>
<SCRIPT LANGUAGE="JavaScript">
var delay = 5000; var choices = new Array(5);
choices[0] = "This is Choice 1";
choices[1] = "This is Choice 2";
choices[2] = "This is Choice 3";
choices[3] = "This is Choice 4";
choices[4] = "This is Choice 5";
function displayRandom() {
    document.writeln(choices[Math.floor(5 * Math.random(choices.length))]);
}
</SCRIPT>
</HEAD>

<BODY onLoad="self.setTimeout('self.location = self.location',delay)">
<SCRIPT LANGUAGE="JavaScript">
displayRandom();
</SCRIPT>
</BODY>
```

This produces results similar to those shown in Figure 8.6.

FIGURE 8.6.

Using setTimeout(), *it is possible to schedule events, such as displaying random text at specified intervals.*

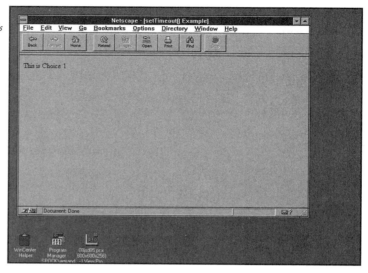

In this example, two simple principles are used. This first is that a script can output text to the document window. The function displayRandom() uses the Math.random() method, discussed earlier when the Math object was examined to randomly select one of the five strings stored in the choices array, then simply writes it to the frame using document.writeln().

The onLoad event handler in the <BODY> tag handles the scheduling of a reload. The setTimout() tag uses the delay variable to specify the length of the delay (in this case 5,000 milliseconds, or five seconds) before evaluating the expression self.location = self.location, which simply reloads the current document into the window.

Managing Cross-Frame Communication

With frames, it is possible to make use of functions and variables stored in other frames. You also can access the properties and methods of objects associated with the documents in other frames.

For example, the following frameset produces a simple calculator in which one frame has all the buttons for keying in numbers and functions and the other window has what amounts to a paper tape record of all entries into the calculator.

The parent frameset looks like the following:

```
<FRAMESET COLS="50%,*">
    <FRAME SRC="control.html">
    <FRAME SRC="output.html" NAME="output">
</FRAMESET>
```

The source code for the file control.html follows:

Listing 8.1. A calculator using frames.

```
<HEAD>
<SCRIPT LANGUAGE="JavaScript">

function nextNumber(number) {

    parent.output.document.displayForm.currentValue.value += number;
    parent.output.document.displayForm.runningTape.value += number;

}

function doAction(action) {

    var toDo = parent.output.document.displayForm.total.value +
            parent.output.document.displayForm.currentAction.value +
            parent.output.document.displayForm.currentValue.value;
    parent.output.document.displayForm.currentValue.value = "";
    parent.output.document.displayForm.currentAction.value = action;
    parent.output.document.displayForm.runningTape.value += action + " \n";
    parent.output.document.displayForm.total.value = eval(toDo);

}

function doEqual() {

    doAction("=");
    parent.output.document.displayForm.runningTape.value += "---------\n";
    parent.output.document.displayForm.runningTape.value +=
    ➥parent.output.document.displayForm.total.value + "\n";
    parent.output.document.displayForm.runningTape.value += "---------\n";
    parent.output.document.displayForm.total.value = "0";
    parent.output.document.displayForm.currentValue.value = "";
    parent.output.document.displayForm.currentAction.value = "+";

}

</SCRIPT>
</HEAD>

<BODY>
<FORM>
<TABLE>
<TR>
<TD>
<INPUT TYPE=button NAME="7" VALUE="7" onClick="nextNumber(this.value)">
</TD>
<TD>
<INPUT TYPE=button NAME="8" VALUE="8" onClick="nextNumber(this.value)">
</TD>
<TD>
<INPUT TYPE=button NAME="9" VALUE="9" onClick="nextNumber(this.value)">
</TD>
<TD>
<INPUT TYPE=button NAME="+" VALUE="+" onClick="doAction(this.value)">
</TD>
</TR>
<TR>
```

continues

Listing 8.1. continued

```
<TD>
<INPUT TYPE=button NAME="4" VALUE="4" onClick="nextNumber(this.value)">
</TD>
<TD>
<INPUT TYPE=button NAME="5" VALUE="5" onClick="nextNumber(this.value)">
</TD>
<TD>
<INPUT TYPE=button NAME="6" VALUE="6" onClick="nextNumber(this.value)">
</TD>
<TD>
<INPUT TYPE=button NAME="-" VALUE="-" onClick="doAction(this.value)">
</TD>
</TR>
<TR>
<TD>
<INPUT TYPE=button NAME="1" VALUE="1" onClick="nextNumber(this.value)">
</TD>
<TD>
<INPUT TYPE=button NAME="2" VALUE="2" onClick="nextNumber(this.value)">
</TD>
<TD>
<INPUT TYPE=button NAME="3" VALUE="3" onClick="nextNumber(this.value)">
</TD>
<TD>
<INPUT TYPE=button NAME="*" VALUE="*" onClick="doAction(this.value)">
</TD>
</TR>
<TR>
<TD>
<INPUT TYPE=button NAME="0" VALUE="0" onClick="nextNumber(this.value)">
</TD>
<TD>
<INPUT TYPE=button NAME="." VALUE="." onClick="nextNumber(this.value)">
</TD>
<TD>
<INPUT TYPE=button NAME="=" VALUE="=" onClick="doEqual()">
</TD>
<TD>
<INPUT TYPE=button NAME="/" VALUE="/" onClick="doAction(this.value)">
</TD>
</TR>
</TABLE>
</FORM>
</BODY>
```

The file output.html looks like the following:

```
<BODY>
<FORM NAME="displayForm">
<INPUT TYPE=hidden NAME="currentValue" VALUE="">
<INPUT TYPE=hidden NAME="currentAction" VALUE="+">
<INPUT TYPE=hidden NAME="total" VALUE="0" SIZE=6>
<TEXTAREA NAME="runningTape" ROWS=30 COLS=10></TEXTAREA><BR>
</BODY>
```

FIGURE 8.7.

Using cross-frame communication, the calculator buttons on the left update the textarea *field in the frame on the right.*

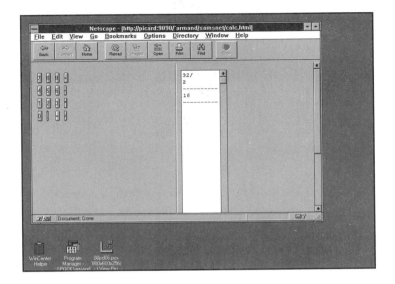

This example demonstrates the basics of cross-frame communication. Although all the logic in the program is in the left-hand frame (control.html), the output occurs in the right-hand frame. In addition, all data for the calculator is stored in hidden fields in the form in the right-hand frame (output.html).

In order to achieve this, the script in control.html references the values stored and displayed in the output form with the following structure:

```
parent.output.displayForm.fieldName.value
```

The program itself breaks down into three simple functions: nextNumber(), doAction(), and doEqual(). nextNumber() displays numbers entered by the user and adds them to the number stored in currentValue. doAction() handles processing when a user clicks one of the four mathematical function buttons. doAction() performs the previously entered action (stored in currentAction) on the value stored in currentValue and the value stored in total. It then updates display and total and stores the new action in currentAction.

Finally, doEqual() completes the last action remaining to be performed, outputs the result and clears total, currentValue, and currentAction to their default state in preparation for a new calculation.

It is clear that with a large number of embedded framesets, handling cross-frame communication can become troublesome, requiring cryptic references to

```
parent.parent.parent.frames[3].frameName.propertyName
```

or

```
parent.parent.frames[2].frames[5].methodName()
```

The best way to handle this is to use a frameset manager—generic JavaScript code that handles cross-frame function calls and, possibly, access to properties and variables across functions.

> **NOTE**
>
> Bill Dortch, well known in the JavaScript world for developing various toolsets to help JavaScript designers (and for running hIdaho Design) has written a publicly-available frameset manager called the hIdaho Frameset, which is available on the Web at `http://www.hidaho.com/frameset/`.

To illustrate how a frameset manager works, the following script is a simple frameset manager that should be included in the top-most frameset in a series of embedded framesets:

```javascript
<SCRIPT LANGUAGE="JavaScript">

var functions = new Array(0);

function registerFunction(objectName,functionName) {

 functions[functionName] = objectName;

}

function callFunction(functionName) {

 var args = callFunction.arguments;
 var argString = "";

 var argList = new Array (args.length);
 for (i = 1; i < args.length; i++) {
  argList[i-1] = args[i];
 }

 for (i = 0; i < argList.length; i++) {
  argString += "argList[" + i + "],";
 }
 argString += "argList[" + argList.length + "]";

 return eval("self." + functions[functionName] + "(" + argString + ")");

}

function alreadyRegistered(functionName) {

 return (functions[functionName] != null);

}

</SCRIPT>
```

In addition, the manager requires the following function in each child frameset:

```
function registerFunction(objectName,functionName) {

        parent.registerFunction(self.name + "." + objectName,functionName);

}
```

The following function is included in each document displayed in a frame that contains functions— which need to be registered with the frameset manager:

```
function registerFunction(functionName) {

        parent.registerFunction(self.name + "." + functionName,functionName);

}
```

The way the frameset manager works is relatively simple: In documents containing functions to register, a call to `registerFunction()` needs to be made with one argument—the function name.

The `registerFunction()` function then calls `registerFunction()` in its immediate parent frameset and passes two arguments: the name of the function with the frame name as a prefix, and the function name itself. In intermediate framesets, `registerFunction()` adds its frame name to the first argument and calls `registerFunction()` in the next parent frameset in the hierarchy.

In the top-level frameset, `registerFunction()` receives the two arguments passed up throughout the child framesets: the complete name of the function, including the frame names needed to call the function from the top-level frameset, and the simple function name itself.

The function then adds the complete function path and name as an entry in the `functions` array, using the simple function name as the array index.

The frameset manager includes two other functions: `callFunction()` and `alreadyRegistered()`. `alreadyRegistered()` simply checks if an entry is in the array functions and returns true or false on the basis of that check.

`callFunction()` does a bit more. It receives two arguments: the name of the function, and arguments to be passed to the function. It then builds a string representing the function call and evaluates it using `eval()` before returning the result.

To demonstrate how the frameset manager works, the following example divides the window into three frames: A button in the right-hand frame calls a function in the bottom-left frame, which displays an alert dialog box.

The parent frameset looks like

```
<HEAD>
<SCRIPT LANGUAGE="JavaScript">

var functions = new Array(0);
```

```
function registerFunction(objectName,functionName) {

 functions[functionName] = objectName;

}

function callFunction(functionName) {

 var args = callFunction.arguments;
 var argString = "";

 var argList = new Array (args.length);
 for (i = 1; i < args.length; i++) {
  argList[i-1] = args[i];
 }

 for (i = 0; i < argList.length; i++) {
  argString += "argList[" + i + "],";
 }
 argString += "argList[" + argList.length + "]";

 return eval("self." + functions[functionName] + "(" + argString + ")");

}

function alreadyRegistered(functionName) {

 return (functions[functionName] != null);

}

</SCRIPT>
</HEAD>
<FRAMESET COLS="50%,*">
        <FRAME SRC="left.html" NAME="left">
        <FRAME SRC="right.html" NAME="right">
</FRAMESET>
```

The file left.html is another frameset file. Notice that the file contains the registerFunction()
function for intermediate framesets:

```
<HEAD>
<SCRIPT LANGUAGE="JavaScript">

function registerFunction(objectName,functionName) {

        parent.registerFunction(self.name + "." + objectName,functionName);

}

</SCRIPT>
</HEAD>
```

```
<FRAMESET ROWS="50%,*">
        <FRAME SRC="top.html" NAME="top">
        <FRAME SRC="bottom.html" NAME="bottom">
</FRAMESET>
```

`bottom.html` holds the function that will be registered with the manager. It includes the `registerFunction()` function for document files and registers the function `doAlert()` by calling it:

```
<HEAD>
<SCRIPT LANGUAGE="JavaScript">

function registerFunction(functionName) {

        parent.registerFunction(self.name + "." + functionName,functionName);

}

registerFunction("doAlert");
function doAlert(toDisplay) {
        alert(toDisplay);
}

</SCRIPT>
</HEAD>

<BODY>
<CENTER>The function is contained in this file.</CENTER>
</BODY>
```

`right.html` contains the button that triggers a cross-frame call after the `alreadyRegistered()` function has been called to confirm that `doAlert()` is loaded and registered:

```
<BODY>
<FORM>
<H3>Call a function in another frame:</H3>
<INPUT TYPE=button VALUE="PUSH ME"
onClick="if (top.alreadyRegistered('doAlert')) { top.callFunction('doAlert',
➥'This was a Cross-frame Alert.') }">
</FORM>
</BODY>
```

The file `top.html` is not functional; it just displays text. The results look like those shown in Figure 8.8.

FIGURE 8.8.

Using a frameset manager makes it easier to make cross-function calls using embedded framesets.

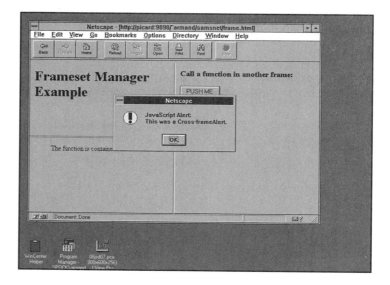

Summary

This chapter covered frames and techniques for working with them. The concept of embedded framesets was discussed in detail, and a basic frameset manager was outlined to ease the management of function calls across frames in embedded framesets.

In Chapter 9, "Using Cookies," cookies—a facility for maintaining client-side state information—are discussed.

Using Cookies

by Arman Danesh

One of the limitations of standard hypertext transfer protocol and the common gateway interface mechanism is that the combination of the two provides no way to maintain client-side state. When developing large, multi-page applications on the Web or for sites that need to maintain user information between user sessions, it is necessary to use complex CGI-BIN scripts and server-side storage to maintain state information.

A simpler solution is offered in cookies—a system for maintaining client-side state available in Netscape Navigator and Microsoft Internet Explorer.

Using JavaScript, it is possible to create and use cookies to maintain client-side state throughout a Web-based application.

This chapter covers the following three topics:

- How Cookies Work
- The `cookie` Property
- A Generic Cookie Manager

Cookie Basics

The cookies mechanism is not a unique feature of JavaScript. Instead, the Cookie definition has been designed to work in an environment of standard HTTP and CGI-BIN.

The basic model for cookies follows:

1. When the server sends a document to the user, an additional entry is added to the HTTP header, instructing the browser to store data in a cookie.
2. The browser stores the data in the cookie.
3. Later, if the user requests a document with an associated cookie, the request is sent with an additional item in the header reflecting the content of the cookie or cookies associated with that page.

Cookies have the following features:

- Cookies can be associated with one or more documents on a particular host. Whenever one of these documents is requested by the user, the browser sends the content of all associated cookies to the server.
- More than one cookie can be associated with a document. All cookies associated with a document are sent to the server when the user requests the document.
- Cookies are named. The complete name-value pairs are sent to the server.
- Cookies have an expiry date associated with them. They can last for as little as the length of the user's current browser session to as much as one year or more.
- The number of cookies stored in a browser and stored for each page is generally limited.

Using this model, Web sites can track user information between pages in a session and between sessions by storing information in cookies. The information can then be processed when the user requests a page, and a custom page can be returned to the user based on the content of the cookie. This enables site developers to avoid other methods of maintaining state across multiple pages in a site, such as forms with numerous hidden fields.

How Cookies Work

Cookies add two header entries to HTTP requests to the server and responses from the server: `Cookie` and `Set-Cookie`.

HTTP header entries take the form of name-value pairs specified with

`Field-name: Data`

These entries are used to communicate information between the client and server, such as the MIME type of the document being sent by the sever. A MIME type header entry might look like

`Type: text/html`

or

`Type: image/gif`

The `Set-Cookie` Header Field

When the server sends a document to the browser with which a cookie needs to be set, the server adds a `Set-Cookie` header entry to the HTTP header sent with the document.

The `Set-Cookie` entry takes the following form:

`Set-Cookie: name=VALUE; expires=DATE; path=PATH; domain=DOMAIN; secure`

The `name=VALUE` pair is a required part of the `Set-Cookie` field. All other entries are optional. Table 9.1 describes the attributes of the `Set-Cookie` field.

Table 9.1. Attributes of the `Set-Cookie` header field.

Attribute	Description
`name=VALUE`	Specifies the name of the cookie and the content to be stored in the cookie. `VALUE` is a string that can't contain semicolons, commas, or spaces.
`expires=DATE`	Specifies the expiry date for the cookie. The client will stop storing the cookie after the date specified by the `expires` attribute. `DATE` takes the form `Wdy, DD-Mon-YY HH:MM:SS` `GMT`—all

continues

Table 9.1. continued

Attribute	Description
	dates are stored in Greenwich Mean Time. The default value for `expires` is the end of the current Navigator session.
path=*PATH*	Specifies the path portion of URLs which the cookie is associated with. A match of both the `path` and `domain` attributes with a requested URL means the cookie is sent to the server along with a document request. The default value for the `path` attribute is the path of the document that set the cookie.
domain=*DOMAIN*	Specifies the domain portion of URLs with which the cookie is associated. The default value for the `domain` attribute is the domain of the document that set the cookie.
secure	Specifies that the cookie should only be transmitted across secure links using the SSL protocol.

Multiple `Set-Cookie` fields can be included in a response header from a server. It is important to remember that cookies with the same `path`, `domain`, and `name` attributes overwrite previously created cookies with the same specifications.

> **TIP**
>
> The ability to overwrite previously set cookies provides a mechanism for deleting cookies by writing a new one with an expiry date in the past.

The `Cookie` Header Field

The `Cookie` header field is used by the browser to include cookies with document requests. It takes the form of a list of `name=VALUE` pairs of cookies associated with the document being requested.

```
Cookie: name1=VALUE1; name2=VALUE2; name3=VALUE3 ...
```

Limitations of Cookies

Navigator limits the number of cookies it will store to a total of 300. Each cookie has a four-kilobyte size limit, including all the optional attributes sent in the `Set-Cookie` header field.

In addition, any single domain can only store 20 cookies. This ensures that one site cannot dominate the cookie mechanism of a browser by flooding it with `Set-Cookie` header fields. When either limit is reached, the browser deletes the least recently used cookie to make room for the new cookie. If a cookie exceeds four kilobytes, it is trimmed to fit.

Application of Cookies

Cookies are used today on the Web for a number of different applications:

- **Custom home pages**: several sites offer the user the ability to customize his home page. The custom parameters are stored in a cookie and each time the user accesses the page, the server uses the cookie data to build a custom home page.

- **Online shopping services**: shopping services can use cookies for a number of different purposes, including keeping track of a user's name, address, and other relevant data between sessions, or for tracking a user's order during a session as the user browses a catalogue.

- **Login information**: Sites that require registration and login procedures can enable a user to automate the process, once the user has registered, by storing the information in a cookie with the `secure` attribute set.

- **Multilingual sites**: Multilingual sites can use cookies to remember the last language selected by a user so that the next time a user accesses the site it uses his preferred language. See Figure 9.1 and Figure 9.2.

FIGURE 9.1.

Multilingual sites can store a user's preferred language in a cookie.

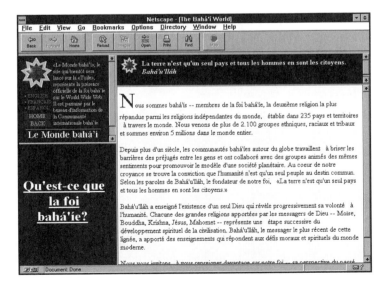

FIGURE 9.2.

The next time a user accesses the site, it will come up in the selected language rather than the default language.

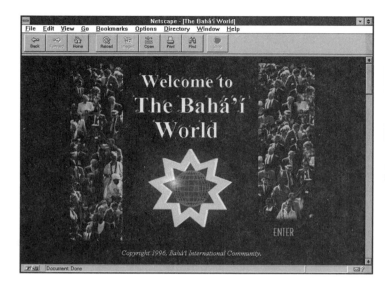

The `cookie` Property

Although the cookie mechanism in itself provides a means to store state information with the client, it still requires the use of CGI-BIN scripting and other server-side processing in order to take advantage of them.

JavaScript provides the `cookie` object so that it is possible to create and use cookies entirely at the client-end without any need for server processing or interaction.

The `cookie` property of the `document` object is the means by which scripts can work with the cookies. It exposes all the attributes of the cookies associated with a document to the script and allows scripts to set cookies.

The property itself is simply a string with the value that would be sent out in a `Cookie` field in the request header for the page in question. Being a string, it can be manipulated like any string object, using all the properties and methods of the `string` object, such as `length`, `charAt()`, and `indexOf()`.

Setting Cookies in JavaScript

Cookies are set in JavaScript by assigning values to `document.cookie`. Unlike regular strings, however, assigning a value to the property does not overwrite existing cookies. Instead, it creates a new cookie for the document.

The value assigned to `document.cookie` should be a string of the same format as is sent in a `Set-Cookie` field in a response header from the server:

```
document.cookie = "cookie1=First_Cookie";
```

The preceding should create a cookie named `cookie1` with a value `"First_Cookie"` that will expire at the end of the current Navigator session. Similarly,

```
document.cookie = "cookie2=Second_Cookie; expires=Mon, 01-Jul-97 12:00:00 GMT;
➥path=/";
```

should create a cookie named `Cookie2` which expires on July 1, 1997, and which is valid for all documents in the domain of the current document.

If these two cookies had been set in the same document, then using `document.write(document.cookie)` should produce results like the following:

```
cookie1=First_Cookie; cookie2=Second_Cookie;
```

Specifying Expiry Dates

Although it is possible to explicitly set expiry dates by building a string of the form

```
Wdy, DD-Mon-YY HH:MM:SS GMT
```

it is easier to use the `Date` object for creating dates.

For instance, to create an expiry date one year from the current date and then set a cookie with that expiry date, the following code could be used:

```
var expires = new Date();
expires.setTime (expires.getTime() + 24*60*60*365*1000);
document.cookie = "cookie3=Third_Cookie; expires=" + expires.toGMTString();
```

Here, an instance of the `Date` object is created for the current date. It is reset to one year in the future by adding the number of milliseconds in a year to the current date, and then it is output as a string in GMT as needed for the cookie's `expires` attributes.

Encoding Values for Cookies

The values stored in a cookie are limited by the fact that they cannot contain spaces, semicolons, or commas. This means that any string value cannot just be assigned directly to a cookie.

Instead, it is necessary to use some type of encoding algorithm on a string before it is stored in a cookie, and then a decoding algorithm needs to be applied when the value is read back from the cookie.

JavaScript provides the built-in `escape()` and `unescape()` methods. `escape()` encodes a string using the scheme used in URL strings. `unescape()` reverses the process. In the preceding example, where `"Third_Cookie"` was stored in a cookie, the string `"Third Cookie"` could have been encoded using `escape()` instead:

```
var expires = new Date();

expires.setTime (expires.getTime() + 24*60*60*365*1000);
var value="Third Cookie";
document.cookie = "cookie3=" + escape(value) + "; expires=" +
expires.toGMTString();
```

A Simple Cookie Application

The following simple personalized Web page illustrates the techniques for working with cookies in JavaScript. If a user comes to the page for the first time or after the relevant cookie has been deleted, he or she is prompted for a name. On future visits the user is welcomed personally without any prompting for a name:

```
<HTML>

<HEAD>

<SCRIPT LANGUAGE="JavaScript">

// SET UP EXPIRY DATE - ONE YEAR IN FUTURE
var expires = new Date();
expires.setTime (expires.getTime() + 24*60*60*365*1000);

// EXTRACT COOKIE
function getCookie(name) {
   var cookieFound = false;
   var start = 0;
   var end = 0;
   var cookieString = document.cookie;

   var i = 0;

   //LOOK FOR name IN cookieString
   while (i <= cookieString.length) {
      start = i;
      end = start + name.length;
      if (cookieString.substring(start,end) == name) {
         cookieFound = true;
         break;
      }
      i++;
   }

   //CHECK IF NAME WAS FOUND
   if (cookieFound) {
      start = end + 1;
      end = cookieString.indexOf(";",start);
      if (end < start)
         end = cookieString.length;
      return unescape(cookieString.substring(start,end));
   }
```

```
    //NAME WAS NOT FOUND
    return "NoName";

}

//CHECK IF USER'S NAME IS STORED
var userName = getCookie("UserName");
if (userName == "NoName") {
    userName = prompt("Please Enter Your Name:","Name");
}
document.cookie = "UserName=" + escape(userName) + "; expires=" +
expires.toGMTString();

</SCRIPT>

</HEAD>

<BODY>

<H1>Personalized Home Page</H1>

<H2>Your Name is: <STRONG>
<SCRIPT LANGUAGE="JavaScript">
document.write(userName);
</SCRIPT>
</STRONG>
</H2>

</BODY>

</HTML>
```

This produces results like those shown in Figures 9.3 and 9.4.

FIGURE 9.3.

The first time a user visits the page, he is prompted for his name.

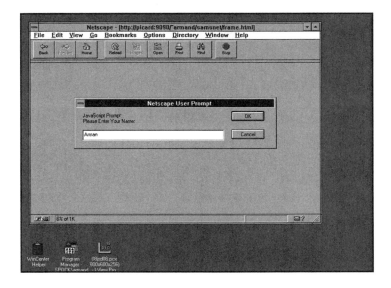

FIGURE 9.4.

On future visits the name is displayed automatically.

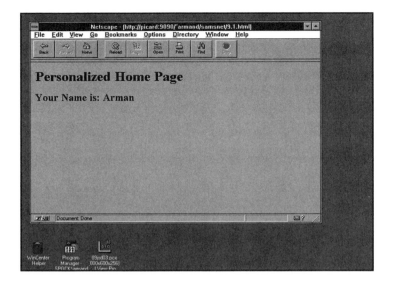

This script has three main parts: the getCookie() function, an initialization process, and the body of the HTML document.

The getCookie() function accepts a cookie name as an argument. It then searches through the cookie string returned by document.cookie for an occurrence of the name and if it finds it, returns the value associated with the name after it is passed through unescape(). If no cookie exists, an empty string is returned.

The script in the header of the document also contains some initialization code that executes before the body of the document is parsed and rendered. This code calls getCookie(), looking for a cookie named UserName. If there is no cookie with that name, then the user is prompted for his or her name. The value contained in userName (either from the cookie or from the user) is written back to the cookie UserName—ensuring that even if the cookie existed, the expiry date is updated to be one year from the current date.

Finally, the user's name is displayed in the body of the document by outputting the value of the variable userName.

A Generic Cookie Manager

Just as framesets benefit from a generic library of code for working with them, so do cookies. Rather than performing the work of setting expiry dates, encoding values, and parsing document.cookie for cookies, a generic cookie manager can provide a complete set of functions for working with cookies.

A cookie toolkit requires several key functions:

■ A function for setting cookies. Given all the attributes a user wishes to set, the function sets a new cookie.

■ A function for reading a cookie. This function was used in the previous example.

■ A function for deleting cookies. This function should reset the cookie with a new expiry date prior to the current date.

Once assembled, a generic cookie toolkit would look like:

```
<SCRIPT LANGUAGE="JavaScript">

//SET A NEW COOKIE
//Arguments:
//  name: cookie name (string)
//  value: cookie value (unencoded string)
//  expiry: expiry date (date)
//  path: document path (string)
//  domain: document domain (string)
//  secure: secure required? (boolean)

function setCookie(name,value,expiry,path,domain,secure) {

    var nameString = name + "=" + value;
    var expiryString = (expiry == null) ? "" : "; expires=" + expires.toGMTString();
    var pathString = (path == null) ? "" : "; path=" + path;
    var domainString = (path == null) ? "" : "; domain=" + domain;
    var secureSring = (secure) ? "; secure" : "";

    document.cookie = nameString + expiryString + pathString + domainString +
secureString;

}

//GET A NEW COOKIE
//Arguments:
//  name: cookie name (string)

function getCookie(name) {
    var cookieFound = false;
    var start = 0;
    var end = 0;
    var cookieString = document.cookie;

    var i = 0;
```

```
      //LOOK FOR name IN cookieString
      while (i <= cookieString.length) {
         start = i;
         end = start + name.length;
         if (cookieString.substring(start,end) == name {
            cookieFound = true;
            break;
         }
         i++;
      }

      //CHECK IF NAME WAS FOUND
      if (cookieFound) {
         start = end + 1;
         end = cookieString.indexOf(";",start);
         if (end < start)
            end = cookieString.length;
         return unescape(cookieString.substring(start,end));
      }

      //NAME WAS NOT FOUND
      return "";

}

//DELETE A COOKIE
//Arguments:
//  name: cookie name (string);

function deleteCookie(name) {

   var expires = new Date();
   expires.setTime (expires.getTime() - 1);

   setCookie(name,"Delete Cookie",expires,null,null,false);

}

</SCRIPT>
```

Summary

Cookies provide a useful mechanism for maintaining client-side state information between pages in a session, and between sessions for the same user.

Using JavaScript, it is possible to create, read, and delete cookies entirely in the client without any recourse to server-side programming and interaction. You can develop a generic cookie toolkit to make the process of managing and working with cookies easier.

In Chapter 10, "Applying Cookies and Frames," frames and cookies are brought together to build an outline manager.

10

Applying Cookies and Frames

by Arman Danesh

Cookies and frames are two very powerful features of the Netscape Navigator which, when used effectively in JavaScript, can greatly enhance Web interfaces and enable the deployment of applications using a Web browser as a delivery agent.

In this chapter you will see the development of an application that applies the information learned in the previous chapters about cookies and frames.

The application is a collapsible menu manager. Increasingly, Web sites provide hierarchical menus of their sites that can be expanded and collapsed in much the same way as Windows 95's Explorer file lists or Windows 3.1's File Manager.

These menus can be implemented in two ways: at the server-end, using CGI-BIN scripts to dynamically build each new page as the user collapses or expands sub-menus, or at the client-end, using JavaScript to refresh the page each time the user selects a new entry.

In building this application, you will see examples of the following:

■ How to use cookies to maintain state information between pages
■ Using frames in JavaScript
■ How to use JavaScript's object-oriented nature to develop structured applications
■ Using JavaScript to build completely dynamic Web pages without any fixed content

Creating a Menu Manager

The menu manager developed in this chapter is designed to enable Web authors to implement collapsible hierarchical menus similar to the system used to display directory structures in Windows 95's Explorer or Windows 3.1's File Manager.

For example, in Windows 95, a system of plus and minus signs next to each directory name allows it to be collapsed or expanded. When collapsed, no sub-directories under the higher-level directory are displayed. When expanded, the first level of sub-directories under a directory are displayed. Figures 10.1 and 10.2 illustrate how this is implemented in Windows 95's Explorer.

For the menu manager, you want to implement a simpler graphical interface with either an "expand" or "collapse" link next to menu entries as appropriate. Figure 10.3 shows how this appears in Netscape Navigator.

Each entry on the menu is a link—after all, that's what a menu is all about—and can have a sub-menu entry, or many entries listed under it. There should be no theoretical limit to the number of menu entries and sub-menu entries, although memory and other system limitations may impose practical limitations on different computers.

FIGURE 10.1.

When directories are collapsed in Explorer, no sub-directories are displayed.

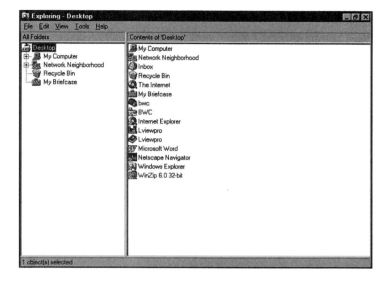

FIGURE 10.2.

If a directory is expanded, the first level of sub-directories is displayed and the plus sign next to the parent directory changes to a minus sign.

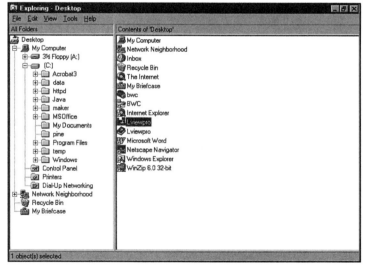

FIGURE 10.3.

The menu manager uses links for the expand and collapse controls (expand controls shown here).

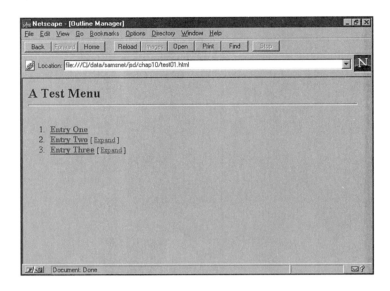

Planning the Program

Some consideration needs to be given to the basic structure of the program.

You need to be able to track information about the menu as a whole as well as tracking each entry on the menu, displaying the menu in its current status, expanding and collapsing menu entries, and creating the menu.

These goals are best done by defining two objects—`sectionObj`, used for entries in the menu, and `menuObj`, used to define the complete menu.

The `sectionObj` Object Definition

Certain basic information and functionality needs to be stored, and provided, for each menu entry, regardless of its level on the list. In particular, you need to know the following about each menu entry:

- Any sub-entries listed below it
- The title to display for the menu entry
- The link to follow if the entry is clicked
- The current status (opened or closed) of the menu entry

In addition, you need to be able to provide several methods:

- a method to display the entry
- a method for opening a collapsed menu entry
- a method for closing an expanded menu entry

This combination of information functionality is a logical candidate for an object that contains properties and methods as appropriate. This is especially true because the program needs to provide this combination for each entry in the menu. The object definition for each menu entry follows:

```
function sectionObj() {

    this.section = new Array();
    this.title = "";
    this.link = "";
    this.display = displaySection;
    this.open = doOpen;
    this.close = doClose;
    pointers[pointers.length] = this;
    this.number = pointers.length - 1;
    if (this.number >= menu.statusString.length) { menu.statusString +=closed; }
    this.status = menu.statusString.charAt(this.number);

}
```

The sub-menu entries for the current menu entry, if there are any, are stored in the property `section`, which is initialized as an empty array. As the section array is populated, each entry is another instance of the `sectionObj` object. If the array isn't populated, it returns a length of zero that provides a means of checking if there are any sub-menu entries under the current menu entry. This is important when it comes time to display the menu (discussed later in this chapter).

You should notice that in addition to the properties and methods listed above, the preceding object definition also contains two lines of code dealing with pointers:

```
pointers[pointers.length] = this;
this.number = pointers.length - 1;
```

These lines of code deal with the need to be able to refer to any particular object directly by a reference number when you build the expand and collapse links later in this chapter. Here, a global array called `pointers` is populated with objects for each menu entry as they are created. This is done by assigning a pointer to the current object to `pointers[pointers.length]` because `pointers.length` should return a value one greater than the index of the last entry in the array. By assigning to `pointers[pointers.length]` you are effectively increasing the length of the array by one. Once this is done, the index number for the current object in the pointer array is stored in the `number` property.

In addition, the technique used to set `this.status` requires some explanation:

```
if (this.number >= menu.statusString.length) { menu.statusString +=closed; }
this.status = menu.statusString.charAt(this.number);
```

As you will see later, whenever a menu entry is expanded or collapsed, the new arrangement is saved in a cookie, which is read when the document is reloaded so that the menu can be displayed with the new status. The current status of the menu is stored as a string of characters in the `statusString` property of the `menu` object, which is an instance of the `menuObj` object definition discussed later.

Thus, each character of the string `statusString` corresponds to the object at the same position in the `pointers` array. `statusString.charAt(this.number)` should match the value of the `status` property of the object indicated by `pointers[this.number]`. In the `sectionObj` object definition, this fact can be used to ensure that you're adding a menu entry that exists in the current `statusString`. It also can be used to ensure that if the menu entry doesn't already exist, it is added. `this.status` can be set to the value of the character at the corresponding place in `statusString`.

Methods of the `sectionObj` Object

The object definition for `sectionObj` refers to three methods:

- `display()`, which points to method definition function `displaySection()`
- `open()`, which points to the method definition function `doOpen()`
- `close()`, which points to the method definition function `doClose()`

The `open()` method is invoked when the user tries to expand a closed menu entry. As the following code shows, this method simply changes the value of the `status` property of the current `sectionObj` object, rebuilds the `statusString` property of the `menu` object, then stores this string in a cookie with the same name as the `name` property of the `menu` object:

```
function doOpen() {

    this.status = open;
    menu.statusString = "";
    for (k = 0; k < pointers.length; k ++) {
        menu.statusString += pointers[k].status;
    }
    setCookie(menu.name,menu.statusString,toExpire,null,null,false);
    self.location = self.location;

}
```

Attention should be given to the way in which `statusString` is rebuilt. First `statusString` is cleared to an empty string and then a `for` loop is used to step through all the objects in the `pointers` array, concatenating the value of the `status` property to the end `statusString` with each iteration of the loop. This effectively rebuilds `statusString` with the newly changed status information.

The `close()` method works in a similar way, except that it sets the `status` property to a closed state rather than an open state:

```
function doClose() {
this.status = closed;
menu.statusString = "";
```

```
for (k = 0; k < pointers.length; k ++) {
menu.statusString += pointers[k].status;
   }
setCookie(menu.name,menu.statusString,toExpire,null,null,false);
self.location = self.location;

}
```

In both doOpen() and doClose() (as well as in sectionObj()) you should notice the use of the open and closed variables, which are defined as constants elsewhere in the script. Their values are "o" and "c" respectively and they're used as the two entries in the statusString string to represent open and closed menu entries.

The last method is display() as defined by displaySection(). This is the most complex method of the sectionObj object:

```
function displaySection() {

   if (this.status == open) {
      document.write("<LI>", this.title.bold().link(this.link), " ");
      toprint = (this.section.length > 0) ? '[
➥<A HREF="javascript:pointers[' + this.number + '].close()"
➥TARGET=_self">Collapse</A> ]' : '';
      document.write(toprint.fontsize(2));
      document.write("<UL>");
      var j = 0;
      for (j = 0; j < this.section.length; j ++) {
         this.section[j].display();
      }
      document.write("</UL>");
   } else {
      document.write("<LI>", this.title.bold().link(this.link), " ");
      toprint = (this.section.length > 0) ? '[
➥<A HREF="javascript:pointers[' + this.number + '].open()"
➥TARGET="_self">Expand</A> ]' : '';
      document.write(toprint.fontsize(2));
   }

}
```

This method first checks to see if the menu is expanded or collapsed by checking the status property.

If the entry is expanded, the method displays the current entry's title as an entry in an unnumbered list with the <LI> tag. The link() method of the string object is used to add the hyperlink stored in the link property of the menu entry object.

Next, this.section.length is tested to see if it's greater than zero. If it is, then a link is built for collapsing the menu entry base. This is done by using the pointers array, with the number property of the current object as an index to refer to the current object in the hypertext link assigned to toprint. If this.section.length isn't greater than zero, the conditional statement assigns an empty string to toprint.

After `toprint` is displayed, a `for` loop is used to run through the `section` property (which is an array of objects for each sub-entry) and calls those objects' `display()` methods in turn. Notice that the `for` loop is surrounded by two `document.write()` calls that output `<UL>` and `</UL>`. This makes the sub-menu entries into nested unnumbered lists, which Netscape indents further than the current level, as shown in Figure 10.4.

FIGURE 10.4.

Nested unnumbered lists produce indented output with each subsequent nested list.

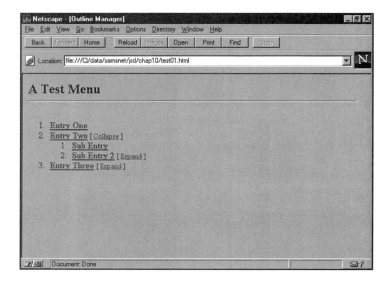

If the `status` property wasn't set to open, then the method prints out the title and link in the same way, creates an `"expand"` link, and displays it if needed.

The `menuObj` Object

The menu itself has several pieces of data and functionality that need to be associated with it, making it a good candidate for being an object. The properties that the `menuObj` needs to have include:

- A list of all top-level menu entries as an array of objects
- A title stored as a string
- A name used for naming the status cookie which will be stored with each change in menu status
- A string representing the current status of the menu

The associated method of the `menuObj` object is a method to initiate display of the whole menu tree. The `menuObj` object definition function looks like the following:

```
function menuObj(menuName) {

    this.statusString = getCookie(menuName);
    this.name = menuName;
```

```
    this.section = new Array();
    this.title = "";
    this.display = displayMenu;
    this.init = initMenu;

}
```

Other than the specific properties and methods of sectionObj, the main difference between the two objects is that menuObj takes an argument for the menu name which can then be used in the status cookie associated with the menu. This name-specific cookie allows multiple menu documents to be created without having cookies for different menus overwriting each other.

The display() method is slightly different than the one that is part of the sectionObj object:

```
function displayMenu() {

    document.write(this.title.fontsize(5).bold());
    document.write("<HR>");
    document.write("<UL>");
    for (i = 0; i < this.section.length; i ++) {
        this.section[i].display();
    }
    document.write("</UL>");

}
```

Here, the title is displayed using the fontsize() and bold() methods of the string object to define the appearance of the text. Next, the top-level unnumbered list is opened by writing out a <UL> tag. Then the function uses a for loop to call the display() method of each top-level menu object.

Global Variables and Other Components

In addition to defining the two objects and their associated properties and methods, the menu manager requires two other components: global variables and a cookie manager.

All work with cookies is done by calling functions such as setCookie() and getCookie(). These are the same functions that were created in the cookie manager at the end of Chapter 9, "Using Cookies." The menu manager needs to include the complete code of the cookie manager in order to work:

```
//SET A NEW COOKIE
//Arguments:
//  name: cookie name (string)
//  value: cookie value (unencoded string)
//  expiry: expiry date (date)
//  path: document path (string)
//  domain: document domain (string)
//  secure: secure required? (boolean)

function setCookie(name,value,expiry,path,domain,secure) {

    var nameString = name + "=" + value;
    var expiryString = (expiry == null) ? "" : "; expires=" + expires.toGMTString();
```

```
    var pathString = (path == null) ? "" : "; path=" + path;
    var domainString = (path == null) ? "" : "; domain=" + domain;
    var secureSring = (secure) ? "; secure" : "";

    document.cookie = nameString + expiryString + pathString + domainString +
secureString;

}

//GET A NEW COOKIE
//Arguments:
//  name: cookie name (string)

function getCookie(name) {
    var cookieFound = false;
    var start = 0;
    var end = 0;
    var cookieString = document.cookie;

    var i = 0;

    //LOOK FOR name IN cookieString
    while (i <= cookieString.length) {
        start = i;
        end = start + name.length;
        if (cookieString.substring(start,end) == name {
            cookieFound = true;
            break;
        }
        i++;
    }

    //CHECK IF NAME WAS FOUND
    if (cookieFound) {
        start = end + 1;
        end = cookieString.indexOf(";",start);
        if (end < start)
            end = cookieString.length;
        return unescape(cookieString.substring(start,end));
    }

    //NAME WAS NOT FOUND
    return "";

}

//DELETE A COOKIE
//Arguments:
//  name: cookie name (string);

function deleteCookie(name) {

    var expires = new Date();
    expires.setTime (expires.getTime() - 1);

    setCookie(name,"Delete Cookie",expires,null,null,false);

}
```

In addition, there are several global variables used throughout the object definitions that need to be defined as part of the menu manager: open, closed, pointers, and toExpire. Their definitions should be as follows:

```
var open = "o";
var closed = "c";
var pointers = new Array();
var toExpire = new Date(); toExpire.setTime(toExpire.getTime() + 1000*60*60*24);
```

open, closed, and pointers are discussed earlier in this chapter. toExpire is used whenever you set cookies to the expiry date 24 hours into the future. There is no need to make the cookie persist too long, but it is useful to have them persist long enough that if a user is using the menu, quits from the browser, and returns a few minutes later the menu comes up in the same configuration in which the menu was last viewed.

Working with the Menu Manager

In order to use the menu manager in an application, it's necessary to define the menu and then call the display() method of the menu object.

The first step in defining a menu is to create an instance of the menuObj object. This instance should be named menu. For example, to create a menu with three top-level menu entries, you could use

```
var menu = new menuObj("JSDmenu");
menu.title = "An Example Menu";
```

This creates an instance of menuObj called menu, with the name "JSDmenu", and assigns the title "An Example Menu" to it.

Once the menu object is instantiated, it's possible to define its menu entries. To do this, a new entry in the section array needs to be created as an instance of sectionObj and then its title and link properties can be set. For example, in a menu with three top-level menu entries, the following code would define the top-level entries:

```
menu.section[0] = new sectionObj();
menu.section[0].title = "First Menu Entry";
menu.section[0].link = "http://first.menu.link/";
menu.section[1] = new sectionObj();
menu.section[1].title = "Second Menu Entry";
menu.section[1].link = "http://second.menu.link/";
menu.section[2] = new sectionObj();
menu.section[2].title = "Third Menu Entry";
menu.section[2].link = "http://third.menu.link/";
```

In order to add two second-level entries under the second menu entry, it's necessary to add entries to the section array of the menu.section[1] object and then assign titles and links to them. The new entries in the array should also be instances of the sectionObj object:

```
menu.section[1].section[0] = new sectionObj();
menu.section[1].section[0].setTitle("Sub-menu Entry One");
```

```
menu.section[1].section[0].link = "http://fourth.menu.link/";
menu.section[1].section[1] = new sectionObj();
menu.section[1].section[1].setTitle("Sub-menu Entry Two");
menu.section[1].section[1].link = "http://fifth.menu.link";
```

Similarly, to add four second-level entries to the third menu entry, you would use the following:

```
menu.section[2].section[0] = new sectionObj();
menu.section[2].section[0].setTitle("Sub-menu Entry Three");
menu.section[2].section[0].link = "http://sixth.menu.link/";
menu.section[2].section[1] = new sectionOj();
menu.section[2].section[1].setTitle("Sub-menu Entry Four");
menu.section[2].section[1].link = "http://seventh.menu.link";
menu.section[2].section[2] = new sectionObj();
menu.section[2].section[2].setTitle("Sub-menu Entry Five");
menu.section[2].section[2].link = "http://eighth.menu.link/";
menu.section[2].section[3] = new sectionOj();
menu.section[2].section[3].setTitle("Sub-menu Entry Six");
menu.section[2].section[3].link = "http://ninth.menu.link";
```

To add a third-level entry under "Sub-menu Entry Four", you need to create an instance of sectionObj as an element of the menu.section[2].section[1].section and then assign it a title and a link:

```
menu.section[2].section[1].section[0] = new sectionObj();
menu.section[2].section[1].section[0].setTitle("Sub-menu Entry Seven");
menu.section[2].section[1].section[0].link = "http://tenth.menu.link";
```

Finally, to display the menu, it's necessary to call menu.displayMenu() from inside the body of the HTML document. The complete menu manager, along with the menu just defined, would look like the following:

```
//SET A NEW COOKIE
//Arguments:
//   name: cookie name (string)
//   value: cookie value (unencoded string)
//   expiry: expiry date (date)
//   path: document path (string)
//   domain: document domain (string)
//   secure: secure required? (boolean)

function setCookie(name,value,expiry,path,domain,secure) {

    var nameString = name + "=" + value;
    var expiryString = (expiry == null) ? "" : "; expires=" + expires.toGMTString();
    var pathString = (path == null) ? "" : "; path=" + path;
    var domainString = (path == null) ? "" : "; domain=" + domain;
    var secureSring = (secure) ? "; secure" : "";

    document.cookie = nameString + expiryString + pathString + domainString +
secureString;

}
```

```
//GET A NEW COOKIE
//Arguments:
//  name: cookie name (string)

function getCookie(name) {
   var cookieFound = false;
   var start = 0;
   var end = 0;
   var cookieString = document.cookie;

   var i = 0;

   //LOOK FOR name IN cookieString
   while (i <= cookieString.length) {
      start = i;
      end = start + name.length;
      if (cookieString.substring(start,end) == name {
         cookieFound = true;
         break;
      }
      i++;
   }

   //CHECK IF NAME WAS FOUND
   if (cookieFound) {
      start = end + 1;
      end = cookieString.indexOf(";",start);
      if (end < start)
         end = cookieString.length;
      return unescape(cookieString.substring(start,end));
   }

   //NAME WAS NOT FOUND
   return "";

}

//DELETE A COOKIE
//Arguments:
//  name: cookie name (string);

function deleteCookie(name) {

   var expires = new Date();
   expires.setTime (expires.getTime() - 1);

   setCookie(name,"Delete Cookie",expires,null,null,false);

}
var toExpire = new Date(); toExpire.setTime(toExpire.getTime() + 1000*60*60*24);

function sectionObj() {

   this.section = new Array();
   this.title = "";
```

```
    this.link = "";
    this.display = displaySection;
    this.open = doOpen;
    this.close = doClose;
    pointers[pointers.length] = this;
    this.number = pointers.length - 1;
    if (this.number >= menu.statusString.length) { menu.statusString +=closed; }
    this.status = menu.statusString.charAt(this.number);

}

function doOpen() {

    this.status = open;
    menu.statusString = "";
    for (k = 0; k < pointers.length; k ++) {
       menu.statusString += pointers[k].status;
    }
    setCookie(menu.name,menu.statusString,toExpire,null,null,false);
    self.location = self.location;

}

function doClose() {

    this.status = closed;
    menu.statusString = "";
    for (k = 0; k < pointers.length; k ++) {
       menu.statusString += pointers[k].status;
    }
    setCookie(menu.name,menu.statusString,toExpire,null,null,false);
    self.location = self.location;

}

function displaySection() {

if (this.status == open) {
     document.write("<LI>", this.title.bold().link(this.link), " ");
     toprint = (this.section.length > 0) ? '[ <A
➡HREF="javascript:pointers[' + this.number + '].close()"
➡TARGET="_self">Collapse</A> ]' : '';
     document.write(toprint.fontsize(2));
     document.write("<UL>");
     var j = 0;
     for (j = 0; j < this.section.length; j ++) {
        this.section[j].display();
     }
     document.write("</UL>");
   } else {
     document.write("<LI>",this.title.bold().link(this.link), " ");
     toprint = (this.section.length > 0) ? '[ <A
➡HREF="javascript:pointers[' + this.number + '].open()"
➡TARGET="_self">Expand</A> ]' : '';
     document.write(toprint.fontsize(2));
   }
```

```
}

function menuObj(menuName) {

    this.statusString = getCookie(menuName);
    this.name = menuName;
    this.section = new Array();
    this.title = "";
    this.display = displayMenu;

}

function initMenu(numSections) {

    for (i = 0; i < numSections; i++) {
        this.section[i] = new sectionObj();
    }

}

function displayMenu() {

    document.write(this.title.fontsize(5).bold());
    document.write("<HR>");
    document.write("<UL>");
    for (i = 0; i < this.section.length; i ++) {
        this.section[i].display();
    }
    document.write("</UL>");

}

var menu = new menuObj("JSDmenu");

menu.title = "An Example Menu";
menu.section[0] = new sectionObj();
menu.section[0].title = "First Menu Entry";
menu.section[0].link = "http://first.menu.link/";
menu.section[1] = new sectionObj();
menu.section[1].title = "Second Menu Entry";
menu.section[1].link = "http://second.menu.link/";
menu.section[2] = new sectionObj();
menu.section[2].title = "Third Menu Entry";
menu.section[2].link = "http://third.menu.link/";
menu.section[1].section[0] = new sectionObj();
menu.section[1].section[0].title = "Sub-menu Entry One";
menu.section[1].section[0].link = "http://fourth.menu.link/";
menu.section[1].section[1] = new sectionObj();
menu.section[1].section[1].title = "Sub-menu Entry Two";
menu.section[1].section[1].link = "http://fifth.menu.link";
menu.section[2].section[0] = new sectionObj();
menu.section[2].section[0].title = "Sub-menu Entry Three";
menu.section[2].section[0].link = "http://sixth.menu.link/";
menu.section[2].section[1] = new sectionObj();
menu.section[2].section[1].title = "Sub-menu Entry Four";
menu.section[2].section[1].link = "http://seventh.menu.link";
```

```
menu.section[2].section[2] = new sectionObj();
menu.section[2].section[2].title = "Sub-menu Entry Five";
menu.section[2].section[2].link = "http://eighth.menu.link/";
menu.section[2].section[3] = new sectionObj();
menu.section[2].section[3].title = "Sub-menu Entry Six";
menu.section[2].section[3].link = "http://ninth.menu.link";
menu.section[2].section[1].section[0] = new sectionObj();
menu.section[2].section[1].section[0].title = "Sub-menu Entry Seven";
menu.section[2].section[1].section[0].link = "http://tenth.menu.link";

</SCRIPT>

</HEAD>

<BODY>

<SCRIPT LANGUAGE="JavaScript">
menu.display();
</SCRIPT>

</BODY>

</HTML>
```

The resulting menu manager would resemble Figures 10.5 and 10.6.

FIGURE 10.5.

Initially the menu is displayed entirely closed.

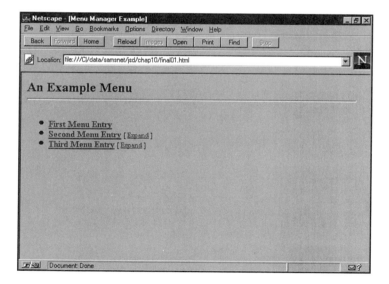

FIGURE 10.6.

The user can use the expand and collapse links to manipulate the menu.

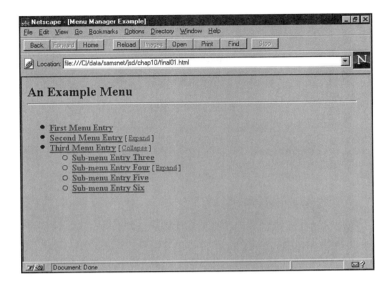

Incorporating a Menu into a Frameset

The menu manager is designed with the assumption that all the links in the menu are intended to be targeted at the same frame or window, which is why no provisions are made to include link targets in the sectionObj object definition.

By default, all the links are targeted at the same window in which the menu appears, which may defeat the purpose of a hierarchical menu like the one produced by the menu manager.

In order to combine a menu into a frameset, it's necessary to specify the target frame for all the links in a menu. This is done with the <BASE> tag, which can be used to set an alternate default target for all links in a document. By using

```
<BASE TARGET="targetFrame">
```

in the HTML header of the menu file, all links in a menu are targeted at another frame.

For example, consider the following frameset:

```
<HTML>

<HEAD>
<TITLE>Menu Frameset</TITLE>
</HEAD>

<FRAMESET COLS="30%,*" BORDER=1>
    <FRAME SRC="menu.html">
    <FRAME SRC="output.html" NAME="output">
</FRAMESET>

</HTML>
```

As a result, the file `menu.html` could include a `<BASE TARGET="output">` tag in the header and a menu definition:

```
var menu = new menuObj("FrameMenu");

menu.title = "FrameSet Menu Example";
menu.section[0] = new sectionObj();
menu.section[0].title = "Document One";
menu.section[0].link = "document1.html";
menu.section[0].section[0] = new sectionObj();
menu.section[0].section[0].title = "Sub-document One";
menu.section[0].section[0].link = "subdocument1.html";
menu.section[0].section[1] = new sectionObj();
menu.section[0].section[1].title = "Sub-document Two";
menu.section[0].section[1].link = "subdocument2.html";
menu.section[1] = new sectionObj();
menu.section[1].title = "Document Two";
menu.section[1].link = "document2.html";
menu.section[2] = new sectionObj();
menu.section[2].title = "Document Three";
menu.section[2].link = "document3.html";
menu.section[2].section[0] = new sectionObj();
menu.section[2].section[0].title = "Sub-document Three";
menu.section[2].section[0].link = "subdocument3.html";
```

This would produce results similar to those shown in Figures 10.7 and 10.8.

FIGURE 10.7.

The menu loads in its own frameset and can be expanded and collapsed without affecting the output *frame.*

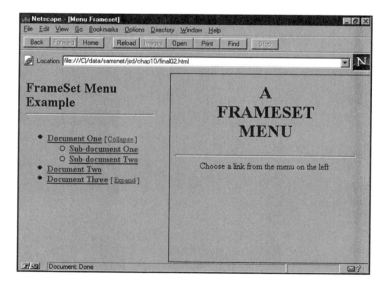

FIGURE 10.8.

Clicking on a link in the menu opens the appropriate document in the output *frame.*

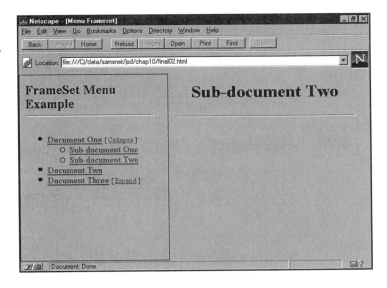

Summary

In this chapter an outline manager has been developed as an example of applying cookies. This application highlights several important principles, including the following:

- ■ The benefit of organizing an application using objects
- ■ How to use cookies to maintain state during a user's session
- ■ How to build a page of dynamic content created entirely in JavaScript

The next chapter moves from client-side JavaScript to server-side JavaScript and takes a look at LiveWire and LiveWire Pro.

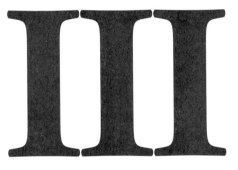

III

JavaScript and LiveWire Pro

11

LiveWire and LiveWire Pro

by Arman Danesh

With the increase in complex client-server applications being deployed on the Web, ranging from shopping basket applications to complete database systems, it's increasingly necessary to have robust server-based development environments.

Netscape meets this need with LiveWire, a server-based, online development environment.

LiveWire provides both site management through a site manager and application development facilities with an application manager.

In addition, LiveWire can wholly replace the need for CGI programming, allowing for the development of more tightly integrated client-server applications.

LiveWire Pro is an extended version of LiveWire that offers additional features for integration with relational databases.

This chapter covers the basics of LiveWire and LiveWire Pro, including the following topics:

- The main features of LiveWire
- Acquiring LiveWire
- Using the Site Manager
- Using the Application Manager

LiveWire Features

LiveWire is a complete server-based site management and application-development environment offered by Netscape.

It requires an installed Netscape server running on Windows NT or certain versions of UNIX (only Solaris was available at the time this book was written) and extends the server to provide the following features:

- **Site Management**: LiveWire includes the Site Manager, a graphical application that enables the drag-and-drop management of a Web site, easy maintenance of hyperlinks, a set of site templates, and a graphical front-end to the LiveWire compiler.
- **Server Extensions**: LiveWire extends Netscape servers, allowing them to run the server-end of client-server applications. This is done by providing an object framework, akin to the Navigator object tree, to access server features and an application manager.
- **Application Management**: Using the server-based Application Manager, it's possible to add, change, start, and stop applications installed on the server.
- **A Development Server**: LiveWire separates the development and deployment servers. This enables the separation of applications under development and applications offered to the end-user. The development and deployment servers can run on the

same physical machine, although performance may be better if they run on distinct machines.

- **WYSIWYG Web Page Editing**: LiveWire includes a copy of Navigator Gold—Netscape's Web browser with an integrated editor. Navigator Gold provides drag-and-drop, editing of HTML and JavaScript, and quick one-button publishing. The Navigator Gold Authoring Guide at Netscape's Web site provides more details about using Navigator Gold for Web page development.

LiveWire Pro adds the following functionality:

- **SQL Support**: LiveWire Pro provides additional support for the Structured Query Language (SQL) by including an SQL database server. The server provides the ability to create and deploy database applications for sites lacking another database system.

- **Report Generation**: LiveWire Pro includes the Crystal Reports report generator, which generates HTML reports from a database.

These two features of LiveWire Pro are beyond the scope of this book. Netscape provides documentation for them when LiveWire Pro is purchased.

Acquiring LiveWire and LiveWire Pro

At the time of writing this book, the release version LiveWire for NT was available. A 60-day demo version can be downloaded from `http://home.netscape.com/comprod/mirror/server_download.html`.

In addition, a beta version for HP-UX, IRIX, and Solaris was available to members of Netscape's DevEdge developer's program. For information about joining the DevEdge developer's program, check out `http://developer.netscape.com/`.

Additional Information

Additional information about LiveWire is available on Netscape's Web site in the LiveWire Developer's Guide at `http://developer.netscape.com/library/documentation/livewire/index.html`.

The Application Manager

The LiveWire application provides the ability to manage applications installed on the server.

Using the Application Manager, it is possible to add new applications, modify an application's configuration, stop and start it, debug and test the application, and uninstall it if needed.

The Application Manager is itself deployed as a LiveWire application and is accessed through a copy of Navigator. The Windows NT version of LiveWire provides a special icon to launch Netscape Navigator and directly connect to the Application Manager.

> **NOTE**
>
> Non-Windows NT versions of LiveWire enable the Application Manager to be launched by accessing http://host.name/appmgr/ from any copy of Navigator.

The Main Application Manager Window

Once the Application Manager is launched, the main screen is displayed. This screen is divided into two frames: a control frame and an information frame. Figure 11.1 shows the main LiveWire window.

FIGURE 11.1.
The main LiveWire screen.

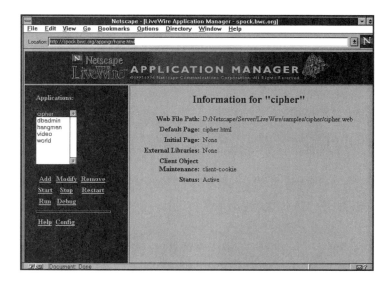

The Control Frame

The left frame of the main window provides the controls necessary for using the Application Manager. The frame provides a scrolling list of installed applications as well as buttons to perform the following actions:

- Add a new application.
- Modify the selected application.

■ Remove the selected application.

■ Start the selected application.

■ Stop the selected application.

■ Restart the selected application.

■ Run the selected application.

■ Debug the selected application.

■ Get help.

■ Configure the Application Manager.

The details of these actions are covered later in this chapter.

The Information Frame

The right frame of the main window is used to display information about the currently selected application. The information displayed includes the following:

■ Application name

■ Application path on the server

■ Page information

■ Libraries used

■ Client object technique (discussed in Chapter 12, "The LiveWire Object Tree")

■ Status (such as active or stopped)

In addition to presenting information about the current application, the right frame is used to perform the tasks associated with the control buttons in the left frame of the main window.

Adding an Application to the Server

To add a new application, simply click on the Add button in the control frame. This causes a form like the one in Figure 11.2 to be displayed in the right frame.

The form asks for the following information:

■ **Name**: The application name. The URL for the application will be `http://host.name/appliction_name`.

■ **Web File Path**: The full file path of the application's Web file. Web files are created when an application is compiled. This is discussed later in this chapter.

■ **Default Page**: The file to load if no page is indicated and this is not the user's first access to the application.

- **Initial Page**: The file to display when the user first accesses the application.
- **External Libraries**: Full file path of external libraries. LiveWire applications can access external libraries. This subject is beyond the brief introduction to LiveWire presented in this book.
- **Client Object Maintenance**: Client-object maintenance techniques are discussed in Chapter 12, where the `client` object is examined.

The Default Page, Initial Page, and External Libraries entries are optional and can be left blank.

When the page is done, simply click the Add button.

FIGURE 11.2.
The Add application form.

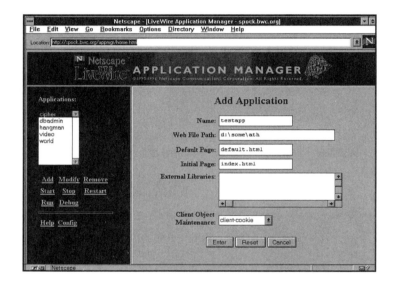

How URLs Work in LiveWire

You will notice in the description of the preceding Name field that application URLs in LiveWire take the form

```
http://host.name/application_name
```

Following this logic, individual pages in an application can be accessed using the following form:

```
http://host.name/application_name/page.html
```

It's important to realize that LiveWire applications are independent of the normal document tree in the Netscape Web server. That is, Web application files can be stored outside the normal document tree of the server.

> **NOTE**
>
> Because applications aren't always part of the normal document tree, it's important to ensure that application names don't conflict with existing document or directory names in the server's normal document tree. If they do, they over-ride the documents from the server's tree.

Modifying an Installed Application

To modify an application, select it from the list in the left frame and click on the Modify button. This opens a form in the right frame similar to the one used to add a new application with all the information filled in to match the current application settings.

It is possible to change any of the values except for the name of an application.

Removing, Starting, Stopping, Restarting, and Running Applications

To remove, start, stop, or restart an application, simply select its name from the list in the left frame and click the appropriate control button.

When an application is removed, its files aren't deleted. An application must be started in order for users to access it.

Running an application opens the application in a new Navigator window. Applications also can be run by directly entering the application's URL in Navigator.

Debugging Applications

The Application Manager provides the ability to debug applications. To debug an application, simply select its name from the list in the control frame and click the Debug button. This displays a trace of the application in a separate frame in the same window as the application or in a separate window altogether. This can be set in the Application Manager's configuration settings.

A separate frame trace looks like Figure 11.3.

FIGURE 11.3.

An application trace in a separate frame.

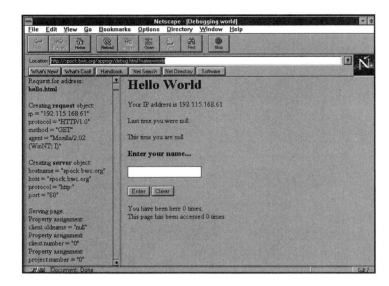

The Site Manager

The Site Manager is a stand-alone application. It doesn't require a Web server or Web browser to use. The Windows NT version can be used on Windows 95, extending LiveWire's site management capabilities to Windows 95 users.

Site Manager provides the following features:

■ Templates for site creation

■ A drag-and-drop interface

■ Automatic tracking and maintenance of links

■ A graphical front-end to the LiveWire application compiler

The next section guides you through a brief tour of Site Manager's features, starting with the basics of the Site Manager interface. More detailed information about Site Manager is available in the LiveWire documentation.

The Site Manager Interface

The basic Site Manager interface consists of a window divided into two frames. The interface is shown in Figure 11.4.

FIGURE 11.4.
The Site Manager window.

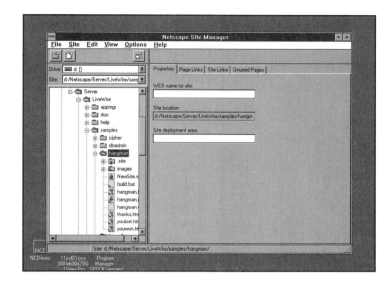

The left frame is used to select and display an application and its document tree. At the top are two drop-down menus for selecting a drive and directory for a site.

Below this is a hierarchical display of documents and directories in a site. This document tree is presented much like the one used to display a disk drive in the Windows 95 Explorer or the File Manager from Windows 3.1 and Windows NT 3.51.

The right pane provides four tabbed pages for managing Site Properties, Pages Links, Site Links, and Unused Pages.

The Properties Tab

The Properties Tab (like the one in Figure 11.4) displays the properties of the object selected in the left frame. This includes the site name, the site's development location, and the deployment location for the Web site.

The Page Links Tab

The Page Links Tab, like the one shown in Figure 11.5, displays a list of links to and from an HTML document selected in the left window.

FIGURE 11.5.
The Page Links Tab.

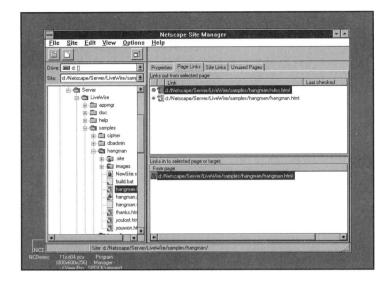

Site Links

Site Manager is able to track links and mark them as valid, invalid, internal, or external links. The Site Links Tab, as shown in Figure 11.6, provides a way to work with links in a site.

FIGURE 11.6.
The Site Links Tab.

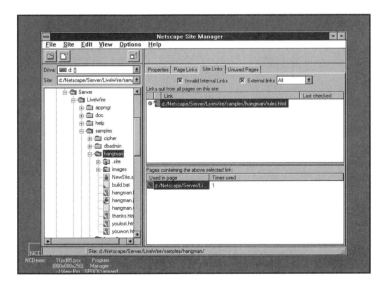

On this tab, it is possible to view all links or a subset such as valid, invalid, or unchecked. Four columns present information, including validity, link type, link name, and the date the link was last checked for validity.

Unused Pages Tab

The Unused Pages Tab, like the one shown in Figure 11.7, displays pages that are not being used in a site—pages that have no other pages pointing to them.

FIGURE 11.7.
The Unused Pages Tab.

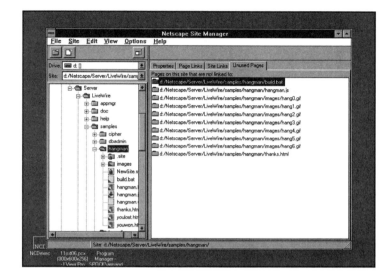

Creating a New Site

New sites are created in Site Manager using the New Site template window. This is done by selecting New Site from the Site menu.

This opens a New Site Window like the one shown in Figure 11.8.

Sites can be created using one of the following options:

- ■ Create a site from a template
- ■ Create a site based on a remote site
- ■ Create an empty site

If you create a site from a template then the create site wizard launches the Site Manager Guru, which guides you through creating a site directory, selecting a template, and configuring the template.

If you choose to base your site on a remote site, then the wizard asks for the URL of the remote site and downloads information about the site and sets up your local site to be managed.

Empty sites also can be created.

The New Site wizard is fairly straightforward and guides you through the steps for creating a new site using any of the preceding three options.

FIGURE 11.8.
The Creating a site window.

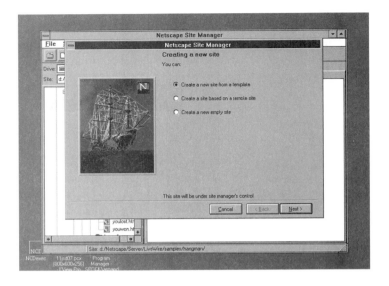

Managing an Existing Site

In addition to creating a new site, it's possible to bring an existing site into Site Manager for management.

This is done by selecting the site's directory in the left frame and then selecting Manage from the Site menu. Site Manager then builds the database of links needed for it to manage the site.

Managing Links in a Site

Site Manager makes it easy to fix invalid links and ensure that internal links are kept valid when you make changes to a site and its structure.

There are four types of actions that constitute site link management:

- Repairing case sensitivity problems
- Checking links
- Modifying links
- Updating the links database

Repairing Case Sensitivity Problems

Filenames in links are case-sensitive. Site Manager can repair case sensitivity problems. Simply select Repair Case Sense Problems from the Site menu. Site Manager then compares links to actual file names in the directory tree and fixes the links to match the actual filenames.

Checking Links

Site Manager tracks links as you move documents around in a site, updating its internal database as documents move and ensuring links in documents match current document locations.

However, external links need to be checked to ensure they are valid. Choose Check External Links from the Site menu to make Site Manager check all external links.

Modifying and Updating the Links Database

If you modify a file using an application other than Site Manager, then the site ceases to correspond to the Site Manager's database for the site.

To fix this, choose Update Site from the Site menu. This causes Site Manager to update its database to match the current status of the site.

The LiveWire Application Compiler

It is necessary to briefly mention the LiveWire compiler.

LiveWire applications are written in server JavaScript, which is actually embedded in the HTML source files of the application.

Where client JavaScript appears between `<SCRIPT>` and `</SCRIPT>` tags, server JavaScript needs to appear between `<SERVER>` and `</SERVER>` tags:

```
<SERVER>
    Server JavaScript code
</SERVER>
```

More information about server JavaScript is discussed in Chapter 12.

JavaScript also can be included in HTML by enclosing it between backquotes. This enables JavaScript to be evaluated in the middle of an HTML tag:

```
<TAG ATTRIB="some value" ATTRIB='some JavaScript code'>
```

Quotes are automatically placed around the attribute value generated by the JavaScript code.

The LiveWire compiler takes the HTML, server JavaScript, and client JavaScript in a file and compiles them into a Web file with a .web extension. This file is used by LiveWire to build the HTML page to send to the client when a page is requested. Only sites that use server JavaScript in some of their files need to be compiled.

There are two ways to compile a Web file:

■ Select Build Web File from Site Manager's Site menu
■ Use the command-line compiler

The command-line compiler is invoked with the command `lwcomp` using the following syntax:

```
lwcomp [-c|-v|-?] [-o output_file.web] [script1.html script2.html ...]
[javascript1.js javascript2.js ...]
```

The options do the following:

Option	Function
`-c:`	Checks syntax but doesn't compile
`-v:`	Specifies Verbose Output
`-?:`	Displays help information
`-o output_file:`	Specifies target .web file

Multiple HTML files and JavaScript libraries can be compiled at the same time with the command-line compiler.

Summary

This chapter examined the LiveWire site management and server development environment from Netscape. LiveWire offers the ability to develop complex client-server applications for deployment on the Web and offers the following features:

■ Site Management

■ Application Management

■ Application Compilation

This chapter also looked briefly at how to use these main features in preparation for the next two chapters, which cover the basics of application development for LiveWire. Chapter 12 covers the LiveWire object tree, the core of server JavaScript, and Chapter 13, "Programming with LiveWire and JavaScript," provides a few brief examples of client-server programming with LiveWire.

12

The LiveWire Object Tree

by Arman Danesh

As in Navigator, LiveWire has a set of objects that are available for developing LiveWire-based applications. The LiveWire object tree consists of four objects:

- The `request` object
- The `client` object
- The `project` object
- The `server` object

These objects have associated methods and properties and can be extended with additional properties. Each object also has a lifetime, which varies based on the object.

The LiveWire Object Tree

The primary purpose underlying the LiveWire object tree is to provide mechanisms for maintaining state when using HTTP, a fundamentally stateless protocol. What this means is that you can track access to a server-based application by a single client across multiple pages. With the highly complex interactive applications being used on the Web, this ability is increasingly important when you're trying to maintain information about a user and his or her session.

To help you do this, LiveWire provides four objects:

- `request`: Provides information about the current HTTP request from the client.
- `client`: Provides information about a given client.
- `project`: Provides information about the entire application and can be used to share information between multiple clients.
- `server`: Provides information that's global to the whole server and can be used to share data across applications and multiple clients.

Object Lifetimes

Before taking a detailed look at the properties and methods of each object, you need to understand the concept of *object lifetimes*. Each object in the LiveWire object tree comes into existence at a specified time and lasts until a specified time. Here is the object lifetime of LiveWire objects, in order from longest lifetime to shortest:

- `server`: Exists from the time the server is started until the time it is stopped.
- `project`: Exists from the time an application is started until it is stopped.
- `client`: Exists for the length of a client's connection to an application.
- `request`: Exists for the duration of a single client request to the server—this is generally less than one second.

In addition, global variables declared in server JavaScript have the same lifetime as the `request` object.

Object Scope and Property Types

Another important concept in using LiveWire objects is that of *scope*. Unlike client JavaScript, LiveWire objects are not global in scope. Within a function, LiveWire objects are inaccessible, which means you must pass objects or their properties to a function as parameters.

Another unique aspect of server JavaScript as it's used in LiveWire is that all properties are stored as strings. So, although you can assign a Boolean or numeric value to a property, once it's assigned, it's a string—it's no longer Boolean or numeric.

For instance, the following JavaScript code would have worked in client JavaScript, but because you're dealing with server JavaScript, it's incorrect:

```
client.property = true;
if (client.property) { JavaScript Code }
```

Because `client.property` is actually a string, the code would have to be this:

```
client.property = true;
if (client.property == "true") { JavaScript Code }
```

Similarly, numbers are also stored as a string, so if an integer were assigned to `client.property` and you wanted to increment it, you would have to use

```
client.property = parseInt(client.property)++
```

instead of `client.property++` or `client.property += 1`.

The `request` Object

The `request` object supplies information about a specific client request. Client requests occur when the user manually opens a URL, selects a bookmark, or clicks on a hyperlink; when client JavaScript navigates to a page or server, JavaScript redirects the browser to a particular page.

The `request` object has four pre-defined properties, as listed in Table 12.1.

Table 12.1. Pre-defined properties of the `request` object.

Property	Description
agent	Name and version of the client. Provides the same information as `navigator.userAgent` in client JavaScript.
ip	Supplies the IP address of the client.
method	Specifies the method used by the client to make the request (that is, GET, POST, or HEAD for HTTP 1.0).
protocol	Returns the protocol and level used by the client to make the request (such as HTTP/1.0).

Other properties of the `request` object are created in two ways:

- By creating form elements. Each element becomes a property of the `request` object; its name is indicated by the NAME attribute of the element's tag.
- Specifying name-value pairs in a URL using the standard syntax used in GET method form submissions. The syntax is: *URL?name1=value1&name2=value2&name3=value3&...* Each property created this way has the name from the name-value pair and takes the value as its value.

For example, in this form,

```
<FORM METHOD="post" ACTION="URL">
Name: <INPUT TYPE="text" NAME="name">
<INPUT TYPE="submit">
</FORM>
```

a property called `request.name` is created when the form is submitted to the server.

Likewise, this hyperlink

```
<A HREF="URL?number=5">The Link</A>
```

would create a `request` property called `number` with the value 5 when the user clicks on the link.

The `client` Object

The `client` object helps to distinguish separate clients accessing an application. It can be used to track persistent state information across multiple pages of an application. A new object is created each time an unknown client accesses an application, and the same client object is provided each time the client reconnects to the application.

The `client` object contains no pre-defined properties. Instead, applications can create their own properties of the `client` object, which then persist across multiple accesses by a client.

For instance, an application could create a property called `name`:

```
client.name = "User's Name";
```

This property would then be available for the rest of the client's connections to the application.

`Client` objects can be stored in several different ways. The method used for a particular application is specified in the LiveWire Application Manager when you install or subsequently modify an application.

At the most basic level, the `client` object can be stored on the client using cookies or URL encoding or on the server using short cookies, URL encoding, or IP address references.

Client Cookies

If client cookies are used to store the `client` object, then each property is stored as a separate cookie with the name `NETSCAPE_LIVEWIRE.propName=propValue`.

The disadvantage of this technique is two-fold: Many clients don't support cookies, and the limitations on the number of cookies may mean that information is destroyed prematurely by other applications from the same server.

Client URL Encoding

In this technique, all the object information is transferred to the client as name-value pairs encoded into the URL with the syntax `URL?name1=value1&name2=value2&...`

With client URL encoding, the server must dynamically generate URLs, and object information must be transmitted each time a request is made.

Server Short Cookies

The short cookie technique stores the client property data on the server under a name generated the first time a client accesses an application. This name is then stored on the client by using cookies and subsequently passed to the server with each client request. The short cookie technique helps overcome the size and number limitations of client cookies.

Server Short URL Encoding

The server-based short URL encoding uses the same generated name technique to store client objects on the server, but then passes the generated name from client to server by encoding it into URLs.

Like client-based URL encoding, this technique requires dynamically generated URLs.

Server IP Addresses

The IP address technique stores `client` object data on the server based on the client's IP address. This works well when each client has a fixed IP address, as in an intranet. However, on the Internet, where many users get dynamically assigned IP addresses each time they connect to their Internet Service Provider, this technique isn't reliable because it's simply not possible to track a single client using IP addresses. Proxy servers also mask the real client IP address, which hinders this technique.

`client` Object Lifetime and Maintenance

The lifetime of the `client` object has a default expiry time that allows LiveWire to clean up old `client` objects that aren't necessary anymore. This is done because once a client accesses an application, there is no guarantee that the user will do so again in the future.

By default, if the `client` object is stored in a cookie on the client, it expires when the user exits the client browser. Server-based storage expires the `client` object by default after 10 minutes of inactivity.

The `client` object provides two methods that allow an application to override these defaults:

- `client.expiration(seconds)`: Specifies the expiration of the `client` object in seconds; *seconds* should be an integer.
- `client.destroy()`: Removes all properties of the `client` object and destroys the object.

The `project` Object

The `project` object offers a way to share data between all clients accessing an application. The data will persist from the time the application is started to the time it's stopped.

Like the `client` object, the `project` object offers no pre-defined properties. Rather, the application can use the object to define its own properties. For instance, this statement

```
project.nextWord = "value";
```

would define a `project` property called `nextWord` that would be available to all clients accessing the application.

Object Locking

Because it's possible for several clients to simultaneously access the `project` object, you need to use *locking* to prevent conflicts from occurring—such as when two clients try to assign values to the same property at the same time.

By default, the `project` object implicitly locks a property when it's being read or set, then unlocks as soon as the action is finished. This works fine if an application wants to either read or set the property. However, if multiple steps are required, such as reading and then setting the same property in sequence, another client could possibly access the property between the reading and setting steps and change its value.

To prevent this, the `project` object provides the `lock()` and `unlock()` methods, which can be used to lock the object, perform several actions, and then unlock it again. These methods would be used like this:

```
project.lock()
   Multiple JavaScript Statements
project.unlock()
```

> **NOTE**
>
> It's important to remember that although one client locks the `project` object by using `lock()`, all other clients are prevented from accessing the entire object. For this reason, the object should be locked for the minimum time possible. In addition, all `lock()` calls should be balanced by an `unlock()` call.

The `server` Object

The `server` object gives you a way to share information among all applications on a server; it also provides several pre-defined properties, outlined in Table 12.2.

Table 12.2. Pre-defined properties of the server object.

Property	Description
hostname	The full host name of the server (including port number)
host	The host name of the server without the port number
protocol	The protocol being used (such as `http:`)
port	The port number of the server

Locking the `server` Object

Like the `project` object, locking needs to be used with the `server` object to ensure that two applications don't try to change or access values of the `server` object at the same time.

The `server` object includes the `lock()` and `unlock()` methods—which are used the same way as the `lock()` and `unlock()` methods of the `project` object—as a means to perform locking. The same caveats about length of locking and balancing `lock()` and `unlock()` calls applies to both the `server` and `project` objects.

Other LiveWire Objects

In addition to the LiveWire object tree described previously, which is associated with requests, clients, applications, and the server itself, there are two other main objects available in server JavaScript: `File` and `database`.

The `File` Object

The `File` object supplies a way to store and retrieve data from files on the server. This is useful when a database server isn't being used and there's a need to store persistent files on the server that last beyond a server shutdown.

The LiveWire `File` object is used strictly to create files on the server. For security reasons, it can't be used to create files on the client.

To work with a file, you create an instance of the `File` object in the same way you create an array:

```
filePointer = new File("file_path");
```

filePointer will be used to refer to the specific instance of the `File` object, and `file_path` is the path on the server of the file to work with (this path corresponds to the application directory).

Methods of the `File` Object

The `File` object offers several methods, outlined in Table 12.3, for working with files.

Table 12.3. Methods of the `File` object.

Method	Description
open()	Opens a file. Takes a single argument specifying the mode to open the file with (see Table 12.4 for a list of file modes for the open() method). Returns true if successful; false if unsuccessful.
close()	Closes a file. Returns true if successful; false if the file is not open.
lock()	Locks a file from access by other users.
unlock()	Unlocks a file.
setPosition()	Positions the pointer in a file. Accepts two arguments: the first, an integer indicating the position in bytes, and the second, a reference that's optional. The values for the reference argument are specified in Table 12.5. Returns true if successful; false if unsuccessful.
getPosition()	Returns the current position in bytes. Returns -1 if there's an error.
eof()	Returns true if the pointer is at the end of the file; otherwise, it returns false.
read()	Reads from the file. Takes one argument—an integer specifying the number of bytes to read. Returns a string.

Method	Description
`readln()`	Reads and returns the next line from the file. The line separator is not included in the returned string.
`readByte()`	Reads and returns the next byte in the file. Returns `-1` if there are no further bytes to read.
`write()`	Writes a string to the file. Takes a single string argument indicating the data to write to the file. Returns `true` if successful, and `false` if not.
`writeln()`	Writes a string to the file followed by a new line. Takes a single string argument and returns `true` or `false`, indicating the success of the operation.
`writeByte()`	Writes a byte to the file. Takes a single integer argument (the value of the byte to write to the file) and returns `true` or `false`.
`flush()`	Writes the buffer to the disk. Returns `true` if successful and `false` if it fails.
`byteToString()`	Converts a number into a one-character string. No object is required—can use `File.byteToString()`. Takes a single integer argument. The empty string is returned if the argument is invalid.
`stringToByte()`	Converts the first character of a string argument into a number. No object is required—can use `File.stringToByte()`. Returns zero if the argument is invalid.
`getLength()`	Returns the number of bytes in a file or `-1` if there are problems performing the action.
`exists()`	Returns `true` if the file exists; `false` otherwise.
`error()`	Returns the error status or `-1` if the file isn't open or can't be opened.
`clearError()`	Clears the error status and the value of `eof()`.

Table 12.4. Mode arguments for the `open()` method.

Mode	Description
`r`	Opens the file for reading. If the file exists, returns `true`; otherwise returns `false`.
`w`	Opens the file for writing. Creates new file if the file doesn't exist.
`a`	Opens the file for appending. Creates a new file if the file doesn't exist.

continues

Table 12.4. continued

Mode	Description
r+	Opens the file for reading and writing from the beginning of the file. If the file exists, returns `true`; otherwise returns `false`.
w+	Opens the file for reading and writing. Creates a new file if the file doesn't exist.
a+	Opens a file for reading and writing from the end of the file. Creates a new file if the file doesn't exist.
b	Opens a file as a binary file (as opposed to a text file). Append this mode to any of the other modes in the `open()` method (for example, `rb` or `a+b`). Relevant only on Windows systems.

Table 12.5. References for the `setPosition()` method.

Reference	Description
0	Sets the position in relation to the beginning of the file.
1	Sets the position in relation to the current position.
2	Sets the position in relation to the end of the file.
Other value	Sets the position in relation to the beginning of the file.
Unspecified	Sets the position in relation to the beginning of the file.

For instance, to open a new file in the /tmp directory called test, then write a line of text to it, and close it, you could use:

```
newFile = new File("/tmp/test");
isOpen = newFile.open("w");
if (isOpen) { newFile.write("Some Text") }
```

Then the file could be opened and the value of the first line written out to the current HTML stream by using this:

```
theFile = new File("/tmp/test");
isOpen = theFile.open("r");
if (isOpen) { write(theFile.readln()) }
```

The database Object

LiveWire Pro gives you the ability to work with a database server and generate SQL queries; it presumes knowledge of, and access to, a database server and is beyond the scope of this book.

Briefly, though, LiveWire gives the database object methods for working with relational databases. The database object is created when an application connects to a database server.

Table 12.6 briefly outlines the methods of the database object. More details are available in the *LiveWire Developer's Guide* available on Netscape's Web site.

Table 12.6. Methods of the database object.

Method	Description
beginTransaction()	Begins an SQL transaction with the database server.
commitTransaction()	Commits the transaction.
connect()	Connects to a database server.
connected()	Returns the status of a connection.
cursor()	Creates a cursor for a specified SELECT statement.
disconnect()	Disconnects from a database server.
execute()	Performs a specified SQL statement.
rollbackTransaction()	Rolls back the transaction.
SQLTable()	Displays query results.
majorErrorCode()	Returns the major error code.
minorErrorCode()	Returns the minor error code.
majorErrorMessage()	Returns the major error message.
minorErrorMessage()	Returns the minor error message.

Server JavaScript Functions

LiveWire provides several built-in JavaScript functions that aren't methods of any of the LiveWire objects:

- write()
- writeURL()
- redirect()
- debug()
- flush()

The write() Function

Like the document.write() method in client JavaScript, the server-side write() function is used to display the results of JavaScript expressions into the HTML stream. The function takes a single expression, which evaluates to a string: write(*expression*).

The source code received at the client end is the actual text or HTML generated by the `write()` call and is treated as static HTML by the client.

The `writeURL()` Function

The `writeURL()` function is used to generate dynamic URLs when either of the URL encoding methods of maintaining the `client` object is being used.

The `writeURL()` function accepts one argument: an expression evaluating to a string that specifies the URL of a page to link to. The result returned by `writeURL()` is the full URL, including all necessary encoded information. For instance, to create a link to the URL `http://some.domain/some/path.html`, you could use

```
write('<A HREF="');
writeURL("http://some.domain/some/path.html");
write('">');
```

or simply

```
<A HREF='writeURL("http://some.domain/some/path.html")'>
```

The `redirect()` Function

This function redirects clients to the URL specified as the argument to the function.

The `debug()` Function

The `debug()` function redirects its output to the trace utility's display. This function was discussed in Chapter 11, "LiveWire and LiveWire Pro."

The `flush()` Function

In general, LiveWire sends output from the `write()` function to the client in 64K blocks of data. Until 64K is available to be sent, the data is stored in a buffer.

The `flush()` function enables you to send the content of the current buffer to the client before it reaches 64K.

Summary

In this chapter, you reviewed the objects and major functions available in LiveWire-based server JavaScript. They give you the means to develop sophisticated applications that, among other things, work with relational databases, maintain persistent state information, and track information about clients using an application.

In the next chapter, you'll see some small examples that demonstrate the applications of LiveWire-based programming.

13

Programming with LiveWire and JavaScript

by Arman Danesh

Now that you have examined the main objects and functions available, you can study some examples of how to use these features in actual applications. In this chapter, you will progressively develop a small client-server application that illustrates how LiveWire can be used to set up interactive applications.

By studying how this simple program works, you will learn about the following:

■ Using the `request` object

■ Maintaining client-specific information with the `client` object

■ Accessing the local file system with the `File` object

In addition, another program is examined. It implements a simple ordering system for a collection of three products, all using a single HTML file. This application demonstrates the following:

■ The difference between the `request` object and the `client` object

■ Tracking client information using the `client` object

■ Generating dynamic content with server JavaScript

IP-Based Authentication

In this chapter, you will create a simple authentication program that decides whether to provide access to a site based on the client's IP address. You will develop this program in four stages:

■ Stage one simply redirects the user to one of two different pages based on the client's IP address. This program includes the list of valid IP addresses in the script itself.

■ Stage two moves the list of valid IP addresses to a separate file but performs the same authentication: When users first access the site, they are directed to one of two pages. This makes configuration easier because the IP addresses are stored as a simple list in a separate file, rather than being embedded in the program's source code. New IP addresses can then be added without recompiling and restarting the application.

■ Stage three gives valid users a way to add an IP address to the list of valid IPs—not necessarily something you would do in a real authentication situation, but it shows how a Web front-end can be used to configure an application.

■ Stage four carries out site-wide authentication, which ensures that a user can't directly jump to a sub-document without first being authenticated.

IP-Based Authentication: Stage One

The following listing sets up a simple IP address authentication:

```
<SERVER>

function myArray(length) {
```

```
    for (i = 0; i < length; i++) {
        this[i] = "";
    }

    this.length = length;

}

var validIPs = new myArray(3);
validIPs[0] = "192.115.168.1";
validIPs[1] = "192.115.168.11";
validIPs[2] = "192.114.74.1";

var gotoURL = "http://spock/authentic/sorry.html";

for (i = 0; i < validIPs.length; i++) {

    if (request.ip == validIPs[i]) {
        gotoURL = "http://spock/authentic/welcome.html";
    }

}

redirect(gotoURL);

</SERVER>
```

This script is actually fairly simple. It's written entirely in server JavaScript, which is placed between <SERVER> and </SERVER> tags. The script relies on the IP property of the request object to find out the client's IP address for the current request. In addition, the redirect() function is used to redirect the client to the appropriate page once validation has taken place.

The script starts by defining the myArray() constructor function because server JavaScript currently lacks the Array() object and you want to store the list of valid IP addresses in an array. The myArray() function accepts the number of elements as an argument, then uses a for loop to assign an empty string to each element, defines the length property, and assigns the value of the length argument to it.

Next, an array called validIPs is created by using the myArray() function, and an IP address is assigned to each element in the array.

A variable called gotoURL is then created to hold the array to which you're redirecting the client. The assumption is made that the client is invalid, so the URL for the page displayed to users without valid IP addresses is assigned to gotoURL.

A for loop is then used to loop through the validIPs array, comparing each entry to request.ip. If a match is found, then the alternative URL is assigned to gotoURL.

When the loop exits, the redirect() function is used to make the client browser access the appropriate page. The results look like those in Figures 13.1 and 13.2.

FIGURE 13.1.

If users have a valid IP address, they are admitted to the site.

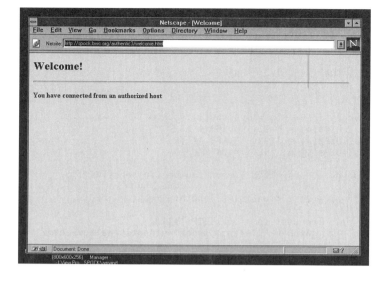

FIGURE 13.2.

Invalid users are informed that they don't have access to the site.

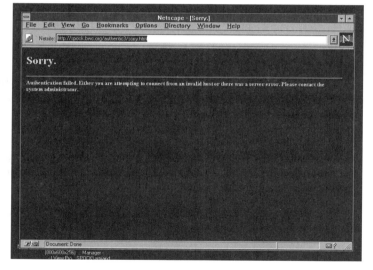

IP Authentication: Stage Two

In this addition to the basic authentication program, you move the list of valid IP addresses to a separate file. This offers easier configuration to the application administrator and enables new IP addresses to be added without requiring a recompilation of the application; a recompilation would be needed in the first stage, where the list of valid IP addresses is an integral part of the application source code.

The following listing performs this authentication:

```
<SERVER>

function myArray(length) {

    for (i = 0; i < length; i++) {

        this[i] = "";

    }

    this.length = length;

}

var validFile = new File("d:/users/armand/livetest/valid2.txt");
var success =validFile.open("r");

if (success) {
    validFile.setPosition(0);
    var numIPs = validFile.readln();
    var getIP = "";

    var validIPs = new myArray(numIPs);

    for (i = 0; i < numIPs; i++) {

        getIP = validFile.readln();
        validIPs[i] = getIP;

    }

    validFile.close();

}

var gotoURL = "http://spock/authentic2/sorry.html";

for (i = 0; i < validIPs.length; i++) {

    if (request.ip == validIPs[i]) {

        gotoURL = "http://spock/authentic2/welcome.html";

    }

}

redirect(gotoURL);

</SERVER>
```

This script doesn't change the actual validation portion at the end of the listing. Rather, the section where the IP addresses were assigned to the validIPs array has been changed to load the list from a file.

The format of this list of files stores each IP address on a separate line; the first line should contain a single integer that indicates the number of IP addresses in the file.

The script first creates a new instance of the `File` object called `validFile`, which points to the file containing the IP list. Next, the object's `open()` method is called, and the result is assigned to `success` to test for the successful completion of the attempt to open the file. The mode for the `open()` method is "r", indicating that the file should be opened from the beginning for reading.

If `success` is `true`, the file is open and the script can continue to read in the values. First, `setPosition()` is called to make sure the pointer is set to the start of the file. Then the first line is read, using the `readln()` method of the `File` object, and stored in `numIPs`, which is used to initialize the `validIPs` array. Finally, a `for` loop is used to read each subsequent line from the file and store it in the array, and the `close()` method is called to close the file.

Because the `length` property of `validIPs` doesn't exist if the file fails to open, authentication will fail in this circumstance because the authentication `for` loop never executes.

IP Authentication: Stage Three

In this stage, you go a step further by enabling valid users to add IP addresses to the list of valid IP addresses. To do this, you need two additional pieces of source code:

■ In the welcome file, you add a form that the user can use to enter an IP address and submit it.

■ When the form is submitted, you call another file that actually adds the IP address to the file.

The welcome file includes the following form:

```
<FORM METHOD=POST ACTION="http://spock/authentic3/add3.html">
<INPUT TYPE=text NAME=ipAddress SIZE=15>
<INPUT TYPE=submit>
</FORM>
```

This produces a form like the one shown in Figure 13.3.

The following script adds the IP address to the file containing the list of addresses:

```
<SERVER>

function myArray(length) {

    for (i = 0; i < length; i++) {

        this[i] = "";

    }

    this.length = length;
```

```
}

var validFile = new File("d:/users/armand/livetest/valid2.txt");
var success = validFile.open("r");

if (success) {
    validFile.setPosition(0);
    var numIPs = validFile.readln();
    var getIP = "";

    var validIPs = new myArray(numIPs);

    for (i = 0; i < numIPs; i++) {

        getIP = validFile.readln();
        validIPs[i] = getIP;

    }

    validFile.close();

    validIPs[numIPs] = request.ipAddress;
    numIPs = 1 + parseInt(numIPs,10);

    var newSuccess = validFile.open("w");

    if (newSuccess) {

        validFile.writeln(numIPs);

        for (i = 0; i < numIPs; i++) {

            validFile.writeln(validIPs[i]);

        }

        validFile.close();

    }

}

redirect("http://spock/authentic3/");

</SERVER>
```

This script resembles the authentication script you used in the second stage. It starts by reading the list of IP addresses into the validIPs array, as you did in the authentication script.

Next, the submitted IP address is assigned to a new entry at the end of the array. The IP address is stored in a property of the request object with the same name as the text field in the form used to submit the IP address. Once this is done, the value of numIPs can be increased by one.

Then the file can be reopened for writing. The "w" mode is used to open the file as an empty text file for writing. The number of addresses and each address can be written on separate lines in the file by using the `writeln()` method of the `File` object.

Finally, after the file is closed, the client is redirected to the main home page, which reauthenticates the client and displays the welcome page.

FIGURE 13.3.

Valid users can submit an IP address to be added to the list of valid IP addresses.

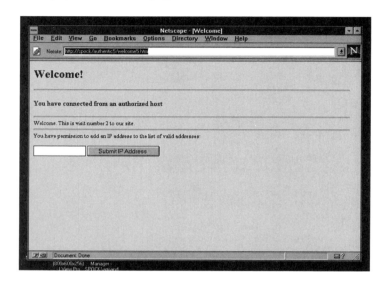

IP Authentication: Stage Four

In this, the final stage of your small authentication program, you add the ability to make sure users can't access a sub-document without first being authenticated by the application's main document. In this way, you can ensure that a user can't directly open the welcome page or any other page without first opening the top-level URL for the application where the IP address authentication takes place.

To do this, you need to add a section to the main authentication script that creates a property to be used throughout clients' sessions to track whether they have been validated.

In addition, you need to add a small header script to all other pages in the application that should be accessible only to validated users.

This is what the final authentication script looks like:

```
<SERVER>

function myArray(length) {

    for (i = 0; i < length; i++) {
```

```
        this[i] = "";

    }

    this.length = length;

}

var validFile = new File("d:/users/armand/livetest/valid2.txt");
var success =validFile.open("r");

if (success) {
    validFile.setPosition(0);
    var numIPs = validFile.readln();
    var getIP = "";

    var validIPs = new myArray(numIPs);

    for (i = 0; i < numIPs; i++) {

        getIP = validFile.readln();
        validIPs[i] = getIP;

    }

    validFile.close();

}

var gotoURL = "http://spock/authentic5/sorry5.html";
client.valid = false;

for (i = 0; i < validIPs.length; i++) {

    if (request.ip == validIPs[i]) {

        gotoURL = "http://spock/authentic5/welcome5.html";
        client.valid = "true";

    }

}

redirect(gotoURL);

</SERVER>
```

This script adds two simple steps. Before the final for loop that performs the actual validation of the IP address, a property of the client object is created called valid. Its initial value is set to false, which assumes that the IP address is invalid. However, if a valid address is found, client.valid is set to true.

The client object and its properties persist either until the end of the client session—in the case of client objects stored in the client—or for 10 minutes of inactivity, in the case of server-stored client objects.

The header of files that need authentication should include the following script:

```
<SERVER>

if (!client.valid ¦¦ client.valid == null) {

    redirect("http://spock/authentic5/");
}

</SERVER>
```

This simply checks the value of client.valid. If it's false or null (meaning that the property has never been defined), then the client is redirected to the main authentication page before the page's content can be displayed.

A LiveWire Ordering System

Another LiveWire example should help you get more of a sense of what the possibilities of LiveWire are. This application implements a simple ordering system for a collection of three products.

The application needs to provide the following functionality:

■ The ability to enter or edit personal data such as names and addresses

■ The ability to individually add or remove any item from the order

■ The ability to view the current status of the user's order

■ An option to place the order when it's ready

In order to do this, a single HTML file has been built, using server JavaScript to dynamically build the appropriate HTML output based on user actions:

```
<HTML>

<HEAD>
<TITLE>
LiveWire Order System
</TITLE>

</HEAD>

<BODY BGCOLOR="cornsilk">
<DIV ALIGN=CENTER>

<SERVER>

client.name = (client.name == null) ? "" : client.name;
client.address1 = (client.address1 == null) ? "" : client.address1;
client.address2 = (client.address2 == null) ? "" : client.address2;
client.phone = (client.phone == null) ? "" : client.phone;
client.fax = (client.fax == null) ? "" : client.fax;
client.email = (client.email == null) ? "" : client.email;
```

```
client.item1 = (client.item1 == null) ? "false" : client.item1;
client.item2 = (client.item2 == null) ? "false" : client.item2;
client.item3 = (client.item3 == null) ? "false" : client.item3;

if (request.newdata == "yes") {

        client.name = (request.name == null) ? client.name : request.name;
        client.address1 = (request.address1 == null) ? client.address1 :
        ➡ request.address1;
        client.address2 = (request.address2 == null) ? client.address2 :
        ➡ request.address2;
        client.phone = (request.phone == null) ? client.phone : request.phone;
        client.fax = (request.fax == null) ? client.fax : request.fax;
        client.email = (request.email == null) ? client.email : request.email;
        client.item1 = (request.item1 == null) ? client.item1 : request.item1;
        client.item2 = (request.item2 == null) ? client.item2 : request.item2;
        client.item3 = (request.item3 == null) ? client.item3 : request.item3;

}

if (client.name == "" || request.action == "data") {

        write('<H1>Personal Data</H1>');
        write('<HR>');
        write('<FORM ACTION="shop2.html" METHOD="GET">');
        write('<TABLE ALIGN=CENTER BORDER=0 CELLPADDING=10 CELLSPACING=1>');
        write('<TR>');
        write('<TD BGCOLOR="black"><FONT COLOR="white">Name:</FONT></TD>');
        write('<TD BGCOLOR="maroon"><INPUT TYPE=text SIZE=30 NAME=name VALUE="' +
        ➡ client.name + '"></TD>');
        write('</TR>');
        write('<TR>');
        write('<TD BGCOLOR="black"><FONT COLOR="white">Address:</FONT></TD>');
        write('<TD BGCOLOR="maroon"><INPUT TYPE=text SIZE=30 NAME=address1 VALUE="'
        ➡ + client.address1 + '">');
        write('<BR><INPUT TYPE=text SIZE=30 NAME=address2 VALUE="' +
        ➡ client.address2 + '"></TD>');
        write('</TR>');
        write('<TR>');
        write('<TD BGCOLOR="black"><FONT COLOR="white">Phone:</FONT></TD>');
        write('<TD BGCOLOR="maroon"><INPUT TYPE=text SIZE=30 NAME=phone VALUE="' +
        ➡ client.phone + '"></TD>');
        write('</TR>');
        write('<TR>');
        write('<TD BGCOLOR="black"><FONT COLOR="white">Fax:</FONT></TD>');
        write('<TD BGCOLOR="maroon"><INPUT TYPE=text SIZE=30 NAME=fax VALUE="' +
        ➡ client.fax + '"></TD>');
        write('</TR>');
        write('<TR>');
        write('<TD BGCOLOR="black"><FONT COLOR="white">E-mail:</FONT></TD>');
        write('<TD BGCOLOR="maroon"><INPUT TYPE=text SIZE=30 NAME=email VALUE="' +
        ➡ client.email + '"></TD>');
        write('</TR>');
        write('<TR>');
        write('<TD ALIGN=CENTER BGCOLOR="midnightblue" COLSPAN=2><INPUT TYPE=SUBMIT
        ➡ VALUE="Save Data"></TD>');
        write('</TR>');
        write('</TABLE>');
```

```
        write('<INPUT TYPE=hidden NAME="action" VALUE="view">');
        write('<INPUT TYPE=hidden NAME="newdata" VALUE="yes">');
        write('</FORM>');

} else if (request.action == null ¦¦ request.action == "view") {

        write('<H1>Current Status</H1>');
        write('<HR>');
        write('<TABLE ALIGN=CENTER BORDER=0 CELLPADDING=10 CELLSPACING=10>');
        write('<TR VALIGN=TOP>');
        write('<TD BGCOLOR="cyan" WIDTH=50%>');
        write('<H2>Personal Data</H2>');
        write('<HR>');
        write('NAME: <EM>' + client.name + '</EM><BR>');
        write('ADDRESS: <EM>' + client.address1 + ', ' + client.address2 + '<
        ➥EM><BR>');
        write('PHONE: <EM>' + client.phone + '</EM><BR>');
        write('FAX: <EM>' + client.fax + '</EM><BR>');
        write('E-MAIL: <EM>' + client.email + '</EM><BR>');
        write('</TD><TD BGCOLOR="#020A33">');
        write('<FONT COLOR="cornsilk">');
        write('<H2>Order Status</H2>');
        write('<HR>');

        var ordered = "false";
        if (client.item1 == "true") {
                write('Item 1 ordered1<P>');
                ordered = "true";
        }
        if (client.item2 == "true") {
                write('Item 2 ordered1<P>');
                ordered = "true";
        }
        if (client.item3 == "true") {
                write('Item 3 ordered1<P>');
                ordered = "true";
        }
        if (ordered == "false") {
                write('No items ordered.');
        }

        write('</TD></TR></TABLE>');

} else if (request.action == "item1") {

        write('<H1>Item One</H1>');
        write('<HR>');
        write('<TABLE BORDER=0 CELLPADDING=10 CELLSPACING=1>');
        write('<TR>');
        write('<TD BGCOLOR="maroon" ALIGN=CENTER><FONT COLOR="white">');
        write('Current Order Status: ');
        if (client.item1 == "true") {
                write("Ordered");
        } else {
                write("Not Ordered");
        }
        write('</FONT></TD></TR>');
        write('<TR>');
```

```
              write('<TD BGCOLOR="cyan" ALIGN=CENTER>');
              if (client.item1 == "true") {
                      write('<A HREF="shop2.html?item1=false&newdata=yes">Remove From
                      ➥ Order</A>');
              } else {
                      write('<A HREF="shop2.html?item1=true&newdata=yes">Add to Order<
                      ➥A>');
              }
              write('</TD></TR></TABLE>');

} else if (request.action == "item2") {

              write('<H1>Item Two</H1>');
              write('<HR>');
              write('<TABLE BORDER=0 CELLPADDING=10 CELLSPACING=1>');
              write('<TR>');
              write('<TD BGCOLOR="maroon" ALIGN=CENTER><FONT COLOR="white">');
              write('Current Order Status: ');
              if (client.item2 == "true") {
                      write("Ordered");
              } else {
                      write("Not Ordered");
              }
              write('</FONT></TD></TR>');
              write('<TR>');
              write('<TD BGCOLOR="cyan" ALIGN=CENTER>');
              if (client.item2 == "true") {
                      write('<A HREF="shop2.html?item2=false&newdata=yes">Remove From
                      ➥ Order</A>');
              } else {
                      write('<A HREF="shop2.html?item2=true&newdata=yes">Add to Order<
                      ➥A>');
              }
              write('</TD></TR></TABLE>');

} else if (request.action == "item3") {

              write('<H1>Item Three</H1>');
              write('<HR>');
              write('<TABLE BORDER=0 CELLPADDING=10 CELLSPACING=1>');
              write('<TR>');
              write('<TD BGCOLOR="maroon" ALIGN=CENTER><FONT COLOR="white">');
              write('Current Order Status: ');
              if (client.item3 == "true") {
                      write("Ordered");
              } else {
                      write("Not Ordered");
              }
              write('</FONT></TD></TR>');
              write('<TR>');
              write('<TD BGCOLOR="cyan" ALIGN=CENTER>');
              if (client.item3 == "true") {
                      write('<A HREF="shop2.html?item3=false&newdata=yes">Remove From
                      ➥ Order</A>');
              } else {
                      write('<A HREF="shop2.html?item3=true&newdata=yes">Add to Order<
                      ➥A>');
              }
```

```
                write('</TD></TR></TABLE>');

    } else if (request.action == "order") {

                write('<H1>Order Placed</H1>');
                write('<HR>');
                write('<TABLE BORDER=0 CELLPADDING=10>');
                write('<TR>');
                write('<TD BGCOLOR="midnightblue"><FONT COLOR="yellow">');

                var ordered = "false";
                if (client.item1 == "true") {
                        write('Item 1 ordered<P>');
                        ordered = "true";
                }
                if (client.item2 == "true") {
                        write('Item 2 ordered<P>');
                        ordered = "true";
                }
                if (client.item3 == "true") {
                        write('Item 3 ordered<P>');
                        ordered = "true";
                }
                if (ordered == "false") {
                        write("No items ordered.");
                }

                write('</FONT></TD></TR></TABLE>.');

    }

</SERVER>

<HR>
<A HREF="shop2.html?action=view">View Status</A> ¦
<A HREF="shop2.html?action=item1">Item 1</A> ¦
<A HREF="shop2.html?action=item2">Item 2</A> ¦
<A HREF="shop2.html?action=item3">Item 3</A> ¦
<A HREF="shop2.html?action=data">Edit Personal Data</A> ¦
<A HREF="shop2.html?action=order">Place Order</A>
</DIV></BODY>

</HTML>
```

This script uses several underlying principles that you need to keep in mind as you analyze how the script works:

■ Properties of the request object can be created using the URL syntax: http://url?name=value&name=value...

■ The GET submission method for a form includes all the values from the form in the URL using the form http://url?name=value&name=value...

■ Properties of the client object persist between each user action until the end of the current browser session.

The script itself is divided into two main portions: The first performs basic initialization and the second determines what HTML code needs to be displayed and then displays it.

Script Initialization

The script initializes by setting up the properties of the client object, which is used to track the user throughout his or her session.

Specifically, you want to track two types of data:

- **Personal data:** this includes `client.name`, `client.address1`, `client.address2`, `client.phone`, `client.fax`, and `client.email`—which consist of string data
- **Order status information:** this consists of three Boolean values: `client.item1`, `client.item2`, and `client.item3`—which indicate if the user wants to order any of the three items available in the application

Initialization takes place in two steps. First, a check is made to see if any of the personal data or order status properties contain a null value. This indicates that the value has never been set and it is likely the initial access to the application by the client. For each property, a conditional expression is used to assign an empty string (or false string in the case of the order status properties) to the property if it's value is null.

Next, a check is made to see if the user has attempted to update the data stored in the personal data or order status properties. Because the same page is repeatedly reloading with each user action, it's possible to pass an expression called `newdata` as a property of the `request` object indicating if you are in fact updating existing data.

If data is being updated, then another set of conditional expressions can be used to assign the new values to the correct properties of the `client` object. This is done by passing the values as properties of the `request` object, with names corresponding to the properties of the `client` object. For each property of the `request` object that isn't a null value, the value of this property is assigned to the corresponding property of the `client` object.

Page Display

After initialization takes place, the appropriate HTML is generated for the user's actions. As the user performs different actions by clicking on links or submitting forms, the requested action is passed as a property of the `request` object called `action`.

The possible actions are:

- **Edit Personal Data**: The user is presented with a form in which he can edit his name and contact information. This is displayed when two conditions exist—the user's name is not set (`client.name == ""`) and the user has requested to update his personal data (`request.action == "data"`).

- **View Status**: The user is presented with a list of personal data and a list of items he has asked to include in his order. This page is loaded when two conditions exist—when no action is specified (`request.action == null`) and when the user explicitly asks to view the status of his order (`request.action == "view"`).
- **Change order for an item**: For each item, the user can view a page where he can change the status of the order for that item. This page loads when it is explicitly asked to load (`request == "item1"`, `request == "item2"` or `request == "item3"`).
- **Place the order**: In the script, the user is informed that the order has been placed and a list of ordered items is displayed. In a real application, the order could be electronically placed with a live online order system. This page is loaded only when the user explicitly requests that the order be placed (`request.action == "order"`).

Editing personal data

When users are editing personal data, they are presented with a form like the one shown in Figure 13.4.

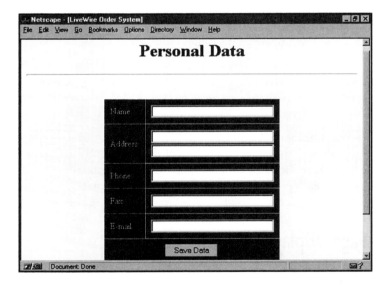

The form has a field for each personal data property of the `client` object. The action for the form is set to reload the current page with the GET method. In this way, the value of each field in the form is appended to the URL and becomes a property of the request object. The form also has two hidden fields: one sets `action` to the value `"view"` and the other sets the `newdata` property of the `request` object so that the new values get assigned to the `client` object when the page is reloaded.

Viewing Order Status

When the order status is being viewed, the information stored in the client object is displayed as formatted HTML.

The actual order status information is displayed either as a list of items being ordered or by a phrase indicating the user hasn't chosen to order any items yet.

The view status page looks like Figure 13.5.

FIGURE 13.5.

Personal data and order status data is displayed when the user decides to view the current status.

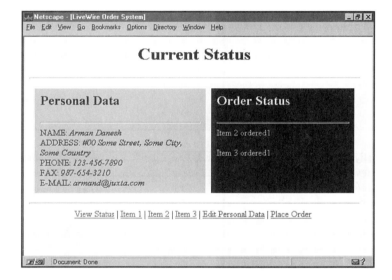

Changing Item Order Status

If a user selected to change the order status of an item, then he or she is presented with two main pieces of information: the order status for the current item plus a link to change the order status of the item.

First the value of the relevant property of the `client` object is checked for the item in question (`client.item1`, `client.item2` or `client.item3`). Based on this value, the order status for the item is displayed.

Then, again based on the value of the same property, one of two links is displayed. These links reload the current page with appended name-value pairs: the relevant item is set to `true` or `false` as appropriate and `newdata` is set to force the new data to be stored in the `client` object when the page is reloaded.

The results look like those shown in Figure 13.6 and 13.7.

FIGURE 13.6.

*If the item is already
ordered, a link enables the
user to choose not to order
the item.*

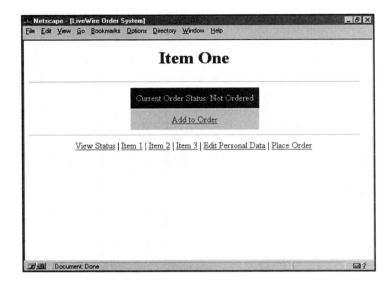

FIGURE 13.7.

*When an item isn't
ordered, a link enables the
user to add the item to the
order.*

Placing the Order

When the user places the order, a list of objects ordered is displayed. If no items have been ordered by the user, then an appropriate message is displayed. Figure 13.8 shows that an order has been placed.

FIGURE 13.8.

When the user places an order, he or she is presented with a list of ordered items.

Global Menu

At the bottom of each page a global control menu is displayed. This menu consists of a set of hyperlinks for each action the user can take. The URL for each of these links reloads the current page with an appended name-value pair setting the `action` property as necessary.

Summary

In this chapter, you have developed two simple programs. One that authenticates clients based on their IP addresses while the other implements a simple online order system. In doing this, you have gained experience working with the following:

■ Pre-defined properties of the `request` object

■ User-defined properties of the `request` object

■ Using the `client` object to track the client's status

■ Generating dynamic HTML content using server JavaScript

■ Reading and writing from the server's file system

Server JavaScript offers more functions than you have covered in this chapter, but the principles are the same as the ones you learned in the previous chapter, where you studied objects available in server JavaScript.

In the next chapter, you move back to the client side and take a look at live objects—Java applets and Netscape plug-ins—and how you can use JavaScript to manipulate them and extend their usefulness. Using LiveConnect, the mechanism that interconnects these three features of JavaScript, you can create sophisticated multimedia interactive applications, using JavaScript as the connecting layer.

IV

Java and Live Objects

14

Introducing Java

by Wes Tatters

For all its capabilities, JavaScript is still very much bound by the existing features of your Web browser. As the name in fact suggests, JavaScript is designed not as a programming language, but as a scripting language that enables you to control elements on your Web pages.

If you are looking for a means to add new functionality to the World Wide Web, you need to turn to Java itself. In this chapter, you will learn about Java by examining the following topics:

- What is Java all about?
- Programming with Java
- Including Java applets on your Web pages

What Is Java All About?

Java was originally developed by a small advanced projects team at Sun Microsystems, as part of a somewhat misdirected attempt to move into the mainstream consumer market. In its early days, Java—originally named OAK, reputedly after the tree outside its creator James Gosling's office window—was designed as the programming language for an interactive controller called a Portable Data Assistant (PDA).

What made this device unique was the fact that the technology it encompassed could be embedded into nearly any type of electronic consumer product. By doing so—due to its built-in graphical user interface and of course OAK—the device could be programmed to perform any operation desired. For example, if used with a VCR, it could replace all the buttons and dials with an easy-to-use graphical display and touch screen that guided people through the steps required to set the time and program their favorite shows. At the lofty heights envisaged by the special projects team, there was no consumer product that could not benefit in some way from the PDA. It has been rumored that there was even a suggestion at one stage that an electric toaster with an infrared receiver could be programmed to deliver the perfect golden-brown piece of toast.

Unfortunately, this wonderful device somehow got lost in the hype surrounding the information superhighway. In its place, the special projects team, which by this stage was known as FirstPerson Inc., set its sights on the interactive set-top television market and the plans of companies such as Time-Warner, who were considering such devices as a means of delivering video on demand and other interactive services through cable.

After many months of negotiations, the team was unable to close any deals with even one potential customer, and as a result, the future of FirstPerson and all the devices it had developed hung in the balance. Eventually all of these projects were abandoned, but there was one resource whose potential had not been fully explored. This resource was the OAK language that had been at the heart of all the devices created by FirstPerson.

Programming the World Wide Web

By the time the activities of FirstPerson were being wound up, the Internet, and more specifically the World Wide Web, was rapidly becoming part of everyday life for companies such as Sun. It was at this time that Bill Joy—one of Sun's cofounders—realized that OAK was an ideal language for the Internet and the World Wide Web.

As a result, after some prodding, James Gosling and Patrick Naughton, who was the catalyst for the original FirstPerson project, began to form OAK into the ultimate Internet development environment. Then, as if to signal the final death of FirstPerson, OAK was renamed Java, and the language found in Navigator 2.0 and 3 was born.

The Java Language

But enough history. What exactly is Java, and why would you want to use it?

At its heart, Java is an object-oriented programming language similar to C++. Unlike C++, however, Java was designed with portability capability. In the Internet world, there are various computer platforms, all of which use different operating systems and require programs written in languages like C++ to be specially crafted to suit their individual needs. As a result, you cannot simply take a C++ program written for a Macintosh computer and run it on your Windows 95–based PC.

Java, on the other hand, was designed so that you can do just that—write a program once and have it run on many different computer platforms. To achieve this goal, Java programs are compiled into what is called an *architecture-neutral byte-code*. What this basically means is that the programs are platform-nonspecific. In this architecture-neutral form, Java programs can be run on any computer platform that supports what is called a Java runtime.

Currently, Java runtime modules are available for Windows 95, Windows NT, Apple Macintosh, and a small number of UNIX-based X Window systems, including HP-UX, SGI IRIX, SunOS 4.1, and Sun Solaris 2.3 or 2.4.

Distributed Programming

The second major feature of Java is the one that makes it such a viable tool for use with the World Wide Web. To use the technical definition, Java is a distributed language.

What this really means is that through the Internet, Java programs can be transferred from computer system to computer system without any intervention by the user or, because of its application-neutral technology, any concern about the type of computer system to which it is being sent.

When this capability is incorporated into a Web browser such as Navigator 3, the true power of Java becomes apparent. Take, for example, the GolfWeb home page shown in Figure 14.1. The small window in the middle of this page contains a window a lot like a ticker tape display. In this window, headlines for all the latest breaking golf news are scrolled across the window from right to left.

FIGURE 14.1.

GolfWeb uses Java to create its online ticker tape displays.

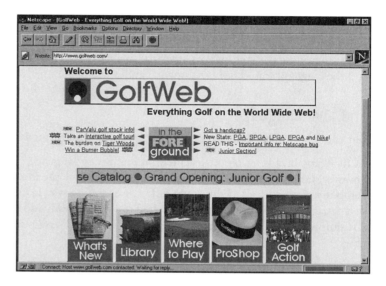

You might have noticed that there has been no mention throughout this book of such a feature in HTML. That's because currently there is no such capability. So how does c|net, producer of GolfWeb, make this magic work? Or more importantly, how do you make it work on your Web browser?

> **NOTE**
>
> The Microsoft Web browser Internet Explorer does include an extension to the HTML that adds an element called <MARQUEE>. This element creates a scrolling area on a Web page, but it lacks many of the features available when you code such a window in Java.

To add the ticker tape display to their Web pages, the developers at c|net wrote a small Java program. This program draws the ticker tape window on the Web page and looks after scrolling the messages.

Writing such a program is not a difficult task. What places Java in a world all its own is that when a Java program (or *applet*) is included as part of a Web page, the applet is automatically transferred and installed on the computer in question, without any user intervention.

What Can Java Be Used For?

Basically, there is very little limitation to the possible applications for Java applets and Java-based applications. To this extent, Sun has even created a Web browser called HotJava that was written entirely using the Java language.

> **NOTE**
>
> Java programs generally fall into one of two specific categories: *Java applets*, which are designed to be embedded inside a Web page, and *Java applications*, which are stand-alone Java programs. These programs are fully self-contained and don't run within a Web browser at all.

In fact, about the only real limitation imposed by Java is in the imaginations of Web developers. And if the crop of Java applets that have sprung up since the launch of Navigator 3 is any indication, some very imaginative minds are at play on the World Wide Web.

Blue Skies Weather Underground

Take for example the Blue Skies Weather Underground, operated by the University of Michigan. (See Figure 14.2.) This site represents one of the best current examples of the incredible interactive capabilities that Java brings to the World Wide Web. The weather map and the various gadgets surrounding it in Figure 14.2 are all part of a single Java applet, which enables you to view the current weather report for major cities by highlighting them with the cursor. In addition, by clicking various regions of the map, you can zoom in for a close-up look at individual weather patterns, or, alternatively, view a movie of the weather pattern for the past 24 hours.

What makes this service so amazing is that it all happens within one easy-to-use screen. Without Java, you would probably need many hundreds of separate Web pages to create a similar service, and even with all these pages, you would still not be able to easily duplicate some features, including the line-drawn U.S. maps over the satellite images that are created on the fly by Java itself.

To experiment with the features offered by the Blue Skies service, point your Web browser to `http://cirrus.sprl.umich.edu/javaweather/`.

FIGURE 14.2.

View the latest weather maps for the mainland U.S. by using Java and Blue Skies.

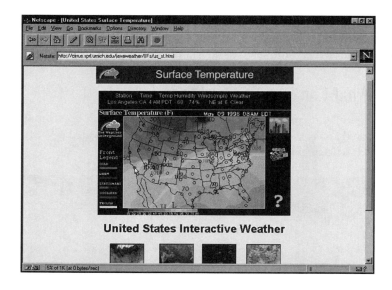

Gamelan

To give yourself an even better idea of the possibilities offered by Java, point your Web browser to http://www.gamelan.com/, as shown in Figure 14.3. This site contains the most up-to-date directory of sites using Java. It also includes a large collection of applets that demonstrate the wide variety of reasons why people are starting to incorporate Java into their Web pages—reasons such as these:

■ Online games

■ Enhanced graphics, including multicolored and animated text

■ Interaction with 3D tools such as VRML

■ Simulations

■ Spreadsheets and advanced mathematical calculations

■ Real-time information retrieval

Netscape and Sun

Apart from Gamelan, both Netscape and Sun also operate their own directories of Java applets along with a wide variety of related information. To visit the Netscape directory shown in Figure 14.4, use http://home.netscape.com/comprod/products/navigator/version_2.0/java_applets/index.html. This index contains pointers to all the latest Netscape-related Java information, along with some of the more popular Java applets.

FIGURE 14.3.

Gamelan is regarded as the repository for Java applets.

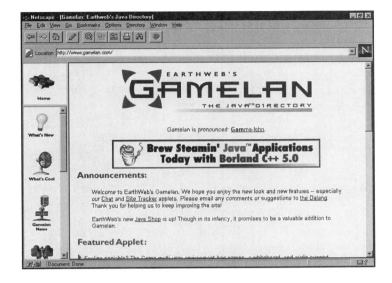

FIGURE 14.4.

Netscape is another good source of information about Java and its capabilities.

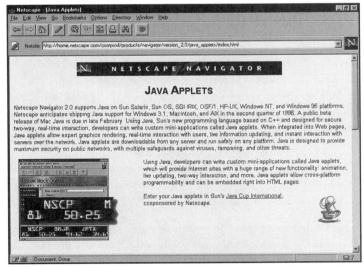

To provide more information about Java, Sun has set up an entire Web site devoted solely to the subject, as shown in Figure 14.5. This site contains up-to-the-minute details covering all aspects of Java development and usage, and it is also the primary source for Java development tools and documentation.

FIGURE 14.5.
`http://`
`java.sun.com/` *is the*
home of Java.

Programming with Java

Due to the size and complexity of the issues involved in using a programming language like Java to its fullest advantage, dealing with all the intricacies of Java programming is beyond the scope of this book. Therefore, instead of dealing with the actual programming techniques involved, in this section you will work through the creation of a simple ticker tape display like the one shown previously in Figure 14.1. In this way, you'll get a better idea of what Java is all about.

For those of you who are keen to learn more about the internals of Java, a copy of the complete Java documentation written by Sun Microsystems has been included on the CD-ROM accompanying this book. To view this documentation you will first need to install a copy of the Adobe Acrobat reader—also available on the CD-ROM on both Macintosh and Windows versions.

NOTE

For a full discussion of Java programming, refer to *Presenting Java* and *Teach Yourself Java in 21 Days*, or *Java Unleashed*, also by Sams.net.

The Java Developers Kit (JDK)

Before you begin creating your own Java applets, you must get a copy of the current version of the Java Developers Kit, known currently as the Java 1.1 JDK. This kit contains all the tools required to compile Java applets, the most up-to-date libraries (called *classes*), a stand-alone applet viewer to test your applets without the need for Navigator 3, and a debugging utility to help locate problems in your Java code.

> **NOTE**
>
> In object-oriented terms, the class is the basic structural framework for all program design. A class is a bit like a library of pre-built instructions, or a template that you can enhance to create new classes and entire applications. Although it is not vitally important that you understand all the concepts surrounding object-oriented design and development as you start to use Java, you might find it very handy to get a good book on the subject.
>
> One such book is *Object-Orientated Analysis and Design with Applications*, by Grady Booch, published by Benjamin/Cummings Publishing Company. Alternatively, you might check out *An Introduction to Object-Oriented Programming*, by Timothy Budd, published by Addison-Wesley Publishing Company. Or you can read *Object-Oriented Technology: A Manager's Guide*, by David A. Taylor, Ph.D., published by Servio Corporation.

To get a copy of the JDK for your particular computer system, point your Web browser to `http://java.sun.com/java.sun.com/products/JDK/index.html`, as shown in Figure 14.6. Sun currently provides JDKs for Windows 95, Windows NT, Mac OS and SPARC/Solaris 2.3, 2.4, or 2.5 systems. JDKs for other systems are expected in the near future.

FIGURE 14.6.

To create Java applets, you must install a copy of the Java Developers Kit on your computer.

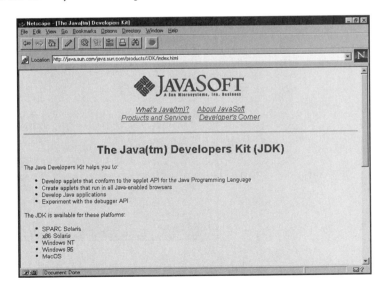

> **NOTE**
>
> An alternative method for compiling Java applets is provided by the Black Star Public Java Compiler—http://mars.blackstar.com/. This site operates a Web page where you can submit Java programs for compilation. For any serious use, however, you really do need to install the JDK on your local computer.

Exercise: Creating a Ticker Tape Applet

After you have downloaded the appropriate JDK, you need to unpack the archive file as described on the JDK Web pages or in the documentation included with the JDK archive. Then you should be ready to start building your first Java applet.

You can write Java programs by using a simple text editor, or alternatively, you might want to use a program editor of some sort. It really does not matter what you use, because Java source code is plain text.

Under Windows 95, however, I currently use a program called PFE (shown in Figure 14.7), which can be obtained from http://www.lancs.ac.uk/people/cpaap/pfe/. The one advantage of using a program like this, over using a normal text editor, is that you can perform actions such as compiling your code from inside the editor itself instead of having to start a separate MS-DOS shell.

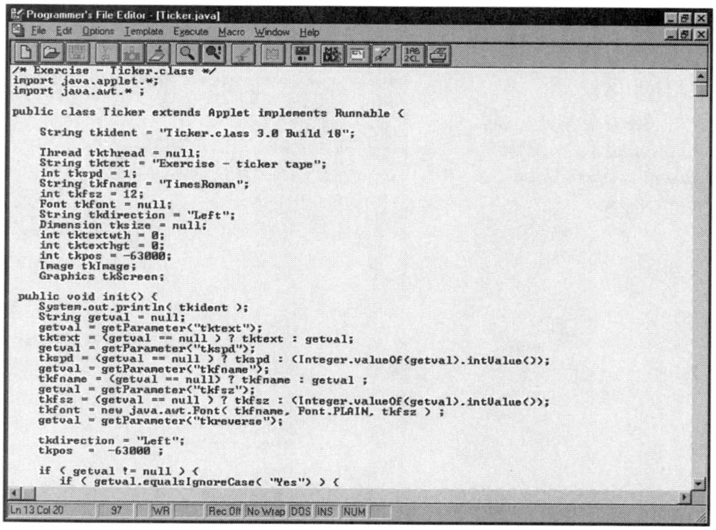

FIGURE 14.7.

Program editors can control repetitive tasks such as compiling your Java code.

Finally, in recent months a number of companies have begun to release what are know as Integrated Development Environments (IDEs) specifically for Java programming. (See Figure 14.8.) These environments incorporate an editor and other tools such as class browsers and a Java compiler into a single application. For more information on such systems, take a look at the Gamelan Web site mentioned previously.

FIGURE 14.8.

Café by Symantec.

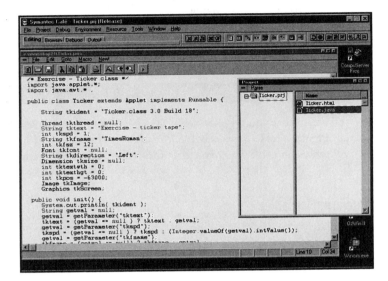

After choosing your editor, create a new directory to hold your Java applets. Start the editor and create a new file called `Ticker.java`. (Be sure to include the capital T because Java is very case specific.)

Java Framework

At its heart, Java is an object-oriented language. As a result, when you are working with Java applets, you are really adding functionality to the basic applet framework defined in the JDK. For this reason, the basic structure of all Java applets looks almost identical.

The basic framework for the Ticker Tape applet looks like the following:

```
/* Exercise - Ticker.class */
import java.applet.*;
import java.awt.* ;
public class Ticker extends Applet implements Runnable {
    Additional functionality goes in here.
}
```

The first line is simply a comment line that describes the name of the Java applet. Any text enclosed between a /* symbol and a corresponding */ symbol is treated as a comment and is ignored by the compiler.

The next two lines of code—the ones starting with import—are used to tell the compiler about any additional class libraries that will be used by your applet. All applets need to use routines from the java.applet.* library, and to display information on-screen, you also need routines from the Advanced Windows Toolkit, as defined by java.awt.*.

The fourth line of text is the one that does all the work of defining your new class as an applet. In this line, you declare the name for your new class—public class Ticker. You tell the system which existing class it is based on—extends applet. And because the Ticker Tape applet needs to run continually, you define a special package called Runnable by using implements Runnable.

CAUTION

Make sure that you type the word Ticker in exactly the same way as you did when naming the Ticker.java text file. If the two names are not identical (case wise), Java will report an error when you attempt to compile the program.

Declaring Variables

Immediately after the class definition, you first need to define some variables for the applet to use. Like most object-oriented languages, Java is a typed language. As a result, you must declare the type of information that a variable will hold before it can be used.

To declare all the variables that are accessible to the entire class, make the following entry after the class declaration:

```
public class Ticker extends Applet implements Runnable {

    String tkident = "Ticker.class 3.0 Build 18"; /* class name and ident */

    Thread tkthread = null;      /* Thread handle needed for  multitasking */
    String tktext = "Exercise - ticker tape";            /* Default text    */
    int tkspd = 1;              /* The default scroll speed (slowest is 1 ) */
    String tkfname = "TimesRoman";                /* The default font name   */
    int tkfsz = 12;                               /* The default font size   */
    Font tkfont = null;             /* Font handle for graphics library */
    String tkdirection = "Left";        /* The default scroll direction   */
    Dimension tksize = null               /* Window dimension handle    */
    int tktextwth = 0;                       /* Text width value  */
    int tktexthgt = 0;                       /* Text height value  */
    int tkpos = -63000;                    /* Scroll position    */
    Image tkImage;                       /* Image object for buffer */
    Graphics tkScreen;                   /* Graphics object for buffer*/
```

The init() Method

Inside every class, there can be any number of different routines called methods. These methods are used to control specific actions that can be taken by a class.

For every class, the first method called when the class is run (or instantiated) is the init() method. This method is used to set up default information for the class and to load variables such as those just defined previously with working values. In the base applet class, an init() method is declared already; however, because you want to add additional functionality to the applet class, you need to override the base init() method with a new one of your own.

To define the init() method for Ticker and set up all the control variables, you write the code given next.

> **NOTE**
>
> The comment lines included in this code are not required to make Ticker operate. They simply explain what each line does. If you are following along with this exercise, you need not include all the comments. Also, you might find it easier to refer to the completed example at the end of the exercise, which has all the comments removed.
>
> Alternatively, you can download the complete source for this exercise from http:// www.cnrstone.com/samsjsd.html. The source code also is on the CD-ROM.

```
/* Declare the init() method      */
public void init() {

/* Print the contents of tkindent to the Java console */
    System.out.println( tkident );

/* Declare a working variable for this method only              */
    String getval = null;

/* Retrieve the text to be displayed by Ticker                  */
/* as defined in the HTML document                              */
    getval = getParameter("tktext");
/* If no text is defined, revert to the default message         */
    tktext = (getval == null ) ? tktext : getval;

/* Retrieve the scroll speed for Ticker                         */
/*as defined in the HTML document                               */
    getval = getParameter("tkspd");
/* If no speed is defined, revert to the default speed         */
    tkspd = (getval == null ) ? tkspd : (Integer.valueOf(getval).intValue());

/* Retrieve the font for Ticker */
/* as defined in the HTML document                              */
    getval = getParameter("tkfname");
/* If no font is defined, revert to the default font           */
    tkfname = (getval == null) ? tkfname : getval ;

/* Retrieve the font size for Ticker   */
/* as defined in the HTML document      */
    getval = getParameter("tkfsz");
/* If no font size is defined, revert to the default size           */
    tkfsz = (getval == null ) ? tkfsz : (Integer.valueOf(getval).intValue());
```

```
/* Create a font class based on the font name and font size          */
   tkfont = new java.awt.Font( tkfname, Font.PLAIN, tkfsz ) ;

/* Check to see if the Reverse parameter has been set.               */
/* If not, set tkdirection to Left                                   */
/* and tkpos to a large negative number                          */
/* Otherwise, set tkdirection to Right                               */
/* and tkpos to a large positive number.                         */
   getval = getParameter("tkreverse");

   tkdirection = "Left";
   tkpos = -63000 ;

   if ( getval != null ) {
      if ( getval.equalsIgnoreCase( "Yes") ) {
         tkdirection = "Right";
         tkpos  = 63000;
         }
      }

/* Create double-buffering image area */
/* Get the size of the Java canvas                               */
/* and assign it to a dimension class called tksize.             */
   tksize = this.size();

/* Create a buffer to hold copy of the screen area */
   tkImage = createImage(tksize.width,tksize.height);
   tkScreen = tkImage.getGraphics();
}
```

CAUTION

Be sure to include all the opening ({) and closing (}) brackets where listed. These curly brackets, or braces, are used by Java to indicate the start and finish of blocks of code, and without them, Java will get very confused indeed.

The start() and stop() Methods

The start() and stop() methods are called when a class is first started and when the class is stopped, as the names suggest.

In this exercise, the start() method needs to be overridden to define Ticker as a self-contained task, one that operates independently of all other activities on your computer. This action allows your operating system to better share its resources among all the programs that are currently running. If this is not done, there is a danger that a routine like Ticker could have a serious impact on the performance of other programs.

However, after you define Ticker as a task, or a thread of its own, you need a way to stop it from running when the applet is no longer needed. To do this, in the stop() method, you include a specific call to the thread to halt its execution.

The code required to perform the start-and-stop tasks follows:

```
/* Declare the start() method                              */
public void start() {

/* Define a new Thread for this task                       */
    tkthread = new Thread(this);
/* start Ticker running as an independent task             */
    tkthread.start();
}

/* Declare the stop() method                               */
    public void stop() {

/* stop the Ticker thread running                          */
    tkthread.stop();
}
```

The run() Method

In the class definition at the start this exercise, you might recall a statement that said implements Runnable. What this statement actually does is define a template for a special method that gets called after the applet has been loaded, following the init() and start() methods. If you have any computer programming experience, you'll find that the run() method is a bit like a main() subroutine.

For everyone else at this stage, all you really need to understand is that this method contains a loop of code that causes the Java screen to be continually redrawn. Each time it gets redrawn, the text in the Ticker window is moved a step to either the left or the right.

The code for the run() method looks like this:

```
/* Declate the run() method                                */
public void run() {

/* Create an infinite loop that continually repaints the Java screen   */
    while (true) {

/* Redraw the contents of the Java applet window */
        repaint();

/* Then send Ticker to sleep so that other programs can get some work done */
        try {
            Thread.sleep( 100 );
        } catch (InterruptedException e){}
    }
}
```

The `update()` Method

The `update()` method is used to control how the contents of the applet window are refreshed. Normally Java controls this process through an internal `update()` method, but to make the contents of a Ticker Tape window scroll smoothly the internal update needs to be overridden with the following code.

```
/* Declare the updatet method                                   */
/* Unlike the other methods, this one receives some information from the */
/* calling routine. This information is assigned to a graphics   */
/* class called g .                                              */

public void update( Graphics g ){

/* call the paint() method with g as an argument  /*
   paint(g);
 }
```

The `paint()` Method

The final method for this exercise is the `paint()` method. Whenever the `repaint()` statement in the `run()` method is reached—each time through the `while` loop—the `paint()` method is the main method that gets run. The `paint()` method is where all the tricky stuff happens to make the text scroll across the screen.

In Java terms, the `paint()` method is where you draw information onto the Java *canvas*, which is a fancy name for the drawing area of a Java applet. The `paint()` method for Ticker looks like the following:

```
/* Declare the paint method                                      */
/* Unlike the other methods, this one receives some information from the */
/* calling routine. This information is assigned to a graphics    */
/* class called tk.                                               */
public void paint(Graphics tk) {

/* Set the font to use to the one defined in the init() method,  */
/* and then get its specs                                        */
/* Note that the tkScreen buffer is used throughout this method   */
/* instead of the applet canvas tk.                              */
   tkScreen.setFont(tkfont);
   FontMetrics tkfm = tkScreen.getFontMetrics();

/* Calculate the height in pixels of the text                    */
/* the first time through the paint method                       */
/* After this, use the previously calculated value.              */
   tktexthgt = ( tktexthgt==0 ) ? tkfm.getHeight() : tktexthgt;

/* Calculate the width in pixels of the text message             */
/* the first time through the paint method                       */
/* After this, use the previously calculated value               */
   tktextwth = ( tktextwth==0 ) ? tkfm.stringWidth( tktext ) : tktextwth;
```

```
/* If the scroll direction is set to Left,                        */
/* use the first set of calculations to determine the             */
/* new location for the text in this pass through paint().        */
/* Otherwise, use the set of calculations following the else statement.  */
    if (tkdirection=="Left") {
        tkpos = ( tkpos <= tktextwth * -1 ) ? tksize.width : tkpos - tkspd;
        }
    else{
        tkpos = ( tkpos > tksize.width ) ? 0 - tktextwth : tkpos + tkspd;
    }

/* Set the color to white                                         */
    tkScreen.setColor(Color.white);

/* fill the screen buffer tkScreen with the color white           */
    tkScreen.fillRect(0,0,tksize.width,tksize.height);

/* Set the text color to black                                    */
    tkScreen.setColor(Color.black);
/* Draw the message in its new position on the Java canvas        */
    tkScreen.drawString( tktext, tkpos, ( tksize.height + tktexthgt ) / 2 );

/* copy the contents of the screen buffer tkImage to the applet canvas  */
tk.drawImage( tkImage,0,0,this );

    }
```

Putting It All Together

As promised earlier, here is the completed Ticker applet, ready to be compiled. All the comments except the one on the first line have been removed, and any unnecessary line spacing is gone as well. The indentations, however, have been left in as a guide to how the various components are related. When you write Java code, using indentations to indicate the separate blocks of text is a very good way of cross-checking that no { or } symbols have been left out.

```
/* Exercise - Ticker.class */
import java.applet.*;
import java.awt.* ;

public class Ticker extends Applet implements Runnable {

    String tkident = "Ticker.class 3.0 Build 18";

    Thread tkthread = null;
    String tktext = "Exercise - ticker tape";
    int tkspd = 1;
    String tkfname = "TimesRoman";
    int tkfsz = 12;
    Font tkfont = null;
    String tkdirection = "Left";
    Dimension tksize = null;
    int tktextwth = 0;
    int tktexthgt = 0;
    int tkpos = -63000;
```

```
    Image tkImage;
    Graphics tkScreen;

  public void init() {
    System.out.println( tkident );
    String getval = null;
    getval = getParameter("tktext");
    tktext = (getval == null ) ? tktext : getval;
    getval = getParameter("tkspd");
    tkspd = (getval == null ) ? tkspd : (Integer.valueOf(getval).intValue());
    getval = getParameter("tkfname");
    tkfname = (getval == null) ? tkfname : getval ;
    getval = getParameter("tkfsz");
    tkfsz = (getval == null ) ? tkfsz : (Integer.valueOf(getval).intValue());
    tkfont = new java.awt.Font( tkfname, Font.PLAIN, tkfsz ) ;
    getval = getParameter("tkreverse");

    tkdirection = "Left";
    tkpos   =   -63000 ;

    if ( getval != null ) {
       if ( getval.equalsIgnoreCase( "Yes") ) {
          tkdirection = "Right";
          tkpos   = 63000;
       }
    }

/* Create double-buffering image area */

    tksize = this.size();
    tkImage = createImage(tksize.width,tksize.height);
    tkScreen = tkImage.getGraphics();

  -

  public void start()
     tkthread = new Thread(this)
     tkthread.start()


  public void stop()
     tkthread.stop()


  public void run()
     while (true)
         repaint()
         try
             Thread.sleep( 100 )
         } catch (InterruptedException e){


  public void update( Graphics g )
     paint(g)
```

```
public void paint(Graphics tk) {
    tkScreen.setFont(tkfont);
    FontMetrics tkfm = tkScreen.getFontMetrics();
    tktexthgt = ( tktexthgt==0 ) ? tkfm.getHeight() : tktexthgt;
    tktextwth = ( tktextwth==0 ) ? tkfm.stringWidth( tktext ) : tktextwth;
    if (tkdirection=="Left") {
        tkpos = ( tkpos <= tktextwth * -1 ) ? tksize.width : tkpos - tkspd;
    } else {
        tkpos = ( tkpos > tksize.width ) ? 0 - tktextwth: tkpos + tkspd;
    }

    tkScreen.setColor(Color.white);
    tkScreen.fillRect(0,0,tksize.width,tksize.height);
    tkScreen.setColor(Color.black);
    tkScreen.drawString( tktext, tkpos, ( tksize.height + tktexthgt ) / 2 );

    tk.drawImage( tkImage,0,0,this );
}
}
```

Compiling `Ticker.java`

After you have entered the code for `Ticker.java` into your text editor and saved a copy onto your hard drive, the next step in the process is compiling it into Java byte-code.

To do this from either the DOS prompt or the UNIX command line, enter this:

```
javac Ticket.java
```

NOTE

This assumes that `javac` is located somewhere in your execution PATH and that `Ticket.java` is located in the current directory. In addition, the HOME and CLASSPATH variables also need to be properly defined in your system environment. See the installation notes that came with the JDK for more information about setting the correct values for these variables.

If everything goes as planned, after a few seconds—or minutes, depending on the speed of your computer—your cursor will return to the command line, and a new file called `Ticker.class` will have been created in the current directory.

On the other hand, if the javac compiler detects any errors, you will see something that looks a bit like this:

```
C:\samsgold\java>javac Ticker.java
Ticker.java:15: ';' expected.
        Dimension tksize = null
                                ^
```

```
Ticker.java:49: ';' expected.
        this.setBackground( Color.white )
                                          ^
2 errors
```

The number following the colon indicates the line where the problem occurred, and the message after the number indicates the reason for the error. On the following line, the source for the problem line is displayed with a caret (^) indicating the fault's position in the line.

If you received any errors, go back and re-edit `Ticker.java` to fix the problems, and then try recompiling the applet. When you have a "good" compile of `Ticker.class`, you are ready to add the applet to your Web pages.

Learning More About Java

The fact that Java is a language that until very recently was somewhat unstable, to say the least, has made the job of writing a definitive text covering all the features of Java something akin to hitting a moving target. Luckily, however, things are now starting to change. Following the freeze of the Java specification at version 1.0, which was done in part to synchronize with the release of Navigator 3, the documentation and specifications for Java are now reasonably stable.

As a result of this stabilization, some very good tutorial documents, including the entire Java 1.0 API specification, are available online from Sun's Java Web site. To view any of this documentation or download a copy in either postscript or HTML form, point your Web browser to `http://java.sun.com/doc/programmer.html`, as shown in Figure 14.9.

FIGURE 14.9.

`http://java.sun.com/doc/programmer.html` *is a very good source of information about writing Java applets and applications.*

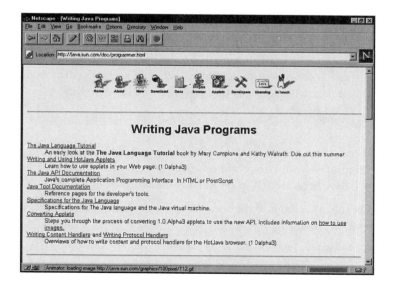

Including Java Applets on Your Web Pages

After you have your new applet compiled, the next thing you will want to do is include it on a Web page to test it. In the final section of this chapter, you will learn how to include the Ticker Tape applet on a Web page and how to include pre-built applets written by other people.

The <APPLET> Tag

When the <APPLET> tag is used on a Web page that is to be viewed using Navigator 3, it takes the following form:

```
<APPLET CODE="name.class" WIDTH=pixels HEIGHT=pixels></APPLET>
```

In the CODE attribute, you place the name of the Java class to be run, and in the WIDTH and HEIGHT attributes, you *must* declare the width and height of the drawing area (or canvas) to be used by the applet. In the current version of Navigator 3, if you do not include the WIDTH and HEIGHT attributes, the applet does not appear on the Web page at all.

Based on this information, you could include the Ticker Tape applet in a Web page by writing the following:

```
<APPLET CODE="Ticker.class" WIDTH=400 HEIGHT=75></APPLET>
```

In this basic form, when you loaded the Web page, the Ticker applet would be displayed by using the default values set in the init() method discussed previously.

NOTE

So that your Web browser can locate the applet code, place the Ticker.class file in the same directory as the Web page.

The <PARAM> Tag

In the init() method of Ticker.class, several calls were made to a method called getParameter(). What this call actually does is interrogate the <APPLET> tag, looking for parameters that match the name declared in the getParameter() call, as shown here:

```
getval = getParameter("tktext");
tktext = (getval == null ) ? tktext : getval;
```

In this example, `getParameter("tktext")` tells Java to look for a parameter called `tktext` between the `<APPLET>` and `</APPLET>` tags. If such a value is located, the text associated with the parameter, rather than the default message text, is scrolled through the Ticker Tape window.

To define `tktext` as a parameter inside the `<APPLET>` tags, you use the `<PARAM>` tag, which takes the following form:

```
<PARAM NAME="tktext" VALUE="Exercise - Scroll this text in the Ticker Tape window">
```

When used inside the `<PARAM>` tag, the `NAME` attribute is assigned the parameter name, and the `VALUE` attribute is assigned the information to be passed to the applet.

If you take a closer look at the `init()` code, you'll see four other parameters that can also be set for `Ticker.class`:

NAME=`"tkspd"`—Set the scroll speed; 1 is the slowest value.

NAME=`"tkfname"`—Set the font name; Times Roman is the default.

NAME=`"tkfsz"`—Set the font size; 12 point is the default.

NAME=`"tkreverse"`—Reverse the scroll direction.

By combining these attributes, you can tailor the appearance of the Ticker Tape window in various ways. For example, when they're used as shown in the following HTML source, the result is a Web page like the one shown in Figure 14.10.

```
<HTML>
<HEAD>
<TITLE>Exercise - Ticker.class</TITLE>
</HEAD>
<BODY>
<H1>Ticker Tape Java Exercise</H1>
<HR>
<P ALIGN=CENTER>
<APPLET CODE="Ticker.class" width=400 height=50>
<PARAM NAME="tktext"
       VALUE="Exercise - Scroll this text in the Ticker Tape window">
<PARAM NAME="tkspd"     VALUE="1">
<PARAM NAME="tkfname"   VALUE="Arial">
<PARAM NAME="tkfsz"     VALUE="28">
<PARAM NAME="tkreverse" VALUE="Yes">
</APPLET>
</P>
<HR>
</BODY>
</HTML>
```

FIGURE 14.10.

`Ticker.class` *adds a scrolling Ticker Tape window to your Web pages.*

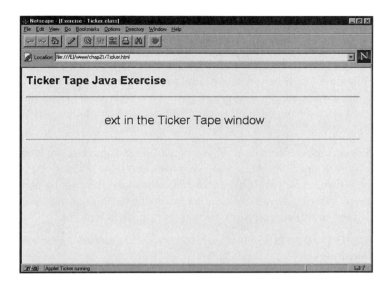

Building on the Ticker Example

With a little extra work, you can add many other features to `Ticker.class`, if you wish. These could include parameters to control the color of the text or background, the ability to display text from a separate HTML document in the Ticker Tape window, or even fancy borders like those in the Ticker Tape window shown in Figure 14.1, at the start of this chapter.

You might be surprised to hear that some good examples of enhanced Ticker Tape classes are already available for download from sites on the World Wide Web—saving you the hassle of coding all these features yourself. To locate most of these sites, take a look at the Gamelan directory mentioned previously—`http://www.gamelan.com/`.

NOTE

Many of the Java classes currently available include source code you can freely use in your own applets. Before using anyone else's code, however, check the copyright requirements the author expects you to meet. Some authors ask for mention and possibly a hyperlink to their site, whereas others expect nothing.

Using Pre-Built Java Applets

If you're starting to feel as though this Java thing is a bit beyond you—maybe the preceding pages look more like a Chinese lottery ticket to you than a computer program—or you just feel as though you don't have the time to spend learning all its intricacies, you might be interested in an alternative way to use Java. This method provides many of the benefits without most of the programming hassles.

The distributed nature of Java means that it is possible to incorporate Java applets that have been developed by other people into your Web pages. In addition, in some cases you don't even need a copy of the Java class on your own computer; you only need to know where it is located.

For example, an enhanced version of the Ticker Tape class you learned about previously is stored on my Web site at `http://www.cnrstone.com/TickerT.class`. To use this class in your own Web pages, you have two options. You can download the class by using FTP and install it at your own Web site, or you can simply include the location of the class as part of your `<APPLET>` tag. If used in this second form, the `<APPLET>` tag will look something like the following:

```
<APPLET CODE="TickerT.class" CODEBASE="http://www.cnrstone.com/" HEIGHT="30"
➥WIDTH="400" >
```

The difference between this example and previous ones is in the inclusion of the `CODEBASE` attribute, which contains a URL that describes the location of the directory where the `Ticker.class` file is located.

> **NOTE**
>
> To find out about the latest features of `TickerT.class`, point your Web browser to `http://www.cnrstone.com/TickerT.html`. This page contains information about the supported parameters and describes how you can download the file yourself. All I ask is that, if you do decide to use this applet on your Web pages, please include a link to my home page at `http://www.cnrstone.com/` as described on the page listed previously.

A quick exploration of the Gamelan site reveals various other sites that also offer classes you can incorporate into your own Web pages. Take, for example, the J_tools site shown in Figure 14.11. This collection includes applets that display animated bullets, multicolored wavy text, and different types of horizontal rules. To find out more about how you can use these applets in your own pages, take a look at `http://www.crl.com/~integris/j_tools.htm`.

A copy of the J_tools applet class has been included on the CD-ROM that accompanies this book, along with a collection of sample applets for you to experiment with. The following list indicates who created each applet.

FIGURE 14.11.
J_tools is a collection of Java applets that enable you to display animated bullets, text, and rules on your Web pages.

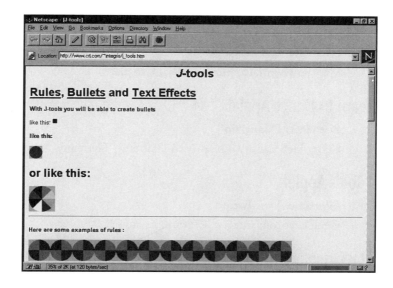

Jumping Frog Applet

Filename: Frogjump.zip

Charles-Edouard Ruault, Association Decouvertes, Paris, France

Stock Trace Applet

Filename: Stock.zip

Christian Dreke, University of Virginia Networks Laboratory, Charlottesville, Virginia

Chernobyl Reactor Applet

Filename: Nplant.zip

Henrik Eriksson, Ph.D., Linköping University, Sweden

Server Socket Example Applet

Filename: Server.zip

Mike Fletcher, Bell South Wireless, Atlanta, Georgia

Clock and GoURL Applets

Filename: Clock.zip and GoURL.zip

Nils Hedström, Linköping University, Sweden

Curve Applet

Filename: Curve.zip

Michael Heinrichs, Burnaby, BC, Canada

Learn to Dance Applet

Filename: Dance.zip

Georg Heßmann, University of Hamburg, Germany

J-Tools Applet

Filename: J-tools.zip

Gene Leybzon, Integris, Clayton, Missouri

Documentation, Form, Jline, Pointer, Ticker, & WAIS Interface Applets

Filename: tw.zip

Thomas Wendt, University of Kessel, Germany

Collections (A Collection of Functions and Utilities)

Filename: Collect.zip

Doug Lea, SUNY at Oswego, New York

Summary

As you have discovered in this chapter, Java has the potential to forever change the face of Web publishing, but at the same time, some effort is required to come to grips with its capabilities. This having been said, at the same time, Java applets are remarkably easy to incorporate into your Web page. All it takes is an `<APPLET>` tag and a few corresponding `<PARAM>` tags.

To learn more about what Java has to offer, point your Web browser to `http://java.sun.com/` and join the journey into the next generation of Web publishing.

There is another aspect of Java that has not yet been examined in detail. This is the fact that Java applets and JavaScript programs can be made to interact with each other and share information and commands. The next chapter examines how JavaScript and Java communicate with each other.

15

Communicating with Java Applets

by Arman Danesh

Now that you've looked at the basics of creating Java Applets, it's time to examine the relationship between JavaScript and Java, and methods of integrating Java Applets into Web pages using JavaScript.

Navigator 3 provides LiveConnect, a mechanism for communicating between JavaScript, Java applets, and plug-ins in a Web page. By using LiveConnect, it's possible to control applets and plug-ins from JavaScript, access JavaScript from applets, and more.

JavaScript provides the glue between applets and plug-ins and the rest of a Web page environment including forms, links, and images. JavaScript also can be used as a middle layer for communication between applets and plug-ins.

This chapter takes a closer look at the role of JavaScript as the Java glue, including the following topics:

- When to use Java and when to use JavaScript
- The applet object
- Calling Java methods from JavaScript
- Calling JavaScript methods from Java

When to Use Java and When to Use JavaScript

As mentioned in the preceding section, Java and JavaScript have distinct but complementary roles to play in the development of interactive Web pages. By effectively combining these two tools, it is possible to enhance the usefulness of both.

For instance, traditionally, an applet may have produced a continuous text ticker-tape across a portion of the screen. Unless the applet itself provided mechanisms for the user to set properties of the ticker-tape, it wasn't possible for a Web author to add controls to the Java Applet without rewriting and compiling from the original source code of the applet.

With JavaScript, scripts can be designed to talk to the applet and effectively extend interactivity beyond the bounds of an applet's own defined interface to the whole Web page.

> **NOTE**
>
> The ability for JavaScript and Java to communicate with each other has only been introduced with the beta releases of Navigator 3. Netscape Navigator 2.0 and its subreleases (2.01 and 2.02) do not support this ability.

The Java Developer's Kit includes the Blink applet, which simply takes a string and blinks it in random colors. Throughout this chapter, this applet is used to demonstrate all the possibilities for JavaScript-Java communication.

The Blink applet takes two parameters: lbl (which represents the text to display) and speed. For example, the HTML code

```
<applet code="Blink.class" width=100 height=35>
<parameter name="lbl" value="Blink">
<parameter name="speed" value="4">
</applet>
```

produces results like those shown in Figure 15.1.

By using JavaScript it's possible to add a form to the Web page that enables the user to start or stop the blinking (as shown in Figure 15.2).

FIGURE 15.1.

The Blink applet blinks a string of text in random colors.

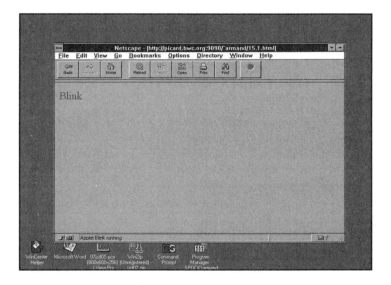

FIGURE 15.2.

JavaScript can be used to control aspects of an applet.

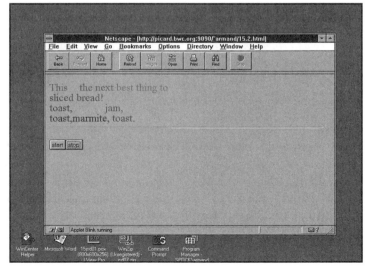

When to Use Java

Being able to interact between Java and JavaScript is not enough. It is important to use the right tool for the right occasion.

Java is ideally suited to particular tasks, including the following:

■ *When it is necessary to perform network access.* Java can work with a variety of protocols, including HTTP and FTP. JavaScript is limited in this respect.

■ *When the interactivity provided by HTML, forms, and image maps is insufficient.* Java can be used to implement editors, spreadsheets, animation tools, and graphic manipulation applications. JavaScript would not be an effective tool for these purposes.

■ *When the algorithms in a task require a more sophisticated and robust object-oriented programming and development environment.* Java is a full-fledged programming language that enables the development of powerful applications and applets. There are also an increasing number of available development tools for Java which are lacking for JavaScript today.

Beyond these roles, Java also can be used when the programmer doesn't want to be tied to only JavaScript-capable platforms—even though the task could ably be performed by JavaScript. Presently, JavaScript is available on a more limited set of platforms than Java, which is supported by more browsers than JavaScript and on dedicated devices such as Java-enabled X-terminals and network computers.

When to Use JavaScript

By comparison, JavaScript is suited to adding interactivity to elements of a Web page, including links, forms, images, applets, and plug-ins.

JavaScript, because it includes objects and methods to address most elements making up an HTML document, can be used for the following:

■ *To add client-end interactivity to forms.* Java is unable to interact directly with page elements such as forms, so it can't be used for form verification, dynamic updating, or other interactivity.

■ *To provide interface extensions to Java applets and plug-ins.* The start and stop buttons are easier to implement as HTML forms with JavaScript event handlers than they would have been in Java. In addition, by taking them out of the applet, control of the page layout is more flexible because the applet is assigned a fixed rectangular space for all of its output.

■ *For quick implementation of simple algorithms.* Because JavaScript at the client-end doesn't require the complete code, compile, test, debug, re-compile cycle for development, scripting simple algorithms may be easier and less tedious using JavaScript, which can go from coding directly to testing and back with compilation cycles.

The `applet` Object

Applets are accessible in JavaScript through an array of `applet` objects called `applets`. The `applets` array is a property of the `document` object. Applets are ordered in the array in the order they appear in the HTML source code—and as would be expected, are indexed starting at zero.

NOTE

Throughout this chapter the interaction between Java and JavaScript is discussed. For the examples to work, it is important for both Java and JavaScript to be enabled in the network preferences dialog box, which is accessed through Navigator's Options menu.

For example, `document.applets[0]` refers to the first applet in a document.

Like other arrays of this nature in JavaScript, such as the `forms` and `frames` arrays, individual applets can be referred to by name. If the Blink applet were included in an HTML document using the `<APPLET>` tag

```
<APPLET CODE="Blink.class" NAME="Blink" WIDTH=300 HEIGHT=100>
```

then the corresponding `applet` object could be referred to by its index number or with `document.Blink`.

Accessing Properties and Methods of an Applet

Each applet is reflected into one `applet` object. The `applet` object provides the means for accessing all public variables in an applet as well as properties and methods.

Properties and methods are reflected into JavaScript as properties and methods of the corresponding `applet` object.

In the Blink applet example introduced in the preceding section, inspection of the Java source code reveals that there are five public methods in the applet:

```
/*
 * Copyright (c) 1994 Sun Microsystems, Inc. All Rights Reserved.
 */

import java.awt.*;
import java.util.StringTokenizer;

/**
 * I love blinking things.
 *
 * @author Arthur van Hoff
 */
```

```
public class Blink extends java.applet.Applet implements Runnable {
    Thread blinker;
    String lbl;
    Font font;
    int speed;

    public void init() {
    font = new java.awt.Font("TimesRoman", Font.PLAIN, 24);
    String att = getParameter("speed");
    speed = (att == null) ? 400 : (1000 / Integer.valueOf(att).intValue());
    att = getParameter("lbl");
    lbl = (att == null) ? "Blink" : att;
    }

    public void paint(Graphics g) {
    int x = 0, y = font.getSize(), space;
    int red = (int)(Math.random() * 50);
    int green = (int)(Math.random() * 50);
    int blue = (int)(Math.random() * 256);
    Dimension d = size();

    g.setColor(Color.black);
    g.setFont(font);
    FontMetrics fm = g.getFontMetrics();
    space = fm.stringWidth(" ");
    for (StringTokenizer t = new StringTokenizer(lbl) ; t.hasMoreTokens() ; ) {
        String word = t.nextToken();
        int w = fm.stringWidth(word) + space;
        if (x + w > d.width) {
        x = 0;
        y += font.getSize();
        }
        if (Math.random() < 0.5) {
        g.setColor(new java.awt.Color((red + y * 30) % 256, (green + x / 3) % 256,
blue));
        } else {
        g.setColor(Color.lightGray);
        }
        g.drawString(word, x, y);
        x += w;
    }
    }

    public void start() {
    blinker = new Thread(this);
    blinker.start();
    }
    public void stop() {
    blinker.stop();
    }
    public void run() {
    while (true) {
    try {Thread.currentThread().sleep(speed);} catch (InterruptedException e){}
        repaint();
    }
    }
}
```

If this Blink applet were included in an HTML document using the following HTML code

```
<applet code="Blink.class" name="Blink" width=300 height=100>
<param name=lbl value="This is the next best thing to sliced bread!
➡Toast, toast, toast, butter, jam, toast, marmite, toast.">
<param name=speed value="4">
</applet>
```

then the various methods in the Java applet could be accessed in JavaScript as

```
document.blink.init()
document.blink.paint()
document.blink.start()
document.blink.stop()
document.blink.run()
```

By way of illustration, the example earlier in this chapter of a start and stop button being added to the Blink applet using JavaScript is achieved with the following source code:

```
<applet code="Blink.class" name="Blink" width=300 height=100>
<param name=lbl value="This is the next best thing to sliced bread!
➡ Toast, toast, toast, butter, jam, toast, marmite, toast.">
<param name=speed value="4">
</applet>
<HR>
<form>
<input type=button value="start" onClick="document.Blink.start()">
<input type=button value="stop" onClick="document.Blink.stop()">
</form>
```

Simple onClick event handlers in the button definitions call the start() and stop() methods of the applet using document.blink.start() and document.blink.stop().

The process can be carried a step further by using JavaScript to dynamically update the text displayed by the applet. To do this requires one change to the Java applet's source code—the lbl variable needs to be declared as a public variable so that it is accessible in JavaScript:

```
public String lbl;
```

Once this changes is made and the applet is recompiled, then the HTML file's source code can be extended:

```
<applet code="Blink.class" name="Blink" width=300 height=100>

<param name=lbl value="This is the next best thing to sliced bread!
➡ Toast, toast, toast, butter, jam, toast, marmite, toast.">
<param name=speed value="4">
</applet>
<HR>
<form>
<input type=text name="label"value="Enter Text Here">
<input type=button value="Change Text" onClick="document.Blink.lbl =
this.form.label.value"><br>
<input type=button value="start" onClick="document.Blink.start()">
<input type=button value="stop" onClick="document.Blink.stop()">
</form>
```

FIGURE 15.3.

By using JavaScript, it is possible to update the value of properties in an applet.

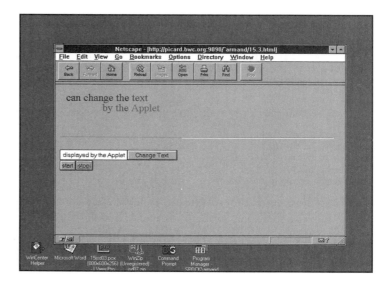

Here, the user enters text in the text field. When the new button is clicked, the value of the text field is assigned to document.Blink.lbl. When the applet next repaints the display, the new text is displayed by the applet.

Accessing Java Classes and Packages

Navigator 3 provides more than just the ability to access variables, properties, and methods in a Java applet. It's possible, using JavaScript, to access any class in the Java package name space.

Java's objects are organized into classes, which are collections of objects. Classes are organized into packages in which subclasses inherit the objects of their immediate parents (or superclasses) and then extend and change the class. Java has a substantial set of classes, all of which can be accessed in JavaScript.

The Java class hierarchy available in Navigator includes three packages: java, sun, and netscape, which provide different subclasses.

NOTE

More information about the Java's native classes can be found at the JavaSoft home page: http://www.javasoft.com.

The JavaScript package name space is reflected in JavaScript under `Packages`. Thus, `Packages.sun` is the top of the Java sun hierarchy. The `java`, `sun`, and `netscape` class hierarchies are also aliased in JavaScript to simply `java`, `sun`, and `netscape`.

Any Java class can be reflected into a JavaScript variable using a simple `var` statement. For instance,

```
var javaSystem = java.lang.System;
```

Here, the variable `javaSystem` is defined to point to the Java class `java.lang.System`, which is part of the `java` package. As a result, it's possible to make calls directly to methods or access properties of the class. For instance, to print text in the Java console, the `println()` method could be used:

```
javaSystem.err.println("JavaScript can print here.");
```

In addition, constructor classes in Java can be used to create instances in JavaScript (as is done with the `Array()` and `Date()`). For instance, instead of using JavaScript's date constructor, the Java date constructor could be used:

```
var javaDate = new java.util.Date();
```

As a result, the methods of the Java date class are available in JavaScript.

By using the ability to directly access Java methods and properties in a JavaScript script, it's possible to perform many Java tasks, such as network access and window manipulation, directly from within a JavaScript script.

By way of illustration, the following script uses Java's AWT class, which handles graphics and windows tasks, to open an empty 300×200 pixel Java window:

```
<script language="JavaScript">

var awt = java.awt;
var javaWin = new awt.Frame("Java Window");
javaWin.setLayout(new awt.BorderLayout(10,20));
javaWin.resize(300,200);
javaWin.show();

</script>
```

First, a reference to the entire `java.awt` class is created. Then, an instance of the `Frame()` constructor class called `javaWin` is created. The methods of `javaWin` are used to define the window's size and display it. Further calls to other methods could have caused buttons, fields, or text, among other things, to be displayed in the window.

The results look like those shown in Figure 15.4.

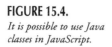

FIGURE 15.4.
*It is possible to use Java
classes in JavaScript.*

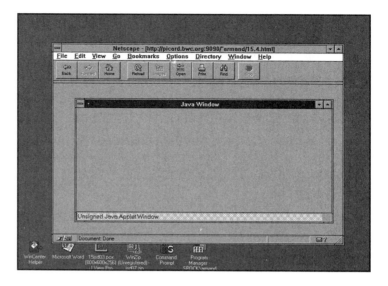

Calling JavaScript from Java

Communication between JavaScript and Java is not a one-way street, however. Not only is it possible to access Java properties, methods, and variables from within a JavaScript script, a Java applet is also capable of calling JavaScript methods and accessing the value of JavaScript properties.

> **NOTE**
>
> In order for an applet to have access to JavaScript properties and methods, it is necessary to explicitly give the applet permission to do this in the <APPLET> tag. This is done with the MAYSCRIPT attribute of the <APPLET> tag: <APPLET CODE="className" WIDTH=width HEIGHT=height NAME="appletName" MAYSCRIPT>.

In order to call a JavaScript method from Java, it is necessary to import the relevant JavaScript package into the applet: netscape.javascript.*.

netscape.javascript.* defines the JSObject class and the JSException object. JavaScript objects are instances of the class netscape.javascript.JSObject.

Once the necessary package is imported, accessing a JavaScript method or property is a two-step process: First a handle to the JavaScript window needs to be created and then the method or property can be accessed.

Handles are created using the getWindow() method of the JSObject object—usually in the applet's init() method:

```
public void init() {
    JSObject handleName = JSObject.getWindow(this);
}
```

Once the handle is created, the getMember() method of the JSObject object can be used to access objects and properties from JavaScript. In order to create a handle to an object that isn't a top-level object in JavaScript, such as the text field document.*formName*.*fieldName*, the getMember() method can be used for each object in the tree:

```
public void init() {
    JSObject handleName = JSObject.getWindow(this);
    JSObject documentHandle = (JSObject) handleName.getMember("document");
    JSObject formHandle = (JSObject) documentHandle.getMember("formName");
    JSObject fieldHandle = (JSObject) formHandle.getMember("fieldName");
}
```

Once the handle to the desired object is created, it's possible to use the getMember() method to access the value of one of the object's properties. In the preceding example, the value property of the text field's object could be assigned to a Java variable called *fieldValue* with

```
String fieldValue = (String) fieldHandle.getMember("value");
```

In order to call a method in JavaScript, a handle to the relevant object needs to be created, as previously outlined. Once this is done, the JSObject object has two methods for calling JavaScript methods:

> call("*methodName*",*arguments*)—the call() method calls *methodName* and passes it the data stored in the *arguments* array as arguments.

> eval("*expression*")—the eval() method evaluates the JavaScript expression *expression*.

For example, the following is a Java applet that simply calls the JavaScript alert() method:

```
import netscape.javascript.JSObject;
import.netscape.javascript.JSException;

public class jsAlert extends java.applet.Applet implements Runnable {

    JSObject windowObject;

    public void init() {
        windowObject = JSObject.getWindow(this);
    }

    public void start() {
        windowObject.eval("alert(\"Hello from Java!\");");
    }

    public void stop() {
    }
```

```
public void paint() {
}

public void run() {
}


}
```

Notice that the windowObject variable is declared outside any method so that it's available in all the methods of the applet. In the init() method the handle to the top-level window object is created and in the start() method the eval() method is used to call JavaScript's alert() method. Notice the use of the backslash to escape the quotation marks in the call to the alert() method.

The results look like those shown in Figure 15.5.

FIGURE 15.5.

By using Java, it is possible to call JavaScript methods.

The following script demonstrates how these techniques can be used to create a simple Java applet to display the value of a field in a form in the Java console.

```
import java.awt.*;
import java.util.StringTokenizer;
import netscape.javascript.JSObject;
import netscape.javascript.JSException;

public class twowayExample extends java.applet.Applet implements Runnable {
    String output;
    Font font;
```

```
JSObject thiswindow;
JSObject thisdocument;
JSObject thisform;
JSObject thisfield;

public void init() {
font = new java.awt.Font("TimesRoman", Font.PLAIN, 24);
thiswindow = JSObject.getWindow(this);
thisdocument = (JSObject) thiswindow.getMember("document");
thisform = (JSObject) thisdocument.getMember("controlForm");
thisfield = (JSObject) thisform.getMember("entryField");
}

public void run() {
}

public void displayField() {
    output = (String) thisfield.getMember("value");
    System.out.println(output);
}

}
```

This applet assumes that it is being used in a page with a form called `controlForm`, with a text field called `entryField`. The applet initializes by reading the parameter output and setting up the font for output. Whenever the method `displayField()` is called, the `output` variable based on the content of the text field entryField and then this value is displayed in the Java console using `System.out.println()`.

Using the `netscape` Package

All the applets in the previous section make use of a Java package called `netscape.javascript`. This package isn't one of the packages that make up the standard class libraries available with the Java Developer's kit.

Instead, it is part of the class libraries that ship with Navigator 3. Navigator 3 comes with a file called `moz3_0.zip`, which includes all of the Java packages needed for Navigator to run. These include the `netscape` packages as well as versions of the standard `java` and `sun` packages, which enhance some of the security of these packages.

> **NOTE**
>
> The file `moz3_0.zip` contains two packages, `netscape.applet` and `netscape.net`, which are replacements for the standard `sun.applet` and `sun.net` packages. Functionally, these are the same as the original packages in the Java Developer's Kit.

In order to compile applets that use `netscape.javascript` (or `netscape.plugins` for communication between applets and plug-ins), it's necessary for the `javac` compiler to know where to find `moz3_0.zip`.

This is done by setting the `CLASSPATH` environment variable to specify the path and filename for both `moz3_0.zip` and `classes.zip`, which is part of the Java Developer's Kit. On Windows-based systems, this path would look something like the following:

```
C:\java\lib\classes.zip;c:\Navigator\Program\java\classes\moz3_0.zip
```

On Windows systems, the `CLASSPATH` environment variable can be created in the System Control Panel applet. On UNIX systems, use the `setenv` command or the corresponding command in your shell.

Once the `CLASSPATH` environment variable is properly set, the `javac` compiler should be able to import `netscape.javascript` and the other packages in `moz3_0.zip`.

Summary

Starting with Navigator 3, JavaScript fulfills its promise as the tool to glue Java applets into Web pages. Using LiveConnect, it's possible for JavaScript to pass information to Java applets, access its properties, and invoke its methods, as well as have full access to Java packages and classes.

This communication is two-way. It is also possible for Java applets to access JavaScript objects and their properties and methods. As you'll see in later chapters, LiveConnect also provides methods for Java and JavaScript to communicate with Navigator plug-ins.

16

Navigator Plug-ins

*by Arman Danesh
and Wes Tatters*

Netscape provides a set of specifications for plug-ins to Navigator. Plug-ins allow Navigator to handle new MIME types not supported natively by the browser but that are different from the helper applications historically used by Web browsers to handle unsupported file formats.

Plug-ins from third-party developers already exist to support numerous standard and proprietary formats, ranging from Microsoft Word documents to a wide range of graphics formats, including TIFF, EPS, and PICT files.

JavaScript provides the plug-in and MIME type objects to allow scripts to be aware of the currently available plug-ins. This can enable a Web author to dynamically produce a page based on supported MIME types and plug-ins.

In this chapter, the details of plug-ins and how to work with them in JavaScript are covered, including the following topics:

■ What Are Plug-ins?
■ Using Plug-ins in JavaScript
■ Creating Your Own Plug-ins

What Are Plug-ins?

As mentioned in the preceding section, plug-ins provide a method of adding support for new file formats and MIME types to Navigator. Plug-ins are small libraries of code written to directly extend the capabilities of Navigator—they work within the Navigator environment to handle new MIME types, display their content and additional information, perform network communication, and more.

When Navigator loads, it searches for available plug-ins and registers the MIME types they support. Then, in the course of browsing, if Navigator receives a file with a MIME type supported by one of the plug-ins, Navigator loads the plug-in and hands the file off to the plug-in for processing.

This is different from the helper applications, which have traditionally been used on the Web to display and handle unsupported file formats. In the case of helper applications, browsers are configured to launch a separate stand-alone application to handle a specified file format. These helper applications aren't integrated into the Navigator environment—they generally can't communicate with Navigator and they can't work with other Navigator components, such as JavaScript and Java applets.

Popular Plug-ins

There are presently numerous popular plug-ins for Navigator (mostly for Windows and the Macintosh platforms—UNIX is behind in this regard). The types of applications these plug-ins perform include the following:

- Real-time audio streaming
- Displaying Adobe Acrobat files
- Viewing and working with spreadsheets on the Internet
- Displaying multimedia interactive presentations, such as those produced with Macromedia Director and Microsoft PowerPoint
- Playing video formats such as QuickTime and MPEG, including real-time audio streaming (see Figure 16.1)
- Displaying word processor files
- Extending the range of image files supported by Navigator to include vector file formats as well as bitmap images

FIGURE 16.1.

Plug-ins extend Navigator to support new file formats, including real-time video streaming.

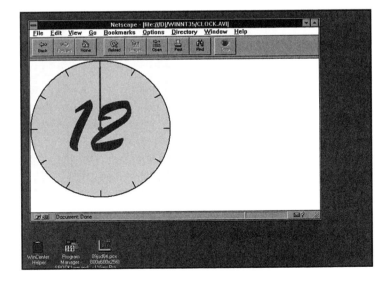

Table 16.1 lists a selection of the major plug-ins available today.

Table 16.1. Selected Navigator Plug-ins.

Plug-in	*Description*
Acrobat Reader	By Adobe. Acrobat Reader allows Portable Document Format (PDF) files to be viewed within a Navigator window. (`http://www.adobe.com`.)
Carbon Copy/Net	By Microcom. Carbon Copy/Net enables users to remotely control another PC on the Internet. (`http://www.microcom.com`.)
CoolFusion	By Iterated Systems. CoolFusion streams and displays AVI video files as they're received by Navigator. (`http://www.iterated.com`.)
EarthTime	By Starfish Software. EarthTime displays the time and date for up to eight locations around the globe at once. (`http://www.starfishsoftware.com`.)
Formula One/NET	By Visual Components. Formula One/NET is an Excel-compatible spreadsheet that enables Navigator users to edit and view spreadsheets within Navigator. (`http://www.visualcomp.com`.)
KEYview for Windows	By FTP Software. This plug-in can view, print and convert 200 file formats including Word, WordPerfect, Excel, and image formats. (`http://www.ftp.com`.)
PointCast Network	By PointCast. A free service that broadcasts news and other information to be accessed from within Navigator. (`http://www.pointcast.com`.)
PowerPoint Animation Player & Publisher	By Microsoft. This PowerPoint plug-in lets users view PowerPoint presentations in Navigator. (`http://www.microsoft.com`.)
RealAudio	By Progressive Networks. RealAudio provides real-time audio on the Internet. (`http://www.realaudio.com`.)
Shockwave for Director	By Macromedia. Allows interaction with Director files in a Navigator window. (`http://www.macromedia.com`.)
ToolVox	By VoxWare. ToolVox can be used to play synthesized speech in a Web page. (`http://www.voxware.com`.)

Plug-in	Description
VDOLive	By VDONet. VDOLive delivers compressed video without reducing quality at as much as 15 frames per second. (`http://www.vdo.net`.)
WebXpresso	By Dataviews. WebXpresso displays two-dimensional and three-dimensional images and controls with support for real-time interaction, continuous updating, and Java native methods. (`http://www.dvcorp.com`.)
Word Viewer	By Inso Corporation. Allows Navigator users to view Microsoft Word 6.0 and Word 7.0 documents inside Navigator. (`http://www.inso.com`.)

A more extensive list of plug-ins is available in Appendix G, "Navigator Plug-ins." Netscape also maintains an extensive list of plug-ins at `http://home.netscape.com/comprod/products/navigator/version_2.0/plugins/index.html`.

The `<EMBED>` Tag

The list of plug-ins in Table 16.1 demonstrates that most plug-ins are triggered when a particular file format is included in an HTML file. In traditional HTML, the `<IMG>` tag provided a mechanism to include images in documents. Similarly, the `<APPLET>` tag allows Java applets to be embedded in Web pages.

Another tag is needed to include the variety of file formats potentially supported by plug-ins in Web documents. This requirement is fulfilled by the `<EMBED>` tag.

The `<EMBED>` tag is similar to the `<IMG>` tag and the `<APPLET>` tag. It allows the embedding of a file supported by a plug-in to be downloaded when the page is being rendered by the browser and displayed within the Web page.

The tag takes the following attributes:

- ■ `HEIGHT`: Specifies the height of the space to allot for the object. `HEIGHT` is specified in the units defined with the `UNITS` attribute.
- ■ `SRC`: Specifies the URL of the object to be embedded.
- ■ `WIDTH`: Specifies the width of the space to allot for the object. `WIDTH` is specified in the units defined with the `UNITS` attribute.
- ■ `HIDDEN`: Specifies whether the plug-in should be visible. Takes the value `true` or `false` and overrides the `HEIGHT` and `WIDTH` tags if set to `true`.

- **PALETTE**: Specifies the color palette mode for the plug-in. Can either be set to `foreground` or `background` and is used only on Windows versions of Navigator.

- **PLUGINSPAGE**: Specifies the URL for a page containing instructions on downloading the plug-in for the embedded type. Used by Navigator's assisted installation feature.

- **TYPE**: Specifies the MIME type for the `<EMBED>` tag. `<EMBED>` tags require either the `SRC` or `TYPE` attribute.

- **NAME**: Specifies a name for the embedded plug-in object.

- **UNITS**: Specifies the unit of measurement for the `HEIGHT` and `WIDTH` attributes. `UNITS` takes the value `pixels`, or `en`—which equals half the point size. `Pixels` is the default value for `UNITS`.

For example, the following HTML code would produce results similar to those shown in Figure 16.2 if a QuickTime-capable plug-in were installed in Navigator:

FIGURE 16.2.

The `<EMBED>` *includes plug-in objects in Web pages.*

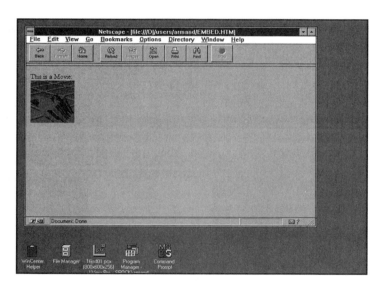

```
<BODY>
This is a QuickTime movie:<BR>
<EMBED SRC="sample.qt" WIDTH=100 HEIGHT=100 UNITS=pixels>
</BODY>
```

By changing the `WIDTH` and `HEIGHT` tags, the size of the displayed image is changed. For instance, changing `WIDTH=100` to `WIDTH=300` stretches the resulting display area on the horizontal axis.

FIGURE 16.3.
The WIDTH *and* HEIGHT
attributes of the <EMBED>
tag can change the size of
the display area.

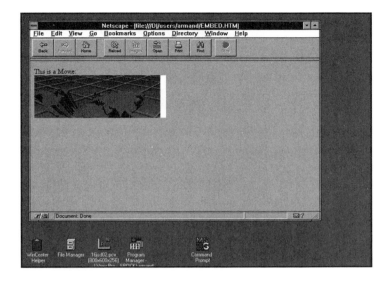

In addition, plug-ins can define their own custom attributes to be included in the <EMBED> tag. Navigator ignores these and passes them straight to the plug-in for processing.

The <NOEMBED> Tag

Similar to frames where the <NOFRAMES> tag provided a mechanism to include alternate HTML code for browsers that don't support frames, the <NOEMBED> tag enables authors to specify HTML code to display in browsers that don't support the <EMBED> tag, and therefore don't support plug-ins.

For example, the HTML code

```
<BODY>
This is a QuickTime movie:<BR>
<EMBED SRC="sample.qt" WIDTH=100 HEIGHT=100 UNITS=pixels>
<NOEMBED>
<H1>Sorry!</H1>
You need a plug-ins capable browser.
</NOEMBED>
</BODY>
```

displays the text Sorry! You need a plug-ins capable browser. in browsers that don't support the <EMBED> tag.

FIGURE 16.4.
The <NOEMBED> *tag defines text to display when a browser doesn't support plug-ins.*

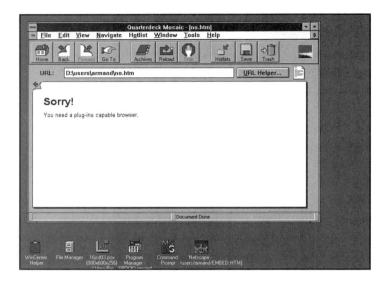

Using Plug-ins in JavaScript

JavaScript includes two objects—plugins and mimeTypes—that can be used in scripts to determine if specific plug-ins or MIME types are supported. Both are properties of the navigator object.

The plugins Object

The plugins object is an array of plug-in objects, reflecting each of the available plug-ins in the browser.

For instance, the first plug-in in a document could be accessed with document.plugins[0]. As with applets, plug-ins also can be referenced with the name specified in the NAME attribute of the <EMBED> tag. For the plug-in object,

```
<EMBED SRC="srcFile" NAME="samplePlugin" HEIGHT=100 WIDTH=100>
```

the associated plugin object is document.samplePlugin.

Each plugin object has five properties:

- name: the name of the plug-in
- filename: the filename of the plug-in on the local system
- description: the description provided by the plug-in
- length: the number of plug-ins
- mimeTypes: an array indicating the MIME types supported by the plug-in—this has the same characteristics as the mimeTypes object discussed later in this chapter.

It is also possible to check for the existence of a particular plug-in by evaluating the plug-in object itself. The code segment

```
if (navigator.plugins["ShockWave"])
   document.writeln('<EMBED SRC="sample.dir" HEIGHT=50 WIDTH=50>');
else
   document.writeln('Install the Shockwave plug-in');
```

outputs the appropriate HTML, based on the existence of the Shockwave plug-in.

FIGURE 16.5.

Using JavaScript, it is possible to embed plug-in files only when the plug-in is available. Otherwise, the user can be told to install the plug-in.

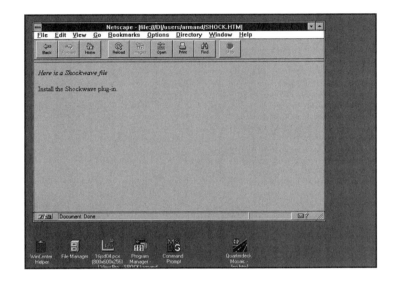

The mimeTypes Object

mimeTypes is an array of all the MIME types supported by the browser through any means, including plug-ins and helper applications. Each MIME type is represented by a mimeType object. The array itself is indexed by number or by MIME type names.

The mimeType object has three properties:

- name: the name of the MIME type such as image/jpeg or video/avi.
- description: a description of the MIME type
- suffixes: a string containing a comma-separated list of file suffixes for the MIME type

For instance, for TIFF images, navigator.mimeTypes["image/tiff"].suffixes might have the value "tiff, tif" and navigator.mimeTypes["images/tiff"].description might be equal to "TIFF Image".

Plug-ins and LiveConnect

Just as LiveConnect allows Java and JavaScript to communicate, LiveConnect provides similar capabilities for plug-ins.

The basic LiveConnect model allows two-way communication between Java and plug-ins, and between Java and JavaScript. Because Java and JavaScript are tightly integrated, JavaScript is able to call plug-in functions that have been made available to the Java environment.

FIGURE 16.6.

LiveConnect puts Java at the center of communication between JavaScript and plug-ins.

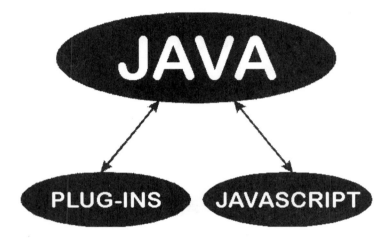

The Java Runtime Interface

The core of LiveConnect is in the Java Runtime Interface (JRI). The JRI makes it possible for so-called native methods written in C or C++ to be called from Java. These native methods can be part of plug-ins.

The technical use of the JRI requires knowledge of C or C++ and is beyond the scope of this book.

Calling Native Methods from Java and JavaScript

Although this book doesn't cover the mechanics of writing native methods into plug-ins, an increasing number of third-party plug-ins make native methods available to the Java environment. Being able to call these methods from JavaScript is important.

The Java environment includes the `netscape.plugin.Plugin` class. Each plug-in is an instance of this class. Individual plug-ins—and their available native methods—can be accessed through the `documents.plugins` array.

For instance, most versions of Navigator 3 come with the LiveVideo plug-in. This plug-in's object is accessible in Java (and therefore in JavaScript).

The LiveVideo plug-in documentation indicates that it makes four native methods available to the Java environment:

- ■ `play()`—Start playing the source file from the current position
- ■ `stop()`—Stop playing the source file
- ■ `seek(position)`—Sets the current position to *position* where *position* indicates a frame number
- ■ `rewind()`—Sets the current position to the start of the video

Using these methods, it is possible to use JavaScript to create a simple control panel for an embedded audio file:

```
<BODY>

<EMBED SRC="demo.avi" NAME="testVideo" HEIGHT=100 WIDTH=100>

<FORM>
<INPUT TYPE=button VALUE="Play" onClick="document.plugins[0].play(false);">
<INPUT TYPE=button VALUE="Stop" onClick="document.testVideo.stop(false);">
</FORM>

</BODY>
```

This file uses JavaScript event handlers to provide control buttons for the video file specified in the `<EMBED>` tag.

FIGURE 16.7.

JavaScript can be used to call native methods in plug-ins.

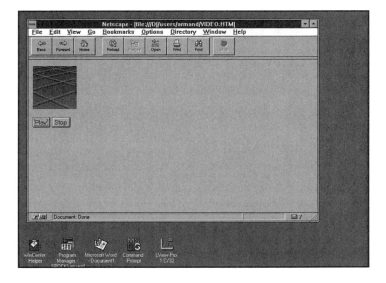

Creating Your Own Plug-ins

The process of creating plug-ins requires knowledge of C or C++ and, as such, is beyond the scope of this book. However, a more general discussion of how plug-ins are created should help you understand the way they fit into Navigator and LiveConnect.

Plug-ins are platform-specific code libraries that are dynamically loaded by the browser as needed. Plug-ins are written based on an Application Programmers Interface provided by Netscape. There are different plug-in APIs for the Windows, Macintosh, and UNIX versions of Netscape and while they are not identical across platforms, Netscape says that the plug-ins are designed to be functionally equivalent across platforms while maintaining flexibility for developers.

The APIs provide several areas of functionality:

- Registering MIME types in Navigator
- Drawing window elements into Navigator and receiving events from windows
- Reading URLs from the network and posting data to URLs
- Generating data for other plug-ins for use by Navigator
- Implementing protocol handlers

> **NOTE**
>
> Netscape's documentation for the plug-in API is available on the Web at `http://home.netscape.com.eng/mozilla/3.0/handbook/plugins/index.html`.

Developers who want to experiment with plug-in development should download the Plug-in Software Development Kit from Netscape. Three kits are available—Windows, Macintosh, and UNIX.

Things Plug-ins Can Do

There are several things that the programmer can do to customize his or her plug-in. Plug-ins can have different appearances, can open data streams from the network or the local file system, can extend the <EMBED> tag to allow HTML files to pass parameters to the plug-in, and can be automatically installed when the user first accesses a new data type.

Plug-in Appearance

In its current form, the plug-in API provides two different appearances to plug-in developers: embedded and full-page.

Embedded plug-ins are used as part of larger HTML documents. The plug-in is given a rectangular space on the page for its display and works strictly within this area. These plug-ins are specified with the <EMBED> tag discussed earlier.

By contrast, full-page plug-ins are for document types that won't be embedded as part of an HTML document. These plug-ins are displayed in the entire inner frame of a Navigator window.

Plug-ins also can be used in a hidden mode by specifying HIDDEN=TRUE in the <EMBED> tag. Hidden plug-ins run in the background without any display. These could be used, for example, for audio players.

Data Streams

One of the primary functions of plug-ins is to perform network access. Plug-ins can request URLs for which a data stream is opened and the data made available to the plug-in as it arrives.

Plug-ins can request as many streams as the host Navigator browser has been configured to allow. The data received in a data stream for a plug-in is cached like other data fetched by the browser.

Streams can be opened in two modes by a plug-in: push mode—where the plug-in is provided data as it arrives from the server, and pull mode—where the plug-in explicitly requests data as it needs it.

Assisted Installation

Plug-ins need to be installed in the correct directory in order to be available to the browser. This can be done manually by the user or automatically, with an installation program provided by the plug-in developer.

Alternately, Netscape provides an assisted installation feature. The system is simple:

1. The HTML page author uses the PLUGINSPAGE attribute of the <EMBED> tag for the document. The attribute specifies a URL for a page, with information about how to download and install the plug-in.
2. When the user requests the page with the embedded document, Navigator presents a dialog box that enables the user to go to the URL containing more information about the plug-in.
3. If the user chooses to go to the URL specified in the PLUGINSPAGE attribute, he or she can download and install the plug-in and then restart Navigator.
4. If the user chooses Cancel in the dialog box, Navigator won't prompt the user with the dialog box in the future.

Summary

Plug-ins extend Navigator's ability to handle new MIME types. Plug-in objects can be embedded in Web pages using the <EMBED> tag, and text for other browsers can be provided with the <NOEMBED> tags.

JavaScript and Java can communicate with plug-ins that have native methods, and plug-ins can make calls back to the Java environment.

In the next section, the methods and technique discussed up to this point will be applied to a variety of sample applications, including a multilingual interface, a solitaire game, and a search engine interface.

V

JavaScript in Practice

17

A Language-Switching Interface

by Arman Danesh

Given the increasingly international character of the Internet, multilingual Web sites are becoming increasingly common.

However, creating an effective mechanism for deploying multilingual sites can be difficult. Generally, if a site offers all its content in multiple languages, then it needs to provide methods for users to switch languages at their current location in the document tree without having to start again from the top level.

There are several ways this can be done:

- Manually building a unique link in every document, linking it to the same document in the other languages—which is time-consuming and hard to maintain.
- Calling a cgi-bin script that decides which document to return—which requires cgi-bin access and adds load to the server.
- Scripting the client end so that the decision about which document to fetch is dynamically made before accessing the server.

In this chapter, you will be pursuing this last option.

Basic Requirements

The scripts you will be writing in this chapter are designed to enable Web authors to easily deploy multilingual sites without complex scripting at the client or server end and without requiring tedious building of manual cross-language links for the whole site.

Your language-switching tools need to provide the following capabilities:

- The ability to switch either a frameset or a single document to the same document in another language.
- The ability to offer at least two methods of switching: from a link within a document and via an intermediate dialog box.
- Optionally, the page author should be able to open a small window that informs the user to wait while the change takes place.
- The author should be able to specify if a page is available in other languages or not.

In order to effectively implement these capabilities, it is important to first define the environment in which the scripts must be used:

- The scripts will be included in a document using the SRC attribute of the `<SCRIPT>` tag so that documents are not too large.
- The different language versions of a single document should be stored in the same directory using the following naming convention: `filename.languagename.extension`. Therefore, a document called `test` that is available in English and French might be named `test.english.html` and `test.french.html`.

There are many sites on the Internet currently using different sorts of language-switching mechanisms for handling multiple languages. Figure 17.1. is an example of a multilingual site.

FIGURE 17.1.
The Bahá'í World
(http://
www.bahai.org/) *uses a*
multi-frame design and a
graphical menu to
implement a multilingual
site.

The Scripts

Three script libraries make up the language-switching toolkit you are developing:

- A set of functions to be included in the parent frameset document or in each document in a non-frames site. These functions provide the actual language-switching mechanism.
- A configuration script to be included in the parent frameset or in each document of a non-frames site.
- A configuration script to be included in each document, but not in a parent frameset.

The source code for these three script libraries follows.

Language-Switching Functions

The first script library consists of the functions that actually perform the language switching. These functions need to be included in the parent frameset of a site using frames or in each document in a non-frames site.

```
// Declare Constants
var dialog = true;
var noDialog = false;
var complete = true;
var notComplete = false;
```

```
var closeChooseDialog = true;
var currentDocument = -1;

// Declare Global Variables

var chooseDialog;
var language = new Array();
var currentLanguage;
var wantWaitDialog;
var waitDialog;


//  Change Language Function - takes zero, one or two argument

function changeLanguage() {

    // Check if there are arguments --
    // This determines what type of change
    // we are making.

    if (changeLanguage.arguments.length > 0) {

        // A language is passed to the function,
        // so we are doing a direct change.

        var newLanguage = changeLanguage.arguments[0];

        // Check if we need to close a dialog box

        if (changeLanguage.arguments.length > 1) {

            chooseDialog.close();

        }

        // Check if language choice is valid

        if (newLanguage < 0 || newLanguage >= language.length) {

            return;

        }

    } else {

        // No language is passed, so let's ask for one.

        selectLanguage();
        return;

    }

    // Check if this is the current language or not.

    if (currentLanguage == newLanguage) {

        // It is the current language.
```

```
        window.alert("You are already reading " + language[newLanguage].displayName +
".");
        return;

    }

    // Check if dialog box is needed.

    if (wantWaitDialog) {

        // Open the box and display a wait message

        waitDialog =
window.open("","wait","toolbar=0,location=0,directories=0,status=0,menubar=0,scrollbars=1,
➡resizable=0,copyhistory=0,width=300,height=200");
        waitDialog.document.open("text/html");
        waitDialog.document.writeln('<HEAD>');
        waitDialog.document.writeln('<TITLE>Please Wait ... Changing to ' +
➡language[newLanguage].displayName + '.');
        waitDialog.document.writeln('</TITLE></HEAD>');
        waitDialog.document.writeln('<BODY BGCOLOR="black" TEXT="yellow">');
        waitDialog.document.writeln('<H1><DIV ALIGN=CENTER>');
        waitDialog.document.writeln('Please Wait ... Changing to ' +
➡language[newLanguage].displayName + '.');
        waitDialog.document.writeln('</DIV></H1>');
        waitDialog.document.writeln('</BODY>');
        waitDialog.document.close();

    }

    // Check if we have frames

    if (self.frames.length < 1) {

        // No frames - just change the current document,
        // but first check if the document is market changeable

        if (change) {
            changeDocument(-1,newLanguage);
        }

    } else {

        // We have frames -- loop throught them and make changes

        for (frameNum = 0; frameNum < self.frames.length; frameNum ++) {

            // Only make changes if the document is marked changeable

            if (self.frames[frameNum].change) {
                changeDocument(frameNum,newLanguage);
            }

        }

    }

    // Check if dialog box needs closing
```

```
     if (wantWaitDialog) {

        // Close the box

        waitDialog.close();

     }

     // Reset the current language

     currentLanguage = newLanguage;

  }


// Switch a Document --  Takes two arguments

function changeDocument(frameNum,newLanguage) {

   // Are we changing the current document?

   if (frameNum == currentDocument) {

      // The current document is changed

      self.location =
replace(self.location.href,language[currentLanguage].fileName,
➥language[newLanguage].fileName);

   } else {

      // Change a frame

      self.frames[frameNum].location = replace(self.frames[frameNum].location.href,
➥language[currentLanguage].fileName,language[newLanguage].fileName);

   }

}


// Replace text in a string -- Takes three arguments

function replace(target,oldTerm,newTerm) {

  var work = target;
  var ind = 0;
  var next = 0;

  // Not case sensitive, so change everything to lowercase

  oldTerm = oldTerm.toLowerCase();
  work = target.toLowerCase();

  // Search for math string in original text -- if we find it, make the change

  while ((ind = work.indexOf(oldTerm,next)) >= 0) {
```

```
        target = target.substring(0,ind) + newTerm +
➡target.substring(ind+oldTerm.length,target.length);
        work = work.substring(0,ind) + newTerm +
➡work.substring(ind+oldTerm.length,work.length);
        next = ind + newTerm.length;
        if (next >= work.length) { break; }

    }

    return target;

}


// Open Language Selection Dialog Box Function

function selectLanguage() {

    // Open the box and display choices

    chooseDialog =
window.open("","choose","toolbar=0,location=0,directories=0,status=0,
➡menubar=0,scrollbars=1,resizable=0,copyhistory=0,width=300,height=350");
    chooseDialog.document.open("text/html");
    chooseDialog.document.writeln("<HEAD>");
    chooseDialog.document.writeln("<TITLE>Select a Language</TITLE>");
    chooseDialog.document.writeln('<SCRIPT LANGUAGE="JavaScript">
➡var mainWindow = window.opener;</SCRIPT>');
    chooseDialog.document.writeln("</HEAD>");
    chooseDialog.document.writeln("<BODY BGCOLOR=black TEXT=yellow>");
    chooseDialog.document.writeln("<DIV ALIGN=CENTER>");
    chooseDialog.document.writeln("<H1>Select a Language:</H1>");
    chooseDialog.document.writeln(buildMenu(dialog,notComplete));
    chooseDialog.document.writeln("</BODY>");
    chooseDialog.document.close();

}


// Build a menu Function -- Takes two arguments

function buildMenu(dialog,complete) {

    var menu = "<TABLE CELLPADDING=5>";
    menu += "<TR><TD BGCOLOR=cornsilk ALIGN=center><BR>";

    menu += "<FORM NAME=chooseForm>";
    menu += "<SELECT SIZE=5 NAME=languageChoice>";

    // Build the option list

    for (thisLang = 0; thisLang < language.length; thisLang ++) {

        // If not the current language, or if complete list
        // is indicated, add to the option list

        if (thisLang != currentLanguage || complete) {
            menu += "<OPTION VALUE=" + thisLang + ">" +
```

```
➥language[thisLang].displayName;
        }

    }

    menu += "</SELECT>";
    menu += "<P>";
    menu += '<INPUT TYPE=button VALUE="Change Language" onClick="if
➥(document.chooseForm.languageChoice.selectedIndex >= 0) { ';

        // If this is a dialog box menu, prepare
        // call across windows, otherwise call parent frame

        if (dialog) { menu += 'mainWindow'; } else { menu += 'parent'; }

        menu += '.changeLanguage(document.chooseForm.languageChoice.
➥options[document.chooseForm.languageChoice.selectedIndex].value';

        // If this is a dialog box menu, then make sure it gets closed

        if (dialog) { menu += ',' + closeChooseDialog; }
        menu += ') }">';
        menu += "</FORM>";

        menu += "</TD></TR></TABLE>";

        return menu;

    }


// Language Object Definition Function -- Takes two arguments

function languageObj(fileName,displayName) {

    this.fileName = fileName;
    this.displayName = displayName;

}
```

This set of functions is the center of the language-switching toolkit. It should be saved in a file named language.js.

Due to its relative complexity, this script requires some detailed analysis.

Variable Declaration

The scripts starts with declarations of global constants and variables. The global constants are used later in the script to make function calls and comparisons and assignments more readable.

The global variables are used for various purposes:

■ chooseDialog: used to track the currently open language-selection dialog box

■ language: an array of language choices available to the user

■ currentLanguage: used to track the current language—the value is the index of the current language in the language array

- wantWaitDialog: used to indicate if a wait dialog box should be displayed while languages are being changed
- waitDialog: used to track the currently open wait dialog box

The changeLanguage() Function

The changeLanguage() function is the heart of the toolkit. It is where all the key decisions are made when a language-change request is made.

The function starts by determining how many arguments are passed to the function and, based on that, follows one of the following courses of action:

- If there are no arguments, the selectLanguage() function is called and then the function exits. This enables the user to select a language.
- If there are one or two arguments, then a language has been passed. This is assigned to the variable newLanguage, after which two things happen: a check is made to see if there is a second argument indicating that a language-selection dialog box needs to be closed, and then a check is made to see if the language selected is a valid language. If it is not valid, the function simply exits.

If the function gets this far, then a language was passed to the function and it is a valid language. The first thing to do before changing languages is to check if the language is the same language as is currently displayed; if it is, then no change should take place. The user is informed with an alert() dialog box, after which the function exits.

Assuming the selected language is not the same as the current language, then the function checks if a wait dialog box is specified in the configuration variable wantWaitDialog. If it is, the dialog box is displayed and the global variable waitDialog is set to point to the window object for the dialog box.

After the dialog box is opened (if needed), then the function is ready to change languages. The way in which this change is made depends on whether or not the site is operating as a frameset or as a single document. This is determined by looking at the value of self.frames.length. If it is greater than zero, you know you are dealing with a frameset.

If the site is not frames-based, then you need to simply switch the current document. First, check to see that the configuration indicates the document is changeable; if it is, call changeDocument(), indicating that you are changing the current document (as opposed to one frame of the frameset).

If the site is frames-based, then things are a little more complicated. A for loop is used to iterate through each separate frame and, if it is marked as changeable, then changeDocument() is called and the index of the frame is passed to it.

After the changes have been made, the wait dialog box is closed, if necessary, and currentLanguage is set to the new language.

The changeDocument() Function

This function is called each time a document needs to be changed. It is called from the changeLanguage() function.

The process is simple. If the frameNum parameter indicated that you are changing the current document, then the value of self.location is set to a new value. If you are dealing with a frame, then self.frames[frameNum].location is set to a new value.

These new values are the URLs of the document in the selected language. These are created by calling the replace() function, which searches the URL of the current document (provided by the href property of the location object) and replaces the current language with the new language.

Notice that the replacement string for the languages is indicated by referencing the fileName property of an object stored in the language array. As you will see later in this chapter when the languageObj object is discussed, values are stored for each language in the language array. The fileName property indicates how the language is indicated in a document name in a URL.

The replace() Function

This function is a simplified version of the replace() function from a set of search-and-replace functions developed in Chapter 10 of *Teach Yourself JavaScript in a Week*, also from Sams.net Publishing.

The principle underlying this function is simple. It relies on the substring() method of the string object to move through the target string, looking for occurrences of the original term and switching them to the new term. Because you are passing a URL and two languages to the function, the function effectively changes the URL to point to the current document in the new language.

For reference, the source code for the complete set of search-and-replace functions is included here:

```
<SCRIPT LANGUAGE="JavaScript">
<!— HIDE FROM OTHER BROWSERS

// SET UP ARGUMENTS FOR FUNCTION CALLS
//
var caseSensitive = true;
var notCaseSensitive = false;
var wholeWords = true;
var anySubstring = false;


// SEARCH FOR A TERM IN A TARGET STRING
//
// search(targetString,searchTerm,caseSensitive,wordOrSubstring)
//
// where caseSenstive is a boolean value and wordOrSubstring is a boolean
// value and true means whole words, false means substrings
//
```

```
function search(target,term,caseSens,wordOnly) {

  var ind = 0;
  var next = 0;

  if (!caseSens) {
    term = term.toLowerCase();
    target = target.toLowerCase();
  }

  while ((ind = target.indexOf(term,next)) >= 0) {
    if (wordOnly) {
      var before = ind - 1;
      var after = ind + term.length;
      if (!(space(target.charAt(before)) && space(target.charAt(after)))) {
        next = ind + term.length;
        continue;
      }
    }
    return true;
  }

  return false;

}

// SEARCH FOR A TERM IN A TARGET STRING AND REPLACE IT
//
// replace(targetString,oldTerm,newTerm,caseSensitive,wordOrSubstring)
//
// where caseSenstive is a Boolean value and wordOrSubstring is a Boolean
// value and true means whole words, false means substrings
//
function replace(target,oldTerm,newTerm,caseSens,wordOnly) {

  var work = target;
  var ind = 0;
  var next = 0;

  if (!caseSens) {
    oldTerm = oldTerm.toLowerCase();
    work = target.toLowerCase();
  }

  while ((ind = work.indexOf(oldTerm,next)) >= 0) {
    if (wordOnly) {
      var before = ind - 1;
      var after = ind + oldTerm.length;
      if (!(space(work.charAt(before)) && space(work.charAt(after)))) {
        next = ind + oldTerm.length;
        continue;
      }
    }
    target = target.substring(0,ind) + newTerm +
        _target.substring(ind+oldTerm.length,target.length);
    work = work.substring(0,ind) + newTerm +
        _work.substring(ind+oldTerm.length,work.length);
    next = ind + newTerm.length;
```

```
      if (next >= work.length) { break; }
   }

   return target;

}

// CHECK IF A CHARACTER IS A WORD BREAK AND RETURN A BOOLEAN VALUE
//
function space(check) {

   var space = " .,/<>?!`';:@#$%^&*()=-¦[]{}" + '"' + "\\\n\t";

   for (var i = 0; i < space.length; i++)
     if (check == space.charAt(i)) { return true; }

   if (check == "") { return true; }
   if (check == null) { return true; }

   return false;

}

// STOP HIDING —>
</SCRIPT>
```

This script library consists of three functions: `search()`, `replace()`, and `space()`:

- `search()`: Searches a string for a search term and returns `true` or `false` based on the result of the search.
- `replace()`: Searches a string for a search term and replaces it with a new term.
- `space()`: Checks for word breaks—is called from `search()` and `replace()`, but not directly by the user.

Instructions for how to correctly use `search()` and `replace()` appear in the preceding source code.

The `selectLanguage()` Function

The `selectLanguage()` function opens a dialog box with a menu in it so that the user can select a language.

When the new window is opened, the `chooseDialog` variable is made to point at the window and then the content is displayed in the window. The bulk of the content is generated by the `buildMenu()` call.

It's important to note that the header of the document being displayed in the dialog box includes a variable definition creating a pointer to the window, which opened the dialog box. This is done using the `window.opener` property. The reason this variable is defined is so that when the user selects a language, it is possible to call back to the main window and trigger a language change.

The `buildMenu()` Function

This function looks complex but is really rather simple. It takes two arguments: `dialog` (which specifies if the menu will be displayed in a dialog box), and `complete` (which specifies if the complete language list should be displayed or the complete list minus the current language).

These parameters are passed so the menu that is built works in the context in which it will be used.

The `dialog` parameter is used to ensure that the call to `changeLanguage()` is made correctly. If the menu is in a dialog box, then `changeLanguage()` is a property of `mainWindow`; if it is not a dialog box, the call is to the parent of the current frameset.

The function itself builds a string called `menu` with all the HTML needed to produce a form with a selection list of all the languages and a button with an `onClick` event handler to call `changeLanguage()` as long as the user has selected a language.

The `languageObj()` Object Definition

The last function in the script library is the `languageObj()` object definition function. It is used to define the objects stored in the language array.

The function defines an object with two properties: `displayName`, which specifies how the name of the language should be displayed to the user, and `fileName`, which indicates how the language name appears in filenames in URLs.

The Configuration Scripts

As indicated earlier, there are two configuration scripts: one included in the parent frameset or each document of a non-frames site, and another included in each document in a site (but not a parent frameset).

The First Configuration Script

The following script needs to be included in the parent frameset document or in each document in a non-frames site:

```
<SCRIPT LANGUAGE="JavaScript">
   language[0] = new languageObj("english","English");
   language[1] = new languageObj("french","French");
   language[2] = new languageObj("spanish","Spanish");
   currentLanguage = 0;
   wantWaitDialog = false;
</SCRIPT>
```

This set of variable assignments declares those universal variables that are used throughout. In this example, languages are assigned to the language array by creating instances of the `languageObj()` object. The first parameter is the language name in files, and the second is the language name displayed for the user.

The particular languages declared here could just as easily be a different number and combination of languages:

```
language[0] = new languageObj("english","English");
language[1] = new languageObj("french","Francais");
language[2] = new languageObj("spanish","Espanol");
```

or

```
language[0] = new languageObj("simplechinese","Simplified Chinese");
language[1] = new languageObj("tradchinese","Traditional Chinese");
language[2] = new languageObj("japanese","Japanese");
language[3] = new languageObj("korean","Korean");
```

After the languages are configured, the `currentLanguage` variable needs to be set. In a parent frameset, this would be set to the language initially displayed in the frames; in a non-frames situation, this would be set to the current document's language. The value assigned to `currentLanguage` should be the index of the language in the `language` array.

Finally, the `wantWaitDialog` variable takes a value of `true` or `false` depending on whether or not a dialog box with a wait message should be displayed each time a language change occurs.

The Second Configuration Script

This script is simple and is included in any displayed document (in other words, not in a parent frameset):

```
<SCRIPT LANGUAGE="JavaScript">
   var change = true;
</SCRIPT>
```

This script simply sets the `change` variable to `true` or `false`. This indicates if the current document should be changed when the user attempts to change languages. This can be used in a frameset to keep the menu frame or some graphical frame from changing.

Using the Scripts

There are several ways to use the scripts. The two basic methods are

■ Non-frames sites
■ Frameset sites with the language controls in a separate frame

Non-Frames Sites

When implementing language-switching functionality in a non-frames site, it is assumed that a language menu will appear in each document.

As previously indicated, three scripts need to be included in each document as follows:

```
<HEAD>
<SCRIPT LANGUAGE="JavaScript" SRC="language.js"></SCRIPT>
<SCRIPT LANGUAGE="JavaScript">
    language[0] = new languageObj("english","English");
    language[1] = new languageObj("french","French");
    language[2] = new languageObj("spanish","Spanish");
    currentLanguage = 0;
    wantWaitDialog = false;
</SCRIPT>
<SCRIPT LANGUAGE="JavaScript">
    var change = true;
</SCRIPT>
<TITLE>The English Document</TITLE>
</HEAD>
```

This header would be used in English documents in the site. The value assigned to currentLanguage would be 1 in French documents and 2 in Spanish documents.

The documents themselves need to include a menu. This can be done by calling buildMenu() in the body of the document:

```
<BODY>
<DIV ALIGN=CENTER>
<H1>The English Document</H1>
<HR>
<SCRIPT LANGUAGE="JavaScript">
document.write(buildMenu(noDialog,complete));
</SCRIPT>
</DIV>
</BODY>
```

This produces results similar to those shown in Figure 17.2.

FIGURE 17.2.

The basic language-changing menu.

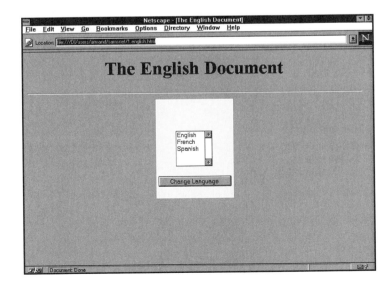

Notice, however, that the menu includes the current language because the constant `complete` was passed to `buildMenu()`. To ensure that the current language is not included, pass `notComplete` instead of `complete` to `buildMenu()`. This produces results such as those in Figure 17.3.

FIGURE 17.3.

The menu can be made to not include the current language.

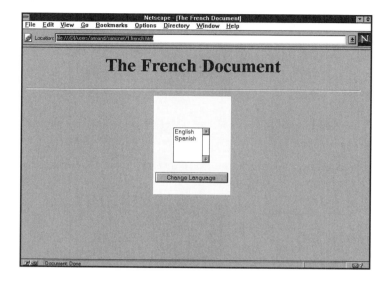

There are two other ways that the menu can be built:

■ By displaying the menu in a dialog box
■ By creating links that call `changeLanguge()` directly

Using a Dialog Box

If the `changeLanguage()` function is called without any arguments, then a dialog box is displayed, prompting users to select a language.

Using this, it is possible to change pages so that the body of the document looks like the following:

```
<BODY>
<DIV ALIGN=CENTER>
<H1>The English Document</H1>
<HR>
<STRONG><A HREF="javascript:changeLanguage()">Change Language</A></STRONG>
</DIV>
</BODY>
```

Then, when a users clicks on Change Language, a language-selection dialog box is displayed. This produces results like those shown in Figures 17.4 and 17.5.

FIGURE 17.4.
A single link can be used for changing languages.

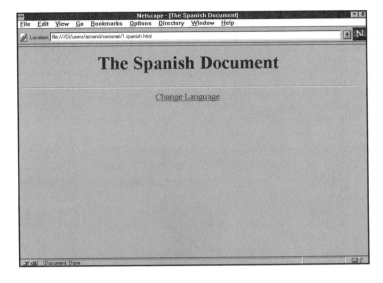

FIGURE 17.5.
When the link is clicked, a dialog box is displayed.

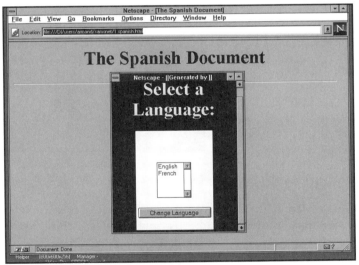

This technique is useful when the list of languages is long or the menu would clutter up a document excessively.

Calling changeLanguage() Directly

Another approach to building a menu requires that a manually built menu, which directly calls changeLanguage(), be included in each document. For instance, the body of the document could look like the following:

```
<BODY>
<DIV ALIGN=CENTER>
<H1>The English Document</H1>
<HR>
<STRONG>
<A HREF="javascript:changeLanguage(1)">Change to French</A>
&#0149;
<A HREF="javascript:changeLanguage(2)">Change to Spanish</A>
</STRONG>
</DIV>
</BODY>
```

This produces a document resembling Figure 17.6.

FIGURE 17.6.

Manually built links can be used for language switching.

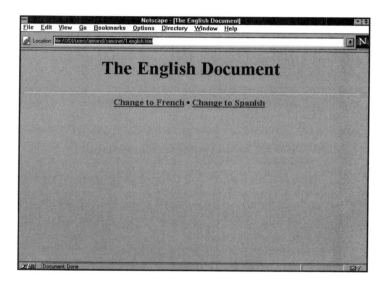

Language Switching in a Frameset

Things work a little differently in a frameset. The parent frameset needs to include the language functions script plus the first configuration script:

```
<HEAD>
<SCRIPT LANGUAGE="JavaScript" SRC="language.js"></SCRIPT>
<SCRIPT LANGUAGE="JavaScript">
    language[0] = new languageObj("english","English");
    language[1] = new languageObj("french","Francais");
    language[2] = new languageObj("spanish","Espanol");
    currentLanguage = 0;
    wantWaitDialog = false;
</SCRIPT>
<TITLE>Multiple Languages</TITLE>
</HEAD>
<FRAMESET COLS="50%,*">
    <FRAME SRC="menu.html">
    <FRAME SRC="text.english.html">
</FRAMESET>
```

Then, the various documents need to include the following script in their headers:

```
<SCRIPT LANGUAGE="JavaScript">
   var change = true;
</SCRIPT>
```

The menu file doesn't need to change when the user changes languages, so it should include the following:

```
<SCRIPT LANGUAGE="JavaScript">
   var change = false;
</SCRIPT>
```

In the menu file, whether you are using `buildMenu()` or `changeLanguage()` links to create your menu, it is important to remember that the functions are in the parent frameset. Calls to `buildMenu` will have to look like the following:

```
document.write(parent.buildMenu(parent.noDialog,parent.complete));
```

Similarly, calls to `changeLanguage()` should be called in the parent frameset.

This produces results that look like Figure 17.7.

FIGURE 17.7.

Language changing in a frameset.

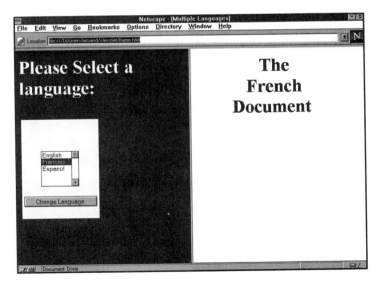

As with the preceding non-frames examples, any of the available menu methods can be used, including opening a dialog box and manually building the menu links.

Summary

In this chapter you built a set of functions that can be used to implement anything from a single-document multilingual interface to multi-frame sites in which all, or some, of the frames change languages.

In doing this, you applied several basic principles, including:

- String manipulation using the `substring()` method
- Object definition and instantiation
- Use of the `frames` array
- Working with windows
- Creating and working with arrays

The next chapter looks at another example, and takes you through the development of a solitaire game in JavaScript that demonstrates several techniques—including interactive forms, object definition and instantiation, and the use of random numbers.

18

Solitaire in JavaScript

by Arman Danesh

Given JavaScript's utility for adding interactivity to Web pages and HTML forms, it is ideally suited for implementing games.

In fact, some of the earliest examples of JavaScript on the Web were games ranging from a simple matches game to a full-text fantasy adventure.

In this chapter, you will learn how to implement a simple solitaire card game, more as an example of interactive forms than of complex game development. This game demonstrates several key JavaScript principles, including the following:

■ Using event handlers
■ Using the `eval()` statement
■ Using the `string` object
■ Creating custom objects
■ Dynamically updating form fields

The chapter begins by examining the game you will be implementing and the requirements this game has in terms of an interface. Then the actual program code and the way it works is reviewed.

The Game

The solitaire game being implemented in this chapter is fairly straightforward:

1. The deck is shuffled.
2. Four cards are dealt face-up in a row.
3. If two cards on the top of any of the four piles form a pair (in other words, the same number—suit is irrelevant), they are discarded.
4. When all pairs are discarded, step two is repeated, dealing on top of the previous cards—if the deck is finished, the game is over.
5. When the deck is finished, if all cards have been discarded, the game is won.

The game is admittedly simple. It requires little in the way of strategy on the part of the user and is easy to learn. For the purposes of this chapter, however, it provides a good example of how to implement an interactive game using JavaScript. And it isn't the worst way to pass idle hours.

Basic Requirements

The key to implementing the game lies in its interface. The game must provide the following:

■ A display of the current top card in each of the four piles
■ Controls to select two cards to attempt to remove

■ Control buttons for the following actions: removing the selected pair, dealing four new cards, starting a new game, and exiting

■ Counters to display both the number of cards left in the deck and the number already discarded

In addition, the user should be informed that the deck is being shuffled and should be told that no cards are left to deal if the user attempts to deal more cards when all cards have been dealt. Any attempt to remove an invalid pair should simply be ignored by the program.

Source Code for the Game

The entire game is implemented in one HTML file with embedded JavaScript:

Listing 18.1. A solitaire game.

```
<HEAD>

<TITLE>
JavaScript Solitaire
</TITLE>

<SCRIPT LANGUAGE="JavaScript">

var cards = "-A23456789TJQK";
var suits = "-HDCS";
var deck = new Array(52);
var card1 = new Array(14);
var card2 = new Array(14);
var card3 = new Array(14);
var card4 = new Array(14);
var cardPoint1, cardPoint2, cardPoint3, cardPoint4;
var currentCard = 0;
var choice1, choice2, value1, value2;
var hands;
var taken = 0;

for (i = 0; i < 52; i++) {

    deck[i] = new cardObj();

}

for (i = 0; i < 14; i++) {

    card1[i] = new cardObj();
    card2[i] = new cardObj();
    card3[i] = new cardObj();
    card4[i] = new cardObj();

}
```

continues

Listing 18.1. continued

```
function cardObj() {

    this.card = -1;
    this.suit = -1;

}


function shuffleDeck() {

    var chooseCard, chooseSuit;

    var dialog = window.open("","dialogBox","height=100,width=300");
    dialog.document.open("text/html");
    dialog.document.writeln("<HEAD><TITLE>");
    dialog.document.writeln("Shuffling cards");
    dialog.document.writeln("</TITLE></HEAD>");
    dialog.document.writeln("<BODY BGCOLOR=#020A33 TEXT=cornsilk>");
    dialog.document.writeln("<H1><DIV ALIGN=CENTER>");
    dialog.document.writeln("Shuffling cards ... please wait");
    dialog.document.writeln("</DIV></H1></BODY>");
    dialog.document.close();

    for (i = 0; i < 52; i++) {

        deck[i].card = -1;
        deck[i].suit = -1;

    }

    for (i = 0; i < 52; i++) {

        chooseCard = Math.ceil(Math.random() * 13);
        chooseSuit = Math.ceil(Math.random() * 4);

        while (cardSelected(chooseCard,chooseSuit,i)) {

            chooseCard = Math.ceil(Math.random() * 13);
            chooseSuit = Math.ceil(Math.random() * 4);

        }

        deck[i].card = chooseCard;
        deck[i].suit = chooseSuit;

    }

    dialog.close();

}


function cardSelected(chosenCard,chosenSuit,currentCounter) {

    for (j = 0; j < currentCounter; j++) {

        if (deck[j].card == chosenCard && deck[j].suit == chosenSuit) {
```

```
            return true;

        }

    }

    return false;

}


function takeCards() {

    getChoices();

    if (checkCards()) {

        removeCards();

    }

    if (checkWin()) {

        if (userWon()) {

            startGame();

        } else {

            self.location = "solbye.html";

        }

    }

}


function userWon() {

    return confirm("You won! Play again?");

}


function checkWin() {

    if (taken == 52) { return true; }

    return false;

}

function getChoices() {

    choice1 = 0;
    while (choice1 < 4) {
```

continues

Listing 18.1. continued

```
            if (document.game.choice1[choice1].checked) { break; }
            choice1 ++;

    }
    choice1++

    choice2 = 0;
    while (choice2 < 4) {

            if (document.game.choice2[choice2].checked) { break; }
            choice2 ++;

    }
    choice2++

    if (choice1 == 5 || choice2 == 5) {

            choice1 = 5;
            choice2 = 5;
            value = 0;
            value = 0;
            return;

    }

    value1 = eval("card" + choice1 + "[cardPoint" + choice1 + "].card");
    value2 = eval("card" + choice2 + "[cardPoint" + choice2 + "].card");

}


function checkCards() {

    if (choice1 == choice2) { return false; }

    if (value1 != value2) { return false; }

    if (value1 == 0 || value2 == 0) { return false; }

    return true;

}


function removeCards() {

    eval("cardPoint" + choice1 + "--");
    eval("cardPoint" + choice2 + "--");
    eval("document.game.choice1[" + --choice1 + "].checked = false");
    eval("document.game.choice2[" + --choice2 + "].checked = false");
    choice1 = 0;
    choice2 = 0;
    taken += 2;
    document.game.taken.value = taken;
    displayCards();

}
```

```
function dealCards() {

    if (hands == 13) {

        alert ("All the cards have been dealt");
        return;

    }

    hands++;
    document.game.hands.value = 52 - (hands * 4);

    card1[++cardPoint1] = deck[currentCard++];
    card2[++cardPoint2] = deck[currentCard++];
    card3[++cardPoint3] = deck[currentCard++];
    card4[++cardPoint4] = deck[currentCard++];

    displayCards();

}



function displayCards() {

    if (cardPoint1 == 0) {

        document.game.card1.value = "";

    } else {
        document.game.card1.value = cards.charAt(card1[cardPoint1].card);
        document.game.card1.value += " of ";
        document.game.card1.value += suits.charAt(card1[cardPoint1].suit);

    }

    if (cardPoint2 == 0) {

        document.game.card2.value = "";

    } else {

        document.game.card2.value = cards.charAt(card2[cardPoint2].card);
        document.game.card2.value += " of ";
        document.game.card2.value += suits.charAt(card2[cardPoint2].suit);

    }

    if (cardPoint3 == 0) {

        document.game.card3.value = "";

    } else {

        document.game.card3.value = cards.charAt(card3[cardPoint3].card);
        document.game.card3.value += " of ";
        document.game.card3.value += suits.charAt(card3[cardPoint3].suit);
```

continues

Listing 18.1. continued

```
        }
        if (cardPoint4 == 0) {
            document.game.card4.value = "";
        } else {
            document.game.card4.value = cards.charAt(card4[cardPoint4].card);
            document.game.card4.value += " of ";
            document.game.card4.value += suits.charAt(card4[cardPoint4].suit);
        }
    }

    function startGame() {
        document.game.choice1[0].checked = false;
        document.game.choice1[1].checked = false;
        document.game.choice1[2].checked = false;
        document.game.choice1[3].checked = false;
        document.game.choice2[0].checked = false;
        document.game.choice2[1].checked = false;
        document.game.choice2[2].checked = false;
        document.game.choice2[3].checked = false;
        hands = 0;
        taken = 0;
        document.game.taken.value = taken;
        currentCard = 0;
        cardPoint1 = 0;
        cardPoint2 = 0;
        cardPoint3 = 0;
        cardPoint4 = 0;
        card1[cardPoint1].card = "";
        card2[cardPoint2].card = "";
        card3[cardPoint3].card = "";
        card4[cardPoint4].card = "";
        shuffleDeck();
        dealCards();
    }

    </SCRIPT>

    </HEAD>

    <BODY onLoad="startGame()" BGCOLOR="white" FGCOLOR="cyan">

    <FORM NAME="game">

    <DIV ALIGN=CENTER>

    <TABLE BORDER=0 CELLPADDING=5>
```

```
<TR>
    <TD COLSPAN=6 ALIGN=CENTER BGCOLOR="midnightblue">
        <FONT SIZE=6 COLOR=yellow>Solitaire</FONT>
    </TD>
</TR>

<TR>
    <TD ALIGN=CENTER BGCOLOR="darkmaroon">
        <FONT SIZE=4 COLOR=white>CARDS</FONT>
    </TD>
    <TD ALIGN=CENTER BGCOLOR="darkgreen">
        <INPUT TYPE=text NAME="card1" SIZE=6 onFocus="this.blur()">
    </TD>
    <TD ALIGN=CENTER BGCOLOR="darkgreen">
        <INPUT TYPE=text NAME="card2" SIZE=6 onFocus="this.blur()">
    </TD>
    <TD ALIGN=CENTER BGCOLOR="darkgreen">
        <INPUT TYPE=text NAME="card3" SIZE=6 onFocus="this.blur()">
    </TD>
    <TD ALIGN=CENTER BGCOLOR="darkgreen">
        <INPUT TYPE=text NAME="card4" SIZE=6 onFocus="this.blur()">
    </TD>
    <TD ALIGN=CENTER BGCOLOR="darkgray" ROWSPAN=7>
        <FONT SIZE=4 COLOR=darkmaroon>CARDS<BR>LEFT<BR>IN<BR>DECK:</FONT><BR>
        <INPUT TYPE=text NAME="hands" SIZE=3 onFocus="this.blur()"><P>
        <HR><P>
        <FONT SIZE=4 COLOR=darkmaroon>CARDS<BR>TAKEN:</FONT><BR>
        <INPUT TYPE=text NAME="taken" SIZE=3 onFocus="this.blur()"><P>
    </TD>
</TR>

<TR>
    <TD ALIGN=CENTER BGCOLOR="darkmaroon">
        <FONT SIZE=4 COLOR=white>CHOICE 1</FONT>
    </TD>
    <TD ALIGN=CENTER BGCOLOR="cornsilk">
        <INPUT TYPE=radio NAME="choice1" VALUE="1">
    </TD>
    <TD ALIGN=CENTER BGCOLOR="cornsilk">
        <INPUT TYPE=radio NAME="choice1" VALUE="2">
    </TD>
    <TD ALIGN=CENTER BGCOLOR="cornsilk">
        <INPUT TYPE=radio NAME="choice1" VALUE="3">
    </TD>
    <TD ALIGN=CENTER BGCOLOR="cornsilk">
        <INPUT TYPE=radio NAME="choice1" VALUE="4">
    </TD>
</TR>

<TR>
    <TD ALIGN=CENTER BGCOLOR="darkmaroon">
        <FONT SIZE=4 COLOR=white>CHOICE 2</FONT>
    </TD>
    <TD ALIGN=CENTER BGCOLOR="cornsilk">
        <INPUT TYPE=radio NAME="choice2" VALUE="1">
    </TD>
    <TD ALIGN=CENTER BGCOLOR="cornsilk">
        <INPUT TYPE=radio NAME="choice2" VALUE="2">
```

continues

Listing 18.1. continued

```
            </TD>
            <TD ALIGN=CENTER BGCOLOR="cornsilk">
                <INPUT TYPE=radio NAME="choice2" VALUE="3">
            </TD>
            <TD ALIGN=CENTER BGCOLOR="cornsilk">
                <INPUT TYPE=radio NAME="choice2" VALUE="4">
            </TD>
        </TR>

        <TR>
            <TD ALIGN=CENTER ROWSPAN=4 BGCOLOR="darkmaroon">
                <FONT SIZE=4 COLOR=white>CONTROLS</FONT>
            </TD>
            <TD COLSPAN=4 ALIGN=CENTER BGCOLOR="black">
                <FONT COLOR=white>
                <INPUT TYPE=button NAME="take" VALUE="TAKE THE PAIR"
➥onClick="takeCards()">
                </FONT>
            </TD>
        </TR>

        <TR>
            <TD COLSPAN=4 ALIGN=CENTER BGCOLOR="black">
                <FONT COLOR=white>
                <INPUT TYPE=button NAME="deal" VALUE="DEAL CARDS"
➥onClick="dealCards()">
                </FONT>
            </TD>
        </TR>

        <TR>
            <TD COLSPAN=4 ALIGN=CENTER BGCOLOR="black">
                <FONT COLOR=white>
                <INPUT TYPE=button NAME="start" VALUE="START OVER"
➥onClick="startGame()">
                </FONT>
            </TD>
        </TR>

        <TR>
            <TD COLSPAN=4 ALIGN=CENTER BGCOLOR="black">
                <FONT COLOR=white>
                <INPUT TYPE=button NAME="exit" VALUE="EXIT" onClick="self.location =
➥'solbye.html'">
                </FONT>
            </TD>
        </TR>

</TABLE>

</DIV>

</FORM>

</BODY>
```

The Interface Form

The first piece of the script to look at is the form that provides the user interface.

The form uses tables and Navigator 3's capability to display different color backgrounds in separate table cells to produce the colorful layout seen in Figure 18.1.

FIGURE 18.1.
The Solitaire user interface.

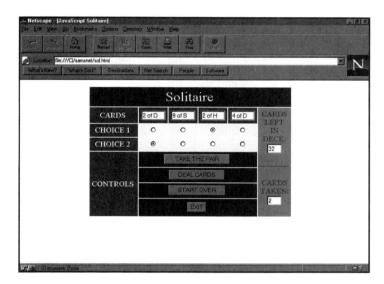

The form itself provides all the fields and buttons described in the basic requirements section earlier in this chapter.

The four cards are each displayed as text labels in three text input fields called card1, card2, card3, and card4. Two sets of radio buttons named choice1 and choice2, respectively, enable the user to select two cards. An additional two text fields called hands and taken provide display space for the remaining cards and discarded cards counters.

The six text fields all have the same event handler to ensure that users can't change the values of these fields:

```
onFocus="this.blur()"
```

Finally, four buttons are provided:

- take is used to discard a selected pair. When the user clicks this button, an onClick event handler calls the takeCards() function.

- deal is used to deal four new cards. When the user clicks this button, an onClick event handler calls the dealCards() function.

- start is used to start a new game. When the user clicks this button an onClick event handler calls the startGame() function.

■ exit is used to finish playing. When the user clicks this button, an HTML document with a good-bye message is loaded by assigning a new URL to self.location.

In addition to the form, the HTML <BODY> tag has an event handler that calls the startGame() function.

Global Variables and Objects

Before looking at the various functions that make up the script, you need to look at the global variables and object definitions used throughout the application.

All the major information in the script is stored in global variables so that it is easily accessible to all functions without having to pass arguments back and forth throughout the script. This makes the data more susceptible to mistaken coding in one function, corrupting data needed by the rest of the script, but it makes writing the script easier.

At the top of the script, the following global variables and constants are defined:

■ cards: A string used to display a letter or number representing a card. Cards themselves are tracked as numbers between 1 and 13 and these indexes correspond to letters in the cards string.

■ suits: Like the cards string, but for the suits.

■ deck: An array of 52 elements used to store the shuffled deck. Each element is an instance of the cardObj object discussed later in this section.

■ currentCard: A counter used to track the index number of the next card available for dealing.

■ card1, card2, card3, card4: These 14-element arrays are used to store cards dealt into a current pile. The maximum number of cards that can be in a pile is 13.

■ cardPoint1, cardPoint2, cardPoint3, cardPoint4: Counters used to track the index numbers of the current card being displayed in each of the four piles.

■ choice1, choice2: Used to store pointers to the two cards selected by the user—these values range from 1 to 4.

■ value1, value2: Used to store the values of the cards selected by the user—these value range from 1 to 13.

■ hands: A counter to track the number of hands dealt. This figure is used to calculate the number of cards remaining in the deck for the user.

■ taken: A counter to track the number of cards successfully discarded by the user.

The script also uses one custom object mentioned above: cardObj. This object has two properties—card and suit, used to store the value and suit of a card. These properties provide an easy way to get at the two attributes of any card.

The startGame() Function

The startGame() function is called when the page first loads from the onLoad event handler of the <BODY> tag. It also is called when the user clicks the Start Over button.

The function first initializes several variables:

■ The checked property of all the radio button objects is set to false in order to clear the buttons if they were selected before the user clicked the Start Over button.

■ The hands and taken counters are set to zero and the value of the taken counter is displayed in the appropriate field of the form.

■ currentCard, cardPoint1, cardPoint2, cardPoint3, and cardPoint4 are reset to zero.

■ The card properties of the first items in the four arrays—card1, card2, card3, and card4—are cleared to the empty string in case they held any values. These first fields are used to indicate when there are no cards in a pile.

After these values are initialized, shuffleDeck() is called to shuffle the cards and then dealCards() is called to deal the first four cards.

The shuffleDeck() Function

The shuffleDeck() function attempts to shuffle the deck using the Math.random() method.

The function starts by opening a window to inform the user that the deck is being shuffled like the one shown in Figure 18.2. This is done because on slower systems the shuffling process causes a noticeable delay in the program.

FIGURE 18.2.
A window is used to inform the user that shuffling is occurring.

Before shuffling occurs, the card and suit of each card in the deck is cleared to a value of -1, indicating that no valid card has been assigned.

The shuffling process takes place within a `for` loop that iterates from 0 to 51—each entry in the `deck` array.

For each entry in the array, the following process is used to select a card: An initial card is selected using `Math.random()`, and then a `while` loop is used to continue selecting cards until a card that hasn't been selected is found.

This test to see if the randomly selected card has already been used is done by calling `cardSelected()` with three arguments: the value and suit of the card plus the index number of the card in the deck.

Once the card is selected, the function closes the message window.

The `cardSelected()` Function

This function is simple. It loops through each card in the deck up to the card currently being selected and compares the `card` and `suit` property to values of the arguments passed to the function. If any card matches, then false is returned by the function, otherwise true is returned.

The `dealCards()` Function

After calling the `shuffleDeck()` function, the `startGame()` function finished by calling `dealCards()` to display the first four cards of the deck. This function is also called by the `onClick` event handler of the Deal Cards button in the form to display the next four cards.

The first step taken by the function is to check the value of the `hands` counter. If it is 13, then all cards have been dealt and an alert dialog like the one shown in Figure 18.3 is used to inform the user, and the function exits.

Otherwise, the dealing process begins. First, the hands counter is incremented by one to reflect a new set being dealt and the value is used to calculate and display the number of cards remaining in the deck for the user.

Next, the four cards are dealt from the `deck` array into the `card1`, `card2`, `card3`, and `card4` arrays.

This is done with four commands similar to this one, used to deal into the first pile:

```
card1[++cardPoint1] = deck[currentCard++];
```

What's worth noting here is the differing uses of the unary increment operator. In the left side of the expression, the counter variable is incremented before using the value because the value of the counter represents the currently displayed card. On the right side, however, the value is used before incrementing because the counter `currentCard` points to the next available card for dealing.

FIGURE 18.3.
An alert box is used to inform the user when there are no more cards left to deal.

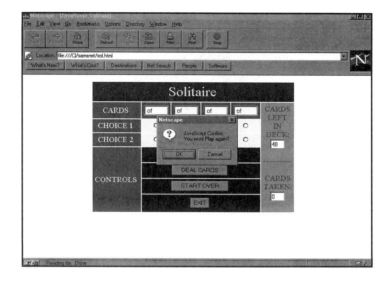

The last step in the dealCards() function is to call displayCards() to display the results of dealing the cards.

The displayCards() Function

This function is called by dealCards() after a new set of cards has been dealt and by removeCards() after a pair is successfully removed by the user.

For each pile, the following steps are taken: If the counter for the current pile (cardPoint1, and so on) is zero, then the pile is empty and an empty string is assigned to the value property of the text field. Otherwise, the card property for the card object pointed to by the counter is used as an argument to the charAt() method of the cards string, as is the suit property used for the suits string to display the card's name in the appropriate field in the form.

The takeCards() Function

The takeCards() function is called by the appropriate button in the form.

The function starts by calling getChoices() to identify the cards selected by the user. Then the cards are checked by calling checkCards(). If the cards are valid, then removeCards() is called to remove the cards.

Next, a check is made to see if the user has won by calling checkWin(). If they have, userWon() is called to inform the user and if the user wants to continue, startGame() is called. If the user doesn't want to continue, then the farewell page is loaded.

The getChoices() Function

This function extracts information about the user's selected cards.

The function first gets the pile numbers of the two selections (a value from one to four). This is accomplished by looking for the index number of the button where the checked property is true and then adding one to the value. A while loop increments the index until a selected button is found.

After the loop, the index is incremented by one. If no index had been found, the index will be four and be incremented to become five, an invalid value, but one that is handled by the next step in the function. This step is to see if either index is five. If it is, both are set to five, the values of the cards are set to zero, and the function exits.

If the two piles are valid selections, then the card values for the piles are assigned to value1 and value2 using the eval() statement. This statement takes a string and evaluates its content as a JavaScript operation. In this case, the card property of the top card is evaluated in a given pile using the value of choice1 or choice2 to select the right array name to work with.

The checkCards() Function

The checkCards() function performs three basic checks to confirm the validity of the cards selected by the user. If choice1 is the same as choice2 (in other words, the user has selected the same card twice), or value1 is different than value2 (meaning that the user has selected cards with different values), or either value1 or value2 is equal to zero (meaning that the user has selected at least one empty pile or forgotten to select one of the cards) then the cards are invalid and false is returned.

Otherwise, true is returned.

The removeCards() Function

This function is used to discard a pair of cards if the user has made a valid selection.

First, the counters for the two piles are decreased by one by using an eval() statement to evaluate the names of the pile arrays based on the values stored in choice1 and choice2.

Then, eval() statements are used to uncheck the two radio buttons.

Next, choice1 and choice2 are cleared to zero and the taken counter is incremented by two and displayed. Finally, displayCards() is called.

The checkWin() Function

This function checks to see whether the user has won by seeing whether all 52 cards have been taken (this is accomplished by looking at the value of the taken counter).

The userWon() Function

This function is called if the user has won. It informs the user of the win and asks the user whether he or she wants to play again. It does this by returning the value of a single confirm() method call.

Summary

In this chapter you were shown how it is possible to implement an interactive game using forms and basic JavaScript. This game provided examples of event handlers, the eval() statement, dynamic form updating, and the random() method.

In the next chapter you will be shown the development of a unified interface to three leading search engines. JavaScript is used to implement a single form that searches all three engines without requiring any server-side scripting.

19

A Search Engine Interface

by Arman Danesh

When JavaScript first became available with beta versions of Navigator 2, some of the earliest applications developed using HTML and JavaScript included search engine front-end pages. These would provide a single form that could be used to select multiple search engines for a single query.

The results would usually be presented in multiple frames in the same window. All the processing to handle the calls to the various search engines was executed at the client end.

This chapter walks you through the development of just such an interface to multiple search engines. This application highlights several techniques, including the following:

■ Changing window focus
■ Dynamically updating select lists
■ Dynamically generating a frameset document

The Search Engine Interface Requirements

The search engine interface you are developing has several basic requirements:

■ It should be easy to adjust the script to handle any number of search engines.
■ The user should be able to search anywhere from one to all available search engines.
■ The search results should be displayed in a separate window.
■ There should be an easy way to flip back to the main window with the search form if the user wants to pursue a new search.

In addition, to keep the queries simple, especially in light of the fact that each search engine has its own way of encoding URLs for Boolean queries, the searches will be restricted to single-term keyword searches.

Source Code for the Search Engine Interface

The source code for this application is divided into two files: the main search form document and a small HTML file. The HTML file provides a control on the search results page, enabling easy access back to the main search form.

The source code for the main search form document is:

```
<HEAD>

<TITLE>JavaScript Web Search Tool</TITLE>

<SCRIPT LANGUAGE="JavaScript">

var url = new Array(4);
url[0] = new urlObj("http://www.altavista.digital.com/cgi-bin/query?
➥pg=q&what=web&fmt=.&q=","AltaVista");
```

```
url[1] = new urlObj("http://www.hotbot.com/search.html?_v=1.0&OP=0&
➥SM=MC&SW=&MOD=0&date=WH&DR=newer&DM=1&DD=1&DY=96&DV=10&DU=years&
➥smiley=&RD=AN&RG=NA&domain=&DC=10&FJS=off&FJA=off&FRA=off&FAC=off&
➥FSW=off&FVR=off&FSU=off&FSM=off&OP=0&MOD=0&search.x=55&
➥search.y=16&MT=","HotBot");
url[2] = new urlObj("http://www.lycos.com/cgi-bin/pursuit?query=","Lycos");
url[3] = new urlObj("http://guide-p.infoseek.com//Titles?
➥col=WW&sv=IS&lk=noframes&qt=","InfoSeek");

function urlObj(url,title) {

    this.url = url;
    this.title = title;

}


function changeNumber(number) {

    var toSelect;

    for (i = 1; i <= number; i++) {

        toSelect = (document.search.elements[i].options[0].text == 'Unavailable') ?
i - 1 : document.search.elements[i].selectedIndex;

        for (j = 0; j < url.length; j++) {

            document.search.elements[i].options[j].text = url[j].title;

        }

        document.search.elements[i].options[toSelect].selected = true;

    }

    for (i = number + 1; i <= url.length; i++) {

        for (j = 0; j < url.length; j++) {

            document.search.elements[i].options[j].text = 'Unavailable';

        }

    }

}


function doSearch(number) {

    var frameSize = Math.floor(85 / number);

    var searchWin = window.open("","searchWindow");
    searchWin.document.open("text/html");
    searchWin.document.write('<FRAMESET ROWS="15%,*');

    for (i = 1; i < number; i++) {
```

```
            searchWin.document.write(',' + frameSize + '%');

    }

    searchWin.document.writeln('">');
    searchWin.document.writeln('<FRAME SRC="control.html">');

    for (i = 0; i < number; i++) {

            searchWin.document.write('<FRAME SRC="' + url[i].url +
document.search.term.value + '">');

    }

    searchWin.document.writeln("</FRAMESET>");
    searchWin.document.close();

    searchWin.focus();

}


function displayMenus() {

    document.write('<TABLE>');

    document.write('<TR>');

    document.write('<TD>');
    document.write('Number of Search Engines:');
    document.write('</TD>');
    document.write('<TD>');
    document.write('<SELECT NAME="number" onChange="changeNumber(this.selectedIndex
+ 1)">');

    for (i = 1; i < url.length; i++) {

        document.write('<OPTION>' + i);

    }
    document.write('<OPTION SELECTED>' + url.length);

    document.write('</SELECT>');
    document.write('</TD>');

    document.write('</TR>');

    for (i = 1; i <= url.length; i++) {

        document.write('<TR>');

        document.write('<TD>');
        document.write('Search Engine ' + i + ':');
        document.write('</TD>');
        document.write('<TD>');
        document.write('<SELECT NAME="engine' + i + '">');

        for (j = 0; j < url.length; j++) {
```

```
            document.write('<OPTION VALUE="' + url[j].url + '"');
            document.write((j == i - 1) ? ' SELECTED>' : '>');
            document.write(url[j].title);

        }

        document.write('</SELECT>');
        document.write('</TD>');

        document.write('</TR>');

    }

    document.write('<TR>');

    document.write('<TD>');
    document.write('Search for the term:');
    document.write('</TD>');
    document.write('<TD>');
    document.write('<INPUT TYPE=text NAME="term" SIZE=20>');
    document.write('</TD>');

    document.write('</TR>');

    document.write('</TABLE>');

    document.write('<HR>');

    document.write('<INPUT TYPE=button NAME="search" VALUE="Start Search"
onClick="doSearch(this.form.number.selectedIndex + 1)">');

}

</SCRIPT>

</HEAD>

<BODY BGCOLOR="cornsilk" TEXT="#020A33">

<DIV ALIGN=CENTER>

<FORM NAME="search">

<H1>Search the Web</H1>
<HR>

<SCRIPT LANGUAGE="JavaScript">
displayMenus();
</SCRIPT>

</FORM>

</BODY>
```

The source code for the control button document is as follows:

```
<HEAD>

<TITLE>JavaScript Search Engine</TITLE>
```

```
</HEAD>

<BODY BGCOLOR=black TEXT=white>
<FORM NAME="controls">
<DIV ALIGN=CENTER>
<INPUT TYPE=button VALUE="New Search" onClick="parent.opener.focus()">
</DIV>
</FORM>
</BODY>
```

The Interface form

The first piece of the script to examine is the form providing the user interface.

The form's main controls are drop-down select lists, defined using the `<SELECT>` and `<OPTION>` tags, plus a text field for the search term and a button to execute the search.

The menu itself is built by calling `displayMenus()`, which produces results similar to those shown in Figure 19.1. This function is discussed later in this chapter.

FIGURE 19.1.

The main menu of the application.

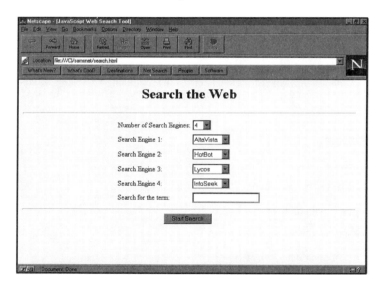

Two event handlers provide the menu's interactivity. The `onChange` event handler in the first menu (Number of Search Engines), adjusts the other menus according to the number selected by the user. The `onClick` event handler for the button calls the `doSearch()` function to execute the search.

Configuring the Search Engines

The first part of the script is where the number, names, and URLs of the search engines to use are configured. The process is simple—an array called `url` needs to be created. Each entry in the array is an instance of the urlObj object defined by the function of the same name. Each of these objects has two properties: url, which indicates how to call the search engine, and title, which provides the name to display for the given search engine in the menus.

Each of the provided URLs should be coded so that simply concatenating a single search term to the end of the URL creates a valid URL for the given search engine.

The property url.length is used throughout the script when the number of search engines is required for processing.

The displayMenus() Function

This function displays the search form based on the number of entries in the url array.

First, a select menu from which the user can choose the number of search engines to search is built by including one <OPTION> tag for the total number of entries in url. This is done by a for loop iterating from zero to the value of url.length.

Next, a separate select menu is built for each entry in the url array. For instance, if url contains four entries, then you want to build four select menus, and so on.

Each menu displays the titles of all the search engines specified in the url array. Each menu, however, has a different search engine selected by default.

This is done using a conditional operator to ensure that in the first menu the first search engine is selected, while in the second menu the second entry is selected, and so on.

Finally, a text field and a button are output by the function, completing the form.

The changeNumber() Function

The changeNumber() function is called when the user changes the number of search engines selected in the first drop-down select menu.

The function is called by the onChange event handler of the menu and takes one argument: one greater than the index number of the entry selected in the menu. A value one greater than the index is passed because if the user chooses three search engines, then the index is two because the indexes start at zero.

The function itself has two roles: It has to correctly display the number of search engine menus specified by the user's choice and then it has to clear the remaining menus to an unavailable state, like the one shown in Figure 19.2.

The first step involves a for loop that iterates from one to the number selected by the user. For each of these iterations, the appropriate menu in the form is redefined to display all the URLs in the url array. The only caveat is that if the menu was not unavailable before calling changeNumber (in other words, it was an active menu), then the user's previous selection should not be removed. If the menu was previously unavailable, then the default selection is displayed.

FIGURE 19.2.

*When a menu is not
available, all its entries are
changed to unavailable.*

The actual process is accomplished by assigning the titles of the URLs to each of the options in the selection list. To do this, the URLs are assigned to the text properties of these options. The selected property of the appropriate option is set to true to force it to be the default selection.

Next, another for loop iterates from the next menu to the last—those that should be unavailable—and sets all the options of each menu to an unavailable state by assigning "Unavailable" to the text properties of those options.

The doSearch() Function

This function is called when the user clicks the Start Search button in the main search form. It takes one argument: one greater than the index of the number of the search engine selected by the user in the first drop-down menu.

The function opens a new window and opens a frameset in it with one frame for each of the search engines, plus an extra frame for a control button.

The frames are in rows, with the top frame taking 15 percent of the available window space and holding the control button. The search engines evenly share the remaining 85 percent of the window space. So, the first step is to define the frame size for each of the search engine frames by dividing 85 by the number of search engines being used and dropping the values after the decimal point using Math.floor().

After this step, a window is opened, and the frameset is defined with the correct number of rows using a for loop to ensure the correct number of entries appear in the value of the ROWS attribute.

Next, the file `control.html`, which contains the control button, is assigned to the first frame and a `for` loop is used to assign the correct search engine URL to each of the subsequent frames.

This is accomplished by getting the index number of the selected entry in each of the active menus and combining the URL at that index in the `url` array with the user's search term.

Finally, after the frameset has been built and the document stream is closed, focus is given to the window by calling the window's `focus()` method to ensure that the window is at the front.

This produces results like those shown in Figure 19.3.

FIGURE 19.3.
The search results window.

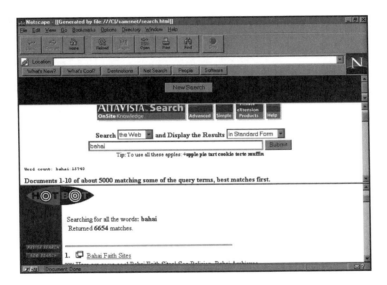

The Control Button

The control button provided in the search results page offers a one-click way to bring the main search form window to the front.

This is accomplished by an event handler for the button that calls the `focus()` method of the window object specified by `parent.opener`. The `opener` property is the object for the window containing the script that opened the current window (in this case, the main search form window).

Summary

In this chapter you learned how to implement a simpler application than those introduced in the two previous chapters.

Still, this simple application demonstrates how a small script, effectively used, can provide a useful and functional application.

In this case, three simple functions and two HTML files created a multi-window interface to any number of search engines. After all, there's no reason why the `url` array can't be defined to include 10 or even 20 search engines rather than the four used throughout this chapter.

The next chapter looks at a fourth application. A client-server application will be developed using server JavaScript running on a LiveWire-based system.

Chapter 20, "Creating a Spreadsheet in JavaScript," will use server JavaScript to enable a user to create a personalized home page that the user can configure and that persists between sessions.

20

Creating a Spreadsheet in JavaScript

by Arman Danesh

In this chapter, you are going to apply what you have learned to developing another application—a general-purpose spreadsheet.

Using forms and cookies, you will create a general-purpose spreadsheet that retains its formulas between sessions.

The Specifications

The spreadsheet has several basic requirements:

- It should have a reasonable number of fields—not so many that users with small displays will have trouble, but not so few as to be less than useful. A good number appears to be roughly 100.
- The columns and rows should be numbered—one with numerals and one with letters.
- Users should be able to create formulas, or expressions, for any of the fields that use values from other fields to calculate their own values.
- Formulas should be able to include mathematical operators, as well as any of the methods of the `Math` object. Basically, any legal JavaScript mathematical expression should be acceptable.
- Users should be able to change or delete any expression.
- Expressions should be saved between sessions so that users can come back and continue using their spreadsheets.

What You Need to Do

In order to implement a spreadsheet with these requirements, you need to do several things before you start writing the script.

First, you need to decide the structure of expressions, how to store expressions, and how to handle changes to information in the spreadsheet.

The obvious choice for saving expressions is using cookies, and Bill Dortch's functions are used to achieve this (these were mentioned when cookies were discussed in Chapter 9, "Using Cookies"). Each function should be stored in a cookie named by the field it is attached to in the spreadsheet.

For instance, if an expression is created for field A6, then a cookie named A6 should be created with the expression stored as a string for the value of the cookie. An expiry date one year in the future is used to ensure that cookies are available between sessions.

Of course, you're limited by the number of cookies that can be stored for a given page and need to keep track of them so you don't accidentally delete important expressions by enabling the user to add too many expressions. This can be accomplished by using one cookie as a counter to keep track of how many expressions have been created so far on the page.

The syntax for expressions is simple: the value of another field can be referenced simply by using the field's name followed by a semicolon. So, the expression A1; * B7; multiplies the value in field A1 by the value in field B7.

Every time the value of a form field is changed, all expressions are reevaluated. Likewise, if the definition of an expression is changed, a new expression is created, or an expression is deleted, all expressions need to be re-evaluated because the change could potentially affect any of the formulas. Listing 20.1 contains the script for the program.

Listing 20.1. A general-purpose spreadsheet.

```
<HTML>

<HEAD>
<TITLE>Chapter 12</TITLE>

<SCRIPT LANGUAGE="JavaScript">
<!-- HIDE FROM OTHER BROWSERS
//
//   cookie Functions - Second Helping   (21-Jan-96)
//   Written by:  Bill Dortch, hIdaho Design <bdortch@netw.com>
//   The following functions are released to the public domain.

//
// "Internal" function to return the decoded value of a cookie
//
function getCookieVal (offset) {
  var endstr = document.cookie.indexOf (";", offset);
  if (endstr == -1)
    endstr = document.cookie.length;
  return unescape(document.cookie.substring(offset, endstr));
}

//
//  Function to return the value of the cookie specified by "name".
//
function GetCookie (name) {
  var arg = name + "=";
  var alen = arg.length;
  var clen = document.cookie.length;
  var i = 0;
  while (i < clen) {
    var j = i + alen;
    if (document.cookie.substring(i, j) == arg)
      return getCookieVal (j);
    i = document.cookie.indexOf(" ", i) + 1;
    if (i == 0) break;
  }
  return null;
}

//
//  Function to create or update a cookie.
//
```

continues

Listing 20.1. continued

```
function SetCookie (name, value) {
  var argv = SetCookie.arguments;
  var argc = SetCookie.arguments.length;
  var expires = (argc > 2) ? argv[2] : null;
  var path = (argc > 3) ? argv[3] : null;
  var domain = (argc > 4) ? argv[4] : null;
  var secure = (argc > 5) ? argv[5] : false;
  document.cookie = name + "=" + escape (value) +
    ((expires == null) ? "" : ("; expires=" + expires.toGMTString())) +
    ((path == null) ? "" : ("; path=" + path)) +
    ((domain == null) ? "" : ("; domain=" + domain)) +
    ((secure == true) ? "; secure" : "");
}

//  Function to delete a cookie. (Sets expiration date to current date/time)
//    name - String object containing the cookie name
//
function DeleteCookie (name) {
  var exp = new Date();
  exp.setTime (exp.getTime() - 1);  // This cookie is history
  var cval = GetCookie (name);
  document.cookie = name + "=" + cval + "; expires=" + exp.toGMTString();
}

// END OF COOKIE FUNCTIONS

// SEARCH AND REPLACE FUNCTIONS
//
// SET UP ARGUMENTS FOR FUNCTION CALLS
//
var caseSensitive = true;
var notCaseSensitive = false;
var wholeWords = true;
var anySubstring = false;


// SEARCH FOR A TERM IN A TARGET STRING
//
// search(targetString,searchTerm,caseSensitive,wordOrSubstring)
//
// where caseSenstive is a boolean value and wordOrSubstring is a boolean
// value and true means whole words, false means substrings
//
function search(target,term,caseSens,wordOnly) {

  var ind = 0;
  var next = 0;

  if (!caseSens) {
    term = term.toLowerCase();
    target = target.toLowerCase();
  }

  while ((ind = target.indexOf(term,next)) >= 0) {
    if (wordOnly) {
      var before = ind - 1;
      var after = ind + term.length;
```

```
      if (!(space(target.charAt(before)) && space(target.charAt(after)))) {
        next = ind + term.length;
        continue;
      }
    }
    return true;
  }

  return false;

}

// SEARCH FOR A TERM IN A TARGET STRING AND REPLACE IT
//
// replace(targetString,oldTerm,newTerm,caseSensitive,wordOrSubstring)
//
// where caseSenstive is a boolean value and wordOrSubstring is a boolean
// value and true means whole words, false means substrings
//
function replace(target,oldTerm,newTerm,caseSens,wordOnly) {

  var work = target;
  var ind = 0;
  var next = 0;

  if (!caseSens) {
    oldTerm = oldTerm.toLowerCase();
    work = target.toLowerCase();
  }

  while ((ind = work.indexOf(oldTerm,next)) >= 0) {
    if (wordOnly) {
      var before = ind - 1;
      var after = ind + oldTerm.length;
      if (!(space(work.charAt(before)) && space(work.charAt(after)))) {
        next = ind + oldTerm.length;
        continue;
      }
    }
    target = target.substring(0,ind) + newTerm +
➥target.substring(ind+oldTerm.length,target.length);
    work = work.substring(0,ind) + newTerm +
➥work.substring(ind+oldTerm.length,work.length);
next = ind + newTerm.length;
    if (next >= work.length) { break; }
  }

  return target;

}

// CHECK IF A CHARACTER IS A WORD BREAK AND RETURN A BOOLEAN VALUE
//
function space(check) {

  var space = " .,/<>?!`';:@#$%^&*()=-¦[]{}" + '"' + "\\\n\t";

  for (var i = 0; i < space.length; i++)
```

Listing 20.1. continued

```
      if (check == space.charAt(i)) { return true; }

   if (check == "") { return true; }
   if (check == null) { return true; }

   return false;

}

// END OF SEARCH AND REPLACE FUNCTIONS

// MAIN BODY OF SCRIPT
//
// Set up global variables
//
var width = 8;
var height = 12;
var letters = "ABCDEFGHIJKLMNOPQRSTUVWXYZ";

// Set up Expiry Date for cookies
//
var expiryDate = new Date();
expiryDate.setTime(expiryDate.getTime() + 365*24*60*60*1000);
var deleteExpiry = new Date();
deleteExpiry.setTime(deleteExpiry.getTime() - 1);

// Function to calculate the spreadsheet
//
function calculate(form) {

   var expField = "";
   var expression = "";

   // Check each field for an expression and if there is one, evaluate it
   for (var x = 0; x < width; x ++) {
     for (var y = 1; y <= height; y ++) {
       expField = letters.charAt(x) + y;
       if ((expression = GetCookie(expField)) != null)
 form[expField.value = evaluateExp(form,expression);
     }
   }

}

// Function to evaluate an expression
//
function evaluateExp(form,expression) {

   var column = "";
   var index = 0;
   var nextExpField;
   var nextExpression = "";
   var nextResult = "";

   // Scan the expression for field names
   for (var x = 0; x < width; x ++) {
     column = letters.charAt(x);
     index = 0;
```

```
    index = expression.indexOf(column,index);


    // If we find a field name, evaluate it
    while(index >= 0) {

        // Check if the field has an expression associated with it
        nextExpField = expression.substring(index,expression.indexOf(";",index));

        // If there is an expression, evaluate--
➡otherwise grab the value of the field
if ((nextExpression = GetCookie(nextExpField)) != null) {
        nextResult = evaluateExp(form,nextExpression);
        } else {
 nextResult = form[nextExpField.value;
        if ((nextResult == "") || (nextResult == null))
           nextResult = "0";
        }

        // Replace the field name with the result
        nextExpField = nextExpField + ";";
        nextResult = "(" + nextResult + ")";
        expression = replace(expression,nextExpField,nextResult,
➡notCaseSensitive,anySubstring);

        // Check if we have reached the end of the expression
        index = index + nextResult.length;
        if (index >= expression.length - 1) { break; }

        // If not, search for another field name
        index = expression.indexOf(column,index);
    }
  }

  // Evaluate the expression
  with (Math) {
    var result = eval(expression);
  }

  // Return the result
  return result;

}

// Function to save an expression
//
function saveExp(form) {

  var numExp = GetCookie("numExpressions");

  // Check the number of saved expressions
  if (numExp == "19") {
    alert("Too many expressions. Delete One first");
  } else {

    // If there is room, save the expression and update
➡the number of expressions
SetCookie(form.expField.value,form.expression.value,expiryDate);
```

continues

Listing 20.1. continued

```
    numExp = parseInt(numExp) + 1;
    SetCookie("numExpressions",numExp,expiryDate);

    // Recalculate the spreadsheet
    calculate(document.spreadsheet);

    alert("Expession for field " + form.expField.value + " is saved.");

  }

}

// Function to delete an expression
//
function deleteExp(form) {

  var numExp = GetCookie("numExpressions");
  var expression = GetCookie(form.expField.value);

  // Check if there is an expression to delete for the field
  if (expression != null) {

    // There is, so set the expiry date
    SetCookie(form.expField.value,"",deleteExpiry);
    numExp = parseInt(numExp) - 1;
    SetCookie("numExpressions",numExp,expiryDate);

    // Update the field and recalculate the spreadsheet
    document.spreadsheet[form.expField.value].value = "";
    calculate(document.spreadsheet);

    alert("Expession for field " + form.expField.value + " is removed.");

  }

}

// Function to build form
//
function buildForm() {

  var numExp = 0;

  // Check if this is a new spreadsheet. If it is,
➥set the number of expressions to zero
  if ((numExp = GetCookie("numExpressions")) == null) {
    SetCookie("numExpressions",0,expiryDate);
  }

  // Build row header
  document.write("<TR><TD></TD>");
  for (var x = 0; x < width; x++) {
    document.write("<TD><DIV ALIGN=CENTER>" +
➥letters.charAt(x) + "</DIV></TD>");
}
  document.write("</TR>");

  // Build each field -- each is the same, with a different name
```

```
  for (var y = 1; y <= height; y++) {
    document.write("<TR><TD>" + y + "</TD>");
    for (var x = 0; x < width; x++) {
      document.write('<TD><INPUT TYPE=text SIZE=10 NAME="' +
➥letters.charAt(x) + y + '" onChange="calculate(this.form);"></TD>');
//SetCookie(letters.charAt(x) + y,"",deleteExpiry);
    }
    document.write("</TR>");
  }

}

// STOP HIDING -->
</SCRIPT>

</HEAD>

<BODY BGCOLOR="iceblue">

<CENTER>

<FORM METHOD=POST NAME="spreadsheet">
<TABLE BORDER=0>

<SCRIPT LANGUAGE="JavaScript">
<!- HIDE FROM OTHER BROWSERS

buildForm();

// STOP HIDING -->
</SCRIPT>

</TABLE>
</FORM>
<HR>

<FORM METHOD=POST>
<TABLE BORDER=1>

<TR>
<TD><DIV ALIGN=CENTER>Field Name</DIV></TD>
<TD><DIV ALIGN=CENTER>Expression</DIV></TD>
</TR>

<TR>
<TD><DIV ALIGN=CENTER><INPUT TYPE=text SIZE=10 NAME="expField"
  onChange="var exp = GetCookie(this.value); this.form.expression.value =
➥(exp == null) ? '' : exp;"></DIV></TD>
<TD><DIV ALIGN=CENTER><INPUT TYPE=text SIZE=50 NAME="expression"></DIV></TD>
<TD><DIV ALIGN=CENTER><INPUT TYPE=button VALUE="Apply"
➥onClick="saveExp(this.form);"></DIV></TD>
<TD><DIV ALIGN=CENTER><INPUT TYPE=button VALUE="Delete"
➥onClick="deleteExp(this.form);"></DIV></TD>
</TR>

</TABLE>
</FORM>
</CENTER>
```

continues

Listing 20.1. continued

```
</BODY>
```

```
</HTML>
```

The results of this script look like those shown in Figures 20.1 and 20.2.

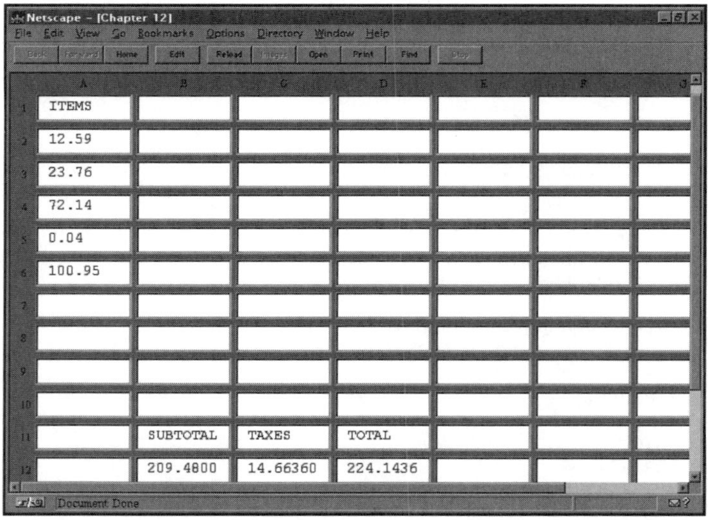

FIGURE 20.1.

Building complex spreadsheets using mathematical expressions.

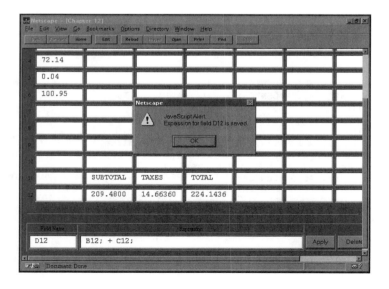

FIGURE 20.2.

The small form at the bottom can be used to create, update, and delete expressions.

The script uses functions to create the spreadsheet application. In addition, Bill Dortch's cookie functions and the search and replace functions provided for reference purposes in Chapter 17, "A Language-Switching Interface," have been included.

Using these, the `calculate()`, `evaluateExp()`, `saveExp()`, `deleteExp()`, and `buildForm()` functions do everything needed.

Before looking at the functions, the body of the HTML document needs to be looked at to understand the different interface components accessible to the user.

The document consists of two forms: the spreadsheet and the expression update form. The spreadsheet form is built dynamically by a small script that calls `buildForm()`. An HTML table is used to create a nicely formatted spreadsheet layout.

The second form also is in a table and is used to create, update, or delete expressions. It contains two text entry fields—one for the field name and one for the expression—and two buttons, Apply and Delete, which invoke the `saveExp()` and `deleteExp()` functions respectively (shown in Figure 20.2).

In addition, when the value of the `expField` field changes, the script checks if there is a stored cookie for that field, and if there is, displays the expression in the `expression` field. Otherwise, you store an empty string in the `expression` field.

Setting Up the Global Variables

In addition to the functions, several global variables are used to keep track of information throughout the script:

```
var width = 8;
var height = 12;
var letters = " ABCDEFGHIJKLMNOPQRSTUVWXYZ ";

// Set up Expiry Date for cookies
//
var expiryDate = new Date();
expiryDate.setTime(expiryDate.getTime() + 365*24*60*60*1000);
var deleteExpiry = new Date();
deleteExpiry.setTime(deleteExpiry.getTime() - 1);
```

The `width` and `height` variables define the size of the spreadsheet. Eight columns and 12 rows fit well on an 800×600 pixel display. Only notebook users with 640×480 displays may need a smaller spreadsheet.

The `letters` string contains the letters of the alphabet that are used to name the columns of the form. Each letter is extracted by its index (the column number minus one) when it is needed. You should include the whole alphabet because this gives you the flexibility to increase the number of columns in the form simply by increasing the value of `width`.

expiryDate and deleteExpiry are the Date objects used for setting and deleting the cookies. expiryDate is set to one year from the current date, and deleteExpiry is set to one millisecond before the current time.

The calculate() Function

The calculate() function is probably the main function of the script. This function is called every time you want to reevaluate the form when a value changes or an expression is added, updated, or deleted. The function takes one argument: the form object for the spreadsheet form.

The structure of the function is quite simple. It uses two nested for loops: one for each column using variable x and one for each row using variable y. For each combination of row and column you build the field name with letters.charAt(x) + y. Notice that the first for statement loops from zero to one less than the number of columns, which means x is the index of the appropriate letter in the letters string.

You then check if there is an expression stored in the cookie with the name of the field. The result of the GetCookie() call is stored in the variable expression and compared null. If it is not null, you have an expression, and it is evaluated by calling evaluateExp(). evaluateExp() returns the evaluated expression, and this can be directly stored in the appropriate field in the form.

The evaluateExp() Function

This is, perhaps, the most heavily used function in the script (with the exception of the cookie functions).

Given two arguments—the form object for the spreadsheet and the expression to be evaluated—the evaluateExp() function returns the value of the expression based on the current content of the spreadsheet.

You start with a for loop which iterates through each of the letters that name the columns. Inside that loop, a check is made to see whether there is an occurrence of the letter in the expression. If there is, it means that there is a reference to a field in that column that you need to handle.

Next, a check for an occurrence of the letter is made by using indexOf() and storing the results in index.

The while loop executes only when a field for the current column has been found—that is, index must be greater than zero.

Inside the loop, you get the field name by using substring() from index to the first occurrence of a semicolon (;), which marks the end of the field name. Given this value, you check whether there is an expression for that field and store the expression in nextExpression. If there is an expression, you call evaluateExp() recursively to get the value for that expression and store the result in nextResult.

If there's no expression for the field, you get the value of nextResult directly from the form. If this value is a null value or an empty string, you change nextResult to zero.

Once you have a value for nextResult, you can replace the occurrence of the field in the expression with the value of nextResult, using the replace() function. You also should replace the semicolon after the field name and add parentheses to nextResult so that when the expression is evaluated, the value of nextResult is correctly evaluated and not affected by the rules of operator precedence.

Once the expression is evaluated, you check whether you have reached the end of the expression by updating index to the character after the newly replaced value and compare this to the index of the last character in the expression.

If the end of the string hasn't been reached, a check for another occurrence of the current letter is made with indexOf() and you are return to the condition at the top of the while loop.

Once the for loop is complete, you're ready to evaluate the expression. with(Math) is used so that any methods from the Math object that occurred in the expression don't require the presence of the Math prefix.

Finally, the expression is evaluated using the eval() statement.

The saveExp() Function

The saveExp() function saves an expression in a cookie when the user clicks the Apply button in the lower form, which is used to create and manipulate expressions. The function takes the form object for the expression as an argument.

The function starts by checking the number of expressions that have already been saved. If the number is already 19, the limit, then the user is informed that she needs to delete another expression if she wants to save this one.

If there is room to save the expression, then it is saved, getting the name of the cookie directly from the appropriate field in the form and getting the expression in the same way. The number of expressions is updated by one and the cookie containing this value is updated (notice the use of parseInt() to change the string returned by GetCookie() into an integer).

Finally, the spreadsheet is recalculated by calling calculate() and then informs the user that the expression has been saved.

The deleteExp() Function

Just as saveExp() saved an expression, deleteExp() deletes the expression indicated by a field name in the form. Again, it takes the form object as an expression and is invoked when the user clicks on the Delete button.

It starts by checking whether there is an expression stored in that field. If there is, it saves a new cookie with the same name but uses `deleteExpiry` as the expiry date. It also decreases the number of expressions by one and updates the cookie containing the number.

Once the cookie has been deleted, the spreadsheet is recalculated and the user is informed that the task is done in the same way as the `saveExp()` function.

The `buildForm()` Function

The `buildForm()` function is the last function in Listing 12.1. It is called from inside the body of the HTML file and builds the HTML of the spreadsheet form, which is displayed in a table.

Using JavaScript to dynamically build the table is the best approach, because each field is repetitive and because you want to be able to build the spreadsheet table to match the `width` and `height` variables if they get changed.

You start determining whether this is a new spreadsheet by checking if there is any value stored in the cookie holding the number of expressions. If there isn't a value, save a zero value there to initialize the spreadsheet.

Next, you build the header row for the table that contains a blank field at the start, and then a field for each column with the appropriate letter centered in the field. This is done with a `for` loop that extracts each letter from the `letters` string.

Once the table header is output, two nested `for` loops are used to build each row of the table with the number in the first field and then blank text input fields in the rest of the table cells in the row.

The names of the text entry fields are created using `letters.charAt(x) + y`.

Beyond the Basic Script

The basic script works, but it has several limitations, including the following:

- **Efficiency**—Most users, especially those on Windows platforms, will notice that your script is a little slow and that actions create a noticeable lag to update the spreadsheet.
- **Error checking**—This script doesn't check that the syntax of the expressions is valid. It doesn't check that fields contain numeric values when it evaluates expressions and doesn't check for circular expressions (expressions that depend on each other to evaluate and cause infinite recursion).
- **Title**—If you tried to create a spreadsheet including titles, you will notice that when you come back to the spreadsheet, the values of these title fields are lost.

There are several features you could add to the spreadsheet to make it more useful:

- **Ranges**—Most spreadsheets enable formulas to include ranges in their expressions. (For instance, A1; ... A5; might be the total of the values in all fields from A1 to A5.)
- **Clear**—This application provides no easy way for the user to clear all the field values and all the expressions and start from scratch.

Improving Efficiency

The main efficiency bottleneck is in the `calculate()` function. In this function, two nested `for` loops are used to iterate through all 96 fields in the form. For each, `GetCookie()` is called to check whether the field has an expression, and if it does, `evaluateExp()` is called.

This is inefficient, however. You end up calling `GetCookie()` for each empty field in the form, which, in the example, means at least 77 unneeded calls to `GetCookie()` each time a value in the form is changed.

If you knew which fields have expressions without checking each field in the spreadsheet, you could avoid all these unnecessary calls to `GetCookie()`.

To do this, you can take one more of the cookies and use it to store a list of fields that contain expressions. For instance, a semicolon delimited list such as A1;B11;C10; could be used.

In order to do this, you need to make changes to `calculate()`, `saveExp()`, and `deleteExp()`.

In the `calculate()` function, make a fundamental change to the logic of the function:

```
function calculate(form) {

  var index = 0;
  var next = 0;
  var expField = "";
  var expression = "";
  var fieldList = GetCookie("fieldList");

  if (fieldList != null) {
    while (index != fieldList.length) {
      next = fieldList.indexOf(";",index);
      expField = fieldList.substring(index,next);
      expression = GetCookie(expField);
      form[expField].value = evaluateExp(form,expression);
      index = next + 1;
    }
  }

}
```

You get the field list from the `fieldList` cookie. If it's `null`, there are no expressions and no evaluation is needed. Otherwise, a `while` loop is entered, continuing until the index reaches the end of the `fieldList` string.

Inside the `while` loop, you scan for the next semicolon using `indexOf()` and extract the substring from `index` to the character before the semicolon. This value is the field name of an expression which you then get from the cookie, evaluate, and store in `form[expField].value`.

`index` is then incremented to the character after the semicolon.

The `saveExp()` and `deleteExp()` functions both have similar changes. In the `saveExp()` function, you need to add a few lines to handle the extra cookie containing the field list, as well as change the maximum number of cookies to 18 to make room for the `fieldList` cookie.

Updating the `fieldList` cookie is handled by first checking if there is a list already. If not, the list is simply created with the current field name. If there is a list, the field name is removed from the list by replacing it with an empty string and then adding it back in. In this way, you don't get double occurrences of any field name in the list.

```
function saveExp(form) {

  var expField = form.expField.value;
  var fieldList = GetCookie("fieldList");
  var numExp = GetCookie("numExpressions");

  // Check the number of saved expressions
  if (numExp == "18") {
    alert("Too many expressions. Delete One first");
  } else {

    // If there is room, save the expression and
➥update the number of expressions
SetCookie(form.expField.value,form.expression.value,expiryDate);
    numExp = parseInt(numExp) + 1;
    SetCookie("numExpressions",numExp,expiryDate);
    expField += ";"
    if (fieldList == null) {
      fieldList = expField;
    } else {
      fieldList = replace(fieldList,expField,"",notCaseSensitive,anySubstring);
      fieldList += expField;
    }
    SetCookie("fieldList",fieldList,expiryDate);

    // Recalculate the spreadsheet
    calculate(document.spreadsheet);

    alert("Expession for field " + form.expField.value + " is saved.");

  }

}
```

The `deleteExp()` function works in a similar manner:

```
function deleteExp(form) {

  var fieldList = GetCookie("fieldList");
  var expField = form.expField.value;
  var numExp = GetCookie("numExpressions");
  var expression = GetCookie(form.expField.value);

  // Check if there is an expression to delete for the field
  if (expression != null) {
```

```
        // There is, so set the expiry date
        SetCookie(form.expField.value,"",deleteExpiry);
        numExp = parseInt(numExp) - 1;
        SetCookie("numExpressions",numExp,expiryDate);
        expField += ";";
        fieldList = replace(fieldList,expField,"",notCaseSensitive,anySubstring);
        SetCookie("fieldList",fieldList,expiryDate);

        // Update the field and recalculate the spreadsheet
        document.spreadsheet[form.expField.value].value = "";
        calculate(document.spreadsheet);

        alert("Expression for field " + form.expField.value + " is removed.");

    }

}
```

To delete the entry from the field list and update the cookie, the `replace()` function is used to delete the name and replace it with an empty string before updating the `fieldList` cookie.

Adding Title Fields

In order to save title fields, treat them as expressions so they get saved as cookies. Have the first character of the title expression be a double-quote character.

This enables you to simply update the `evaluateExp()` function to return the rest of the string when it encounters the following syntax:

```
function evaluateExp(form,expression) {

  var column = "";
  var index = 0;
  var nextExpField;
  var nextExpression = "";
  var nextResult = "";

  if (expression.charAt(0) == '"') {
    return(expression.substring(1,expression.length));
  }

  // Scan the expression for field names
  for (var x = 0; x < width; x ++) {
    column = letters.charAt(x);
    index = 0;
    index = expression.indexOf(column,index);

    // If we find a field name, evaluate it
    while(index >= 0) {

      // Check if the field has an expression associated with it
      nextExpField = expression.substring(index,expression.indexOf(";",index));

      // If there is an expression, evaluate.
➥Otherwise grab the value of the field
if ((nextExpression = GetCookie(nextExpField)) != null) {
```

```
      nextResult = evaluateExp(form,nextExpression);
    } else {
      nextResult = form[nextExpField].value;
      if ((nextResult == "") || (nextResult == null))
        nextResult = "0";
    }

    // Replace the field name with the result
    nextExpField = nextExpField + ";";
    nextResult = "(" + nextResult + ")";
    expression = replace(expression,nextExpField,
➥nextResult,notCaseSensitive,anySubstring);

    // Check if we have reached the end of the expression
    index = index + nextResult.length;
    if (index >= expression.length - 1) { break; }

    // If not, search for another field name
    index = expression.indexOf(column,index);
    }
  }

  // Evaluate the expression
  with (Math) {
    var result = eval(expression);
  }

  // Return the result
  return result;

}
```

Only one step has been added to the `evaluateExp()` function. Before evaluating the expression as a mathematical expression, the first character is checked for a double quotation mark. If one is found, the rest of the `expression` string is returned.

Checking for Errors

By way of example, some very basic error checking is performed.

There are two places you need to check for errors. First, you need to make sure that the user has entered a legitimate expression in the expression field.

Here, if the user has entered a mathematical expression, you check basic syntax—that is, that the field names use capital letters and end with a semicolon and also that there isn't a circular expression.

To make the script easier to read, do this in a separate function and call the function from the main `if` statement in `saveExp()`:

```
if (numExp == "18") {
  alert("Too many expressions. Delete One first");
} else {

  if (!checkExp(form.expression.value,expField + ";")) { return }
```

```
        // If there is room, save the expression and
➡update the number of expressions
SetCookie(form.expField.value,form.expression.value,expiryDate);
        numExp = parseInt(numExp) + 1;
        SetCookie("numExpressions",numExp,expiryDate);
        expField += ";"
        if (fieldList == null) {
          fieldList = expField;
        } else {
          fieldList = replace(fieldList,expField,"",notCaseSensitive,anySubstring);
          fieldList += expField;
        }
        SetCookie("fieldList",fieldList,expiryDate);

        // Recalculate the spreadsheet
        calculate(document.spreadsheet);

        alert("Expession for field " + form.expField.value + " is saved.");

    }
```

The line

```
if (!checkExp(form.expression.value,expField + ";")) { return }
```

calls checkExp(), which checks the expression in question and, if it finds an error, alerts the user, and returns false. Otherwise, it returns true. By checking whether you get a false value from checkExp(), you are able to exit out of the function before saving the new expression.

The main work of error checking takes place in the function checkExp():

```
function checkExp(expression,expField) {

  var index =0;
  var next = 0;
  var checkNum = 0;
  var otherExpField = ""
  var otherExp = "";
  var lowerColumn = ""

  if (expression.charAt(0) == '"') { return true; }

  for (var x = 0; x < width; x++) {
    index =0;
    column = letters.charAt(x);
    lowerColumn = column.toLowerCase();

    // Check for field in this column
    index = expression.indexOf(column,0);
    if (index < 0) {
      index = expression.indexOf(lowerColumn,0);
    }

    // If we have a reference to this column, check the syntax
    while (index >= 0) {

      next = index + 1;

      // Check if letter is followed by a number,
```

```
➥if not assume it is a Math method
checkNum = parseInt(expression.charAt(next));
        if ((checkNum == 0) && (expression.charAt(next) != "0") &&
➥(expression.charAt(index) == lowerColumn)) {
if (next + 1 == expression.length) { break; }
          index = expression.indexOf(column,next+1);
          if (index < 0) {
            index = expression.indexOf(lowerColumn,next+1);
          }
          continue;
        }

        // It is not a Math method so check that the letter was uppercase
        if (expression.charAt(index) == lowerColumn) {
          alert("Field names must use uppercase letters.");
          return false;
        }

        // The letter was uppercase, so check that we have
➥only numbers followed by a semicolon
while(expression.charAt(++next) != ";") {
          checkNum = parseInt(expression.charAt(next));
          if ((checkNum == 0) && (expression.charAt(next) != "0")) {
            alert("Field name format is incorrect (should be like A12; or B9;).");
            return false;
          }
          if (next == expression.length - 1) {
            alert("Field name format is incorrect (should be like A12; or B9;).");
            return false;
          }
        }

        otherExpField = expression.substring(index,next);

        // Check for a circular expression
        otherExp = GetCookie(otherExpField);
        if (otherExp != null) {
          if (search(otherExp,expField,caseSensitive,anySubstring)) {
            alert("You have created a circular expression
➥with field " + otherExpField + ".");
return false;
          }
        }

        if (next + 1 == expression.length) { break; }

        index = expression.indexOf(column,next+1);
        if (index < 0) {
          index = expression.indexOf(lowerColumn,next+1);
        }

    }

  }

  return true;

}
```

This function is divided into several steps. It starts by checking whether you have a string expression (which starts with a double quotation mark). If you do, it returns `true`.

If you don't have a string expression, then you need to check the mathematical expression according to the criteria previously outlined. To do this, a `for` loop is used, which loops through each of the letters that are column names and performs a series of checks based on that column.

You first assign the column name to the variable `column`. The lowercase version of the same letter also is assigned to `lowerColumn` because you also will need to deal with lowercase versions of the same letter.

You then check for an occurrence of either the uppercase or lowercase letter, using `indexOf()`, and assign the index to the variable `index`. You then enter a `while` loop that performs the main checking. The condition of the `while` loop means it will repeat as long as it continues to find instances of the letter.

The first check in the `while` loop is to see if the character immediately following the letter is a number. If it isn't a number—which would make it the start of a field reference—assume it refers to a method or property from the `Math` object.

> **NOTE**
>
> This is not a perfect assumption. To correctly check, you would need to assure that whatever character string you find is actually part of the `Math` object. This could be done using the `typeof` operator.

This check is performed by passing the character through `parseInt()` and then checking if the result is zero. If it is, a check is made to see if the actual character is zero and make sure that the letter is lowercase (because all the `Math` methods start with lowercase letters).

Having passed all these conditions, an assumption is made that this is a `Math` method, and you scan forward for another occurrence of the letter then return to the top of the loop with the `continue` statement.

If you get by the first `if` statement, you know you have a letter followed by a number, which means the user is trying to reference a field name. The first thing you do is check if the user is using an uppercase letter; if not, the user is alerted and a `false` value is returned.

Next, you move forward through the expression, checking each character. If you find a non-numeric character before you reach a semicolon, then you know that you have an invalid reference, so you alert the user and return a `false` value. Likewise, if you reach the end of the expression without hitting a semicolon, you also know you have an incorrect form and do the same thing.

The last check performed is to look for a circular expression. The field name that you are currently looking at is extracted and used to get any existing expression for that field. If the field has an expression, it is searched using search() to see if the expression refers back to the field to which you are trying to add an expression. If it does, you have a circular expression. The user is informed and a false value is returned again.

For instance, if the user is trying to define the expression A1-B1 in field A1, this would create a circular expression. The user needs to be informed, and the expression should not be saved.

Finally, a check is made to see if the end of the expression has been reached. If not, a search is made for another occurrence of the letter, the index is stored in index, and you're returned to the top of the while loop.

The other place that error checking needs to be performed is in the evaluateExp() function. Here, you need to make sure that the values of fields being used in expressions are numeric. This is done in the main if statement in the while loop:

```
if ((nextExpression = GetCookie(nextExpField)) != null) {
  nextResult = evaluateExp(form,nextExpression);
  if ("" + nextResult == "error") {
    return "error";
  }
} else {
  nextResult = form[nextExpField].value;
  if ((nextResult == "") || (nextResult == null)) {
    nextResult = "0";
  } else {
    // Check if this is a numeric expression
    var checkNum = parseInt(nextResult);
    if ((checkNum == 0) && (nextResult.charAt(0) != "0")) {
      return "error";
    }
  }
}
```

When you get back a value of calling evaluateExp(), a check is made to see that the result is not "error". If it is "error", "error" is simply returned back up the chain of function calls.

If you're getting a value directly from a form field and the field isn't empty, a check is performed to see whether the value is a number by applying parseInt() to the value and checking the result. If you don't have a numeric expression, "error" is returned.

Summary

In this chapter you have seen a complete, workable spreadsheet application put together using only the commands and JavaScript objects learned in this book. This demonstrates the power of JavaScript as an easy-to-use and flexible scripting language.

To help you put together the program, the complete source code of the programs is included in Listing 20.2, including all the changes you just made.

Listing 20.2. The final spreadsheet script.

```
<HTML>

<HEAD>
<TITLE>Chapter 12</TITLE>

<SCRIPT LANGUAGE="JavaScript">
<!-- HIDE FROM OTHER BROWSERS
//
//   cookie Functions - Second Helping  (21-Jan-96)
//   Written by:  Bill Dortch, hIdaho Design <bdortch@netw.com>
//   The following functions are released to the public domain.

//
// "Internal" function to return the decoded value of a cookie
//
function getCookieVal (offset) {
  var endstr = document.cookie.indexOf (";", offset);
  if (endstr == -1)
    endstr = document.cookie.length;
  return unescape(document.cookie.substring(offset, endstr));
}

//
//   Function to return the value of the cookie specified by "name".
//
function GetCookie (name) {
  var arg = name + "=";
  var alen = arg.length;
  var clen = document.cookie.length;
  var i = 0;
  while (i < clen) {
    var j = i + alen;
    if (document.cookie.substring(i, j) == arg)
      return getCookieVal (j);
    i = document.cookie.indexOf(" ", i) + 1;
    if (i == 0) break;
  }
  return null;
}

//
//   Function to create or update a cookie.
//
function SetCookie (name, value) {
  var argv = SetCookie.arguments;
  var argc = SetCookie.arguments.length;
  var expires = (argc > 2) ? argv[2] : null;
  var path = (argc > 3) ? argv[3] : null;
  var domain = (argc > 4) ? argv[4] : null;
  var secure = (argc > 5) ? argv[5] : false;
  document.cookie = name + "=" + escape (value) +
    ((expires == null) ? "" : ("; expires=" + expires.toGMTString())) +
    ((path == null) ? "" : ("; path=" + path)) +
    ((domain == null) ? "" : ("; domain=" + domain)) +
    ((secure == true) ? "; secure" : "");
}
```

continues

Listing 20.2. continued

```
//  Function to delete a cookie. (Sets expiration date to current date/time)
//    name - String object containing the cookie name
//
function DeleteCookie (name) {
  var exp = new Date();
  exp.setTime (exp.getTime() - 1);  // This cookie is history
  var cval = GetCookie (name);
  document.cookie = name + "=" + cval + "; expires=" + exp.toGMTString();
}

// END OF COOKIE FUNCTIONS

// SEARCH AND REPLACE FUNCTIONS
//
// SET UP ARGUMENTS FOR FUNCTION CALLS
//
var caseSensitive = true;
var notCaseSensitive = false;
var wholeWords = true;
var anySubstring = false;


// SEARCH FOR A TERM IN A TARGET STRING
//
// search(targetString,searchTerm,caseSensitive,wordOrSubstring)
//
// where caseSenstive is a boolean value and wordOrSubstring is a boolean
// value and true means whole words, false means substrings
//
function search(target,term,caseSens,wordOnly) {

  var ind = 0;
  var next = 0;

  if (!caseSens) {
    term = term.toLowerCase();
    target = target.toLowerCase();
  }

  while ((ind = target.indexOf(term,next)) >= 0) {
    if (wordOnly) {
      var before = ind - 1;
      var after = ind + term.length;
      if (!(space(target.charAt(before)) && space(target.charAt(after)))) {
        next = ind + term.length;
        continue;
      }
    }
    return true;
  }

  return false;

}

// SEARCH FOR A TERM IN A TARGET STRING AND REPLACE IT
//
// replace(targetString,oldTerm,newTerm,caseSensitive,wordOrSubstring)
```

```
//
// where caseSenstive is a boolean value and wordOrSubstring is a boolean
// value and true means whole words, false means substrings
//
function replace(target,oldTerm,newTerm,caseSens,wordOnly) {

  var work = target;
  var ind = 0;
  var next = 0;

  if (!caseSens) {
    oldTerm = oldTerm.toLowerCase();
    work = target.toLowerCase();
  }

  while ((ind = work.indexOf(oldTerm,next)) >= 0) {
    if (wordOnly) {
      var before = ind - 1;
      var after = ind + oldTerm.length;
      if (!(space(work.charAt(before)) && space(work.charAt(after)))) {
        next = ind + oldTerm.length;
        continue;
      }
    }
    target = target.substring(0,ind) + newTerm +
➥target.substring(ind+oldTerm.length,target.length);
work = work.substring(0,ind) + newTerm +
➥work.substring(ind+oldTerm.length,work.length);
next = ind + newTerm.length;
    if (next >= work.length) { break; }
  }

  return target;

}

// CHECK IF A CHARACTER IS A WORD BREAK AND RETURN A BOOLEAN VALUE
//
function space(check) {

  var space = " .,/<>?!`';:@#$%^&*()=-¦[]{}" + '"' + "\\\n\t";

  for (var i = 0; i < space.length; i++)
    if (check == space.charAt(i)) { return true; }

  if (check == "") { return true; }
  if (check == null) { return true; }

  return false;

}

// END OF SEARCH AND REPLACE FUNCTIONS

// MAIN BODY OF SCRIPT
//
// Set up global variables
```

continues

Listing 20.2. continued

```
//
var width = 8;
var height = 12;
var letters = "ABCDEFGHIJKLMNOPQRSTUVWXYZ";

// Set up Expiry Date for cookies
//
var expiryDate = new Date();
expiryDate.setTime(expiryDate.getTime() + 365*24*60*60*1000);
var deleteExpiry = new Date();
deleteExpiry.setTime(deleteExpiry.getTime() - 1);

// Function to calculate the spreadsheet
//
function calculate(form) {

  var index = 0;
  var next = 0;
  var expField = "";
  var expression = "";
  var fieldList = GetCookie("fieldList");

  if (fieldList != null) {
    while (index != fieldList.length) {
      next = fieldList.indexOf(";",index);
      expField = fieldList.substring(index,next);
      expression = GetCookie(expField);
      form[expField].value = evaluateExp(form,expression);
      index = next + 1;
    }
  }

}

// Function to evaluate an expression
//


function evaluateExp(form,expression) {

  var column = "";
  var index = 0;
  var nextExpField;
  var nextExpression = "";
  var nextResult = "";

  if (expression.charAt(0) == '"') {
    return(expression.substring(1,expression.length));
  }

  // Scan the expression for field names
  for (var x = 0; x < width; x ++) {
    column = letters.charAt(x);
    index = 0;
    index = expression.indexOf(column,index);

    // If we find a field name, evaluate it
```

```
  while(index >= 0) {

    // Check if the field has an expression associated with it
    nextExpField = expression.substring(index,expression.indexOf(";",index));

    // If there is an expression, evaluate--otherwise grab the value of the field
    if ((nextExpression = GetCookie(nextExpField)) != null) {
      nextResult = evaluateExp(form,nextExpression);
    } else {
      nextResult = form[nextExpField].value;
      if ((nextResult == "") || (nextResult == null))
        nextResult = "0";
    }

    // Replace the field name with the result
    nextExpField = nextExpField + ";";
    nextResult = "(" + nextResult + ")";
    expression =
replace(expression,nextExpField,nextResult,notCaseSensitive,anySubstring);
    // Check if we have reached the end of the expression
    index = index + nextResult.length;
    if (index >= expression.length - 1) { break; }

    // If not, search for another field name
    index = expression.indexOf(column,index);
  }
}

  // Evaluate the expression
  with (Math) {
    var result = eval(expression);
  }

  // Return the result
  return result;

}

// Function to save an expression
//
function saveExp(form) {

  var expField = form.expField.value;
  var fieldList = GetCookie("fieldList");
  var numExp = GetCookie("numExpressions");

  // Check the number of saved expressions
  if (numExp == "18") {
    alert("Too many expressions. Delete One first");
  } else {

    if (!checkExp(form.expression.value,expField + ";")) { return }

    // If there is room, save the expression and
➥update the number of expressions
SetCookie(form.expField.value,form.expression.value,expiryDate);
    numExp = parseInt(numExp) + 1;
```

continues

Listing 20.2. continued

```
    SetCookie("numExpressions",numExp,expiryDate);
    expField += ";"
    if (fieldList == null) {
      fieldList = expField;
    } else {
      fieldList = replace(fieldList,expField,"",notCaseSensitive,anySubstring);
      fieldList += expField;
    }
    SetCookie("fieldList",fieldList,expiryDate);

    // Recalculate the spreadsheet
    calculate(document.spreadsheet);

    alert("Expession for field " + form.expField.value + " is saved.");

  }

}

// Function to delete an expression
//
function deleteExp(form) {

  var fieldList = GetCookie("fieldList");
  var expField = form.expField.value;
  var numExp = GetCookie("numExpressions");
  var expression = GetCookie(form.expField.value);

  // Check if there is an expression to delete for the field
  if (expression != null) {

    // There is, so set the expiry date
    SetCookie(form.expField.value,"",deleteExpiry);
    numExp = parseInt(numExp) - 1;
    SetCookie("numExpressions",numExp,expiryDate);
    expField += ";";
    fieldList = replace(fieldList,expField,"",notCaseSensitive,anySubstring);
    SetCookie("fieldList",fieldList,expiryDate);

    // Update the field and recalculate the spreadsheet
    document.spreadsheet[form.expField.value].value = "";
    calculate(document.spreadsheet);

    alert("Expression for field " + form.expField.value + " is removed.");

  }

}

// Function to build form
//
function buildForm() {

  var numExp = 0;

  // Check if this is a new spreadsheet. If it is,
➥set the number of expressions to zero
if ((numExp = GetCookie("numExpressions")) == null) {
```

```
    SetCookie("numExpressions",0,expiryDate);
  }

  // Build row header
  document.write("<TR><TD></TD>");
  for (var x = 0; x < width; x++) {
    document.write("<TD><DIV ALIGN=CENTER>" +
➥letters.charAt(x) + "</DIV></TD>");
}
  document.write("</TR>");

  // Build each field — each is the same, with a different name
  for (var y = 1; y <= height; y++) {
    document.write("<TR><TD>" + y + "</TD>");
    for (var x = 0; x < width; x++) {
      document.write('<TD><INPUT TYPE=text SIZE=10 NAME="' +
➥letters.charAt(x) + y + '" onChange="calculate(this.form);"></TD>');
}
    document.write("</TR>");
  }

}


// Function check expressions
//

function checkExp(expression,expField) {

  var index =0;
  var next = 0;
  var checkNum = 0;
  var otherExpField = ""
  var otherExp = "";
  var lowerColumn = ""

  if (expression.charAt(0) == '"') { return true; }

  for (var x = 0; x < width; x++) {
    index =0;
    column = letters.charAt(x);
    lowerColumn = column.toLowerCase();

    // Check for field in this column
    index = expression.indexOf(column,0);
    if (index < 0) {
      index = expression.indexOf(lowerColumn,0);
    }

    // If we have a reference to this column, check the syntax
    while (index >= 0) {

      next = index + 1;

      // Check if letter is followed by a number, if not assume it is a Math method
      checkNum = parseInt(expression.charAt(next));
      if ((checkNum == 0) && (expression.charAt(next) != "0") &&
(expression.charAt(index) ==
```

continues

Listing 20.2. continued

```
➥lowerColumn)) {
        if (next + 1 == expression.length) { break; }
        index = expression.indexOf(column,next+1);
        if (index < 0) {
          index = expression.indexOf(lowerColumn,next+1);
        }
        continue;
      }

      // It is not a Math method so check that the letter was uppercase
      if (expression.charAt(index) == lowerColumn) {
        alert("Field names must use uppercase letters.");
        return false;
      }

      // The letter was uppercase, so check that we have only numbers followed by a
➥semicolon
      while(expression.charAt(++next) != ";") {
        checkNum = parseInt(expression.charAt(next));
        if ((checkNum == 0) && (expression.charAt(next) != "0")) {
          alert("Field name format is incorrect (should be like A12; or B9;).");
          return false;
        }
        if (next == expression.length - 1) {
          alert("Field name format is incorrect (should be like A12; or B9;).");
          return false;
        }
      }

      otherExpField = expression.substring(index,next);

      // Check for a circular expression
      otherExp = GetCookie(otherExpField);
      if (otherExp != null) {
        if (search(otherExp,expField,caseSensitive,anySubstring)) {
          alert("You have created a circular expression with field " +
➥otherExpField + ".");
          return false;
        }
      }

      if (next + 1 == expression.length) { break; }

      index = expression.indexOf(column,next+1);
      if (index < 0) {
        index = expression.indexOf(lowerColumn,next+1);
      }

    }

  }

  return true;

}

// STOP HIDING -->
</SCRIPT>
```

```
</HEAD>

<BODY BGCOLOR="iceblue">

<CENTER>

<FORM METHOD=POST NAME="spreadsheet">
<TABLE BORDER=0>

<SCRIPT LANGUAGE="JavaScript">
<!-- HIDE FROM OTHER BROWSERS

buildForm();

// STOP HIDING -->
</SCRIPT>

</TABLE>
</FORM>
<HR>

<FORM METHOD=POST>
<TABLE BORDER=1>

<TR>
<TD><DIV ALIGN=CENTER>Field Name</DIV></TD>
<TD><DIV ALIGN=CENTER>Expression</DIV></TD>
</TR>

<TR>
<TD><DIV ALIGN=CENTER><INPUT TYPE=text SIZE=10 NAME="expField"
    onChange="var exp = GetCookie(this.value); this.form.expression.value =
➥(exp == null) ? '' : exp;"></DIV></TD>
<TD><DIV ALIGN=CENTER><INPUT TYPE=text SIZE=50 NAME="expression"></DIV></TD>
<TD><DIV ALIGN=CENTER><INPUT TYPE=button VALUE="Apply"
➥onClick="saveExp(this.form);"></DIV></TD>
<TD><DIV ALIGN=CENTER><INPUT TYPE=button VALUE="Delete"
➥onClick="deleteExp(this.form);"></DIV></TD>
</TR>

</TABLE>
</FORM>
</CENTER>

</BODY>

</HTML>
```

VI

JavaScript and Microsoft's Internet Explorer

21

Microsoft Internet Explorer

by Arman Danesh

JavaScript is no longer strictly limited to Netscape's browsers. The leading competition in terms of features, including JavaScript, is Internet Explorer 3.0 from Microsoft, which was released in the summer of 1996.

Internet Explorer 3 offers many of the features found in Navigator 3, including JavaScript, Java applet support, and frames. On top of this, Internet Explorer includes some features not found in Navigator 3, including ActiveX support and support for additional scripting languages.

Given the strength of Microsoft's marketing capabilities, Internet Explorer is likely to gain a foothold next to Netscape in the browser market. For this reason, Web page authors who want to take advantage of interactive Web features such as frames and JavaScript need to be aware of Internet Explorer and its capabilities.

This chapter examines Internet Explorer and compares it with Navigator 3. It covers the following topics:

- Overview of Internet Explorer
- Features common with Navigator 3
- Features not found in Navigator 3
- Navigator 3 features missing in Internet Explorer
- Future prospects for Internet Explorer

Overview of Internet Explorer

Even a quick glance at the feature set of Internet Explorer 3 reveals that one of Microsoft's main goals with this release was to play catch up and offer all of the features that currently make Navigator the most popular Web browser—both with users and with page designers who want to take advantage of the latest interactive technologies.

That wasn't enough for Microsoft, however. The company also has invested a lot of effort in trying to differentiate Internet Explorer 3 from its Netscape counterpart. These steps include ActiveX and VBScript to help draw current Microsoft application developers into the Internet Explorer fold, and stating commitments to open standards. The following features are among those that differentiate Internet Explorer:

- The ActiveX scripting model that includes VBScript and JavaScript as well as support for additional scripting languages
- Support for OLE objects that have been renamed ActiveX controls
- New security features, such as Authenticode
- Multilingual capabilities
- A commitment to standards

The first four are discussed in more detail later in this chapter. The issue of standards, however, deserves consideration.

Internet Explorer and Standards

An issue that is held to be vital by HTML and Web purists—one for which Netscape has received a lot of criticism—is adherence to the standards laid down by standards bodies on the Internet.

The argument goes something like this: All producers of browsers and Web servers should strictly adhere to the defined standards. This ensures the openness and interoperability of the Web so that any document can easily be viewed on any browser.

However, leading software vendors such as Netscape have taken it upon themselves to push the standards envelope by defining and implementing features and extensions to HTML and, once they're adopted by the page developers and users, submitting them to the standards bodies for addition to the defined standards.

The problem this has generated is that leading-edge browsers often have incompatible tags and features, making it difficult to develop a single HTML file that takes advantage of new technology while being compatible with a wide range of client browsers.

Although Netscape expresses support for open standards, it has been the focus of a lot of criticism on the Internet exactly because Netscape has taken it on themselves to push the standards envelope. In the past, Microsoft has done the same thing. With Internet Explorer 2, for instance, Microsoft introduced a handful of custom HTML tags that were neither part of the HTML definition or supported by Netscape.

With the release of Internet Explorer 3, however, Microsoft has changed its tune, voicing a commitment to standards as laid down by the World Wide Web Consortium (W3C).

As expressed by Microsoft, this commitment means they plan to implement all approved Internet standards, identify not-yet-approved tags in their documentation, and submit new extensions to the W3C before shipping them.

Of course, this doesn't guarantee that Internet Explorer will be fully compliant with a standard because the software can—and does—include yet-to-be-approved tags, any of which could end up not being included in the standard HTML definition.

Common Features of Navigator 3

Some of the most notable additions to Internet Explorer 3 are those new features that match those found in Navigator 3:

- JavaScript
- Java support
- Frames
- Plug-in support
- Security features

JavaScript

Microsoft takes a different approach to scripting than Netscape does. They have implemented ActiveX scripting—a low-level scripting engine on top of which any ActiveX-enabled scripting language can be plugged in. In this way, Microsoft has implemented two scripting languages in Internet Explorer 3: VBScript (discussed later in this chapter) and JScript (a JavaScript-compatible scripting language).

This implementation of JavaScript is close to the one found in Navigator 3. Some of its unique differences are discussed in Chapter 22, "The Internet Explorer Object Model," when the Internet Explorer Object Model is examined.

Java Support

Both Navigator 3 and Internet Explorer 3 now support embedded Java applets. Where Netscape integrates the support into Navigator, Microsoft distributed the support as a separate extension to beta versions of Internet Explorer, but the result is the same.

This Java support provides the requisite Java Virtual Machine for running Java applets in an interpreted mode and, like Navigator 3, adds a just-in-time Java compiler. Microsoft has taken a different approach than Netscape, allowing any JIT compiler to be used in Internet Explorer—not just the one provided by Microsoft. Navigator, on the other hand, only supports the Borland JIT Java compiler.

On top of this, Java can be used to build ActiveX controls. ActiveX controls are discussed later in this chapter.

Frames

It's hard to avoid frames these days. Numerous Web sites use them to enhance their interfaces, and many browsers have made moves toward adding support for frames.

Microsoft has added full frame support to Internet Explorer 3 as well as experimenting with additional features such as in-line frames, borderless frames, and other features not found in Navigator 3, such as floating frames. Figure 21.1 shows an example of an in-line frame.

Plug-In Support

It's hard to ignore the role that plug-ins have come to play in the popularity and success of Navigator 2 and 3. Plug-ins have enabled users to add numerous features, including expanded file-format support, new interface elements, and complete applications, to their Navigator browsers.

Given the popularity of plug-ins among software vendors, with a long list of companies offering plug-ins for everything from Microsoft Word viewing capabilities to world clocks, it is inevitable that Microsoft has included support for plug-ins.

FIGURE 21.1.

In-line frames in Internet Explorer.

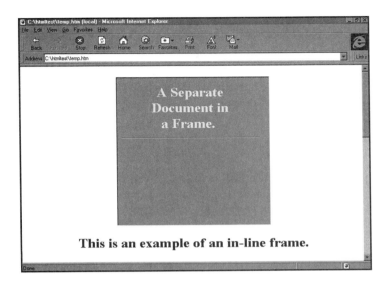

Microsoft has implemented this support in such a way that plug-ins currently installed in Navigator will be detected and used by Internet Explorer when needed. In addition, new plug-ins can be installed either in Navigator or Internet Explorer, and Internet Explorer will be able to use them.

FIGURE 21.2.

Netscape plug-ins like this one from Corel can be used in Internet Explorer.

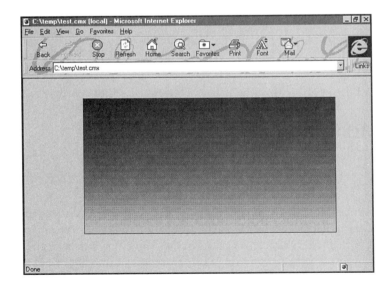

Security Features

In addition to some of its own security features discussed later in this chapter, Microsoft has implemented the server and client authentication features found in Navigator 3. In addition, Secure Sockets Layer technology, Netscape's protocol for secure communication on the Internet used by many sites, is supported by Internet Explorer.

Features Not Found in Navigator 3

While it includes features common to Navigator 3, Internet Explorer 3 also includes several features not found in Netscape's browser:

- VBScript
- ActiveX controls
- HTML layouts
- HTML extensions
- New security features
- Multilingual capabilities

VBScript

Using the ActiveX scripting engine, Microsoft has added a second scripting language to Internet Explorer called VBScript. A subset of the widely used Visual Basic programming language, VBScript is optimized for programming Web pages and client-end interactivity in Internet Explorer.

VBScript is discussed in detail in Chapter 23, "Programming with VBScript."

ActiveX Controls

Object linking and embedding technology has been present in Windows and now Windows 95 for some time. Microsoft has repackaged and renamed the technology ActiveX for its application to network computing on the Internet and intranets.

ActiveX controls is another name for OLE objects. ActiveX controls provide an alternative to Java applets for including small, embedded pieces of software in Web pages. These controls can be built in any language, including Visual C++ or Java, and can be built for a variety of purposes, such as supporting new file formats, extending the Internet Explorer interface, and more. Figures 21.3 and 21.4 are examples of ActiveX controls.

FIGURE 21.3.

Microsoft's Marquee controls allow a scrolling marquee to be included in a Web page.

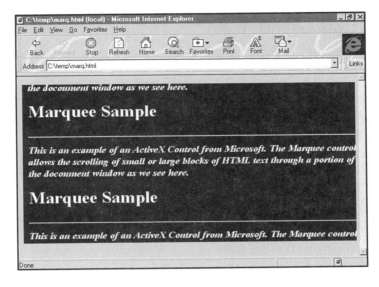

FIGURE 21.4.

ActiveX controls can create special graphics effects, such as this gradient.

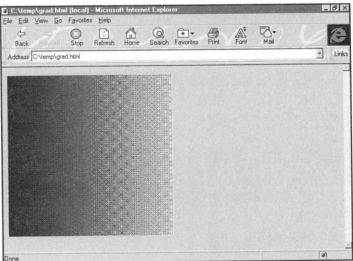

The fact that ActiveX and OLE are essentially the same technology means that Internet Explorer can be made to take advantage of OLE-compliant applications and that these applications can take advantage of pieces of Internet Explorer in order to gain Internet capabilities.

ActiveX controls are discussed in more detail in Chapter 25, "Using the ActiveX Control Pad."

HTML Layouts

HTML layouts offer a degree of design and creative flexibility previously available only in CD-ROM–based applications. Using the HTML Layout Control—an ActiveX control that extends Internet Explorer—it's possible to design a complex layout, bringing together animated effects, interface elements, other ActiveX controls, and embedded objects, along with drag-and-drop capabilities—all in a fixed spatial relationship. This definition of a layout can then be included in an HTML page as an embedded object.

Producing HTML layouts is discussed in more detail in Chapter 26, "JavaScript and the Future," where the ActiveX Control Pad is looked at in more detail.

HTML Extensions

Because of Netscape's commitment to implementing the entire body of approved HTML, which is currently HTML 3.2, as well as to introducing new features not yet approved by the standards bodies, there are several HTML features which have yet to be implemented (or fully implemented) in Navigator.

These include:

- The complete table definition
- The W3C <OBJECT> tag
- Style sheets that offer desktop-publishing–like control over the appearance of a Web page
- Scrolling marquees

New Security Features

In addition to the support for the security features found in Navigator 3—which were described earlier in this chapter—Microsoft has added additional security features to Internet Explorer 3:

- **Code Signing**: Using Authenticode, Internet Explorer enables providers of software components such as applets and ActiveX controls to digitally sign their software so that users can decide if they actually want to download and install a component. This can help users ensure that they aren't downloading and running unattributed and potentially malicious software.
- **CryptoAPI**: This provides mechanisms for secure channels and code signing. This is a low-level layer designed to be leveraged by developers who want to include encryption capabilities in their software.
- **PCT**: This is Microsoft's own protocol that, like SSL, is designed for secure communication across TCP/IP networks.

Multilingual Capabilities

Microsoft offers more international localized versions of Internet Explorer than Netscape does for Navigator.

Microsoft has announced or made available Internet Explorer 3 in 25 localized versions, ranging from simplified Chinese to Brazilian Portuguese to Norwegian. By comparison, Netscape can lay claim to only a little over 11 localized versions.

On top of this, Internet Explorer can accept language extension modules so that, for example, an English copy of the browser could access and display a Web page in Hungarian or Japanese or any other language.

Limitations of Internet Explorer 3

Even with all its features, Internet Explorer still suffers from some limitations.

Foremost among these limitations is the lack of available platforms for Internet Explorer. Netscape Navigator 3 is currently available on 16 platforms including all versions of Windows, Macintosh, and a broad range of UNIX flavors, including Linux, Solaris, and HP-UX.

Internet Explorer 3, on the other hand, is only available for Windows 95 and Windows NT 4.0 at the time this book was written. Microsoft was working on a Macintosh version, but it was only available in a beta version, and there were no clear plans for UNIX ports of Internet Explorer.

This gives Netscape the upper hand in that, theoretically at least, one version of a Web site can be viewed on any platform using Navigator 3.

In addition to this, Internet Explorer does have some other limitations:

- **Lack of integrated mail and news**: Mail and news support is not built into the core of Internet Explorer. This means that a second package—with the mail and news extensions—needs to be downloaded and installed to provide this functionality.
- **Size**: Internet Explorer seems to require more disk space than Navigator for a fully loaded implementation.
- **Speed**: Netscape, at least, is able to produce figures that show that Navigator 3.0 performs the same tasks somewhat faster. This is really a subjective issue because many users report that Internet Explorer feels more "lightweight" when they use it.

Future Prospects for Internet Explorer

Given the easy availability of Internet Explorer and the dominance of Microsoft as the operating system vendor of choice in the home and small office markets, it seems likely that Microsoft will make strong in-roads against Netscape in the Web browser market.

While it is unlikely that Microsoft will be unable to completely usurp Netscape for the dominant market position, it seems likely that Internet Explorer is well-placed to break the complete hold that Netscape enjoys over the Web browser market.

This means that the future Web browser market is likely to be more evenly split, with Netscape and Microsoft sharing the two leading spots for some time to come.

This means that you will likely see an increasing number of sites sporting "Designed for Internet Explorer" slogans as you do now for Netscape Navigator. Some of the technology Microsoft has introduced in Internet Explorer 3.0 will likely find its way into future releases of Netscape Navigator.

Summary

This chapter has shown you how Microsoft has taken a large step towards effectively competing with Netscape.

Given the strong feature-set and the likely increased use of Internet Explorer 3.0, it's important for developers who want to use interactivity tools such as JavaScript to understand the fundamentals of Internet Explorer 3.0.

The next few chapters cover several key features of Internet Explorer, including:

- The Internet Explorer Object Model
- VBScript
- ActiveX controls

22

The Internet Explorer Object Model

by Arman Danesh

Like Netscape Navigator, Internet Explorer has an object hierarchy designed to provide the programmer with the tools needed to interact with the Internet Explorer environment.

Microsoft has designed the model to ensure compatibility with the object model in Navigator. In addition, Microsoft hopes that the model will help to ease the transition from JavaScript to VBScript because all the objects can be used in both JavaScript and VBScript, as well as in any other ActiveX scripting language which may be developed in the future.

This chapter looks at the Internet Explorer Object Model and provides information about:

- Incorporating scripts in Web pages in Explorer
- The objects available in the model
- Key differences between the objects in the current versions of Navigator and Internet Explorer
- How to use the objects in JavaScript

Including Scripts in Web Pages in Explorer

Before exploring the Internet Explorer Object Model, this chapter looks at the available methods for including a script in a Web page in Internet Explorer. Internet Explorer offers the same methods as Netscape Navigator but also provides alternative techniques for incorporating scripts.

Basic Methods for Incorporating Scripts in Web pages

Internet Explorer provides the same basic mechanisms for including scripts in Web pages as Navigator:

- Scripts can be enclosed inside a `<SCRIPT>` tag
- Short JavaScript code can be included as part of a `javascript:` URL
- Scripts can be included as part of an event handler attribute such as `onLoad` or `onClick`

In the first and last case, it's important to specify the language of the script with a `LANGUAGE` attribute so that Internet Explorer knows which scripting language is being used:

```
<SCRIPT LANGUAGE="JavaScript">
Script Here
</SCRIPT>
```

or

```
<INPUT TYPE=button NAME="example" VALUE="Click Here" onClick="pressed"
➥LANGUAGE="VBScript">
```

This is different from Netscape Navigator where it is still possible—although bad style—to omit the `LANGUAGE` attribute of the `<SCRIPT>` tag. Another difference is that the `LANGUAGE` attribute isn't used in element tags such as `<BODY>` or `<INPUT>` in Navigator.

Like Netscape Navigator, scripts are compiled as the page is rendered so that the scripts are available for execution later. This means that both VBScript and JavaScript scripts can exist on the same page, making the LANGUAGE attribute more important. The following example produces a form with two buttons—one with a VBScript event handler and one with a JavaScript event handler:

```
<HTML>
<HEAD>
<TITLE>VBScript and JavaScript Example</TITLE>

<SCRIPT LANGUAGE="JavaScript">
function jsClick() {
alert("You clicked on the JavaScript Button");
}

</SCRIPT>
<SCRIPT LANGUAGE="VBScript">
Sub vbClick
MsgBox "You clicked on the VbScript Button"
End Sub
</SCRIPT>
</HEAD>
<BODY>
<H1>VBScript and JavaScript Example</H1>
<HR>
<FORM NAME="example">
<INPUT TYPE=button NAME="jsButton" VALUE="Click for JavaScript"
onClick="jsClick()" LANGUAGE="JavaScript">
<INPUT TYPE=button NAME="vbButton" VALUE="Click for VBScript"
onClick="vbClick" LANGUAGE="VBScript">
</FORM>

</BODY>
</HTML>
```

This page includes two script definitions in the header of the file: one with a VBScript procedure and one with a JavaScript button. The form includes two buttons—one triggers the JavaScript function when pressed and the other calls the VBScript procedure when the user clicks on it. This page produces results like Figures 22.1 and 22.2.

NOTE

The details of programming VBScript are covered in the Chapter 23, "Programming with VBScript."

The javascript: URL

The javascript: URL can be used to invoke a script using the format javascript:*script-code*. For example, in the example above, you could change the JavaScript button to a hypertext link defined as

```
<A HREF="javascript:jsClick()">JavaScript Link</A>
```

FIGURE 22.1.

If the user clicks the JavaScript button an alert box is displayed.

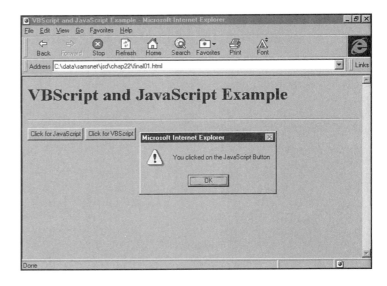

FIGURE 22.2.

If the user clicks the VBScript button a message box is displayed.

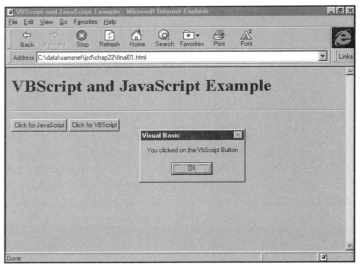

Although the current version of Internet Explorer 3 only supports this syntax for JavaScript code, the final release will support script URLs for all scripting engines supported by Internet Explorer. For example, a VBScript URL might look like

```
<A HREF="vbscript:vbClick">VBScript Link</A>
```

> **NOTE**
>
> Because this feature is not presently supported for VBScript, the final form of a VBScript URL may not exactly match this example.

An Additional Method for Including Scripts in Web Pages

In addition to supporting the same methods as Navigator for including scripts in Web pages, Internet Explorer also provides additional attributes for the <SCRIPT> tag—FOR and EVENT:

- FOR: Specifies the object name with which the script is associated
- EVENT: Specifies the event that will trigger script execution

These scripts effectively enable the creation of event handlers without using the event handler attributes of the actual elements.

For instance, the two-button page in the previous example could be rewritten as follows:

```
<HTML>
<HEAD>
<TITLE>VBScript and JavaScript Example</TITLE>
</HEAD>

<BODY>
<H1>VBScript and JavaScript Example</H1>
<HR>
<FORM NAME="example">
<INPUT TYPE=button NAME="jsButton" VALUE="Click for JavaScript">
<SCRIPT FOR="jsButton" EVENT="onClick" LANGUAGE="JavaScript">
alert("You clicked on the JavaScript Button");
</SCRIPT>
<INPUT TYPE=button NAME="vbButton" VALUE="Click for VBScript">
<SCRIPT FOR="vbButton" EVENT="onClick" LANGUAGE="vbScript">
MsgBox "You clicked on the VbScript Button"
</SCRIPT>
</FORM>

</BODY>
</HTML>
```

You should notice that these scripts are defined in such a way as to be attached to specific events of specific objects. In addition, the scripts break one of the fundamental rules of HTML scripting: include all scripts in the header of the HTML document, unless it is necessary to render content to the document window.

In order to move these two scripts out of the body of the HTML document to the header, you need to understand the context in which scripts can exist. Because the scripts in the previous example are defined inside of the form definition, their context is that of the form. So, when the FOR attributes refer to the names of the button objects, it's assumed they are referring to the names of properties of the specific form object.

If, however, the scripts are moved outside of the form definition—as they would be if they were moved to the header—then it's necessary to fully qualify the object names in the FOR attributes as document.example.jsButton and document.example.vbButton (remember, the form object is a property of the document object):

```
<HTML>
<HEAD>
<TITLE>VBScript and JavaScript Example</TITLE>

<SCRIPT FOR="document.example.jsButton" EVENT="onClick" LANGUAGE="JavaScript">
alert("You clicked on the JavaScript Button");
</SCRIPT>
<SCRIPT FOR="document.example.vbButton" EVENT="onClick" LANGUAGE="vbScript">
MsgBox "You clicked on the VbScript Button"
</SCRIPT>
</HEAD>

<BODY>
<H1>VBScript and JavaScript Example</H1>
<HR>
<FORM NAME="example">
<INPUT TYPE=button NAME="jsButton" VALUE="Click for JavaScript">
<INPUT TYPE=button NAME="vbButton" VALUE="Click for VBScript">
</FORM>

</BODY>
</HTML>
```

The Internet Explorer Object Model

The Internet Explorer object tree closely resembles the one found in Netscape Navigator. The top-level parent is the window object and its children include a frame object, a history object, a navigator object, a location object, a script object, and a document object (which also has children such as the link, anchor, and form objects).

Although most of the object specifications in the Internet Explorer Object Model match their counterparts in Netscape Navigator, a few fundamental differences do exist in the current version of Internet Explorer. These are highlighted throughout this chapter.

The window Object

The window object is the top-level object for every window. As with Netscape Navigator, it is possible to refer to the properties and methods of the window object without explicitly referring to the window itself. For instance, window.alert() can be simply invoked as alert().

The window object in Internet Explorer closely resembles the one provided in Navigator 3, with a few differences:

- The length property isn't available
- An additional method—navigate—is included

- The `name` property isn't correctly implemented
- The `status` and `defaultStatus` properties aren't currently implemented
- The `open()` and `close()` methods aren't currently implemented

The `name` Property

Unlike current versions of Navigator 3, the current beta of Internet Explorer returns "Microsoft Internet Explorer" as the value of the `name` property of all windows, regardless of the actual name of window.

This is actually useful for situations in which a script needs to provide special code for Internet Explorer because of differences between the JavaScript implementations in the current versions of Navigator and Internet Explorer. By simply checking the value of `window.name`, it is possible to determine which browser's in use.

However, Microsoft will likely update their implementation of the `name` property in future releases to correctly reflect window names, so it's better to use properties of the `navigator` object to determine if the user's browser is Navigator or Internet Explorer.

The `navigate()` Method

The navigate method provides an alternative to setting `window.location` or calling `window.open()` to open a new URL in the current window. The syntax of `navigate()` method is simple:

```
navigate("URL");
```

This method is not available in Navigator 3.

> **NOTE**
>
> If your script requires `window.open()` to open new windows, it won't work in the current version of Internet Explorer. If you're using `window.open()` to open a document in an existing window, you may want to try setting `window.location` instead of calling `window.open()`. This way, your script should work on both Navigator 3 and Internet Explorer 3.

The `document` Object

The `document` object provides the properties and methods for working with the current HTML document. As with the `window` object, certain key differences exist between Navigator 3's document object and the current implementation in Internet Explorer:

- Internet Explorer doesn't support active link coloring, so `alinkColor` has no effect.
- The `open()` method only supports the `text/html` Mime type.

The `alinkColor` Property

Navigator 3 supports three distinct link colors: an unfollowed link color, a followed link color, and an active link color. Active links occur when the mouse button is pressed down over the link. In the current version, Navigator changes the color of the link to the active link color until the button is released.

This color is reflected in and can be set using `document.alinkColor`. However, Internet Explorer doesn't use active link colors. Therefore, `alinkColor` is only provided for compatibility and won't have any functional effect on the appearance of a Web page in Internet Explorer.

The `open()` Method

In Navigator, it's possible to open a new document stream for any Mime type supported by the browser. The default is `text/html`, but specifying an alternative Mime type is possible using the following command:

```
document.open("mime-type");
```

For instance, opening a document stream with `document.open("text/plain")` would create a stream for plain text, which means the text would be displayed as-is by Navigator.

Internet Explorer's `document.open()` method currently defaults to the `text/html`, effectively ignoring the Mime type attribute if it's provided.

For instance, the following frameset uses the `onLoad` event handler to clear the document in the right frame and open a `text/plain` document stream in that frame. The document is displayed as plain text in Navigator but is treated as HTML by Internet Explorer:

```
<HTML>
<HEAD>
<TITLE>document.open() Example</TITLE>

<SCRIPT LANGUAGE="JavaScript">
function doOpen() {
self.right.document.clear();
self.right.document.open("text/plain");
self.right.document.writeln("<H1>Example</H1>");
self.right.document.writeln("<HR>");
self.right.document.writeln("A test of document.open()");
self.right.document.close();

}

</SCRIPT>
</HEAD>
<FRAMESET COLS="50%,*" onLoad="doOpen()">
<FRAME SRC="left.html">
<FRAME SRC="blank.html" NAME="right">
</FRAMESET>
</HTML>
```

Figures 22.3 and 22.4 show how the document stream is treated differently in Navigator and Internet Explorer.

FIGURE 22.3.

In Navigator the text/ plain *document stream isn't treated as HTML.*

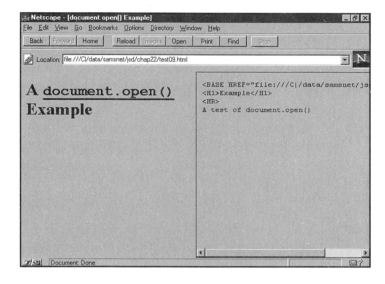

FIGURE 22.4.

In Internet Explorer, the Mime type is ignored and the document stream is treated as HTML.

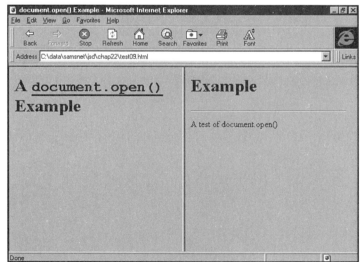

The form Object

There are several basic differences between Netscape Navigator's form object and the current implementation in Internet Explorer:

■ Setting the `target` property doesn't change the target of the form.

■ The `hidden` property hasn't been implemented in the current version of Internet Explorer.

The `location` Object

There are two differences between the `location` object in Navigator and Internet Explorer:

■ The `pathname` property doesn't return the leading slash ("/") the way it does in Navigator.

■ The `hash` property only returns the hash symbol ("#") but not the text following the hash symbol in the URL.

The `link` Object

There are several differences between the `link` object in the two browsers:

■ The `search` property doesn't return the leading question mark ("?").

■ An additional `mouseMove` event handler is provided in Internet Explorer.

■ The `onMouseOver` event handler isn't implemented in the current version of Internet Explorer.

■ The `onClick` event handler isn't implemented in the current version of Internet Explorer.

More important than this difference, however, is the inconsistency between the `link` object properties and the `location` object properties in Internet Explorer:

■ The `hash` property of the `link` object returns the complete hash portion of the link, including the leading hash symbol ("#").

■ The `pathname` property includes the leading slash ("/"), which was omitted in the `location` object's `pathname` property.

■ The leading question mark ("?") is returned by `location` object's `search` property but not by the `link` object's `search` property.

The `anchor` Object

The `anchor` object includes one property not available in Navigator: `name`—a string reflecting the name of the anchor set by the NAME attribute of the <A> tag.

The `element` Object

In Internet Explorer, all embedded objects, including form fields and controls, ActiveX objects, and Java applets are reflected into the scripting environment as instances of the `element` object. These objects can be referred to by name or by their index number in the `elements` array of the `form` object.

Depending on what type of object is being reflected by an instance of the `element` object, the object will have different properties, methods, and event handlers. Table 22.1 outlines which objects take which properties, methods, and event handlers.

Table 22.1. Properties, methods, and event handlers of the `element` object.

Element	Properties	Methods	Event Handlers
button	form, name, value, enabled	click, focus	onClick, onFocus
reset	form, name, value, enabled	click, focus	onClick, onFocus
submit	form, name, value, enabled	click, focus	onClick, onFocus
checkbox	form, name, value, checked, defaultChecked, enabled	click, focus	onClick, onFocus,
radio	form, name, value, checked, enabled	click, focus	onClick, onFocus
combo	form, name, value, enabled, listCount, list, multiSelect, listIndex	click, focus, removeItem, addItem, clear	onClick, onFocus
password	form, name, value, defaultValue, enabled	focus, blur, select	onFocus, onBlur
text	form, name, value, defaultValue, enabled	focus, blur, select	onFocus, onBlur onChange, onSelect
textarea	form, name, value, defaultValue, enabled	focus, blur, select	onFocus, onBlur onChange, onSelect
select	name, length, options, selectedIndex	focus, blur	onFocus, onBlur onChange
hidden	name, value		

Internet Explorer has properties, methods, and objects that aren't offered in Navigator 3:

■ The `enabled`, `listCount`, `multiSelect`, and `listIndex` properties
■ The `removeItem()`, `addItem()`, and `clear()` methods

The `enabled` Property

The `enabled` property can be used to see if an object or form element is enabled and can be used to change the status of an object or form element. The value of `enabled` is `true` when a control is enabled and `false` if it is disabled. This property is not yet implemented in Internet Explorer 3 beta 2.

The `combo` Properties

The `listCount`, `multiSelect`, and `listIndex` properties only apply to the `combo` object type. `listCount` returns the count of the number of elements in the combo's list. `multiSelect` indicates if the `combo` element is `multiselect` or not as a Boolean value and can be set by a script. `listIndex` returns the index of the first selected element in the list.

The `combo` Methods

The `removeItem()`, `addItem()`, and `clear()` methods only apply to the `combo` object type. `removeItem()` and `addItem()` respectively remove an item at a specified index from the list and add an item before the item at the specified index on a list. The `clear()` method clears the contents of the item at the specified index.

The `history` Object

This `history` object is not fully implemented in Internet Explorer 3 beta 2. The following problems exist:

■ The `length` property always returns zero.
■ `back()`, `forward()`, and `go()` can only move one item on the list in either direction—for instance, `history.back(4)` moves one item back on the history list.

The `navigator` Object

The `navigator` object in Internet Explorer works in the same way as its counterpart in Navigator 3. The values returned by the four properties, however, are different from those of Navigator 3. Table 22.2 outlines the expected values to be returned by the properties of the `navigator` object in Internet Explorer 3 beta 2.

Table 22.2. Values for properties of the `navigator` object.

Property	Value in Internet Explorer 3 beta 2
appCodeName	Mozilla
appName	Microsoft Internet Explorer
appVersion	2.0 (compatible; MSIE 3.0A; Windows 95)
userAgent	Mozilla/2.0 (compatible; MSIE 3.0A; Windows 95)

These properties, particularly `appName`, prove useful in determining if the browser running a given script is Internet Explorer. This is important until several of the incomplete or unavailable JavaScript properties and methods are implemented in Internet Explorer.

Summary

This chapter looked briefly at the Internet Explorer Object Model. Being familiar with the Internet Explorer Object Model is important if you intend to write JavaScript code that doesn't conflict with the few small gaps in the current version of Internet Explorer.

In addition, if you intend to develop applications specifically for Internet Explorer, this chapter highlighted the unique features of the Internet Explorer Object Tree which are not available in Navigator 3.

As the next chapter examines programming in VBScript, you will be making calls to the methods learned in this chapter, and accessing the properties discussed here as well.

If you need more information about the object model, Microsoft, like Netscape, maintains extensive reference resources about developing for Internet Explorer on its Web site. Complete reference documents about the Internet Explorer Object Model are available at `http://www.microsoft.com/intdev/sdk/docs/scriptom/local.htm`.

23

Programming with VBScript

by Arman Danesh

VBScript provides an alternative to JavaScript for client-end programming in Internet Explorer. VBScript is a subset of Visual Basic—Microsoft's well-known Windows programming language—specially designed for Internet client scripting.

Like JavaScript, VBScript is included in Web pages and is compiled when a page is loaded. VBScript can access all the objects in the Internet Explorer Object Model. VBScript and JavaScript offer similar capabilities, but where JavaScript more closely resembles Java (and through that C and C++), VBScript looks more like Basic.

In this chapter you will learn about VBScript, including the following topics:

■ Variables and data types in VBScript
■ VBScript operators and expressions
■ Loops and comparison in VBScript
■ Procedures

Basic VBScript Concepts

Before looking at the details of VBScript programming, take a look at certain conventions of VBScript programming, including naming standards, code format, and command syntax.

Naming Standards

Visual Basic—and by extension VBScript—has well-established naming conventions to help make programs and scripts more readable. By contrast, JavaScript is too new to have well-established conventions—and while there are some conventions in Java, these often don't show up in most JavaScript scripts.

The rules fall into four basic areas:

■ *Constants*—Constants should be named all in uppercase with underscores ("_") between words.
■ *Variables*—Variable names should be descriptive combinations of upper- and lower-case letters starting with a capital letter. Standard prefixes are described in the section "Variable Name Prefixes" later in this chapter.
■ *Procedures*—Procedure names should be descriptive combinations of upper- and lowercase letters starting with a capital letter.
■ *Objects*—Object names should be descriptive combinations of upper- and lowercase letters starting with a capital letter. Standard prefixes describing object types are described in the section "Object Name Prefixes" later in this chapter.

Variable Name Prefixes

Microsoft recommends using prefixes to variable names to specify the type of data stored in a variable and the scope of a variable. Table 23.1 outlines the prefixes for the variable data subtypes in VBScript.

Table 23.1. Variable subtype prefixes in VBScript.

Subtype	Prefix
Boolean	bln
Byte	byt
Date (Time)	dtm
Double	dbl
Error	err
Integer	int
Long	lng
Object	obj
Single	sng
String	str

For example, if you wanted to create a variable to store the user's name in a script and the variable was supposed to contain string data, then the naming conventions suggest it should be named strUserName.

Further, variables in VBScript can have either script-level scope or procedure-level scope (just as they can have global scope or function-level scope in JavaScript). The naming conventions suggest that an "s" be added to the start of the name of a script-level variable. This prefix should come before the subtype prefix so that if the preceding username variable had script-level scope, then its name should be sstrUserName.

Object Name Prefixes

Just as variables take prefixes to specify the subtype and scope of a variable, Microsoft recommends using the prefixes in Table 23.2. to specify the types of objects in a name.

Table 23.2. Object name prefixes.

Object Type	Prefix
3D Panel	pnl
Animated button	ani

continues

Table 23.2. continued

Object Type	Prefix
Checkbox	chk
Combo box/Drop-down list	cbo
Command button	cmd
Common dialog	dlg
Frame	fra
Horizontal scrollbar	hsb
Image	img
Label	lbl
Line	lin
List box	lst
Spin	spn
Text box	txt
Vertical scrollbar	vsb
Slider	sld

So, a text box for user comments could be called `txtUserComments`.

Formatting and Syntax Conventions

Microsoft's VBScript documentation also outlines standards for script formatting, comments, and basic syntax.

Comments in VBScript start with a single apostrophe (`'`) and continue to the end of the line, much like single-line comments in JavaScript start with a double-slash (`//`) and continue to the end of the line. Microsoft recommends that important variable declarations should be accompanied by a comment and that the script and each procedure should include overview comments.

In terms of laying out program code, nested blocks should be indented four spaces and overview comments should be indented one space. Lines don't end in a semicolon the way they do in JavaScript.

Variables and Data Types in VBScript

VBScript handles data types somewhat differently than JavaScript. VBScript has one data type—the variant—which in turn has several subtypes. Because a variant can contain any data type, when the data looks like a number it is treated as a number and when it looks like a string it is treated as a string.

In addition, numbers can be made to be treated like a string by enclosing them in quotation marks (`""`).

The number of data subtypes in VBScript are more than the basic types in JavaScript:

- *Empty*—Zero for numeric variables or an empty string (`""`)
- *Null*—Like the `null` value in JavaScript
- *Boolean*—Like JavaScript, Boolean variables can be either `true` or `false`
- *Byte*—An integer between 0 and 255
- *Integer*—An integer between –32,768 and 32,767
- *Long*—An integer between –2,147,483,648 and 2,147,483,647
- *Single*—A single-precision, floating-point number (the exact size is available in Microsoft's VBScript reference material at `http://www.microsoft.com/vbscript`)
- *Double*—A double-precision, floating-point number (the exact size is specified on Microsoft's Web site)
- *Date (Time)*—A number representing a date between January 1, 100, and December 31, 9999
- *String*—A string of up to roughly 2 billion characters
- *Error*—An error number

Converting Between Variant Subtypes

Even though variants can hold any type of data, it is useful to be able to convert between data types. VBScript includes several built-in functions for performing this work:

- `Cbool`—Converts its argument to a Boolean value
- `Cbyte`—Converts its argument to a Byte value
- `Cdate`—Converts its argument to a Date value
- `CDbl`—Converts its argument to a Double value
- `Cint`—Converts its argument to an Integer value
- `CLng`—Converts its argument to a Long value
- `CSng`—Converts its argument to a Single value
- `CStr`—Converts its argument to a String value

For instance, `CStr(15)` returns `"15"` and `Cbyte("15")` returns 15.

In addition, some other conversion functions in VBScript include the following:

- `Abs`—Returns the absolute value of its argument (that is, `Abs(-5)` returns 5)

- ■ `Asc`—Returns the ASCII value of its character argument (that is, `Asc(" ")` returns 32)
- ■ `Chr`—Returns the ASCII character specified by the integer argument to `Chr` (that is, `Chr(32)` returns `" "`)
- ■ `Int`—Returns the integer value of the floating-point argument (that is, `Int(3.75)` returns 3)

Testing Data Types

In addition to being able to convert between data types, VBScript provides a series of functions that can be used by scripts to determine some information about data stored in a variant.

The following list highlights the major functions in VBScript that can test various properties of the data stored in a variant:

- ■ `IsArray(Argument)`—Tests if *Argument* is an array; returns `true` if it is, `false` if it is not.
- ■ `IsDate(Argument)`—Tests if *Argument* is a date variant subtype; returns `true` if it is, `false` if it is not.
- ■ `IsEmpty(Argument)`—Tests if *Argument* is the empty variant subtype; returns `true` if it is, `false` if it is not.
- ■ `IsNull(Argument)`—Tests if *Argument* is the null value; returns `true` if it is, `false` if it is not.
- ■ `IsNumeric(Argument)`—Tests if *Argument* is a numeric variant subtype such as long, integer, or byte; returns `true` if it is, `false` if it is not.

Working with Variables in VBScript

In JavaScript, variables are declared using the `var` keyword. The process is similar in VBScript except that the `Dim` statement is used to declare a variable. For instance,

```
Dim bytOneVariable
```

declares a single variable and

```
Dim bytOneVariable, strTwoVariables, blnThreeVariables
```

declares three variables.

> **NOTE**
>
> Variable names must begin with a letter, cannot contain a period, and must not be longer than 255 characters.
>
> Each array can contain only 127 variables. There can be only 127 script-level variables per script.

Values are assigned to variables using a simple equal sign (=) as in JavaScript:

```
bytOneVariable = 45
strTwoVariable = "A String"
blnThreeVariable = true
```

Arrays in VBScript

Unlike JavaScript, VBScript is not inherently object-oriented. Arrays in VBScript, therefore, are not instances of objects. Rather, arrays are declared using the Dim statement, just as with regular scalar variables.

Fixed-sized arrays are created by specifying the number of last index in the array in parentheses after the variable name in the Dim statement. Arrays start with index zero, as in JavaScript, so Dim AnArray(7) creates an array with eight elements.

In JavaScript, arrays are not of fixed size like this. Instead they dynamically change size as values are assigned to them. In VBScript, array size can be changed with the ReDim statement, which enables the size of an array to be extended. For instance, if an array is created with Dim AnArray(), then ReDim AnArray(20) would create 21 elements in the array.

If data is already stored in an array, the Preserve statement can be combined with ReDim to change the size of the array without destroying the existing content. For instance, AnArray() could be expanded further to 41 elements with ReDim Preserve AnArray(40).

VBScript Operators

VBScript has a similar set of operators to JavaScript, although the exact symbols for them differ. The operators are outlined in order of precedence in Table 23.3.

Table 23.3. VBScript operators in order of precedence.

Symbol	Type	Description
^	Arithmetic	Exponentiation (for example, 3 ^ 2 returns 9)
-	Arithmetic	Unary negation
*	Arithmetic	Multiplication
/	Arithmetic	Division
\	Arithmetic	Integer division
Mod	Arithmetic	Modulo (for example, 7 Mod 3 returns 1)
+	Arithmetic	Addition
-	Arithmetic	Subtraction
&	String	Concatenation (for example, "A" & "B" returns "AB")

continues

Table 23.3. continued

Symbol	Type	Description
=	Comparison	Equality (for example, `"A" = "B"` returns `false`)
<>	Comparison	Inequality (for example, `"A" <> "B"` returns `true`)
<	Comparison	Less than (for example, `1 < 2` returns `true`)
>	Comparison	Greater than (for example, `1 > 2` returns `false`)
<=	Comparison	Less than or equal to (for example, `1 <= 2` returns `true`)
>=	Comparison	Greater than or equal to (for example, `1 >= 2` returns `false`)
Is	Comparison	Object equivalence (Checks if two object references point to the same object)
Not	Logical	Logical negation (for example, `Not true` returns `false`)
And	Logical	Logical conjunction (for example, `true And false` returns `false`)
Or	Logical	Logical disjunction (for example, `true Or false` returns `true`)
Xor	Logical	Logical exclusion (for example, `true Xor true` returns `false`)
Eqv	Logical	Logical equivalence
Imp	Logical	Logical implication

Loops and Comparison in VBScript

VBScript offers similar looping and `If`-statement capabilities as JavaScript.

The basic `If`-`Then`-`Else` construct in VBScript closely resembles JavaScript's. Looping in VBScript, on the other hand, provides more flexibility than in JavaScript.

The `If`-`Then`-`Else` Construct

The basic `If`-`Then` construct looks like:

```
If condition Then
    VBScript code
End If
```

It can be extended to include an `Else` component:

```
If condition Then
    VBScript code
Else
    More VBScript code
End If
```

The key differences to note are that the condition is not contained in parentheses as in JavaScript, a Then statement starts the command block, and the End If statement closes the command block. Command blocks in VBScript are not delimited by curly braces as they are in JavaScript.

For instance, the code

```
If bytAnInteger = 11 Then
    bytAnInteger = 1
Else
    bytAnInteger = bytAnInteger + 1
End If
```

checks if bytAnInteger equals 11. If it does, then the value is reset to 1. Otherwise, the value of bytAnInteger is increased by one. In JavaScript, this if statement could have been written

```
if (anInteger == 11) {
    anInteger = 1;
} else {
    anInteger ++;
}
```

Loops in VBScript

VBScript provides more flexible looping capabilities than JavaScript. There are three basic loops in VBScript:

◼ While-Wend loops

◼ Do-Loop loops

◼ For-Next loops

While-Wend Loops

The While-Wend loops corresponds to the while loop in JavaScript. The basic structure of a While-Wend loop is

```
While condition
    Some VBScript Code
Wend
```

For example,

```
While bytAnInteger <= 10
    bytAnotherInteger = bytAnotherInteger + 10
    bytAnInteger = bytAnInteger + 1
Wend
```

would continue increasing the value of bytAnotherInteger by 10 until the value of bytAnInteger exceeds 10. In JavaScript, this loop would have looked like

```
while (anInteger <= 10) {
    anotherInteger += 10;
    anInteger ++;
}
```

Do-Loop **Loops**

The Do-Loop loop provides flexibility missing in the While-Wend loop and Microsoft's documentation recommends using it in favor of the While-Wend loop.

The Do-Loop loop can be used in two different ways: looping while a condition is true (as with the While-Wend loop) and repeating until a condition is true (similar to Pascal's Repeat-Until loop).

The former's structure is

```
Do While condition
    VBScript code
Loop
```

or

```
Do
    VbScript code
Loop While condition
```

The difference between these is that in the first structure, the condition is tested before the loop; if the condition is false, then the loop doesn't execute. In the second option, the condition is tested after the loop executes; with a false condition, the loop executes at least once.

The While-Wend loop in the last section could be rewritten as

```
Do While bytAnyInteger <= 10
    bytAnotherInteger = bytAnotherInteger + 10
    bytAnInteger = AnInteger + 1
Loop
```

or

```
Do
    bytAnotherInteger = bytAnotherInteger + 10
    bytAnInteger = AnInteger + 1
Loop While bytAnInteger <= 10
```

An alternative use of the Do-Loop structure is to loop until a condition is true (as opposed to *while* a condition is true). This usage has two forms as well:

```
Do Until condition
    VBScript code
Loop
```

or

```
Do
    VBScript code
Loop until condition
```

In the first, if the condition is true entering the loop, the body of the loop is never executed. In the latter, the loop would be executed once if the condition were true.

For instance, the While-Wend loop from before could be rewritten as

```
Do Until bytAnInteger > 10
    bytAnotherInteger = bytAnotherInteger + 10
    bytAnInteger = AnInteger + 1
Loop
```

or

```
Do
    bytAnotherInteger = bytAnotherInteger + 10
    bytAnInteger = AnInteger + 1
Loop Until bytAnInteger > 10
```

Do-Loop loops can be exited early using an Exit Do statement.

For-Next Loops

The For-Next loop corresponds to JavaScript's for loop. Its basic structure is

```
For variable = lower To higher
    VBScript code
Next
```

where variable is the loop *variable* and *lower* and *higher* are the start and end of the range to count through. As with traditional BASIC for loops, the For-Next loop increases the *variable* by one through the range. So,

```
For bytAnyInteger = 1 To 10
    bytAnotherInteger = bytAnotherInteger + 10
Next
```

would count from 1 to 10 using bytAnInteger as a counter variable and increase bytAnotherInteger by 10 with each iteration of a loop.

To count by a large increment or to decrease the counter variable with each iteration of the loop, the Step statement is used:

```
For bytAnInteger = 1 To 10 Step 2
    bytAnotherInteger = bytAnotherInteger + 10
Next
```

This would count from 1 to 10, as in the previous example, but would increase bytAnInteger by two with each iteration of the loop. Similarly,

```
For bytAnInteger = 10 To 1 Step -1
    bytAnotherInteger = bytAnotherInteger + 10
Next
```

would decrease bytAnInteger by one with each iteration of the loop.

The For-Next loop can be exited early using the Exit For statement, which is similar to the Exit Do statement.

The VBScript For-Next loop offers less flexibility than JavaScript's for loop, which resembles the C and C++ for loops.

Procedures in VBScript

VBScript handles procedures and functions in the way that languages such as Pascal do: It separates procedures from functions. This is different from JavaScript and languages such as C and C++, which have only functions.

The fundamental difference between procedures and functions is that functions are able to return a value, but procedures do not return values.

Procedures

A procedure is defined by a Sub statement and ends with an End Sub statement. As with JavaScript functions, a procedure can take arguments.

A procedure is defined using the following structure:

```
Sub ProcedureName(ArgumentList)
    VbScript Code
End Sub
```

where ArgumentList is an optional, comma-separated list of arguments to the procedure. If ArgumentList is omitted, the parentheses are still required, as they are in JavaScript function definitions. Procedures can be exited early using the Exit Sub statement.

For instance,

```
Sub DisplayName(strFirstName, strLastName)
    alert("Welcome " & strFirstName & " " & strLastName)
End Sub
```

would produce results similar to those in Figure 23.1 using the alert() method of the window object.

In order to call a procedure, it is sufficient to simply use the name of the procedure:

```
DisplayName "Arman", "Danesh"
```

Procedures also can be called using the Call statement:

```
Call DisplayName("Arman", "Danesh")
```

Notice that without the Call statement, the argument list has no parentheses around it but when using the Call statement, the parentheses must be used. Both of these forms produce the same result.

FIGURE 23.1.

Procedures can accept arguments and work with them.

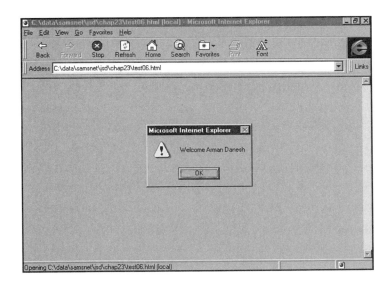

Functions

Functions are enclosed between `Function` and `End Function` statements and can take an optional argument list like a `Sub` procedure. The basic form of a function definition is as follows:

```
Function FunctionName(ArgumentList)
    VBScript Code
End Function
```

Functions can be exited early with the `Exit Function` statement.

As mentioned earlier, functions can return values, and this is generally how they are used. Values are returned by functions by assigning a value to the function's name inside the body of the function. For instance, the following function returns a single string, which is the combination of the first and last name passed to the function as arguments:

```
Function CompleteName(strFirstName, strLastName)
    CompeteName = StrFirstName & " " & strLastName
End Function
```

Calls to functions enclose the arguments in parentheses but don't use the `Call` statement. Function calls should occur on the right side of variable assignments or in expressions. To highlight how this works, the `DisplayName` procedure from the previous section could be rewritten

```
Sub DisplayName(strFirstName, strLastName)
    Dim TheName
    strTheName = CompleteName(strFirstName, strLastName)
    alert("Welcome " & strTheName)
End Sub
```

or simply

```
Sub DisplayName(strFirstName, strLastName)
    alert("Welcome " & CompleteName(strFirstName, strLastName))
End Sub
```

User Interface Functions in VBScript

VBScript does not offer many of the user-interface functions offered in Visual Basic or Visual Basic for Applications because the interface functionality is really provided through the Internet Explorer Object Model in the form of form elements, dialog boxes, and so on. Because VBScript can call all the methods in the Internet Explorer Object Hierarchy (as seen in the next section), there is little reason to duplicate this functionality with internal functions in VBScript.

VBScript does provide two user interface functions: InputBox and MsgBox.

InputBox is a VBScript function that takes a prompt string as an argument, asks the user for input in a dialog box displaying the prompt string, and then returns the value input by the user. InputBox resembles the functionality of the window.prompt() method. Because it is a function, its argument must be enclosed in parentheses:

VariableName = InputBox(*Argument*)

MsgBox, on the other hand, is a procedure that displays the argument in a simple dialog box with a single OK button. The procedure can be called in two ways:

MsgBox *Argument*

or

Call MsgBox(*Argument*)

The MsgBox procedure resembles the window.alert() method from the Object Hierarchy.

Although InputBox and prompt() are almost interchangeable and MsgBox and alert() achieve the same result, the visual appearance of the dialog boxes is different, as demonstrated in Figures 23.2 through 23.5.

FIGURE 23.2.
An InputBox *dialog box.*

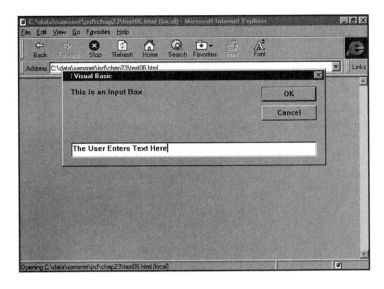

FIGURE 23.3.
A prompt() *dialog box.*

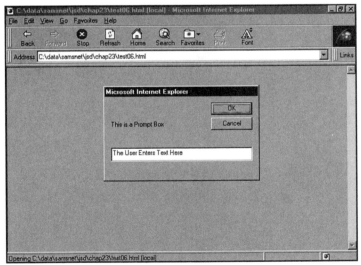

FIGURE 23.4.
A MsgBox *dialog box.*

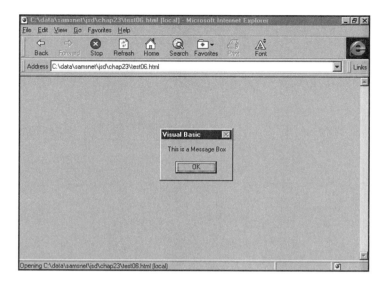

FIGURE 23.5.
An alert() *dialog box.*

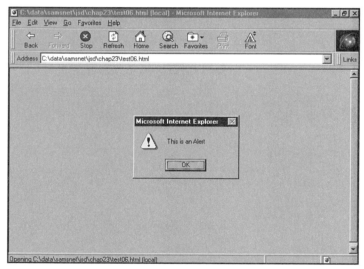

Accessing the Object Model in VBScript

Properties and methods of the Internet Explorer Object Model can be accessed in VBScript just as they are in JavaScript. For instance, the JavaScript script

```
<SCRIPT LANGUAGE="JavaScript">
var TestVar = document.forms[2].elements[3].value;
alert (TestVar);
</SCRIPT>
```

is functionally equivalent to the VBScript script

```
<SCRIPT LANGUAGE="VBScript">
Dim TestVar
TestVar = document.forms[2].elements[3].value
alert (TestVar)
</SCRIPT>
```

A VBScript Example

To highlight the use of VBScript in producing interactive applications, this section shows the development of a simple tic-tac-toe program using VBScript.

This script provides the following features:

- **A forms-based interface**: Nine buttons provide the whole interface. The buttons have blank labels until the user clicks on one or the computer makes a move, at which point the label changes to an "X" or an "O."
- **A computer opponent**: Users will play against the computer.

The game is implemented with the following script:

```
<HTML>

<HEAD>
<TITLE>VBScript Tic-Tac-Toe</TITLE>

<SCRIPT LANGUAGE="VBScript">

Dim strPlayerSymbol
strPlayerSymbol = " X "
Dim strComputerSymbol
strComputerSymbol = " O "
Dim strEmptySymbol
strEmptySymbol = ""

Dim GameBoard(2,2)
Dim BoardPoint(2,2)


Sub InitializeGame

        MsgBox "Welcome to VBScript Tic-Tac-Toe"

        Set BoardPoint(0,0) = document.board.elements(0)
        Set BoardPoint(1,0) = document.board.elements(1)
        Set BoardPoint(2,0) = document.board.elements(2)
        Set BoardPoint(0,1) = document.board.elements(3)
        Set BoardPoint(1,1) = document.board.elements(4)
        Set BoardPoint(2,1) = document.board.elements(5)
        Set BoardPoint(0,2) = document.board.elements(6)
        Set BoardPoint(1,2) = document.board.elements(7)
        Set BoardPoint(2,2) = document.board.elements(8)
```

```
                BuildBoard

        End Sub


        Sub BuildBoard

                For i = 0 to 2
                        For j = 0 to 2
                                BoardPoint(i,j).value = GameBoard(i,j)
                        Next
                Next

        End Sub


        Sub ClearBoard

                EmptyBoard

                BuildBoard

                MsgBox "Ready to Play!"

        End Sub


        Sub EmptyBoard

                For i = 0 To 2
                        For j = 0 To 2
                                GameBoard(i,j) = strEmptySymbol
                        Next
                Next

        End Sub


        Function Win(CheckI,CheckJ)

                Dim Result
                Result = False

                ' CHECK ROWS
                If GameBoard(0,CheckJ) = GameBoard(1,CheckJ) And GameBoard(1,CheckJ) =
                ➥GameBoard(2,CheckJ) Then
                        Result = True
                End If

                ' CHECK COLUMNS
                If GameBoard(CheckI,0) = GameBoard(CheckI,1) And GameBoard(CheckI,1) =
                ➥GameBoard(CheckI,2) Then
                        Result = True
                End if

                ' CHECK DIAGONALS
                If CheckI = CheckJ Then
                        If GameBoard(0,0) = GameBoard(1,1) And GameBoard(1,1) =
```

```
➥GameBoard(2,2) Then
                    Result = True
            End If
    End If

    If CheckI + CheckJ = 2 Then
            If GameBoard(0,2) = GameBoard(1,1) And GameBoard(1,1) =
            ➥GameBoard(2,0) Then
                    Result = True
            End If
    End If

    Win = Result

End Function


Sub Play(PlayI,PlayJ)

    Dim NewI
    Dim NewJ
    Dim Done
    Done = False

    If GameBoard(PlayI,PlayJ) <> strEmptySymbol Then

            MsgBox "This square is taken."
            Exit Sub

    End If

    GameBoard(PlayI,PlayJ) = strPlayerSymbol

    BuildBoard

    If Win(PlayI,PlayJ) = True Then

            MsgBox "Good Play! You Win!"
            ClearBoard

    Else

            For NewI = 0 to 2

                    For NewJ = 0 to 2

                            If GameBoard(NewI,NewJ) = strEmptySymbol Then
                                    GameBoard(NewI,NewJ) = strComputerSymbol
                                    If Win(NewI,NewJ) = True Then

                                            Done = True
                                            Exit For

                                    End If

                                    GameBoard(NewI,NewJ) = strEmptySymbol

                            End If

                    Next
```

```
                    If Done = True Then

                            Exit For

                    End If

            Next

            If Done = True Then

                    BuildBoard
                    MsgBox "The Computer Just Won!"
                    ClearBoard

            Else

                    For NewI = 0 to 2

                            For NewJ = 0 to 2

                                    If GameBoard(NewI,NewJ) = strEmptySymbol
                                    ➥Then
                                            GameBoard(NewI,NewJ) =
                                            ➥strPlayerSymbol
                                            If Win(NewI,NewJ) = True Then

                                                    Done = True
                                                    Exit For

                                            End If

                                            GameBoard(NewI,NewJ) =
                                            ➥strEmptySymbol

                                    End If
                            Next

                            If Done = True Then

                                    Exit For

                            End If

                    Next

                    If Done = True Then

                            GameBoard(NewI,NewJ) = strComputerSymbol
                            BuildBoard

                    Else

                            For NewI = 0 to 2

                                    For NewJ = 0 to 2

                                            If GameBoard(NewI,Newj) =
                                            ➥strEmptySymbol Then
                                                    GameBoard(NewI,NewJ) =
```

```vbscript
                                        ➥strComputerSymbol
                                        Done = True
                                        Exit For
                                End If

                        Next

                        If Done = True Then

                                Exit For

                        End If

                Next

                BuildBoard

            End If

        End If

    End If

End Sub
```

```html
</SCRIPT>

</HEAD>

<BODY BGCOLOR="white" onLoad="InitializeGame" LANGUAGE="VBScript">

<FORM NAME="board">

<DIV ALIGN=CENTER>

<TABLE CELLPADDING=10 CELLSPACING=10>

<TR>
<TD COLSPAN=3 BGCOLOR="#020A33" ALIGN=CENTER>
<FONT COLOR="white"><H2>VBScript Tic-Tac-Toe</H2></FONT>
<TD>
</TR>

<TR>
<TD BGCOLOR="cyan">
<INPUT TYPE=button VALUE="    " NAME="00" onClick="call Play(0,0)"
➥LANGUAGE="VBScript">
</TD>
<TD BGCOLOR="cyan">
<INPUT TYPE=button VALUE="    " NAME="01" onClick="call Play(1,0)"
➥LANGUAGE="VBScript">
</TD>
<TD BGCOLOR="cyan">
<INPUT TYPE=button VALUE="    " NAME="02" onClick="call Play(2,0)"
➥LANGUAGE="VBScript">
</TD>
</TR>

<TR>
```

```
<TD BGCOLOR="cyan">
<INPUT TYPE=button VALUE="   " NAME="10" onClick="call Play(0,1)"
➡LANGUAGE="VBScript">
</TD>
<TD BGCOLOR="cyan">
<INPUT TYPE=button VALUE="   " NAME="11" onClick="call Play(1,1)"
➡LANGUAGE="VBScript">
</TD>
<TD BGCOLOR="cyan">
<INPUT TYPE=button VALUE="   " NAME="12" onClick="call Play(2,1)"
➡LANGUAGE="VBScript">
</TD>
</TR>

<TR>
<TD BGCOLOR="cyan">
<INPUT TYPE=button VALUE="   " NAME="20" onClick="call Play(0,2)"
➡LANGUAGE="VBScript">
</TD>
<TD BGCOLOR="cyan">
<INPUT TYPE=button VALUE="   " NAME="21" onClick="call Play(1,2)"
➡LANGUAGE="VBScript">
</TD>
<TD BGCOLOR="cyan">
<INPUT TYPE=button VALUE="   " NAME="22" onClick="call Play(2,2)"
➡LANGUAGE="VBScript">
</TD>
</TR>

<TR>
<TD COLSPAN=3 ALIGN=CENTER BGCOLOR="maroon">
<INPUT TYPE=button VALUE="Start A New Game" onClick="ClearBoard">
</TD>
</TR>

</TABLE>

</DIV>

</FORM>

</BODY>

</HTML>
```

This script is fairly simple, but highlights several capabilities of VBScript, including the following:

■ Procedures and functions
■ Arrays
■ Accessing the `form` object
■ `If-Then-Else` statements

The script itself is divided into five procedures and one function. Before looking at each of these, take a look at the HTML form that defines the user interface.

The User Interface

The user interface for the tic-tac-toe game consists of a grid of nine buttons. Each of these represents one of the squares in the game. A tenth button enables users to start a new game.

The nine buttons making up the play area all start empty, representing a new game, as shown in Figure 23.6. As the player plays, the button labels change to "X" or "O" as appropriate (see Figure 23.7).

FIGURE 23.6.

The play area consists of nine blank HTML buttons.

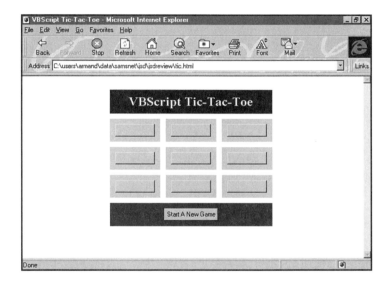

FIGURE 23.7.

As play proceeds, the button labels display either "X" or "O."

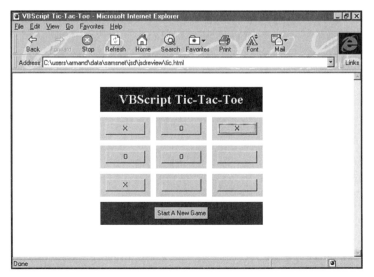

When a user clicks on a blank button to make a play, the `Play` subroutine is called. This subroutine makes the user's play and then chooses a play for the computer if the user hasn't won. The `Play` procedure is discussed later in this chapter.

Global Variables

The script itself starts by declaring global variables and constants. Three global constants—`strPlayerSymbol`, `strComputerSymbol`, and `strEmptySymbol`—represent the strings displayed in the play buttons when the player plays, when the computer plays, and when no play has been made in a square. These are used throughout the script for readability rather than using explicit string literals throughout the script.

Two global arrays—`GameBoard()` and `BoardPoint()`—are also declared. `GameBoard()` reflects the contents of the game board displayed to the user. The values in the array reflect the values displayed in each of the buttons. All work is done with the `GameBoard()` array and then these values are reflected into the user interface using the `BuildBoard` procedure, discussed later in this chapter.

`BoardPoint()` serves a different purpose than `GameBoard()`. The entries in the `BoardPoint()` array point directly to the `button` objects associated with the buttons in the game board.

The `InitializeGame` Procedure

The `InitializeGame` procedure is called only when the document is loaded. It is invoked through the `onLoad` event handler of the `<BODY>` tag.

The procedure starts by displaying a dialog box welcoming the user. Rather than using the `alert()` method of the `window` object, the `MsgBox` procedure built into VBScript is used. This looks like Figure 23.8. Next, each of the entries in `BoardPoint()` is made to point at one of the play buttons in the user interface.

The `Set` command is used to create these pointers to the `button` objects. It isn't possible to simply assign the `button` objects to the `BoardPoint()` array without the `Set` keyword. Notice that the `elements()` array of the `form` object is used to access each of the nine play buttons from the form.

Finally, the `BuildBoard` procedure is called to display the current state of the game (which should consist of nine empty buttons).

The `BuildBoard` Procedure

The `BuildBoard` procedure reflects the contents of the `GameBoard()` array into the actual playing form displayed for the user. This is done with two nested `For` loops that loop through the `GameBoard()` and `BoardPoint()` arrays, assigning the values in `GameBoard()` to the value properties of each of the `button` objects pointed to by the `BoardPoint()` array.

FIGURE 23.8.

The user is welcomed with a dialog box created using the MsgBox *procedure.*

The ClearBoard Procedure

The ClearBoard procedure is called whenever the playing area needs to be cleared for a new game. This is done when the user clicks on the "Start a New Game" button or when either the user or the computer wins a game.

The procedure is simple. It calls the EmptyBoard procedure, calls BuildBoard to display the new empty board, then displays a message box telling the user that the board is ready for play.

The EmptyBoard Procedure

The EmptyBoard procedure clears the GameBoard() array by using nested for loops to assign strEmptySymbol to each entry in the array.

The Win() Function

This function is designed to check if a play leads to a win for either the computer or the user. It takes two parameters: CheckI and CheckJ, which represent the row and column of the play which you need to check for a win.

The function is fairly simple. It starts by creating a variable called Result and setting its value to false. This makes the assumption that no win has happened.

The function then checks across the row the play has been made in to see if all squares in the row contain the same value. If all squares match, then Result is set to true.

Next, the column is checked using a similar technique. Finally, diagonals are checked if the user's play falls on a diagonal. You can check if the play is on a diagonal as follows: If `CheckI` and `CheckJ` are equal, then the play is on the diagonal from top-left corner to bottom-right. If `CheckI` and `CheckJ` add to a value of two, then play lies on the other diagonal.

Finally, once all the checks have been made, the value of `Result` is returned by the function.

The `Play()` Procedure

The `Play()` procedure is the central portion of the script. It's where a user's play is made and the computer decides where to play. It takes two parameters: `PlayI` and `PlayJ`, representing the square the user is trying to play into.

The procedure first checks if a play has already been made in the user's selected position. If the value in this position is not `strEmptySymbol` then the user is told the square is taken and the procedure is exited using `Exit Sub`.

If the square is empty, then the user's play is made by assigning `strPlayerSYmbol` to the selected square.

Next a check is made to see if the player has won by calling `Win()`. If the player has won, the player is informed, the board is cleared, and a new game is ready to be played.

Failing this, an appropriate play for the computer needs to be found. This is a three-fold process. Using nested `For` loops, you loop through all the squares looking for empty positions. For each of these positions a test is made to see if the computer could win by playing in the position. If the computer can win with a play, that play is made and the board is redrawn.

If the computer can't win with a single play, the code next loops through all the positions to see if the user can win on her next move. If she can, the computer needs to play in this position to block the user's win.

Finally, if the computer can't win and there is no potential user win to block, the computer plays in the first available empty square.

VBScript into the Future

Although VBScript is based on the widely used Visual Basic programming language and development environment, it still suffers from the shortcoming that there are no strong examples on the Internet of VBScript in action.

In addition, the Internet Explorer Object Model is not yet fully usable from VBScript (for instance, using some objects that work in JavaScript on Internet Explorer may not yet work in VBScript) and the examples of built-in functions and features of VBScript on Microsoft's Web site are limited.

Still, given the popularity of Visual Basic, it seems likely that there are sufficient programmers who will adopt VBScript as their Web scripting language of choice with time.

Summary

This chapter covered the basics of VBScript—Microsoft's alternative to JavaScript for client-side scripting of Web pages. VBScript offers a familiar and easy-to-use programming environment, which should be able to be used to achieve results similar to JavaScript after it is completely implemented.

The next chapter takes a look at ActiveX objects, the other unique feature of Internet Explorer. ActiveX objects provide interactive functionality similar to that in Java and can be used for everything from animation to viewing OLE files such as Word and Excel files.

24

ActiveX Controls

by Arman Danesh

In addition to VBScript and the Internet Explorer Object Model, which are used for scripting client-side events within the context of HTML documents, Internet Explorer also offers ActiveX controls (or objects).

Based on Microsoft's OLE (Object Linking and Embedding) technology, used for inter-application document sharing and interaction in the Windows environment, ActiveX objects offer an alternative to Java for embedding highly interactive controls and applets in Web pages.

In this chapter, you will learn about ActiveX controls and their place in the Internet Explorer framework. Specifically, you will see the following:

- An overview of ActiveX controls
- Examples of ActiveX controls
- Using ActiveX objects in Web pages
- ActiveX object development information

An Introduction to ActiveX Controls

ActiveX—essentially another name for Microsoft's OLE technology—is made up of several components, including:

- ActiveX controls
- ActiveX documents (such as Excel, Word, or other non-HTML documents)
- Active Scripting (such as VBScript or JavaScript)
- Java Virtual Machine
- ActiveX Server Framework (providing functions like security and database access)

In this chapter, you're covering ActiveX controls, which are components, similar to Java applets, that adhere to Microsoft's OLE standards. They can be inserted in Web pages and also used in programs developed in any of Microsoft's programming and database languages.

Internet Explorer's support for ActiveX objects allows it to be easily extended with new features—including formatting and animation support—by plugging in new ActiveX controls.

The ActiveX model used in Internet Explorer is based on Component Object Model (COM) technology, which allows components built in different languages—such as Visual Basic, C++, and Java—to work together. This ability gives development flexibility currently lacking with Java applets because developers familiar with other development tools should be able to develop ActiveX controls.

Internet Explorer itself is, essentially, a set of ActiveX controls. All the pieces of Internet Explorer, such as the scripting engine, are ActiveX objects that can be used in other applications to give them Internet capabilities, just as Internet Explorer can use other ActiveX applications to extend its functionality.

Unlike Navigator plug-ins, which generally are installed by running a setup program, ActiveX controls operate more like Java applets—they are downloaded when needed. Unlike applets, once they're downloaded and installed, they remain in place for future use, but applets generally disappear at the end of the current session and need to be downloaded again for future use.

Internet Explorer comes with several controls, including

- Controls to help in authoring Web pages, including one that displays a "New!" message until a specified date
- Controls that display data in new ways, such as charts and angled text
- Controls for adding functions like timers and animation

Some ActiveX Controls

Like Navigator plug-ins, the list of available ActiveX controls, both from Microsoft and third-party vendors, is growing rapidly. A selection is listed in Table 24.1.

Table 24.1. Selected ActiveX controls.

Name	Company	Description
Acrobat	Adobe Systems	Adobe is implementing an Acrobat viewer as an ActiveX control.
ActiveMovie	Microsoft	Allows AVI, QuickTime, MPEG, WAV, AU, AIFF, and MIDI files to be embedded in pages.
Billboard Manager	NCompass Labs	Displays several images as a billboard with a large selection of transitions between images.
Chart	Microsoft	Displays graphs and charts from a set of data.
Chart FX	Software FX	Creates scriptable business and scientific charts.
EarthTime	Starfish Software	This ActiveX control from Starfish Software can display the time in multiple cities at the same time. (See Figure 24.1.)

continues

Table 24.1. continued

Name	Company	Description
HTML Layout Control	Microsoft	Enables support for HTML layouts (discussed in Chapter 21, "Microsoft Internet Explorer").
Label	Microsoft	Can display text at any angle as well as displaying on custom paths. (See Figure 24.2.)
Look@Me	Farallon Communications	View the screen of another computer running Look@Me or Timbuktu Pro.
Marquee Control	Microsoft	Allows the content of an HTML document to be scrolled through in a frame at a set speed.
PowerPoint Animation Player	Microsoft	Plays PowerPoint animations in Web pages (animations are created with PowerPoint Animation Publisher—a freely available extension for PowerPoint for Windows 95). (See Figure 24.3.)
RealAudio Control	Progressive Networks	Enables Internet Explorer to play streamed RealAudio sound files.
Shockwave	Macromedia	Macromedia is making its Shockwave viewers available as ActiveX controls.
Stock Ticker	Microsoft	Provides a stock ticker.
SylvanMaps	Sylvan Ascent	Display and analyze geographic data. (See Figure 24.4.)
UniVerse	Gamma Productions	A Unicode-based editor. (See Figure 24.5.)
VDOLive	VDOnet	Provides real-time, streamed audio and video on the Internet.

Name	Company	Description
VRML Control	Microsoft	Provides Virtual Reality Modeling Language support in Internet Explorer.

A more complete list of ActiveX controls is available on Microsoft's Web site at `http://www.microsoft.com/activex/controls/`.

FIGURE 24.1.
The EarthTime control.

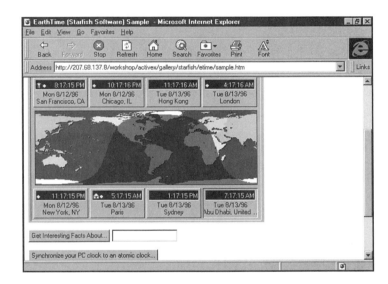

FIGURE 24.2.
The Label control.

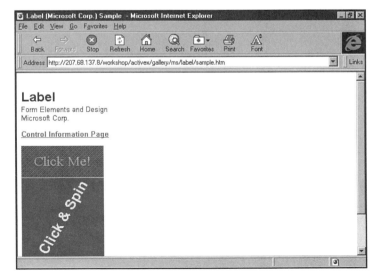

FIGURE 24.3.
*The PowerPoint
Animation Player.*

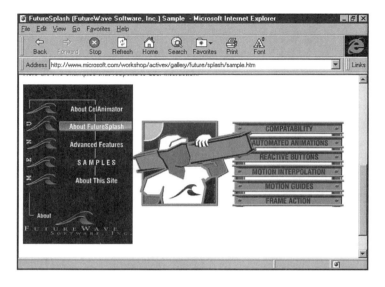

FIGURE 24.4.
The SylvanMaps control.

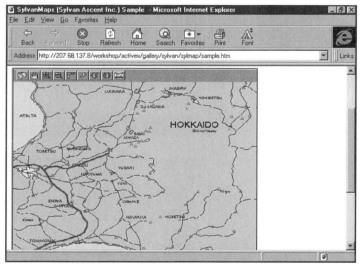

ActiveX Controls in Navigator 3

Although Navigator 3 doesn't include built-in support for ActiveX objects, a third-party plug-in from NCompass Labs offers ActiveX support in Netscape Navigator. With this plug-in, you can view pages that include ActiveX controls in Navigator as well as Internet Explorer. The ActiveX plug-in is available from NCompass's Web site at `http://www.ncomapsslabs.com/`.

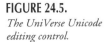

FIGURE 24.5.

The UniVerse Unicode editing control.

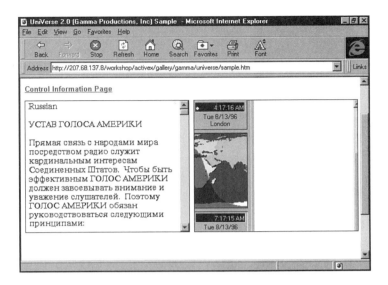

ActiveX Support

ActiveX is currently supported on Windows systems, and work is underway to offer ActiveX support on Macintosh systems and UNIX environments.

In addition, Microsoft announced in the summer of 1996 that it will transfer ownership, control, and future development of ActiveX technology to a standards body. By doing this, it's likely that ActiveX will overcome its biggest criticism in the Web community—that it is proprietary technology—and ensure its position next to HTML, Java, and other open solutions for interactive content on the Internet.

Working with Active Controls

Active controls are included in Web pages by using the `<OBJECT>` tag, which takes several attributes, listed in Table 24.2.

Table 24.2. Attributes of the `<OBJECT>` tag.

Attribute	Description
ALIGN	Specifies the alignment for the object. Possible values are `BASELINE`, `CENTER`, `LEFT`, `MIDDLE`, `RIGHT`, `TEXTBOTTOM`, `TEXTMIDDLE`, and `TEXTTOP`.
BORDER	Specifies the width of the object's border in pixels.

continues

Table 24.2. continued

Attribute	Description
CLASSID	Identifies the object implementation. Registered controls take a value of the form CLSID:*class-identifier* where *class-identifier* is a complex alphanumeric string identifying the control.
CODEBASE	Specifies the code base for the object.
CODETYPE	Specifies the Internet media type.
DATA	Indicates the location of the data for the control to use.
DECLARE	Declares an object without activating an instance of it.
HEIGHT	Specifies the height of the object in pixels.
HSPACE	Specifies the horizontal margin in pixels.
NAME	Specifies the name of the object.
SHAPES	Indicates that the object has shaped hyperlinks. Takes no values.
STANDBY	Indicates a message to display while the object is loading. Takes a string value.
TYPE	Specifies the Internet media type of the data.
USEMAP	Specifies an image map to use with the object.
VSPACE	Specifies the vertical margin in pixels.
WIDTH	Specifies the width of the object in pixels.

In addition to the <OBJECT> tag, the <OBJECT> tag acts as a container that can include <PARAM> tags for any parameters that need to be passed to control—just like the <PARAM> tag is used to pass values to a Java applet in Navigator.

For instance, to include a world clock in a page using the EarthTime control from Starfish Software, you could use a tag like this:

```
<OBJECT ID="EarthTime1" WIDTH=297 HEIGHT=199
 CLASSID="CLSID:9590092D-8811-11CF-8075-444553540000">
    <PARAM NAME="_Version" VALUE="65536">
    <PARAM NAME="_ExtentX" VALUE="7858">
    <PARAM NAME="_ExtentY" VALUE="5239">
    <PARAM NAME="_StockProps" VALUE="0">
</OBJECT>
```

This produces results like the ones shown in Figure 24.6.

Note that the correct use of the CLSID value and other <PARAM> settings is important for the control to work, so for practical purposes it isn't realistic to include controls in pages by manually writing the <OBJECT> tags. Effective coding of a complex <OBJECT> tag is better done by using the ActiveX Control Pad rather than manual coding. The ActiveX Control Pad is a development tool that can be used to include controls, build HTML layouts, and produce VBScript and JavaScript scripts. The ActiveX Control Pad is discussed in detail in Chapter 25, "Using the ActiveX Control Pad."

FIGURE 24.6.
The <OBJECT> tag can be used to include ActiveX controls in a page.

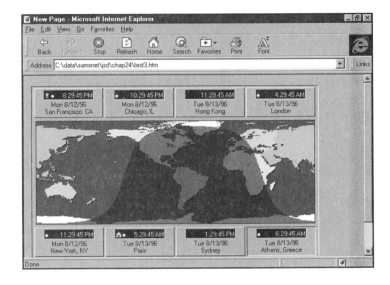

Scripting ActiveX Controls

Like most other objects, ActiveX controls generally have properties and methods available for use in JavaScript or VBScript scripts. Each control has its own set of properties and methods; information about them is available from producers of ActiveX controls.

For instance, the EarthTime control offers the following properties and methods:

- AboutBox()
- CenterMapBySelectedClock()
- ChangeCity()
- ChooseAsHomeClock()
- ChooseAsLocalClock()
- ClockSettings()
- Conversions()
- FactsAboutTheCity()
- ModifyCityInformation()
- SyncClock()
- TimeDifference()
- City

For most, the name of the method or property explains its purpose. For instance, `ChangeCity()` opens a Change City dialog box like the one in Figure 24.7, and `FactsAboutTheCity()` opens an information box like the one in Figure 24.8 for the currently selected city. The City property evaluates to the name of the currently selected city as a string.

FIGURE 24.7.

The EarthTime Change City dialog box.

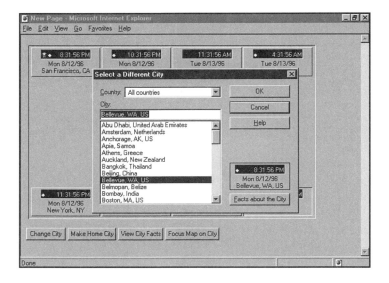

FIGURE 24.8.

The EarthTime City Facts dialog box.

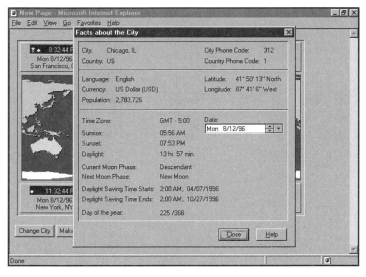

Using these methods, you can create a page that includes the EarthTime control, as well as extra buttons for the following functions:

■ Changing a city

■ Selecting a city as the home city

■ Viewing facts about a city

■ Shifting the map to focus on a city

To do this, you simply need to create an HTML form with buttons for each of these functions and call the appropriate methods of the EarthTime object from the buttons' event handlers:

```
<HTML>
<HEAD>
<TITLE>Scripting a Control</TITLE>
</HEAD>
<BODY>
    <OBJECT NAME="EarthTime1" WIDTH=533 HEIGHT=335
            CLASSID="CLSID:9590092D-8811-11CF-8075-444553540000">
    <PARAM NAME="_Version" VALUE="65536">
    <PARAM NAME="_ExtentX" VALUE="14111">
    <PARAM NAME="_ExtentY" VALUE="8855">
    <PARAM NAME="_StockProps" VALUE="0">
    </OBJECT>
    <FORM NAME="controls">
        <INPUT LANGUAGE="JavaScript" TYPE=button VALUE="Change City"
➥ONCLICK="EarthTime1.ChangeCity()"
        NAME="cityChange">
        <INPUT LANGUAGE="JavaScript" TYPE=button VALUE="Make Home City"
➥ONCLICK="EarthTime1.ChooseAsHomeClock()"
        NAME="homeClick">
        <INPUT LANGUAGE="JavaScript" TYPE=button VALUE="View City Facts"
        ONCLICK="EarthTime1.FactsAboutTheCity()" NAME="viewFacts">
        <INPUT LANGUAGE="JavaScript" TYPE=button
➥ONCLICK="EarthTime1.CenterMapBySelectedClock()"
        NAME="focusCity" VALUE="Focus Map on City">
    </FORM>
</BODY>
</HTML>
```

This produces a page with the four buttons under the EarthTime control, like the one shown in Figure 24.9.

The scripting is simple—the EarthTime object is referred to by the name specified in the NAME attribute of the <OBJECT> tag, and the event handlers for each button in the form make one call to a method of the EarthTime object.

In addition to properties and methods, many controls have event handlers of their own, many with robust sets of scriptable events. For instance, the Label control provides handlers for the following events:

■ BeforeDragOver

■ BeforeDropOrPaste

■ Click

■ DblClick

FIGURE 24.9.

Scripts can be used to extend the user interface of an ActiveX control.

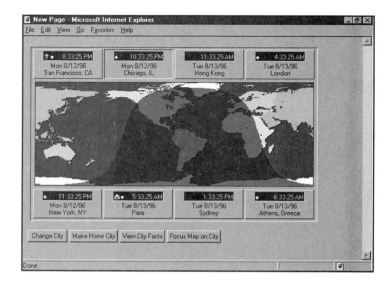

■ Error

■ MouseDown

■ MouseMove

■ MouseUp

Using these events, you can create interactive text labels. For instance, change the text style by scripting event handlers for the MouseDown and MouseUp events, or change other properties, such as the text of the label on clicks or double clicks:

```
<HTML>
<HEAD>
<TITLE>New Page</TITLE>
</HEAD>
<BODY>
    <SCRIPT LANGUAGE="JavaScript" FOR="Label1" EVENT="MouseUp(Button, Shift, X,
➥Y)">
    <!--
    Label1.Font.Italic = false
    -->
    </SCRIPT>
    <SCRIPT LANGUAGE="JavaScript" FOR="Label1" EVENT="MouseDown(Button, Shift, X,
➥Y)">
    <!--
    Label1.Font.Italic = true
    -->
    </SCRIPT>
    <OBJECT ID="Label1" WIDTH=192 HEIGHT=171
     CLASSID="CLSID:978C9E23-D4B0-11CE-BF2D-00AA003F40D0">
        <PARAM NAME="ForeColor" VALUE="2147483669">
        <PARAM NAME="Caption" VALUE="This is a test">
        <PARAM NAME="PicturePosition" VALUE="262148">
```

```
                <PARAM NAME="Size" VALUE="5075;4493">
                <PARAM NAME="BorderColor" VALUE="2147483670">
                <PARAM NAME="BorderStyle" VALUE="1">
                <PARAM NAME="FontName" VALUE="Technical">
                <PARAM NAME="FontEffects" VALUE="1073741825">
                <PARAM NAME="FontHeight" VALUE="320">
                <PARAM NAME="FontCharSet" VALUE="0">
                <PARAM NAME="FontPitchAndFamily" VALUE="2">
                <PARAM NAME="ParagraphAlign" VALUE="3">
                <PARAM NAME="FontWeight" VALUE="700">
        </OBJECT>
<BR>
        <SCRIPT LANGUAGE="JavaScript" FOR="Label2" EVENT="Click()">
        <!--
        Label2.Caption = "Clicked."
        -->
        </SCRIPT>
        <SCRIPT LANGUAGE="JavaScript" FOR="Label2" EVENT="DblClick(Cancel)">
        <!--
        Label2.Caption = "Double Clicked."
        -->
        </SCRIPT>
        <OBJECT ID="Label2" WIDTH=97 HEIGHT=24
         CLASSID="CLSID:978C9E23-D4B0-11CE-BF2D-00AA003F40D0">
                <PARAM NAME="VariousPropertyBits" VALUE="268435483">
                <PARAM NAME="Caption" VALUE="Another Test">
                <PARAM NAME="Size" VALUE="2566;635">
                <PARAM NAME="SpecialEffect" VALUE="1">
                <PARAM NAME="FontHeight" VALUE="240">
                <PARAM NAME="FontCharSet" VALUE="0">
                <PARAM NAME="FontPitchAndFamily" VALUE="2">
                <PARAM NAME="FontWeight" VALUE="0">
        </OBJECT>
</BODY>
</HTML>
```

Two text labels are displayed. In the first, holding the mouse button down changes the text style to italic; releasing it changes the text back to straight, non-italic text. This is done by assigning true or false to the Italic property of the Font object of the Label control.

Similarly, the second label changes its displayed text by assigning new values to the caption property of the Label object, based on whether the user clicks or double-clicks on the text.

This script produces results like those shown in Figure 24.10.

Notice that the special syntax of the <SCRIPT> tag with the FOR and EVENT attributes is used to script the event handlers for the objects.

FIGURE 24.10.

*Objects have scriptable
event handlers.*

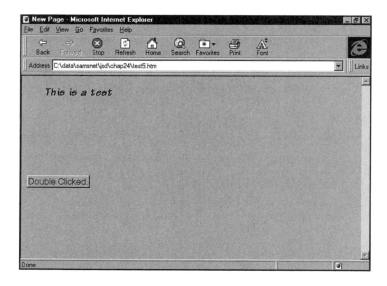

Developing ActiveX Controls

As with Navigator plug-ins, developing ActiveX controls requires more programming knowledge than scripting Web pages does and is beyond the scope of this book. Microsoft offers the ActiveX Software Developer's Kit, which includes tools and documentation, for those who want to take a stab at developing ActiveX controls. You can get more information about the ActiveX SDK from the Microsoft Web site at `http://www.microsoft.com/intdev/sdk/`.

To take advantage of the SDK, you need the following:

- Internet Explorer 3.0 beta 2 or above
- A compiler compatible with the SDK (such as Visual C++ 4.1 from Microsoft)
- Windows 95 or NT 4.0
- The Win32 SDK for Windows NT 4.0, which is available to members of the Microsoft Developer's Network. Information about MSDN is available at `http://www.microsoft.com/msdn/`.

NOTE

The main resource for ActiveX information on the Web is at `http://www.microsoft.com/activex/`.

Summary

In this chapter, you learned about ActiveX controls and their place in the Internet Explorer Framework. ActiveX controls provide an alternative to Java applets and Navigator plug-ins—based on Microsoft's OLE technology—for adding component-level interactivity and file support to Internet Explorer.

You were introduced to some sample controls and learned how to combine them into Web pages, then used JavaScript to write scripts that extend their interfaces, in much the way you can for applets and plug-ins.

In the next chapter, you will take a closer look at the ActiveX Control Pad, which gives you an ideal tool for developing Web pages that combine ActiveX controls, HTML layouts, and scripts.

25

Using the ActiveX Control Pad

by Arman Danesh

With the combination of HTML Layouts, standard HTML, ActiveX controls, JavaScript, VBScript and Java applets, developing Web pages is getting increasingly complex.

In order to ease the process of developing Web-based applications for Internet Explorer, Microsoft has developed ActiveX Control Pad, which offers a degree of point-and-click simplicity to developing Web pages that include HTML layouts and ActiveX objects as well as scripts.

This chapter looks at using ActiveX, focusing on the following:

■ The ActiveX Control Pad interface
■ Basic HTML editing
■ Adding ActiveX objects to pages
■ Adding HTML layouts to pages
■ Scripting events in pages
■ Special features of the Script Wizard
■ Finding more information about the ActiveX Control Pad

This chapter doesn't attempt to cover all features of the ActiveX Control Pad and its components. Rather, it examines enough of the features of the ActiveX Control Pad so that someone familiar with HTML, JavaScript, or VBScript and the principles of ActiveX controls and HTML layouts will be able to take advantage of the application.

ActiveX Control Pad Basics

The ActiveX Control Pad provides four main tools for creating integrated Web pages:

■ **HTML editor**: A basic text editor that can be used for editing the results produced by the other tools (see Figure 25.1).
■ **ActiveX Control Editor**: Enables a single ActiveX control to be inserted into an HTML document and its properties to be edited (see Figure 25.2).
■ **HTML Layout Editor**: Enables drag-and-drop development of HTML layouts consisting of multiple objects and controls (see Figure 25.3).
■ **Scripting Wizard**: Can be used to create scripts for events associated with objects in the current HTML document—scripts can be entirely built by selecting from lists rather than by manual coding (see Figure 25.4).

FIGURE 25.1.

The HTML editor window.

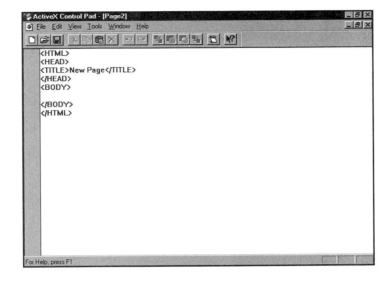

FIGURE 25.2.

The ActiveX Control Editor.

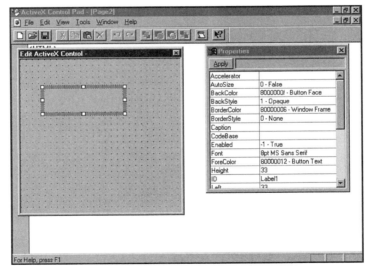

FIGURE 25.3.
The HTML Layout Editor.

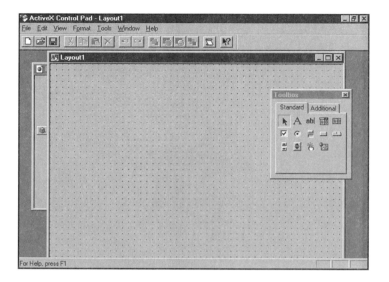

FIGURE 25.4.
The Scripting Wizard.

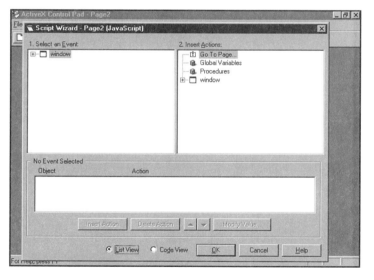

The ActiveX Control Pad Toolbar

Like most Windows 95 and NT applications available today, the ActiveX Control Pad includes a toolbar with buttons for many frequent actions, such as opening and saving files, cutting and pasting, undoing and redoing actions, and adjusting the placement of objects in a layout.

Figure 25.5 highlights the functions of the buttons on the toolbar.

FIGURE 25.5.

The ActiveX Control Pad toolbar.

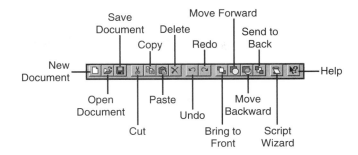

The HTML Editor

The ActiveX Control Pad isn't designed as an HTML editor. It contains none of the features of sophisticated HTML editors, such as syntax checking, toolbars for easily inserting tags, or WYSIWYG HTML editing and development.

Rather, because an HTML document is the core of building pages with objects and scripts, the ActiveX Control Pad provides its HTML editing window as a way to view—and change—the code automatically generated by the Control Pad's other development tools.

The HTML editing window acts as a simple GUI text editor similar to Windows' own Notepad text editor. The only functionality feature beyond this is that objects, layouts, and scripts in the file have a small icon next to them that can be used to directly edit the script or object using the relevant tool in the ActiveX Control Pad. Figure 25.6 shows an HTML file in the ActiveX HTML editing window with a script and an embedded object. Next to the script and object are icons that can be used to launch the relevant Control Pad editing tool. If the user clicks on the icon next to the `<OBJECT>` tag, the relevant window is opened (see Figure 25.7).

In addition to using the icon next to the relevant section of the HTML file, when the cursor is inside the relevant section of the HTML source code, the Edit menu includes a choice to launch the relevant editing tool. For instance, in the example in Figure 25.6, if the cursor were inside the JavaScript script, then the `Edit` menu would include an `Edit Script` entry, as shown in Figure 25.8.

Editing Features of the HTML Editor

The HTML editor window provides standard editing features such as cutting and pasting, available on the `Edit` menu, from the toolbar and by using keystroke combinations. Table 25.1 shows how each of these commands can be invoked.

FIGURE 25.6.

The ActiveX Control Pad's HTML editing window provides icons to launch the script and control editors.

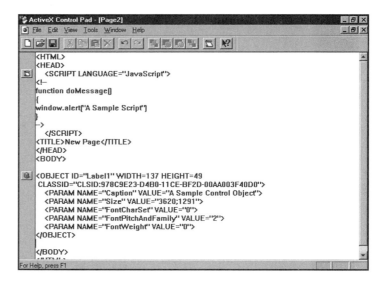

FIGURE 25.7.

If the user clicks on an icon next to a script, control, or HTML layout in the HTML editing window, the relevant editing tool is launched.

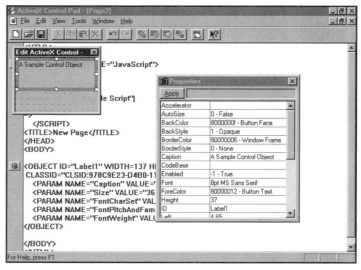

FIGURE 25.8.

The Edit menu can be used instead of the icons to launch editing tools.

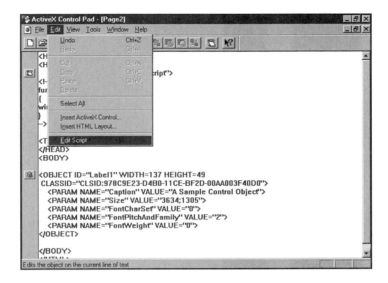

Table 25.1. Editing commands.

Command	Edit Menu Selection	Keystroke	Toolbar Button
Undo Action	Undo	Ctrl-Z	
Redo Action	Redo	Ctrl-R	
Cut Item	Cut	Ctrl-X	
Copy Item	Copy	Ctrl-C	
Paste Item	Paste	Ctrl-V	
Delete Item	Delete	Del	

In addition to these standard editing commands, the Edit menu also provides a Select All command that selects all the text in the HTML window or all objects in a layout.

The ActiveX Control Editor

The Control Pad provides two ways to include ActiveX controls. One is to include individual controls and the other is to build a layout that includes multiple controls in an HTML Layout.

To include a single control, the Control Editor is used.

Inserting an ActiveX Control

An ActiveX control is inserted into a document by choosing `Insert ActiveX Control ...` from the `Edit` menu. When this command is chosen it invokes the Control Editor. When inserting a new control, the Editor first provides a list of available controls, as shown in Figure 25.9.

FIGURE 25.9.

When inserting an ActiveX control, a list of available controls is presented.

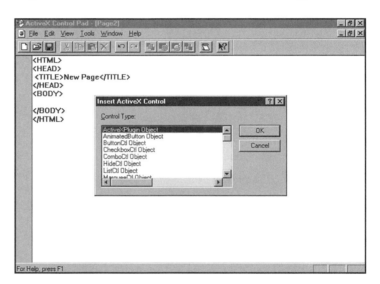

Any control can be chosen from the list. Pressing the OK button opens the Control Editor for the selected ActiveX control.

For instance, choosing `PopupMenu` object from the control list and pressing OK opens an editor that looks like Figure 25.10.

The Control Editor Windows

Once an object is selected, the Control Editor is opened with two windows like those shown in Figure 25.10.

FIGURE 25.10.

The PopupMenu *Object in the Control Editor.*

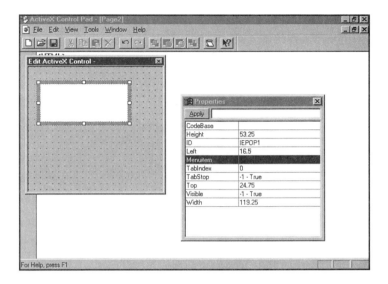

The first window is an Edit window. Here, the object can be resized and positioned. By dragging on the corners of the object box, the control can be resized. Dragging the object moves it.

The other window, the Properties window, provides a table of the object's properties and their values. These values can be edited and changed in this window. To do this, simply select the field to be changed and enter a new value in the text entry field next to the Apply button at the top of the window. Finally, click on the Apply button to apply the changes.

In some cases, a field can take a fixed list of values, such as True and False. In these cases, the text entry field next to the Apply button becomes a drop-down list like the one shown in Figure 25.11.

In some cases, ActiveX objects provide an alternative way to edit their properties. For instance, the UniCode editor control from Gamma Software provides an alternative interface, like the one shown in Figure 25.12, to change property values by selecting from forms.

These alternative property editing boxes can be opened by right-clicking on the object in the editing window and selecting Properties.

Inserting and Editing the Control

Once all the properties have been set, the object can be inserted into a Web page by closing the editor window. When this is done, an <OBJECT> tag with the appropriate parameters is inserted wherever the cursor is in the HTML file. An icon appears next to the tag, enabling the Control Editor to be launched quickly if needed.

FIGURE 25.11.

The Text Entry field in the properties menu can become a drop-down menu.

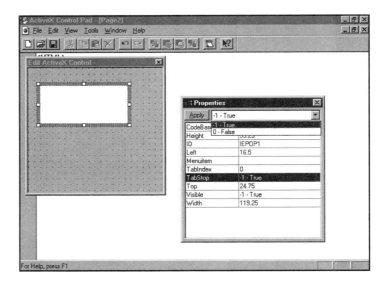

FIGURE 25.12.

Some controls have alternative property editing interfaces.

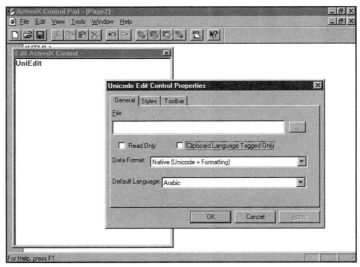

In order to edit the control, you can directly change the HTML code that appears in the HTML window or click on the icon next to the <OBJECT> tag to re-open the Control Editor and the Properties window.

The HTML Layout Editor

The HTML Layout Editor is similar to the Control Editor you just looked at, but it provides the extra functionality needed to create an HTML layout file to be subsequently inserted into an HTML document.

Creating an HTML Layout

New HTML layouts are created by selecting New HTML Layout from the File menu. This opens the HTML Layout Editor, which consists of two main windows: a main layout window, which looks like the Control Editor window, used to insert an ActiveX control, and a Toolbox window like the one shown in Figure 25.13, with two tabbed lists of ActiveX controls that can be included in the layout.

FIGURE 25.13.

The HTML Layout Editor includes a toolbox.

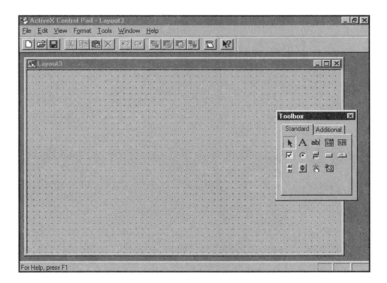

Designing a Layout

The process of designing an HTML layout is simple. Controls are selected from the toolbox and are then placed into the layout by clicking and dragging the rectangular space they should occupy.

Once a control is inserted, its properties can be edited by right-clicking on the object and selecting Properties from the pop-up menu. This either opens the standard properties box used in the ActiveX Control Editor, or a custom properties box like the ones used by the UniCode Editor from Gamma Software.

The toolbox itself has two tabs—each with a set of icons representing different controls that can be included in a layout. The two tabs are for "standard" and "additional" tools. Initially, the collection of controls in these sets may be limited. Additional controls can be added by right-clicking in the body of one of the tabs and selecting Additional Controls from the pop-up menu that appears.

This opens a dialog box with a list of controls like the one shown in Figure 25.14. Controls can be selected or removed from the list for the tab in question by clicking in the checkbox to the left of the control's name.

FIGURE 25.14.

Users can add controls to the toolbox in the HTML Layout Editor.

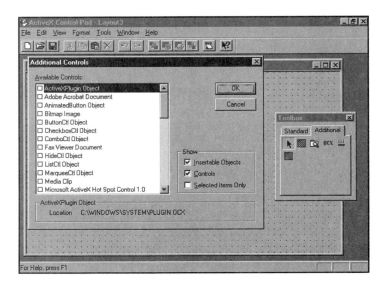

Once controls and objects are in the layout and their properties have been edited, the layout itself can be designed using the conventional principles of most Windows-based graphics-capable applications. Clicking and dragging with the left button of the mouse moves objects. Clicking on an object and then clicking and dragging one of the resizing controls allows the object to be resized.

The Format menu provides basic layout functions, including the following:

■ Object alignment functions
■ Automatic sizing capabilities
■ Spacing controls

Customizing the HTML Layout Editor's Grid

The Layout window can include a grid to help align objects and design pages. The grid can be set by selecting Options from the Tools menu and then selecting HTML Layout ... from the sub-menu. This opens a dialog box where the size of the horizontal and vertical grid can be set and checkboxes are provided to make the grid visible and to force objects to snap to the grid.

Adding Scripts to Controls

Scripts for events associated with objects in an HTML layout can be added by right-clicking on an object in the Layout window and selecting Script Wizard from the pop-up menu. This launches the Script Wizard described later in this chapter, which can be used to create and edit scripts for the various objects in the layout.

Saving and Incorporating HTML Layouts in Documents

When a layout is ready, it can be saved by selecting the save button from the tool bar or the Save As ... entry or Save entry from the File menu. Layout files should be saved with an .ALX extension.

Once saved, a layout file is ready to be included in a document. First place the cursor in the appropriate place in an HTML document and select Insert HTML Layout ... from the Edit menu. This opens a file dialog box where you can choose the appropriate .ALX file. The layout is included in the HTML document as an <OBJECT> tag with a layout icon next to it to easily jump to the HTML Layout Editor to edit the layout.

The Script Wizard

The ActiveX Control Pad provides the Script Wizard, which can help minimize the amount of manual VBScript and JavaScript coding that needs to be done when interactive Web pages are being built.

The underlying assumption of the Script Wizard is that it's designed to write scripts to associate with events and event handlers of objects available in a page. Scripting can be done entirely by selecting from lists and answering questions in dialog boxes, if desired.

Working with the Script Wizard Window

The Script Wizard window is divided into three sections—an event list, a list of possible actions, and the script itself—as indicated in Figure 25.15.

The Script Wizard can be operated in two modes: List View or Code View. In List View, scripts for various events appear as a list of actions to take for various objects (see Figure 25.16) while in Code View, the actual JavaScript or VBScript program code is displayed in the script section of the window (see Figure 25.17).

FIGURE 25.15.

The Script Wizard window.

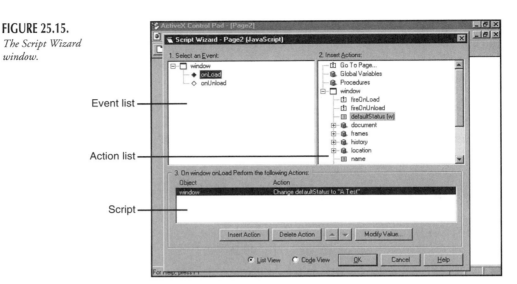

Event list ——

Action list ——

Script ——

NOTE

List View is well-suited to attaching simple actions or a series of actions to an event using a point-and-click interface. It prompts for most of the information it needs, such as values to be assigned to properties. The Code View, on the other hand, is designed for more detailed, extensive coding but provides an easy way to specify objects, methods, and properties without having to type their complete references. It allows for complete manual coding of a script or procedure if needed.

The List View can only create event handlers for the following actions: methods with no arguments, methods with the same number of arguments as the event handler, the special actions in the Script Wizard (which are discussed later in this chapter), and assigning values to properties or global variables. Anything beyond this needs to be done in the Code View.

NOTE

The Script Wizard can be used to create both VBScript and JavaScript scripts. The scripting language used by the Script Wizard is specified before invoking the Script Wizard. From the ActiveX Control Pad, select the Tools menu, select the Options menu, and then select Script .... This opens the Script Options window like the one shown in Figure 25.18. The window can be used to set the default view, the default scripting language, and the font used by the Script Wizard.

FIGURE 25.16.
List View of the Script Wizard window.

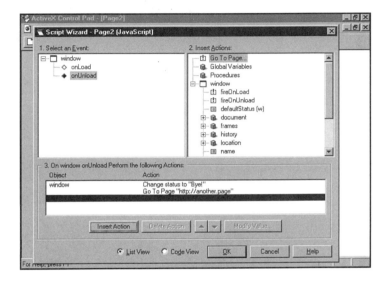

FIGURE 25.17.
Code View of the Script Wizard window.

Scripting an Event

In order to demonstrate how to script an event, the following simple form is used:

```
<FORM NAME="testForm">
   <INPUT TYPE=text NAME="testText">
   <INPUT TYPE=button NAME="testButton" VALUE="Submit">
</FORM>
```

The form attempts to script one simple event: If focus is removed from the text field and there is no text, then the user is alerted to enter text and focus is returned to the field.

FIGURE 25.18.

The Script Options window.

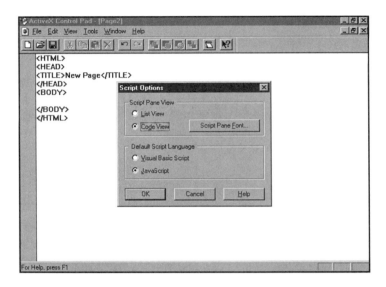

Creating a Procedure

The Script Wizard is designed to help force scripts to be developed in a modular fashion. For instance, when an event is scripted, the Script Wizard is best optimized to assign a single action. When multiple actions need to be taken, they should be invoked by calling a single function or procedure. For this reason, the action list includes a list of all global procedures and variables available in a document.

It's possible to add a procedure or variable to the list by right-clicking inside the action list and selecting either New Global Variable ... or New Procedure from the drop-down menu.

If New Procedure is selected while in code view, the shell for a procedure appears in the bottom part of the window. Here the default name of the function can be changed and then the function can be created. In this case, you can change Procedure1 to CheckField.

First you can select the properties you're testing from the action list. Here you want to test the value property of the testField object. This causes Document.testForm.testField.value to appear in the script. Because conditions and commands such as if don't appear on the action list, they need to be written manually by typing them into the script, resulting in the following:

```
if (Document.testForm.testField.value == "") {
```

If the condition is true, you want to display an alert box so that you can select the alert action from the window object in the action list. When this is double-clicked, the following appears in the script:

```
window.alert(msg)
```

msg can be replaced with some text like the following:

```
window.alert("Please Enter Some Text")
```

Finally, to bring focus back to the field, the `focus` method of the text field is selected from the action list and the `if` statement is closed by typing } into the script. The final result looks like Figure 25.19.

FIGURE 25.19.

The completed `CheckField` *function.*

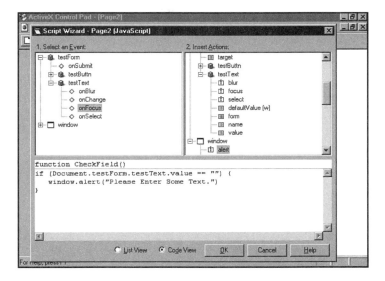

As you can see in Figure 25.19, the procedure now appears in the action list. If you want to edit the procedure later, right-click on the procedure name in the action list and select `Edit` from the drop-down menu.

NOTE

It's important to note that creating custom global procedures like this one can only be done in the Code View. The List View cannot display custom multiline scripts.

Selecting an Event

The first step in scripting an event is to select an event from the event list. The event list includes all events associated with all objects, as well as ActiveX controls and HTML Layouts, in a document.

If the Script Wizard is opened from inside the HTML Layout Editor (rather than the source editor), then the objects in the particular HTML layout are available.

In this example, the blur event of the text field needs to be scripted. This is done by selecting the onBlur event handler of the testText text field. Figure 25.20 shows the selection of an event handler.

FIGURE 25.20.

Selecting an event.

Scripting the Event

Now that the event is selected, you can script its action. In this case, the action is simple: the CheckField function created earlier in this chapter. All you need to do is double-click on CheckField in the event list and it appears in the script. This can be done in the Code View or the List View.

The List View is useful for attaching multiple simple actions to an event. For instance, after selecting CheckField from the action list, the same message could be displayed in the status bar by double-clicking on the status property of the window object in the List View. The Script Wizard prompts for the value to be assigned to status when this is done in List View (see Figure 25.21).

Notice that the order of the actions in the List View can be changed with the arrow buttons and that individual actions can be deleted with the Delete Action button. The final code generated for this event handler would look like the following:

```
CheckField()
window.status = 'Please Enter Some Text'
```

When you create a script for an event, the diamond next to the event in the event list is filled in to indicate that an event handler is associated with an event. If you want to completely remove an event handler from an event, simply right-click on the name of the event in the event list and select Delete Event Handler from the drop-down menu.

FIGURE 25.21.

The List View prompts for values to assign to properties.

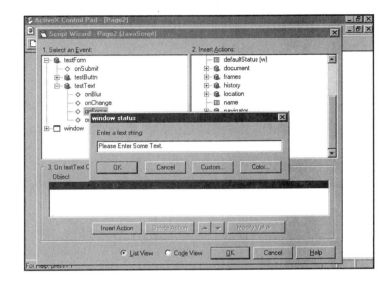

Generating the Scripts

Finally, the scripts can be added to the open HTML file by selecting OK in the Script Wizard. All the scripts will be generated and the end result will be similar to the following:

```
<HTML>
<HEAD>
    <SCRIPT LANGUAGE="JavaScript">
<!--
function CheckField()
{
if (Document.testForm.testField.value == "") {
window.alert("Please Enter Some Text")
Document.testForm.testField.focus()
}
}
-->
    </SCRIPT>
<TITLE>New Page</TITLE>
</HEAD>
<BODY>
    <FORM NAME="testForm">
        <INPUT LANGUAGE="JavaScript" TYPE=text ONBLUR="CheckField()
window.status = 'Please Enter Some Text'"
        NAME="testField">
        <INPUT TYPE=button VALUE="Verify" NAME="testButton">
    </FORM>
</BODY>
</HTML>
```

Special Features of the Script Wizard

The Script Wizard provides several features to ease certain common tasks. Specifically, these are shortcuts that provide the following functions:

■ Going to another page

■ Hiding or showing a control

■ Changing the order of controls (front/back order)

Going to Another Page

The Action list includes a special entry called Go To Page .... By using this action, it is possible to assign a jump to another page as an action to an event.

In the List View, double-clicking on the Go To Page ... action causes a prompt to be displayed, asking for the URL of the destination page, as shown in Figure 25.22.

FIGURE 25.22.

Scripting a jump to another page.

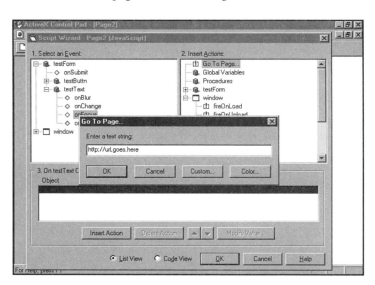

In the Code View, an empty assignment to `window.location.href` is inserted into the script, which can then be completed by the user building the script.

Hiding or Showing a Control

ActiveX controls can be dynamically displayed or hidden by a script. The Script Wizard provides a Hide Control and Show Control action for control objects in a document.

By double-clicking on either of these actions, it's possible to script this action for an event. In the Code View, the JavaScript code displayed for these actions would be `objectName.visible = false` or `objectName.visible = true`.

Changing the Order of Controls

ActiveX controls all have a relative front-back position known as a z-order. Controls can be brought to the front or sent to the back by selecting the `Bring to Front` or `Send to Back` actions in the Action list.

Limitations of the Script Wizard

The current version of the Script Wizard has some limitations:

- It can't script `<A>` and `<FRAMESET>` tags.
- It can only script the `window.location.href` property of the `window` object in an HTML layout. In an HTML file, the complete `window` object is available.
- When the Script Wizard is started, it parses the HTML file for existing scripts. If it finds a `Dim` or `var` line with more than one variable on it, then the variables cannot be deleted or changed. In addition, the `SRC` attribute of the `<SCRIPT>` tag isn't supported, and generates a warning when the Script Wizard is started.

More Information About the ActiveX Control Pad

The help files that come with the ActiveX Control Pad provide detailed information about using the application as well as a complete developer's reference covering the Internet Explorer Object Model.

In addition, Microsoft's Web site includes the Site Builder Workshop, which offers information about the Control Pad at `http://www.microsoft.com/workshop/author/cpad/cpad.htm`.

The Control Pad itself can be downloaded from `http://www.microsoft.com/workshop/author/cpad/download.htm`.

Summary

This chapter covered the basics of using the ActiveX Control Pad to develop Web pages that take advantage of the features of both Internet Explorer 3 and Navigator 3.

Using the Control Pad, it is possible to

- Edit HTML source code
- Insert ActiveX controls
- Design HTML layouts
- Produce scripts for event handlers

The next chapter wraps up with a discussion of JavaScript's position for the future, in light of its acceptance by many industry players.

26

JavaScript and the Future

*by Arman Danesh
and Wes Tatters*

While the changes brought about in the JavaScript language following the release of Netscape Navigator 3, and more significantly its LiveConnect capabilities, place JavaScript at the forefront of Web publishing languages, Netscape Communications is not a company that likes to rest on its laurels.

In fact, a quick browse through the JavaScript newsgroup at `snews://secnews.netscape.com/netscape.devs-javascript` reveals that plans are already underway for JavaScript enhancements in future versions on Netscape Navigator, possibly under the name Netscape Navigator 4.0.

This final chapter takes a look at the future of JavaScript and also explores some other major World Wide Web developments currently underway, by discussing the following topics:

- Where next for JavaScript?
- Customization with LiveConnect
- Microsoft Internet Explorer 3

Where Next for JavaScript?

When JavaScript was first released in version 2.0 of Netscape Navigator, it offered a number of useful capabilities. However, for many Web publishers it was the shortcomings of JavaScript that meant JavaScript was often relegated to the level of oddity or toy.

But now, with the addition of capabilities like LiveConnect and Java-to-JavaScript communications, not to mention the possibilities provided by server-side JavaScript using LiveWire, JavaScript has moved well and truly into the mainstream. Having said that, however, there are still a number of areas where JavaScript could possibly be enhanced. The following sections explore some of the features that may appear in future releases of JavaScript.

Dynamic Table Updating

The capability to alter the appearance of pictures and images on a Web page without having to reload or redraw the entire page was greeted by the JavaScript community with a considerable amount of excitement, as was the capability to dynamically update the contents of selection lists and pop-up lists on a form.

While these enhancements are certainly of great value, there is at least one other area of Web page development that is ideally suited to the use of dynamic updates. This is the area of tables.

Currently the only way to alter the text contents of a cell within a table is to redraw the entire page or alternatively place all of your text within text area fields inside a form. Using the latter technique, it's possible to approximate the effect of altering the contents of a single cell, but using such an approach is somewhat clumsy.

By far the most effective approach to this task is to enable the contents and appearance of each cell to be altered programmatically under JavaScript control. Not only can the contents of the cell be altered by using such an approach, but other items such as the new Cell background color attribute can be altered as well.

Disabled Objects

Programmers and other users familiar with Windows-like environments will no doubt have encountered fields, buttons, and other elements in different programs which from time to time take on a *grayed-out*, or disabled, appearance, preventing the user from entering information into the field or selecting the button or item.

In the original JavaScript documentation produced by Netscape Communications for Navigator 2.0, a `disable()` method was proposed for all form objects that would have allowed input fields on a Web page to be enabled or disabled under program control. Unfortunately, due to the various priorities placed on the JavaScript development team, this feature isn't yet available.

There are, however, strong indications that either a `disable()`/`enable()` method combination or possibly an `enabled` property will finally make the cut for the next release of JavaScript.

Debuggers and Integrated Development Environments

As a programming language that operates by embedding code into existing HTML documents, there are a few unique developmental issues that still need to be resolved by Netscape Communications.

Debugging Tools

The first of these is the lack of any real debugging tools for client JavaScript. Readers familiar with other high-level programming languages, such as C++ and even more recently Java, will be aware that when trying to track down errors or other problems in a piece of running code, the best approach is to use some sort of debugging tool. Such tools enable you to step through a block of code line-by-line and test the contents of variables and properties at each stage of the code's execution.

At this stage, however, no such debugging tools are being provided by Netscape Communications for JavaScript. Having said this, there are currently at least two major third-party tools being developed, and both go at least part of the way toward resolving this situation.

The first of these is the MLI Technology JavaScript Debugger, shown in Figure 26.1. It can be used to inspect the contents of objects and variables in a running JavaScript-aware Web document. To learn more about MLI's debugger, point your Web browser to `http://www.media.com/users/public/jsdb.html`.

FIGURE 26.1.
*The MLI Technology
JavaScript Debugger.*

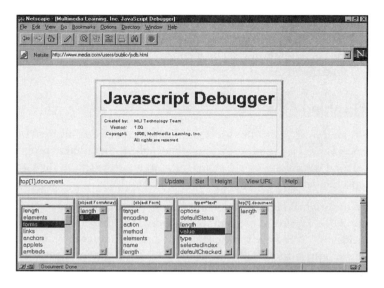

The second is the JSInspector debugging tool, shown in Figure 26.2. Like the MLI tool, JSInspector also enables you to investigate the contents of a JavaScript-aware Web page. However, at the time of this writing there were some unresolved problems between JSInspector and Navigator 3 that made JSInspector's use somewhat problematic. These problems will probably be resolved before the final release of 3. You can explore JSInspector for yourself at http://www.anaya.es/I-D/debug/JSInspector.html.

FIGURE 26.2.
*The JSInspector debugging
tool.*

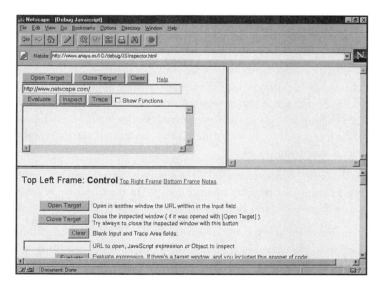

NOTE

While the two tools mentioned above go part of the way towards providing debugging tools for JavaScript, as things stand currently there's a need for Netscape Communications to do some additional work in this area itself.

Netscape has made some initial steps towards this with the development of LiveWire, which provides some debugging tools for client-server applications deployed using LiveWire and a Netscape Web server.

Using the debug() function in server JavaScript and the trace facilities provided by LiveWire's Application Manager, limited debugging functionality is possible, although this still isn't a complete debugging solution.

Integrated Development Tools

Programmers who have worked with languages like Visual Basic, Visual C++, or even the Symantec Café environment for Java (see Figure 26.3) will no doubt be aware of the benefits of using an Integrated Development Environment (IDE) that enables a programmer to edit and execute applications using a single development tool.

FIGURE 26.3.
Symantec Café for Java.

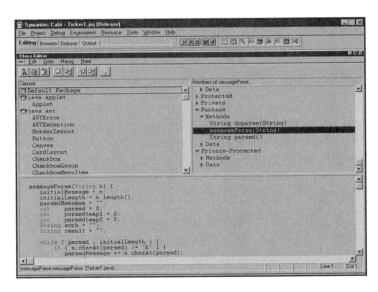

Currently, Netscape Communications provides at least part of the benefits of an IDE through Netscape Gold 3 (see Figure 26.4). Using Netscape Gold, you can enter your JavaScript code directly into a Web page along with the HTML code for the page, then test it immediately using the integrated Web browser. Unfortunately, as mentioned previously, there's no way to debug the JavaScript program itself once you have the code written.

FIGURE 26.4.

Netscape Gold 3 enables you to enter your JavaScript code directly into a Web page.

Customizing with LiveConnect

As you discovered in Part IV, "Java and Live Objects," by using Netscape's LiveConnect technology you can create JavaScript code that communicates directly with both Java applets and Netscape plug-ins.

What was not discussed in any great depth, however, is the fact that in addition to working with the LiveConnect-ready plug-ins that come bundled with Netscape 3, it's also possible to create your own LiveConnect-compatible plug-ins by taking advantage of the LiveConnect Software Developers Kit (SDK) provided by Netscape Communications.

The LiveConnect SDK

To use the LiveConnect SDK you first need to have a reasonable amount of experience working with the C++ programming language, and more particularly, a good knowledge of the development tools appropriate to each of the computer platforms with which you intend to work.

Assuming you have this knowledge, you need to obtain a copy of the LiveConnect SDK for each separate computer platform you want to support. Currently there are SDKs for Windows, Macintosh, and UNIX, all of which can be obtained from `http://home.netscape.com/comprod/ development_partners/plugin_api/index.html`, as shown in Figure 26.5.

FIGURE 26.5.

The LiveConnect SDK contains all the libraries and information you need in order to create LiveConnect-aware plug-ins.

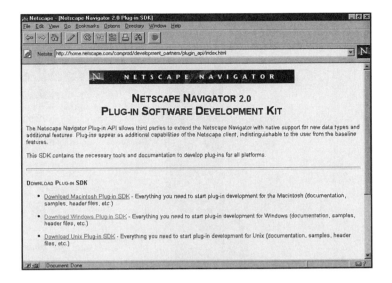

Each SDK contains all of the runtime libraries and related information you need to create LiveConnect-aware plug-ins. This includes a set of HTML documents that discuss the concept of LiveConnect and plug-ins in detail, as well as examining the development process.

> **NOTE**
>
> Even if you don't plan to create your own plug-ins in the future, you may find that a quick read through the documentation included with the SDK is of great assistance in better understanding the relationship between each of the LiveConnect elements—JavaScript, Java, and plug-ins.

Microsoft Internet Explorer 3

Until recently, JavaScript was considered by many people to be a peculiarity of the Netscape Navigator. For this reason it was often strongly argued that, as such, it didn't truly deserve to be treated as an integral part of the World Wide Web.

This all changed, however, when Microsoft announced that version 3 of its Internet Explorer Web browser, shown in Figure 26.6, would include native support for both Java and JavaScript. Internet Explorer is discussed in detail in Part VI, "JavaScript and Microsoft's Internet Explorer."

FIGURE 26.6.
Microsoft's Internet Explorer 3 Web browser.

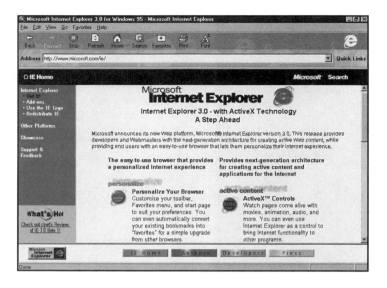

In addition to JavaScript support, Internet Explorer 3 (IE3) also supports many other previously Netscape-specific features which were also discussed in Part VI.

This is an important development because it lends impetus to JavaScript and other Netscape-derived features, such as frames, and helps to establish their role as possible standards for the Web, helping Web developers to produce one version of their site that is equally interactive across all, or most, browsers.

This is helped by Microsoft's stated support for standards and its commitment toward pursuing adoption of the features of Internet Explorer in standards controlled by various standards agencies on the Internet.

In addition, Microsoft's implementation of JavaScript as a plug-in scripting language to its ActiveX Scripting engine means that JavaScript can potentially be deployed as the scripting language of choice for applications other than Web browsers that provide ActiveX scripting capabilities.

At the same time that Internet Explorer provides support for JavaScript and Netscape plug-ins, Microsoft has included alternatives to these Netscape features in the form of VBScript—an alternative ActiveX scripting language derived from Visual Basic—and ActiveX controls (or OLE objects).

If Microsoft has its way, VBScript and ActiveX controls will usurp JavaScript and plug-ins as the preferred tools for Web developers. It's too early to say if this will happen and many in the industry are skeptical because Navigator is currently supported on all major computing platforms while Internet Explorer 3 is only available on 32-bit Windows platforms, and there are no clear indications if features such as VBScript and ActiveX support will make it onto other platforms in the foreseeable future.

Netscape ONE

While Microsoft has been making big noises about its commitment to open standards with the release of Internet Explorer 3, Netscape hasn't been quiet.

In the summer of 1996, Netscape introduced Netscape ONE (Open Network Environment) as a network-based development environment based, Netscape says, on public open standards.

Netscape ONE combines several key core technologies, including HTML, Java, JavaScript, LiveConnect, Netscape's Internet Foundation classes—a set of Java classes and APIs that enable deployment of network-oriented applications—and support for a broad range of communication, collaboration, and security protocols.

It is Netscape's hope that this environment, if widely adopted, will allow applications to be developed once and then deployed on any platform supporting Netscape ONE and in any environment, from a small self-contained LAN to the Internet.

Netscape ONE comes with a suite of tools including LiveWire, a Software Developer's Kit, and the Netscape Administration Kit, enabling the configuration of Navigator for intranet deployment. In addition, Netscape has begun developing commercial applications that extend Netscape ONE. These include Netscape Wallet, LivePayment, and the Netscape Merchant System.

More detailed information about Netscape ONE is available on Netscape's Web site.

Summary

With JavaScript now in its second major release, it is starting to become a fairly stable and complete language. However, there are still a few areas where work remains to be done. This chapter has examined some of these areas and looked briefly at one of the ways in which JavaScript's capabilities can be expanded by the development of LiveConnect-compatible plug-ins.

And finally, to complete the chapter and the book as well, a brief look was taken at the new capabilities of Microsoft's Internet Explorer 3 as well as Netscape ONE, a network development environment from Netscape that includes JavaScript.

A

Netscape Navigator and Netscape Gold

by Wes Tatters

Netscape Communications currently has two main versions of its Navigator Web browser—Netscape Navigator and Netscape Navigator Gold. As Web browsers, both versions are basically identical, but in addition to being a Web browser, Gold is also a Web publishing and HTML editing tool.

This appendix provides a brief introduction to Netscape Navigator and Netscape Navigator Gold. For a more detailed introduction to the use of Netscape's Navigator products refer to the online documentation provided by Netscape.

The following topics are explored in this appendix:

- Netscape Navigator 3
- Netscape Navigator Gold 3
- Working with Netscape Navigator
- Configuring Netscape Navigator
- Advanced capabilities

Netscape Navigator 3

Since its initial release, Netscape Navigator has been through three major development cycles, each of which has brought significant improvements in performance and many new features. The current version of Navigator was originally referred to by the code name Atlas, but has since become known as Netscape Navigator 3.

For many people, Netscape Navigator is the *only* World Wide Web browser. In fact, recent surveys have indicated that Navigator is now used by more than 75 percent of the Web community.

On the surface, the look and feel of Navigator is more than a little similar to NCSA Mosaic—the Web browser regarded as the grand-daddy of all Web browsers—possibly because many of the original NCSA personnel who developed Mosaic are now working for Netscape Communications, the company responsible for the Netscape Navigator.

There are, however, a number of features offered by Navigator that Mosaic does not support. These include the use of windows and multiple frames, JavaScript and Java support, and also Live Objects.

With Netscape enhancing Navigator's capabilities and releasing updates on an almost monthly basis, it is now regarded by many people as the most powerful and fully featured Web browser available. At the same time, its dominance of the marketplace means that many users will soon expect Web sites to take advantage of all these new features in the very near future.

System Requirements for Netscape 2

For those of you who are not currently using Navigator 3, the following section of this appendix describes how you can obtain a copy.

> **NOTE**
>
> Unlike previous versions of the Netscape Navigator, which could be used for personal purposes without the payment of a licensing fee, Navigator 3 is a commercial product. When you download a copy, you are granted permission to use the program for up to 90 days for evaluation purposes. If you continue to use Navigator 3 after this time, you are expected to purchase a software license from Netscape Communications.

Before you install a copy of Navigator 3 on your computer system, you should keep a few requirements in mind. These requirements tend to vary for each of the computer platforms that Netscape Communications supports, so the following sections present each in turn.

Windows 3.x

Although the World Wide Web started as a tool designed mainly for UNIX-based computer systems that support the X Window (X11) standard, in recent years many of the new World Wide Web developments have revolved around the Microsoft Windows platform.

Navigator 3 runs quite comfortably on a Windows 3.1-based computer system. However, there are a few technical issues that need to be resolved first.

16-Bit Operation

With the introduction of Windows NT, and more recently Windows 95, a definition has been coined to describe programs that work on the various Microsoft Windows platforms.

Programs designed specifically for Windows NT and Windows 95 are *32-bit programs*, a designation that relates to the way they use memory and other technical aspects of operation. On the other hand, Windows 3.1 and 3.11 applications are *16-bit programs*. If you want to run Navigator 3 under Windows 3.1 or 3.11, you need to download the 16-bit version.

Winsock

To explore the World Wide Web using Navigator 3 and Microsoft Windows, you need a TCP/IP-based connection to the Internet. These connections come in a variety of forms, including SLIP, PPP, and ISDN connections. To link a TCP/IP connection with Netscape Navigator, you also need a special program called a Winsock. This program looks after all the TCP/IP communications between your computer and the Internet.

> **NOTE**
>
> TCP/IP is the network protocol used by computer systems to communicate with each other over the Internet and SLIP, and PPP and ISDN represent common methods of connecting computers together using the telephone system.

A number of different Winsock programs are available, some commercially and others as shareware or public domain software. Of these, by far the most well-known is Peter Tattam's Trumpet Winsock.

> **NOTE**
>
> Because a full discussion of the use and installation of Winsock is outside the scope of this book, you may want to check out Sams' *Teach Yourself the Internet in a Week, 2nd Edition*, by Neil Randall, ISBN: 0-672-30735-9.

Memory Requirements

To run Navigator 3 on a Windows 3.*x*-based system, you need to have at least 4MB of RAM installed. Although running Navigator 3 is possible with only 4MB, for all practical purposes you need 8MB of RAM to see the browser running at its full potential.

In addition to hardware-based memory, you also need to configure Windows virtual memory properly. Make sure that you have allocated at least 10MB of permanent virtual memory if your disk has enough space available to handle it. (Refer to your Windows Users Guide for more information.)

> **NOTE**
>
> At the time of this writing, the Windows 3.*x* version of Navigator 3 does not support the use of Java—the new, portable Internet-based language—however there are indications that such support will be available in the near future.

Windows 95

Unless you live on the far side of the moon, you have heard some mention of Windows 95 in the last 12 months. For Internet users, Windows 95 opens up a new level of support and functionality that greatly simplifies connecting to the Internet and significantly improves the performance of many Internet applications.

Currently two versions of Navigator 3 work under Windows 95. The first is the 16-bit application mentioned previously, and the second is a 32-bit application that uses Windows 95-specific capabilities. Naturally, there are a few special requirements for the use of this version.

> **NOTE**
>
> Although some 32-bit programs will work on a computer running Windows 3.11—provided a utility called WIN32s is installed—this is not the case for the Windows 95 version of Navigator 3. It can be run only on a machine using Windows 95.

TCP/IP and Winsock

As with the 16-bit version of Navigator 3, you need a Winsock application to complete the connection with the Internet. But unlike the 16-bit version, which can use a variety of Winsock programs, the Windows 95-specific version of Navigator 3 requires the Winsock program provided with Windows 95. For more information on installing the Windows 95 version of Winsock and the underlying TCP/IP communications software it contains, point your Web browser to `http://www.windows95.com/connect/index.html`. Once you get there, follow the TCP/IP installation link.

> **NOTE**
>
> Under Windows 95, you can still use the 16-bit version of Navigator 3 with other Winsock programs, but you will lose access to many of the performance benefits that come with the 32-bit version, including Java support.

Memory Requirements

The issue of memory and Windows 95 is a delicate subject at the best of times. According to its technical specifications, Windows 95 will work with as little as 4MB of memory. Most tests indicate, however, that 8MB is the minimum you should use, with 16MB being the preferred base.

When you add applications to the mix, the amount of memory required increases again. Netscape recommends that you have at least 8MB of memory when running Navigator 3, but you will find that having 16MB greatly improves overall performance.

Apple Macintosh

Netscape Navigator 3 is also well supported on the Apple Macintosh using both MacOS and the newer PowerPC operating systems. The minimum requirements for using Navigator 3 on a Macintosh computer are as follows:

- Macintosh System 7
- MacTCP
- Memory Requirements

Macintosh System 7

Although many Macintosh users may still be opting to stay with version 6 of the Macintosh operating system, only those people with System 7 or greater can use Navigator 3 on their computers.

MacTCP

As with Microsoft Windows, you need a program that acts as the glue between your computer and the Internet. The most popular and most readily available program is a system tool called MacTCP. If you have version 7.5 of the Macintosh operating system, MacTCP is included as a part of the package. Others should contact their nearest Apple support center to obtain a copy of MacTCP.

Memory Requirements

To run Navigator 3 on a Macintosh computer system, you need at least 4MB of RAM, although 8MB is the preferred amount. You also should be careful using programs such as RAMDoubler, which increase the amount of memory available to your programs by using compression techniques. Some older versions of this program are known to cause problems with MacTCP.

UNIX

Because Netscape Navigator 3 is a graphical Web browser, not all versions of UNIX currently support it. To use Navigator 3 under UNIX, your system must be configured to support the X Window specification known commonly as X11.

Supported Platforms

If they support X11, the following computers systems can run Navigator 3:

- Digital Equipment Corporation Alpha computers (OSF/1 2)
- Hewlett-Packard 700 series computers (HP-UX 9.03)
- IBM RS/600 computers (AIX 3.2)
- Silicon Graphics IRIX 5.2 systems
- Sun SPARC computer systems (Solaris 2.4 and SunOS 4.1.3)
- 386/486/Pentium-based computers running BSDI
- Some Linux-based systems

Memory Requirements

The memory requirement for UNIX systems are a little more straightforward than those for other platforms. To run Navigator 3 on any UNIX-based system, as a rule you need at least 16MB of memory.

Obtaining a Copy of Netscape Navigator

There are three ways by which you can obtain a copy of Netscape Navigator 3 that is suitable for your computer system:

- Download a copy using a Web browser
- Download a copy using FTP
- Purchase a copy from a retail outlet

Downloading Navigator 3 Using a Web browser

If you already have an older version of Netscape Navigator or some other Web browser, the simplest way to obtain a copy of the latest version of Navigator 3 is to point your existing browser to `http://home.netscape.com/comprod/mirror/index.html`.

Downloading 3 Using FTP

If you don't have a Web browser yet, but you have access to an FTP client, you can download a copy of Netscape Navigator 3 using anonymous FTP.

Netscape Communications operates an anonymous FTP server that can be reached at `ftp.netscape.com`. However, due to the number of people who visit this site every day, you may find that the main site is very busy. If this is the case, you should try `ftp2.netscape.com` or `ftp3.netscape.com`, and on up to `ftp8.netscape.com`. These sites are mirror images of the main FTP site.

Purchasing a Copy from a Retail Outlet

With the rapid growth of popularity in the Internet and, more specifically, the World Wide Web, many computer suppliers and software houses now carry copies of Netscape Navigator as a regular part of their inventory. Alternatively, you can also purchase a copy direct from Netscape Communications by calling (415) 528-2555. Costs vary: the price for the electronic edition of Navigator 3 (direct from Netscape) is $49, while the price of Navigator 3 Gold, packaged with the authoring guide, is $99.

> **NOTE**
>
> You can, of course, purchase only the latest commercially released version from retail
> outlets. If you want to gain access to prerelease and beta versions of Navigator, you will
> need to do so online.

Installing Netscape Navigator on Your Computer

After you have obtained a copy of Navigator 3, you need to install it on your computer before
you can use it. The file that you obtained, either online or on disk, won't start the Navigator
program for you.

Windows 95

If you downloaded Navigator 3 from Netscape using Windows Explorer or your file manager
utility of choice, locate the directory where the Navigator 3 installation file was stored during
the download. Once you have found it, double-click on the file to commence the installation
process.

After a few seconds, an installation program launches, guiding you through a series of simple
steps that install Navigator 3 on your computer.

Apple Macintosh

Installing Navigator 3 on a Macintosh is even simpler than installing it on a Windows-based
computer. All you need to do is double-click the Netscape Installer icon, located in the folder
where you put Navigator 3 when you downloaded it, or on the floppy disk, depending on how
you obtained your copy.

Except for a few questions about which folder you want Navigator 3 to be stored in, the entire
installation process is fully automated.

UNIX Versions

Unfortunately, installing programs on UNIX-based computer systems is often a little more
complicated than installation on Macintosh- or Windows-based machines.

As a result, each version of the UNIX Navigator contains a small readme file that explains the
steps needed for that particular machine. To view the readme file, copy the Navigator 3 for
UNIX file you obtained previously into a new directory and then type the following on the
command line:

```
zcat filename.tarZ ¦ tar xvf -
```

You will need to replace `filename.tarZ` with the name of the file you downloaded. After the contents of the file have been unpacked, the readme file can be found in the same directory where you saved the original file.

Netscape Navigator Gold 3

Shortly before the final release of Navigator 2, Netscape Communications announced that it planned to release a new version of its Navigator product under the name Netscape Navigator Gold 2. This new version included not only all the powerful World Wide Web navigation features of Navigator 2, but also built-in Web page editing tools.

Following in this trend, the release of Netscape 3 has also resulted in the release of a new Netscape Gold 3 which again includes all the Web navigation tools and significantly enhanced Web editing tools.

> **NOTE**
>
> In this book, Netscape Navigator Gold 3 is referred to simply as Netscape Gold, while Netscape Navigator 3 is referred to as Navigator 3.

Writing HTML documents by hand in a text editor is probably the most cumbersome way to write HTML. You must type all the tags, remember what the elements are called, remember to close your two-sided tags, remember to include closing quotation marks on attributes, and remember a host of other details. And, of course, you must know something about which tags can go where. With all that to keep in mind as you produce an HTML page, it sometimes becomes difficult to remember what you're actually writing.

To ease the amount of work required to create a Web page, a number of HTML editors, utilities, and assistants have begun to appear on the market. These programs look after many of the more mundane tasks usually associated with creating Web pages, and in some cases they also give you a visual approximation of what your final Web page will look like.

However, until recently, if you went looking for an HTML editor that enabled you to see the results of your work quickly, insert links and anchors and inline graphics easily, or manage the publication of multiple sets of documents, you would have drawn a blank. With the introduction of Netscape Gold, Netscape Communications is making moves to redress this problem.

System Requirements for Netscape Gold

Most of the system requirements for Netscape Gold are identical to those for Netscape Navigator, however, there are a few minor differences, which are examined in this section.

> **NOTE**
>
> Like the current version of Navigator 3, Netscape Gold is a commercial product. When you download a copy, you are granted permission to use the program for up to 90 days for evaluation purposes. If you continue to use Netscape Gold after this time, you are expected to purchase a software license from Netscape Communications.

Computer Platforms

Unlike Netscape Navigator, which is currently available across a wide range of computer platforms, there are only two computer platforms supported for Netscape Gold. These are 32-bit windows—Windows 95 and Windows NT— and the Apple Macintosh.

Working with the Netscape Navigator

In the following sections, many of the major features of Netscape Navigator and Netscape Gold Web browser are examined. However, because this is an appendix, if you want to explore the specifics of Web navigation using Netscape Navigator or Netscape Gold in detail, you should refer to any of the very good books devoted specifically to Netscape 3. Of these, *Netscape Unleashed* by Sams.net is a very good place to start.

> **NOTE**
>
> The following discussions refer generally to the features found both in Netscape Navigator and Netscape Gold. Where features are specific to Netscape Gold, a note or comment to such effect will be made.

Starting the Browser

To start either Netscape Navigator or Netscape Gold, all you need to do is locate the folder or directory where it was saved during the installation process. After you locate the program, double-click its icon to activate the browser. This assumes of course, that you have already obtained access to the Internet through an Internet service provider, School or College, your employee, or some other method.

> **CAUTION**
>
> Netscape Navigator and Netscape Gold do not connect your computer to the Internet. This step is looked after by the TCP/IP software installed on your computer. When

Netscape Navigator starts, it expects to find an Internet connection. If it does not find one, you may encounter an error message. (On some systems the TCP/IP software will attempt to create a connection when Netscape Navigator starts. If this is the case, and if the connection is successful, Netscape Navigator starts normally. Otherwise you again receive some sort of error message.)

When Netscape Navigator or Netscape Gold first starts, by default, the Web browser screen is opened. This screen should be very familiar to anyone who has used Netscape Navigator before.

The Document Area

The most important part of any Web browser is the *document area.* This is the area on-screen where Web pages are displayed. With Netscape Navigator, as with most Web browsers, the middle section of the screen is devoted to displaying Web pages as they are retrieved from the Internet. Regardless of which Web browser you use—whether it's the Macintosh or Windows version—the document area is basically the same.

In fact, the similar appearance of the document area, regardless of what system is displaying the document, is one of the most important features of the World Wide Web. When the concept of the Web was first proposed, one of the guiding principles of the project was the idea that any Web page developed on any computer platform must be viewable on any other computer platform, including the most basic text-based computer terminal. Naturally, you could not expect a text-based terminal to display computer graphics such as inline images, but the text and hypertext links for those images needed to be viewable.

You'll occasionally notice some aesthetic differences between Web browsers in the areas of layout and physical display, but, ultimately, a hyperlink is still a hyperlink, and clicking one causes a new page to be loaded.

TIP

You may occasionally find that the information contained on a Web page is larger than the space provided by the Web browser. To view this information, use the scroll bars at the top and sides of the document area.

Hyperlinks

The first thing you need to know when working with any Web browser is how to recognize a hyperlink. With the Netscape Web browser, by default all hyperlinks are highlighted in blue text and are further enhanced by an underline. In addition, any graphics that have hyperlinks associated with them are normally highlighted by a blue border.

When you click any of these hyperlinks, Netscape Navigator opens a copy of the document that the link points to and displays it on-screen in place of the current page.

TIP

Netscape's Web browser supports an optional function that enables the default colors of hyperlinks to be altered by both the user and Web developer. For this reason, most people now use underlines as the preferred method for displaying text-based hyperlinks.

NOTE

When you select a hyperlink to explore a new page, Netscape Navigator "remembers" the original page for the duration of your current session. If you return to the original page again, any of the hyperlinks that you have visited during the current session are displayed as purple text instead of blue text, or in the case of graphical hyperlinks, are surrounded by a purple box.

The Control Console

The area at the top of the Netscape Navigator main window above the document area is often referred to as the control console. You can easily navigate the World Wide Web by using the tools provided in this area.

The Menu Bar

Like all Windows-based programs, Netscape Navigator has a menu bar across the top of its main window. To access the options provided by this menu bar, click the various menu options listed. When you do this, a pull-down menu appears, displaying the available options:

File
The File menu contains functions to open new documents located on either your hard drive or any Web server connected to the Internet. You also can print copies of the page you are currently viewing and create messages to be sent over e-mail. Finally, the file menu enables you to open additional browser windows.

The Netscape Gold version also provides an Edit Document option along with the means for creating a new Web page.

Edit
There are commands on the Edit menu to copy the contents of a Web page onto the Windows Clipboard, and copy URLs to and from the document line.

	There also is a built-in search option that can quickly locate specific text in the current Web page.
View	Most of the options on the View menu refresh the contents of different parts of the Document window.
	This menu also provides options that enable you to display the HTML source (information used to describe the content of a Web page) for the current frame and document, along with other information relating to the document.
Go	This menu duplicates the basic navigational options provided by the toolbar, and also displays a list of Web pages you have visited during your current session.
Bookmarks	With the bookmarks feature of Netscape Navigator, you can keep a list of sites that you visit on a regular basis. After a site is added to the bookmarks list, it is automatically displayed on the Bookmarks menu so that you can easily return to the site whenever you want. When you select a page listed on this menu, Netscape Navigator opens it as if you had selected the link by clicking on a hyperlink in a Web page.
Options	From this menu you can select any of the options that tailor the way Netscape Navigator looks and operates. (See "Configuring Netscape Navigator" later in this appendix for more information.)
Directory	This menu contains a list of handy links maintained by Netscape Communications, giving you immediate access to Netscape's home page, What's News pages, What's Cool pages, Web search tools, the Yahoo Internet directory, and Netscape's own "Galleria" commerce directory.
Window	With the options on this menu, you can open the Mail and News windows, the address book, bookmarks, and history windows. You also can switch between any other Netscape Navigator-specific windows that are currently open.
Help	This menu provides access to the Netscape online help system. It also has an option for sending feedback to the developers at Netscape Communications.

The Toolbar

The toolbar displayed below the menu bar gives you access to many of the functions you will regularly use while exploring the World Wide Web.

By default, the toolbar contains both a graphical and textual description of its purpose. As you become more familiar with the use of Navigator, you will probably want to adjust the settings so that only the graphical elements are displayed. This can be achieved by altering the settings in the General Preferences dialog on the Options menu. By doing this, you increase the amount of space available in the document area for displaying Web pages.

The options provided by the toolbar are as follows:

Back	As you begin to move around the World Wide Web, Netscape Navigator keeps track of where you have been. If you click this button, the last page you accessed before the current one is recalled.
Forward	Click this button to return to the most recently visited page.
Home	When Netscape Navigator is first installed, clicking this button opens the Netscape Communications home page; however, you can alter this default setting at any time to point to any page you choose.
Edit	This button is a new addition for Netscape Gold. Clicking on it tells Netscape Gold that you want to edit the contents of the currently displayed Web page. When you do this, Netscape Gold opens the current page in an Editor Window. (This button is not included on the standard Navigator browser.)
Reload	Clicking this button forces Netscape Navigator to reload the current page. If you stopped the retrieval of a large page, for example, you can use this button to retrieve the missing information.
Images	If you have configured Netscape Navigator so that it does not load the images associated with a page, you can click this button to load the images associated with the current page. (See the "Auto Load Images" topic later in this appendix for more details about the loading of images.
Open	This icon opens a small dialog box. If you enter the URL of a Web page in the field provided, then click the Open button, Navigator retrieves a copy of the page and displays it in either the Web browser or the Editor window.
Print	When you click this button, Navigator sends a copy of the current page to your printer.
Find	When you open a large Web page, it is sometimes handy to be able to search quickly through the contents of the page. The Find button enables you to open a small dialog box where you can enter the text to search for on the current page.
Stop	If you need to halt the loading of a document, click this icon.

Document Title

Immediately above the menu bar is an area that displays the title of the current Web Page. Most Web pages have a title associated with them, but for those that don't, the URL for the page is listed instead.

Document Location

The URL of the Web page currently displayed in the document area is—by default—shown in the document URL field, which is located just below the toolbar. It is the field with the `Location:` label in front of it. (In some older versions of Netscape Navigator the document URL field may also be labelled as `Netsite:`.)

You also can use this field to directly enter a URL for a Web page. When you do this, the Web browser attempts to retrieve the page as though you had selected it with a hyperlink (note that when you start to enter a new URL, the `Location:` label in front of the document URL field is changed to `Go to:`).

> **NOTE**
>
> By clicking the drop-down arrow to the right of this field, you can call up a history list similar to the one provided by the Go menu. This time, however, you see a list of URLs instead of document titles.

Location Icon

To the immediate left of the Document Location field is a small icon that looks somewhat like an anchor chain. By double-clicking on this icon you can copy the current URL to the clipboard. In addition, by clicking on the icon you can drag the URL into a bookmark or editor window. (No location icon is displayed in the standard Netscape Navigator version.)

Logo Animation

Apart from giving you something to look at, the animated logo to the right of the document URL field indicates when Netscape Navigator is retrieving a Web page. If the animation is running, Netscape Navigator is busy. If it is static, no pages are currently being retrieved.

Status Bar

The last area of the Netscape Navigator screen is the status bar, located below the main document display area. The status bar displays a variety of information depending on what the browser is doing. When you place your mouse pointer over a hyperlink, the URL of the page or server that it points to is displayed on the left side of the status bar. Alternately, when a new page is being loaded, a counter is displayed in this area to indicate the page size and the number of bytes already retrieved. At the same time, on the right side of the status bar, a bar graph is displayed to represent the percentage of the page that has been loaded.

Configuring Netscape Navigator

The Options menu provides a list of menu commands that enable you to tailor the way Netscape Navigator looks and operates. In the following sections, these menu items are briefly discussed.

General Preference...

Selecting the General Preferences item opens a dialog box where you can adjust settings that control how the Web browser component of Netscape Navigator operates. The options available through this dialog box are separated into the following categories:

> **NOTE**
>
> Apart from being a Web browser and Web publisher, Netscape Gold can also send and receive e-mail, and read or post articles to Usenet Newsgroups. In previous versions of Navigator these features were included as a part of the Web browser window, but as of version 2, they have been split into separate components that use different windows.

Appearance	This area controls whether images or text are displayed on the toolbar, stores the location of the Web browser home page, and indicates whether hyperlinks are indicated using an underline.
Fonts	This area is used to configure the default fonts for displaying text on Web pages.
Colors	The default colors for links, text, and the background of Web pages can be altered in this area.
Images	The setting in this area controls whether images are displayed as they load, or after they have finished loading. You also can control how Netscape Navigator displays images on screens that can only handle a limited number of colors, by setting the Choose color options.
Apps	This area is used to select the external programs that are used when you click on a hyperlink that points to a Telnet or TN3270 connection. In addition, you also can set the default program for viewing the current Web page's HTML source code, and define the directory to be used for temporary storage.

Helpers   This area contains a list of programs that work in concert with
               Netscape Navigator. These programs include an audio player, image
               browsers, file compression utilities, and video players.

Language   Netscape is currently starting to enhance Netscape Navigator's support
               for foreign languages. In this area, you can control which languages you
               want to see when viewing multilingual web pages.

Editor Preferences...

To give you control over the way the Netscape Gold editor operates, an Editor Preferences
dialog box has been added to the Options menu. For those readers who are familiar with Navigator 2, this is one of the few areas that looks different from what you have previously seen.
(This option does not appear on the standard Netscape Navigator menu.)

The options available through this dialog box cover the following categories:

General   This area is used to define the name of the Web author, the location of
               external Text and Image editors, and the location where templates for
               new Web pages are stored.

Appearance   Like the Colors area of the General Preferences dialog box, this
               Appearance area lets you control the colors of Web pages. In this case,
               however, you are setting the default colors for the Web editor. These
               colors are used whenever a new Web page is created.

               In addition, you also can define a background image to be associated
               with each new Web page as well.

Publish   This last area is for use with a new Netscape Gold feature called One
               Click Publishing.

Mail and News Preferences...

Two of the major changes for Netscape Navigator with the release of version 2 were greatly
improved support for newsgroups, and e-mail. Both changes were carried into version 3. As a
reflection of this greatly enhanced support, a separate Mail and News Preferences dialog box
has been added to the Options menu.

The options that this dialog box manages include the following:

Appearance   Use this area to configure the font and text styles used by Netscape
               Navigator when it displays e-mail messages and newsgroup articles.

Composition   When you compose a new e-mail message or newsgroup article,
               Netscape Navigator needs to be told how to handle the message.
               The composition area is where you do this.

Server	Use this area to tell Netscape Navigator the location of your personal Internet mailbox and the domain name of the Usenet News server you are using.
Identity	The Identity area is where you store personal information about yourself, including your e-mail address, a default signature file for outgoing messages, and the name of your business or organization.
Organization	The settings in this area control the order in which new e-mail messages and newsgroup articles are displayed. The order can be sorted by date, subject, or sender.

Network Preferences...

Unlike stand-alone applications such as word processors, which need to communicate only with you and occasionally a printer, programs such as Netscape Navigator need to communicate with thousands of different computer systems all around the world. While many of these activities occur automatically, Netscape Navigator provides a number of preferences and other settings that enable you to tailor its performance across the Internet.

Network Preferences include the following:

Cache	Netscape Navigator stores a copy of each page that you visit on your computer's hard drive in what is called a local cache. This allows the pages to be reloaded without having to query the remote server again to download the pages. The Cache area controls the amount of memory and disk space used for cache purposes. The more memory and disk space you allocate, the more pages can be held in the local cache.
Connections	When Netscape Navigator encounters a Web page that includes images, it starts downloading several images at the same time. Doing this allows the rest of the Web page to be displayed even though inline images are only partially downloaded. The Connections area is where you tell Navigator how many separate images and files it should attempt to download at the same time.

NOTE

Raising the number of connections can slow down the time it takes to display a web, depending on the speed of your connection and computer. As a result, you really need to test out this setting for yourself to determine an optimum value.

Proxies   A number of businesses and other organizations connect their computer systems to the Internet through what are known as *firewalls*. Firewalls protect computer systems at the site from invasions by unwanted guests.

If you are connected to the Internet by a firewall, you will usually need a proxy server to communicate with the World Wide Web and other Internet services. The Proxies area enables you to configure Netscape Navigator for use with a proxy server.

Protocols   With the increased use of Cookies and e-mail based forms, some users have demanded greater control over the use of such capabilities. The protocols area enables you to request the display of warning messages whenever a cookie is requested of a form submitted by e-mail.

Languages   These options let you enable or disable support for Java and JavaScript programs.

Security Preferences...

As more businesses move onto the World Wide Web, the issue of security has become a dominant factor in many Internet discussions. To cater to this growing area of concern, Netscape Communications has developed new security features that enable business transactions to be conducted on the Web with a high level of protection.

The Security Preferences settings, in the following list, enable you to tailor the level of security provided by Netscape Navigator to your specific needs:

General   These settings control the alert message that Navigator displays when secure or unsecured data is sent to or from your Web browser.

In addition, there are also controls to configure the level of SSL data encryption supported by the Web browser.

Passwords   To prevent illegal use of your Web browser by other people, you can assign passwords that are requested whenever secure data is to be transmitted from your Web browser.

Personal Site Certificates   Navigator 3 introduces support for personal site certificates. See the Verisign site at http://www.verisign.com/ for more information about obtaining a personal site certificate.

Site Certificates   This area contains a list of site certificates for computer systems and people you want to communicate with in a secure manner. Site certificates are a bit like an electronic fingerprint, which can be used to sign and encrypt messages so that only certain people can view their contents.

Unlike traditional encryption systems, which simply scramble the information so that it is unreadable by prying eyes, a Site certificate also can be used as proof of identity, something which guarantees that the site or person you are sending information to is actually who they say they are.

> **NOTE**
>
> The implementation of security certificates is still in a state of constant flux. As a result, the options provided by this dialog box may very well change by the time you read this book. However, the basic principals involved still remain the same. Refer to the release notes and online documents provided by Netscape Communications for more details. In addition, the VeriSign site at `http://www.verisign.com/` contains information about obtaining your own security certificate.

Show Toolbar

Selecting this menu item controls whether the toolbar is displayed below the Menu area. The Show Toolbar item is on a toggle switch: Select it once to display the Toolbar and select it again to hide it. When the option is active—the default—a small check mark or tick is displayed beside the menu item.

Show Location

This menu item controls whether the document URL field is displayed below the toolbar. Like the Show Toolbar item, the Show Location item is also a toggle switch. Select it once to display the document URL field and again to hide it. When the option is active—the default—a small check mark or tick is displayed beside the menu item.

Show Directory Buttons

Selecting this menu item adds an extra toolbar below the document URL field. This toolbar duplicates the links provided by the Directory menu. When you click any of the buttons on this toolbar, Netscape Navigator immediately retrieves the selected Web page. When the option is active—the default—a small check mark or tick is displayed beside the menu item.

Show Java Console

This option is provided as a tool for people developing Java applications for use on the World Wide Web. If you activate this option, a window that reports on the progress of running Java applets is displayed. When the option is active—de-activated is the default—a small check mark or tick is displayed beside the menu item.

Auto Load Images

If you deselect the Auto Load Images item, Netscape Navigator loads only the text of the document and inserts placeholders where all the inline images are meant to go. When the option is active—the default—a small check mark or tick is displayed beside the menu item.

The main advantage of doing this is timesaving. Loading a Web page with placeholders takes only a matter of seconds. When you consider that some pages may take up to 10 minutes to load using slower modems, deselecting the Auto Load Images option makes a lot of sense.

> **NOTE**
>
> The only disadvantage of not loading images is that you will not be able to use image maps. You can get around this, however, by using the Load Images button on the toolbar to retrieve images on pages where they are used.

Document Encoding

With the development of support for languages such as Japanese and Chinese, there is a need for new methods of encoding and representing Web documents.

With Document Encoding on the Options menu, you can tell Netscape Navigator what encoding method it should use.

B

by Wes Tatters

This appendix is a reference to the HTML tags you can use in your documents, according to the HTML 2.0 specification. In addition, tags defined in both the HTML 3.2 and Netscape Navigator 2.0 specification are listed. Tag supported by HTML 3.2 and Navigator 2.0 are listed as (HTML 3.2), while tags that are currently only available in Navigator 2.0 are listed as (NHTML). There are also several tags listed that Navigator 2.0 does not yet support. These are listed as (HTML 3.2 only).

> **NOTE**
>
> If you are new to HTML and Web publishing, you should obtain a copy of my book *Teach Yourself Netscape 2 Web Publishing in a Week* for more detailed coverage of Web publishing techniques.

HTML Tags

This section covers all of the major tags relating to publishing text on a Web page. This includes all the document formatting tags, character formatting tags, and paragraph formatting tags.

Comments

Comments tags are special tags that have no effect on the appearance or content of a Web page. They exist entirely for descriptive or informative purposes.

`<!--...-->`

Any text enclosed within a comment tag is completely ignored by the Web browser. This includes tags, elements, and entities.

`<!DOCTYPE HTML PUBLIC "-//Netscape Comm. Corp.//DTD HTML//EN">`

Used with HTML document validation systems such as Halsoft at `http://www.halsoft.com/html-val-svc/` to indicate the level of HTML support included in a document. If included in a document, this tag must be placed on the very first line, before the `<HTML>` tag.

`<!DOCTYPE HTML PUBLIC "-//Netscape Comm. Corp. Strict//DTD HTML//EN">`

Used to indicate a stricter set of compliance tests for validation systems such as Halsoft. For more information, visit the Halsoft site listed previously. This site contains both the document validation system and a range of files covering *document type definitions* (DTD) and HTML standards.

Structure Tags

The structure tags do not affect the actual appearance of a Web page, but are instead used to define separate section of the HTML code used when writing a Web page.

<HTML>...</HTML>

Encloses the entire HTML document.

Can Include: <HEAD> <BODY> <FRAMESET>

<HEAD>...</HEAD>

Encloses the head of the HTML document.

Can Include: <TITLE> <ISINDEX> <BASE> <NEXTID> <LINK> <META> <SCRIPT>

Allowed Inside: <HTML>

<BODY>...</BODY>

Encloses the body (text and tags) of the HTML document.

Attributes:

BACKGROUND="..."	(HTML 3.2) The name or URL for an image to tile on the page background
BGCOLOR="..."	(NHTML) The color of the page background
TEXT="..."	(NHTML) The color of the page's text
LINK="..."	(NHTML) The color of unfollowed links
ALINK="..."	(NHTML) The color of activated links
VLINK="..."	(NHTML) The color of followed links

Can Include: <H1> <H2> <H3> <H4> <H5> <H6> <P> <OL> <UL> <DIR> <MENU> <DL> <PRE> <BLOCKQUOTE> <FORM> <ISINDEX> <HR> <ADDRESS> <TABLE> <SCRIPT> <APPLET> <EMBED>

Allowed Inside: <HTML>

Tags That Can Be Included Inside the *<HEAD>* Block

The *<HEAD>* block traditionally contains tags that describe the contents of a Web page but which have no actual effect on the Web page's appearance.

<TITLE>...</TITLE>

Indicates the title of the document.

Allowed Inside: <HEAD>

<BASE>

Defines base values for the current document. Required in HTML 3.2.

Attributes:

HREF="..."   Overrides the base URL of the current document.

TARGET="..."   Defines a default target window for all links in the current document.

Allowed Inside: <HEAD>

<ISINDEX>

Indicates that this document is a gateway script that enables searches.

Attributes:

PROMPT="..."   (HTML 3.2) The prompt for the search field

Allowed Inside: <BLOCKQUOTE> <BODY> <DD> <FORM> <HEAD> <LI> <TABLE>

<LINK>

Indicates the relationship between this document and some other document. Generally used only by HTML-generating tools.

Attributes:

HREF="..."   The URL of the referenced HTML document

REL="..."   The forward relationship

REV="..."   A reverse relationship, usually the mailto: address of the document's author

TITLE="..."   The link's title

Allowed Inside: <HEAD>

<META>

Used to simulate HTTP response header messages in an HTML document.

Attributes:

HTTP-EQUIV="..."   HTTP response header name

CONTENT="..."   Value assigned to the response header

NAME="..."   Meta-information name

Allowed Inside: <HEAD>

`<NEXTID>`

Indicates the "next" document to this one (as might be defined by a tool to manage HTML documents in series).

Attributes:

N="…"

Allowed Inside: `<HEAD>`

Headings

Heading tags are used to format the appearance of text that represent headings on a Web page. All heading tags have the following characteristics:

Attributes:

ALIGN="CENTER"	(HTML 3.2) Centers the heading
ALIGN="LEFT"	(HTML 3.2) Left-justifies the heading
ALIGN="RIGHT"	(HTML 3.2) Right-justifies the heading
ALIGN="JUSTIFY"	(HTML 3.2 only) Block-justifies the heading where possible

Can Include: `<A>` `<IMG>` `<BR>` `<BIG>` `<B>` `<BLINK>` `<I>` `<SMALL>` `<SUB>` `<SUP>` `<TT>` `<CITE>` `<CODE>` `<DFN>` `<EM>` `<KBD>` `<SAMP>` `<STRONG>` `<VAR>`

Allowed Inside: `<BLOCKQUOTE>` `<BODY>` `<FORM>`

`<H1>…</H1>`

A first-level heading.

`<H2>…</H2>`

A second-level heading.

`<H3>…</H3>`

A third-level heading.

`<H4>…</H4>`

A fourth-level heading.

`<H5>…</H5>`

A fifth-level heading.

`<H6>...</H6>`

A sixth-level heading.

Paragraphs

Blocks of text displayed on a Web page can be physically separated using paragraph formatting tags. These tags also can be used to define the justification of text within a paragraph.

`<P>...</P>`

A plain paragraph. The closing tag (`</P>`) is optional.

`ALIGN=CENTER`	(HTML 3.2) Centers the paragraph
`ALIGN=LEFT`	(HTML 3.2) Left-justifies the paragraph
`ALIGN=RIGHT`	(HTML 3.2) Right-justifies the paragraph
`ALIGN=JUSTIFY`	(HTML 3.2 only) Block-justifies the paragraph where possible

Can Include: `<A>` `<IMG>` `<BR>` `<BIG>` `<B>` `<BLINK>` `<I>` `<SMALL>` `<SUB>` `<SUP>` `<TT>` `<CITE>` `<CODE>` `<DFN>` `<EM>` `<KBD>` `<SAMP>` `<STRONG>` `<VAR>`

Allowed Inside: `<BLOCKQUOTE>` `<BODY>` `<DD>` `<FORM>` `<LI>` `<TABLE>`

`<DIV>...</DIV>`

Declares a block of text, but unlike the `<P>` tag, the `<DIV>` tag does not add a trailing double-line space.

`ALIGN=CENTER`	(HTML 3.2) Centers the text defined by the division
`ALIGN=LEFT`	(HTML 3.2) Left-justifies the text defined by the division
`ALIGN=RIGHT`	(HTML 3.2) Right-justifies the text defined by the division
`ALIGN=JUSTIFY`	(HTML 3.2 only) Block-justifies the text defined by the division where possible

Can Include: `<A>` `<IMG>` `<BR>` `<BIG>` `<B>` `<BLINK>` `<I>` `<SMALL>` `<SUB>` `<SUP>` `<TT>` `<CITE>` `<CODE>` `<DFN>` `<EM>` `<KBD>` `<SAMP>` `<STRONG>` `<VAR>` `<TABLE>`

Allowed Inside: `<BLOCKQUOTE>` `<BODY>` `<DD>` `<FORM>` `<LI>` `<TABLE>`

Links

Hyperlinks form the basis of the navigation system used by the World Wide Web to move from Web page to Web page and from Web site to Web site. The link tag `<A>` is use to indicate which text and images on a Web page are used as links.

\<A\>...\</A\>

When used with the HREF attribute the \<A\> tag creates a hyperlink to another document or anchor. Alternatively, when it is used with the NAME attribute, creates an anchor that enables links.

Attributes:

HREF="..."	The URL pointed to by a link
TARGET="..."	The target window for the new document
NAME="..."	The anchor name for a reference anchor

Can Include: \<IMG\> \<BR\> \<BIG\> \<B\> \<BLINK\> \<I\> \<SMALL\> \<SUB\> \<SUP\> \<TT\> \<CITE\> \<CODE\> \<DFN\> \<EM\> \<KBD\> \<SAMP\> \<STRONG\> \<VAR\> \<TABLE\>

Allowed Inside: \<ADDRESS\> \<BIG\> \<B\> \<BLINK\> \<I\> \<SMALL\> \<SUB\> \<SUP\> \<TT\> \<CITE\> \<CODE\> \<DFN\> \<EM\> \<KBD\> \<SAMP\> \<STRONG\> \<VAR\> \<BLOCKQUOTE\> \<DD\> \<FORM\> \<LI\> \<TABLE\>

Lists

To create either a numbered list, a bullet list, or a definition list on a Web page, you need to use a combination of the following list tags.

\<OL\>...\</OL\>

An ordered (numbered) list.

Attributes:

TYPE="..."	(NHTML) The type of numerals to label the list with. Possible values are A, a, I, i, and 1.
START="..."	(NHTML) The value to start this list with.

Can Include: \<LI\>

Allowed Inside: \<BLOCKQUOTE\> \<BODY\> \<DD\> \<FORM\> \<LI\> \<TABLE\>

\<UL\>...\</UL\>

An unordered (bulleted) list.

Attributes:

TYPE="..."	(NHTML) the bullet dingbat to use to mark list items. Possible values are DISC, CIRCLE, and SQUARE.

Can Include: \<LI\>

Allowed Inside: \<BLOCKQUOTE\> \<BODY\> \<DD\> \<FORM\> \<LI\> \<TABLE\>

`<MENU>`…`</MENU>`

A menu list of items. (Note: Removed from the HTML 3.2 specification.)

Can Include: `<LI>`

Allowed Inside: `<BLOCKQUOTE>` `<BODY>` `<DD>` `<FORM>` `<LI>` `<TABLE>`

`<DIR>`…`</DIR>`

A directory listing; items are generally smaller than 20 characters. (Note: No longer supported in the HTML 3.2 specification.)

Can Include: `<LI>`

Allowed Inside: `<BLOCKQUOTE>` `<BODY>` `<DD>` `<FORM>` `<LI>` `<TABLE>`

`<LI>`

A list item for use with `<OL>`, `<UL>`, `<MENU>`, or `<DIR>`

Attributes:

`TYPE="…"`	(NHTML) The type of bullet or number to label this item with. Possible values are `DISC`, `CIRCLE`, `SQUARE`, `A`, `a`, `I`, `i`, and `1`.
`VALUE="…"`	(NHTML) The numeric value this list item should have (affects this item and all below it in `<OL>` lists).

Can Include: `<A>` `<IMG>` `<BR>` `<BIG>` `<B>` `<BLINK>` `<I>` `<SMALL>` `<SUB>` `<SUP>` `<TT>` `<CITE>` `<CODE>` `<DFN>` `<EM>` `<KBD>` `<SAMP>` `<STRONG>` `<VAR>` `<P>` `<DIV>` `<OL>` `<UL>` `<DIR>` `<MENU>` `<DL>` `<PRE>` `<BLOCKQUOTE>`

Allowed Inside: `<DIR>` `<MENU>` `<OL>` `<UL>`

`<DL>`…`</DL>`

A definition or glossary list. The `COMPACT` attribute specifies a formatting that takes less whitespace to present.

Attributes: `COMPACT`

Can Include: `<DT>` `<DD>`

Allowed Inside: `<BLOCKQUOTE>` `<BODY>` `<DD>` `<FORM>` `<LI>` `<TABLE>`

`<DT>`

A definition term, as part of a definition list.

Can Include: `<A>` `<IMG>` `<BR>` `<BIG>` `<B>` `<BLINK>` `<I>` `<SMALL>` `<SUB>` `<SUP>` `<TT>` `<CITE>` `<CODE>` `<DFN>` `<EM>` `<KBD>` `<SAMP>` `<STRONG>` `<VAR>`

Allowed Inside: `<DL>`

`<DD>`

The corresponding definition to a definition term, as part of a definition list.

Can Include: `<A>` `<IMG>` `<BR>` `<BIG>` `<B>` `<BLINK>` `<I>` `<SMALL>` `<SUB>` `<SUP>` `<TT>` `<CITE>` `<CODE>` `<DFN>` `<EM>` `<KBD>` `<SAMP>` `<STRONG>` `<VAR>` `<P>` `<OL>` `<UL>` `<DIR>` `<MENU>` `<DL>` `<PRE>` `<BLOCKQUOTE>` `<FORM>` `<ISINDEX>` `<TABLE>`

Allowed Inside: `<DL>`

Character Formatting

Character formatting tags are used to indicate that a section or block of text on a Web page should be displayed in a special style. All the character formatting tags have these features:

Can Include: `<A>` `<IMG>` `<BR>` `<BIG>` `<B>` `<BLINK>` `<I>` `<SMALL>` `<SUB>` `<SUP>` `<TT>` `<CITE>` `<CODE>` `<DFN>` `<EM>` `<KBD>` `<SAMP>` `<STRONG>` `<VAR>`

Allowed Inside: `<A>` `<ADDRESS>` `<BIG>` `<B>` `<BLINK>` `<I>` `<SMALL>` `<SUB>` `<SUP>` `<TT>` `<CITE>` `<CODE>` `<DFN>` `<EM>` `<KBD>` `<SAMP>` `<STRONG>` `<VAR>` `<DD>` `<DT>` `<H1>` `<H2>` `<H3>` `<H4>` `<H5>` `<H6>` `<LI>` `<P>` `<PRE>` `<TABLE>`

`<BIG>`...`</BIG>`

Big text: Text uses larger font than standard text.

`<B>`...`</B>`

Bold: Bold text

`<BLINK>`...`</BLINK>`

Blinking: Blinking text

`<I>`...`</I>`

Italic: Italic text

`<SMALL>`...`</SMALL>`

Small Text: Text uses smaller font than standard text

`<SUB>`...`</SUB>`

Subscript: Text is subscripted

`<SUP>...</SUP>`

Superscript: Text is superscripted

`<TT>...</TT>`

Typewriter: Text uses monospaced typewriter font

`<CITE>...</CITE>`

Citation: For quotes and references

`<CODE>...</CODE>`

Program code: For computer program source code

`<DFN>...</DFN>`

Defined: For word definitions

`<EM>...</EM>`

Emphasis: When italic emphasis is required

`<KBD>...</KBD>`

Keyboard: When showing text people need to type in (like a typewriter)

`<SAMP>...</SAMP>`

Sample: For examples

`<STRONG>...</STRONG>`

Strong: When bold text is required

`<VAR>...</VAR>`

Variable: For names of program variables

Other Text Layout Elements

The following text layout tags don't fall into any pre-defined category. However, they can all be used to affect the appearance or layout of a Web page.

`<HR>`

A horizontal rule line.

Attributes:

SIZE="…"	(NHTML) The thickness of the rule, in pixels.
WIDTH="…"	(NHTML) The width of the rule, in pixels.
ALIGN="…"	(NHTML) How the rule line is aligned on the page. Possible values are LEFT, RIGHT, and CENTER.
NOSHADE="…"	(NHTML) Causes the rule line to be drawn as a solid color with no shading.

Allowed Inside: <BLOCKQUOTE> <BODY> <FORM> <PRE> <TABLE>

A line break.

Attributes:

CLEAR="…"	(HTML 3.2) Causes the text to stop flowing around any images. Possible values are RIGHT, LEFT, and ALL.

Allowed Inside: <A> <ADDRESS> <BIG> <B> <BLINK> <I> <SMALL> <SUB> <SUP> <TT> <CITE> <CODE> <DFN> <EM> <KBD> <SAMP> <STRONG> <VAR> <DD> <DT> <H1> <H2> <H3> <H4> <H5> <H6> <LI> <P> <PRE> <TABLE>

<NOBR>…</NOBR> (NHTML)

Causes the enclosed text not to wrap at the edge of the page.

Allowed Inside: <A> <ADDRESS> <BIG> <B> <BLINK> <I> <SMALL> <SUB> <SUP> <TT> <CITE> <CODE> <DFN> <EM> <KBD> <SAMP> <STRONG> <VAR> <DD> <DT> <H1> <H2> <H3> <H4> <H5> <H6> <LI> <P> <PRE> <TABLE>

<WBR> (NHTML)

Wrap the text at this point only if necessary.

Allowed Inside: <A> <ADDRESS> <BIG> <B> <BLINK> <I> <SMALL> <SUB> <SUP> <TT> <CITE> <CODE> <DFN> <EM> <KBD> <SAMP> <STRONG> <VAR> <DD> <DT> <H1> <H2> <H3> <H4> <H5> <H6> <LI> <P> <PRE> <TABLE>

<BLOCKQUOTE>… </BLOCKQUOTE>

Used for long quotes or citations.

Can Include: <BLOCKQUOTE> <IMG> <H1> <H2> <H3> <H4> <H5> <H6> <P> <OL> <UL> <DIR> <MENU> <DL> <PRE> <FORM> <ISINDEX> <HR> <ADDRESS> <TABLE>

Allowed Inside: <BLOCKQUOTE> <BODY> <DD> <FORM> <LI> <TABLE>

<CENTER>...</CENTER>

All the content enclosed within these tags is centered. This tag is being phased out in favor of
<P ALIGN=CENTER> and <DIV ALIGN=CENTER>.

Can Include: <A> <IMG> <ADDRESS> <BIG> <B> <BLINK> <I> <SMALL> <SUB> <SUP> <TT> <CITE>
<CODE> <DFN> <EM> <KBD> <SAMP> <STRONG> <VAR> <DD> <DT> <H1> <H2> <H3> <H4> <H5> <H6>
<LI> <P> <PRE> <TABLE>

Allowed Inside: <BLOCKQUOTE> <BODY> <DD> <FORM> <LI> <TABLE>

<ADDRESS>...</ADDRESS>

Used for signatures or general information about a document's author.

Can Include: <A> <IMG> <BIG> <B> <BLINK> <I> <SMALL> <SUB> <SUP> <TT> <CITE> <CODE>
<DFN> <EM> <KBD> <SAMP> <STRONG> <VAR> <DD> <DT> <H1> <H2> <H3> <H4> <H5> <H6> <LI>
<P> <PRE> <TABLE>

Allowed Inside: <BLOCKQUOTE> <BODY> <FORM>

Font Sizes (NHTML)

The <FONT> tag introduced by Netscape Communications enables you to define the size and
color of blocks of text displayed on a Web page.

<FONT>...</FONT>

Changes the size or color of the font for the enclosed text.

Attributes:

SIZE="..."   The size of the font, from 1 to 7. Default is 3. Can also be
                  specified as a value relative to the current size, for example, +2.

COLOR="..."   The color of the font. See Appendix E, "Colors by Name and
                  Hex Value," for more information.

Can Include: <A> <IMG> <BIG> <B> <BLINK> <I> <SMALL> <SUB> <SUP> <TT> <CITE> <CODE>
<DFN> <EM> <KBD> <SAMP> <STRONG> <VAR> <DD> <DT> <LI> <P> <PRE> <TABLE>

Allowed Inside: <A> <ADDRESS> <BIG> <B> <BLINK> <I> <SMALL> <SUB> <SUP> <TT> <CITE>
<CODE> <DFN> <EM> <KBD> <SAMP> <STRONG> <VAR> <DD> <DT> <H1> <H2> <H3> <H4> <H5> <H6>
<LI> <P> <PRE> <TABLE>

<BASEFONT>

Sets the default size of the font for the current page.

Attributes:

SIZE="..."   The default size of the font, from 1 to 7. Default is 3.

Allowed Inside: <A> <ADDRESS> <BIG> <B> <BLINK> <I> <SMALL> <SUB> <SUP> <TT> <CITE>
<CODE> <DFN> <EM> <KBD> <SAMP> <STRONG> <VAR> <DD> <DT> <LI> <P> <PRE> <TABLE>

Images

Text is not the only type of information that your can include on a Web page. The tags in this
section let you place images on a Web page and describe the layout of image maps.

<IMG>

Insert an inline image into the document.

Attributes:

ISMAP   This image is a clickable image map.

SRC="..."   The URL of the image.

ALT="..."   A text string that is displayed in browsers that cannot support
                      images.

ALIGN="..."   Determines the alignment of the given image. If LEFT or RIGHT
                      (HTML 3.2, NHTML), the image is aligned to the left or right
                      column, and all following text flows beside that image. All other
                      values, such as TOP, MIDDLE, BOTTOM, or (NHTML) TEXTTOP,
                      ABSMIDDLE, BASELINE, and ABSBOTTOM, determine the vertical
                      alignment of this image with other items in the same line.

VSPACE="..."   The space between the image and the text above or below it.

HSPACE="..."   The space between the image and the text to its left or right.

WIDTH="..."   (HTML 3.2) The width, in pixels, of the image. If WIDTH is not
                      the actual width, the image is scaled to fit.

HEIGHT="..."   (HTML 3.2) The width, in pixels, of the image. If HEIGHT is not
                      the actual height, the image is scaled to fit.

BORDER="..."   (NHTML) Draws a border of the specified value in pixels to be
                      drawn around the image. In the case of images that are also links,
                      BORDER changes the size of the default link border.

LOWSRC="..."   (NHTML) The path or URL of an image that is loaded first,
                      before the image specified in SRC. The value of LOWSRC is usually a
                      smaller or lower-resolution version of the actual image.

USEMAP="...   (NHTML) Used to associate an image with a client-side image
                      map specified by <MAP NAME=mapname>.

Allowed Inside: <A> <ADDRESS> <BIG> <B> <BLINK> <I> <SMALL> <SUB> <SUP> <TT> <CITE> <CODE> <DFN> <EM> <KBD> <SAMP> <STRONG> <VAR> <DD> <DT> <H1> <H2> <H3> <H4> <H5> <H6> <LI> <P> <PRE> <TABLE>

<MAP>...</MAP>

Define a map for a client-side image map.

Attributes:

NAME="..."	Used to define the map's name.

Can Include: <AREA>

Allowed Inside: <BODY>

<AREA>...</AREA>

Define a clickable region for a client-side image map.

Attributes:

TYPE="..."	Used to indicate the type of region bounded by the <AREA> tag. Possible values are RECT, POLY, and CIRCLE.
COORDS="..."	This attribute describes the points bounding the region described by the <AREA> tag.
HREF="..."	The URL to load when the region bounded by the <AREA> tag is clicked.

Allowed Inside: <MAP>

Forms

The most common way to obtain information from users who visit a Web page is with forms. This section describes the tags you use to define a form and its contents.

<FORM>...</FORM>

Indicates a form.

Attributes:

ACTION="..."	The URL of the script to process this form input.
METHOD="..."	How the form input is sent to the gateway on the server side. Possible values are GET and POST.
ENCTYPE="..."	Only values currently supported are application/x-www-form-urlencoded and multipart/form-data (NHTML).

| TARGET="…" | (NHTML) Target window for response following form submission. |

Can Include: `<H1>` `<H2>` `<H3>` `<H4>` `<H5>` `<H6>` `<P>` `<OL>` `<UL>` `<DIR>` `<MENU>` `<DL>` `<PRE>` `<BLOCKQUOTE>` `<ISINDEX>` `<HR>` `<ADDRESS>` `<INPUT>` `<SELECT>` `<TEXTAREA>` `<TABLE>`

Allowed Inside: `<BLOCKQUOTE>` `<BODY>` `<DD>` `<LI>`

`<INPUT>`

An input widget for a form.

Attributes:

TYPE="…"	The type for this input widget. Possible values are CHECKBOX, FILE (NHTML), HIDDEN, PASSWORD, RADIO, RESET, SUBMIT, TEXT, or IMAGE (HTML 3.2 only).
NAME="…"	The name of this item, as passed to the gateway script as part of a name/value pair.
VALUE="…"	For a text or hidden widget, the default value; for a checkbox or radio button, the value to be submitted with the form; for Reset or Submit buttons, the label for the button itself.
SRC="…"	The source file for an image.
CHECKED	For checkboxes and radio buttons, indicates that the widget is checked.
SIZE="…"	The size, in characters, of a text widget.
MAXLENGTH="…"	The maximum number of characters that can be entered into a text widget.
ALIGN="…"	For images in forms, determines how the text and image align (same as with the `<IMG>` tag).

Allowed Inside: `<FORM>`

`<TEXTAREA>`…`</TEXTAREA>`

Indicates a multiline text entry widget.

Attributes:

NAME="…"	The name to be passed to the gateway script as part of the name/value pair.
ROWS="…"	The number of rows this textarea displays.
COLS="…"	The number of columns (characters) this textarea displays.

WRAP="OFF"	Wrapping doesn't happen. Lines are sent exactly as typed.
WRAP="VIRTUAL"	The display word wraps, but long lines are sent as one line without new lines.
WRAP="PHYSICAL"	The display word wraps, and the text is transmitted at all wrap points.

Allowed inside: <FORM>

<SELECT>...</SELECT>

Creates a menu or scrolling list of possible items.

Attributes:

NAME="..."	The name passed to the gateway script as part of the name/value pair.
SIZE="..."	The number of elements to display. If SIZE is indicated, the selection becomes a scrolling list. If no SIZE is given, the selection is a pop-up menu.
MULTIPLE	Enables multiple selections from the list.

Can Include: <OPTION>

Allowed Inside: <FORM>

<OPTION>

Indicates a possible item within a <SELECT> widget.

Attributes:

| SELECTED | With this attribute included, the <OPTION> is selected by default in the list. |
| VALUE="..." | The value to submit if this <OPTION> is selected when the form is submitted. |

Allowed Inside: <SELECT>

Tables (HTML 3.2)

Before the <TABLE> was introduced to the HTML 3.2 specification, there was no easy way to reliably format lists or tables on a Web page. This section describes the tags used to describe the contents and appearance of a table.

<TABLE>...</TABLE>

Creates a table, which can contain a caption (<CAPTION>) and any number of rows (<TR>).

Attributes:

BORDER="..."	Indicates whether the table should be drawn with or without a border. In Netscape, BORDER also can have a value indicating the width of the border.
CELLSPACING="..."	(NHTML) The amount of space between the cells in the table.
CELLPADDING="..."	(NHTML) The amount of space between the edges of the cell and its contents.
WIDTH="..."	(NHTML) The width of the table on the page, in either exact pixel values or as a percentage of page width.
ALIGN="..."	Determines the alignment of the given table. If LEFT or RIGHT (HTML 3.2, NHTML), the image is aligned to the left or right column, and all following text flows beside that image. If CENTER, then table is aligned with the center of the page (HTML 3.2 only).
BGCOLOR="..."	The color of the background for the entire table. See Appendix E for more information.

Can Include: <CAPTION> <TR>

Allowed Inside: <BLOCKQUOTE> <BODY> <DD> <LI> <TABLE>

<CAPTION>...</CAPTION>

The caption for the table.

Attributes:

ALIGN="..."	The position of the caption. Possible values are TOP and BOTTOM.

<TR>...</TR>

Defines a table row, containing headings and data (<TR> and <TH> tags).

Attributes:

BGCOLOR="..."	The color of the background for an entire row—overrides the table color. See Appendix E for more information.
ALIGN="..."	The horizontal alignment of the contents of the cells within this row. Possible values are LEFT, RIGHT, and CENTER.

VALIGN="…"   The vertical alignment of the contents of the cells within this row. Possible values are TOP, MIDDLE, BOTTOM, and BASELINE (NHTML).

Can Include: <TH> TD>

Allowed Inside: <TABLE>

<TH>…</TH>

Defines a table heading cell.

Attributes:

BGCOLOR="…"   The color of the background for the indicated heading row—overrides the table color. See Appendix E for more information.

ALIGN="…"   The horizontal alignment of the contents of the cell. Possible values are LEFT, RIGHT, and CENTER.

VALIGN="…"   The vertical alignment of the contents of the cell. Possible values are TOP, MIDDLE, BOTTOM, and BASELINE (NHTML).

ROWSPAN="…"   The number of rows this cell will span.

COLSPAN="…"   The number of columns this cell will span.

NOWRAP   Do not automatically wrap the contents of this cell.

WIDTH="…"   (NHTML) The width of this column of cells, in exact pixel values or as a percentage of the table width.

Can Include: <H1> <H2> <H3> <H4> <H5> <H6> <P> <OL> <UL> <DIR> <MENU> <DL> <PRE> <BLOCKQUOTE> <FORM> <ISINDEX> <HR> <ADDRESS> <TABLE>

Allowed Inside: <TR>

<TD>…</TD>

Defines a table data cell.

Attributes:

ALIGN="…"   The horizontal alignment of the contents of the cell. Possible values are LEFT, RIGHT, and CENTER.

VALIGN="…"   The vertical alignment of the contents of the cell. Possible values are TOP, MIDDLE, BOTTOM, and BASELINE (NHTML).

BGCOLOR="…"   The color of the background for the indicated cell—overrides table, row, and heading colors. See Appendix E for more information.

ROWSPAN="…"   The number of rows this cell will span.

COLSPAN="…"	The number of columns this cell will span.
NOWRAP	Do not automatically wrap the contents of this cell.
WIDTH="…"	(NHTML) The width of this column of cells, in exact pixel values or as a percentage of the table width.

Can Include: <H1> <H2> <H3> <H4> <H5> <H6> <P> <OL> <UL> <DIR> <MENU> <DL> <PRE> <BLOCKQUOTE> <FORM> <ISINDEX> <HR> <ADDRESS>

Allowed Inside: <TR>

Frame Tags

The use of frames within a Web pages introduces a new level of usability to the World Wide Web. With frames, parts of a Web page can be updated while other sections remain on-screen. This section discusses the tags used to format frames.

<FRAMESET>…</FRAMESET> (NHTML)

Encloses a frameset definition in an HTML document.

Attributes:

| COLS="…" | (NHTML) Defines the number of frame columns and their width in a frameset. |
| ROWS="…" | (NHTML) Defines the number of frame rows and their height in a frameset. |

Can Include: <FRAME> <NOFRAMES>

Allowed Inside: <HTML>

<FRAME> (NHTML)

Used to define the contents of a frame within a frameset.

Attributes:

SRC="…"	The URL of the document to be displayed inside the frame.
MARGINWIDTH="…"	The size in pixels of the margin on each side of a frame.
MARGINHEIGHT="…"	The size in pixels of the margin above and below the contents of a frame.
SCROLLING="…"	Enable or disable the display of scroll bars for a frame. Values are YES, NO, and AUTO.
NORESIZE	Don't enable the user to resize frames.

Allowed Inside: <FRAMESET>

<NOFRAMES>...</NOFRAMES> (NHTML)

Used to define a block of text that will be displayed by Web browsers that don't support frames.

Allowed Inside: <FRAMESET>

Can Include: <A> <IMG> <ADDRESS> <BIG> <B> <BLINK> <I> <SMALL> <SUB> <SUP> <TT> <CITE> <CODE> <DFN> <EM> <KBD> <SAMP> <STRONG> <VAR> <DD> <DT> <H1> <H2> <H3> <H4> <H5> <H6> <LI> <P> <PRE> <TABLE>

Programming Tags

This section discusses the tags used to include JavaScript code, Java applets, and plug-in elements on a Web page.

<SCRIPT>...</SCRIPT>

Encloses a Client JavaScript program definition and related functions. (Note that Client-side code is ignored by Web servers.)

Attributes:

LANGUAGE="..."	Either JavaScript or LiveScript.
SRC="..."	The URL of a JavaScript program stored in a separate file.

Allowed Inside: <HEAD> <BODY>

<NOSCRIPT>...</NOSCRIPT> (NHTML)

Used to define a block of text that will be displayed by Web browsers that don't support JavaScript or which have JavaScript support disabled.

Allowed Inside: <HEAD> <BODY>

Can Include: <A> <IMG> <ADDRESS> <BIG> <B> <BLINK> <I> <SMALL> <SUB> <SUP> <TT> <CITE> <CODE> <DFN> <EM> <KBD> <SAMP> <STRONG> <VAR> <DD> <DT> <H1> <H2> <H3> <H4> <H5> <H6> <LI> <P> <PRE> <TABLE>

<SERVER>...</SERVER>

Encloses a Server JavaScript program definition and related functions. (Note that Server-side code is treated as plain text by Client JavaScript.)

Attributes:

LANGUAGE="..."	Either JavaScript or LiveScript.
SRC="..."	The URL of a JavaScript program stored in a separate file.

Allowed Inside: <HEAD> <BODY>

<APPLET>...</APPLET> (NHTML)

Used to incorporate a Java applet into a Web page.

Attributes:

CODE="…"	The name of the Java class to be included.
CODEBASE="…"	The URL of the directory where the Java class is stored if it is not located in the same directory as the HTML document.
WIDTH="…"	The width in pixels of the area taken up by the applet.
HEIGHT="…"	The height in pixels of the area taken up by the applet.

Can Include: <PARAM>

Allowed Inside: <BODY>

<PARAM> (NHTML)

Used to define values (or parameter) to be passed to the Java applet.

Attributes:

NAME="…"	The name of the parameter to be passed to the Java class.
VALUE="…"	The value of the parameter.

Allowed Inside: <APPLET>

<EMBED> (NHTML)

Use to embed files supported by plug-ins. Netscape calls such files *live objects*.

Attributes:

SRC="…"	A URL that describes the location and file name to be handled by a plug-in. The file extension specified in this attribute determines which plug-in module is loaded.
WIDTH="…"	The width in pixels of the area taken up by the live object.
HEIGHT="…"	The height in pixels of the area taken up by the live object.
Plug-in specific	Each individual plug-in defines its own list of attributes. Refer to the appropriate documentation for additional information.

Allowed Inside: <BODY> <TABLE>

<NOEMBED>...</NOEMBED> (NHTML)

Used to define a block of text that will be displayed by Web browsers that don't support plug-ins.

Allowed Inside: `<BODY>`

Can Include: `<A>` `<IMG>` `<ADDRESS>` `<BIG>` `<B>` `<BLINK>` `<I>` `<SMALL>` `<SUB>` `<SUP>` `<TT>` `<CITE>` `<CODE>` `<DFN>` `<EM>` `<KBD>` `<SAMP>` `<STRONG>` `<VAR>` `<DD>` `<DT>` `<H1>` `<H2>` `<H3>` `<H4>` `<H5>` `<H6>` `<LI>` `<P>` `<PRE>` `<TABLE>`

C

JavaScript Language Reference

by Arman Danesh

The first part of this reference is organized by object, with properties and methods listed by the object to which they apply. The second part covers independent functions in JavaScript not connected with a particular object, as well as operators in JavaScript.

> **NOTE**
>
> In this section the following codes are used to indicate which platforms support any given command, object, property, method, function, event handler, or statement: C-Client JavaScript, S-Server JavaScript, 2-Navigator 2, 3-Navigator 3, I-Internet Explorer 3.

The anchor Object [C | 2 | 3 | I]

The anchor object reflects an HTML anchor.

Properties

- **name**—A string value indicating the name of the anchor. [Not 2|3]

The applet Object [C | 3]

The applet object reflects a Java applet included in a Web page with the APPLET tag.

Properties

- **name**—A string reflecting the NAME attribute of the APPLET tag.

The area Object [C | 3]

The area object reflects a clickable area defined in an imagemap. area objects appear as entries in the links array of the document object.

Properties

- **hash**—A string value indicating an anchor name from the URL.
- **host**—A string value reflecting the host and domain name portion of the URL.

■ **hostname**—A string value indicating the host, domain name, and port number from the URL.

■ **href**—A string value reflecting the entire URL.

■ **pathname**—A string value reflecting the path portion of the URL (excluding the host, domain name, port number, and protocol).

■ **port**—A string value indicating the port number from the URL.

■ **protocol**—A string value indicating the protocol portion of the URL, including the trailing colon.

■ **search**—A string value specifying the query portion of the URL (after the question mark).

■ **target**—A string value reflecting the TARGET attribute of the AREA tag.

Event Handlers

■ **onMouseOut**—Specifies JavaScript code to execute when the mouse moves outside the area specified in the AREA tag.

■ **onMouseOver**—Specifies JavaScript code to execute when the mouse enters the area specified in the AREA tag.

The Array Object [C | 3 | I]

Provides a mechanism for creating arrays and working with them. New arrays are created with *arrayName* = new Array() or *arrayName* = new Array(*arrayLength*).

Properties

■ **length**—An integer value reflecting the number of elements in an array.

■ **prototype**—Provides a mechanism to add properties to an Array object.

Methods

■ **join(*string*)**—Returns a string containing each element of the array separated by *string*. [Not I]

■ **reverse()**—Reverses the order of an array. [Not I]

■ **sort(*function*)**—Sorts an array based on function that indicates a *function* defining the sort order. *function* can be omitted, in which case the sort defaults to dictionary order. [Not I]

The button Object [C | 2 | 3 | I]

The button object reflects a push button from an HTML form in JavaScript.

Properties

- **enabled**—A Boolean value indicating if the button is enabled. [Not 2|3]
- **form**—A reference to the form object containing the button. [Not 2|3]
- **name**—A string value containing the name of the button element.
- **type**—A string value reflecting the TYPE attribute of the INPUT tag. [Not 2|I]
- **value**—A string value containing the value of the button element.

Methods

- **click()**—Emulates the action of clicking the button.
- **focus()**—Gives focus to the button. [Not 2|3]

Event Handlers

- **onClick**—Specifies JavaScript code to execute when the button is clicked.
- **onFocus**—Specifies JavaScript code to execute when the button receives focus. [Not 2|3]

The checkbox Object [C | 2 | 3 | I]

The checkbox object makes a checkbox from an HTML form available in JavaScript.

Properties

- **checked**—A Boolean value indicating if the checkbox element is checked.
- **defaultChecked**—A Boolean value indicating if the checkbox element was checked by default (reflects the CHECKED attribute).
- **enabled**—A Boolean value indicating if the checkbox is enabled. [Not 2|3]
- **form**—A reference to the form object containing the checkbox. [Not 2|3]
- **name**—A string value containing the name of the checkbox element.
- **type**—A string value reflecting the TYPE attribute of the INPUT tag. [Not 2|I]
- **value**—A string value containing the value of the checkbox element.

Methods

- ■ **click()**—Emulates the action of clicking the checkbox.
- ■ **focus()**—Gives focus to the checkbox. [Not 2|3]

Event Handlers

- ■ **onClick**—Specifies JavaScript code to execute when the checkbox is clicked.
- ■ **onFocus**—Specifies JavaScript code to execute when the checkbox receives focus. [Not 2|3]

The client Object [S]

The client object provides information about the current client accessing the server.

Methods

- ■ **destroy()**—Removes all properties from the client object and destroys the client.
- ■ **expiration(*seconds*)**—Sets the client object's expiration to *seconds* seconds from the current time.

The combo Object [C | I]

The combo object reflects a combo field into JavaScript.

Properties

- ■ **enabled**—A Boolean value indicating if the checkbox is enabled. [Not 2|3]
- ■ **form**—A reference to the form object containing the checkbox. [Not 2|3]
- ■ **listCount**—An integer reflecting the number of elements in the list.
- ■ **listIndex**—An integer reflecting the index of the selected element in the list.
- ■ **multiSelect**—A Boolean value indicating if the combo field is in multiselect mode.
- ■ **name**—A string value reflecting the name of the combo field.
- ■ **value**—A string containing the value of the combo field.

Methods

- ■ **addItem(*index*)**—Adds an item to the combo field before the item at *index*.
- ■ **click()**—Simulates a click on the combo field.

- **clear()**—Clears the contents of the combo field.
- **focus()**—Gives focus to the combo field.
- **removeItem(*index*)**—Removes the item at *index* from the combo field.

Event Handlers

- **onClick**—Specifies JavaScript code to execute when the mouse clicks the combo field.
- **onFocus**—Specifies JavaScript code to execute when the combo field receives focus.

The cursor Object [S]

The cursor object reflects the answer returned by an SQL statement from a database.

Properties

- **cursortColumn**—An array reflecting the columns in the data returned from the server. Each array entry is an object with the following methods:

blob(*FileName*)	Assigns BLOB data from *FileName* to the column.
blobImage(*format*,*altText*, *align*,*width*,*height*,*border*, *ismap*)	Displays BLOB data from the column as a data where *format* is a string indicating the image format, *altText* is displayed if the browser doesn't support images, *align* is a string specifying the images alignment, *width*, *height*, and *border* are integer values in pixels, and *ismap* is a Boolean value indicating if the image is an imagemap.
BlobLink(*mimeType*, *text*)	Returns a hyperlink to a binary file containing the BLOB data. *MimeType* indicates the type of the file and *text* is text that should be displayed for the link.

Methods

- **close()**—Closes a cursor.
- **columnName(*index*)**—Returns the name of column specified by *index*.
- **columns()**—Returns the number of columns in a cursor.
- **deleteRow(*table*)**—Deletes a row from *table*.
- **insertRow(*table*)**—Inserts a row into *table*.

■ **next()**—Navigates to the next row in a cursor.
■ **updateRow(*table*)**—Updates the current row in table with the current row from the cursor.

The database **Object [S]**

The database object provides methods for connecting to a database server.

Methods

■ **beginTransaction()**—Starts a transaction with the SQL server.
■ **commitTransaction()**—Commits the transaction to the server.
■ **connect(*type*, *name*, *user*, *password*, *database*)**—Connects to *database* on a server of type *type* named *name* using the username *user* and providing *password* for access.
■ **connected()**—Returns a Boolean value indicating if the application is connected to a database.
■ **cursor(*statement*, *update*)**—Creates a cursor for the specified *statement* and uses the Boolean value *update* to indicate if the cursor is updateable.
■ **disconnect()**—Disconnects from the database.
■ **execute(*statement*)**—Executes *statement*.
■ **rollbackTransaction()**—Rolls back the transaction.
■ **SQLTable(*statement*)**—Display query results for *statement*.
■ **majorErrorCode()**—Returns the major error code from the database server.
■ **minorErrorCode()**—Returns the minor error code from the database server.
■ **majorErrorMessage()**—Returns the major error message from the database server.
■ **minorErrorMessage()**—Returns the minor error message from the database server.

The Date **Object [C | S | 2 | 3 | I]**

The Date object provides mechanisms for working with dates and times in JavaScript. Instances of the object can be created with the syntax

newObjectName = new Date(*dateInfo*)

dateInfo is an optional specification of a particular date and can be one of the following:

> *month day*, *year hours*:*minutes*:*seconds*
>
> *year*, *month*, *day*
>
> *year*, *month*, *day*, *hours*, *minutes*, *seconds*

The latter two options represent integer values.

If no *dateInfo* is specified, the new object represents the current date and time.

Properties

- **prototype**—Provides a mechanism for adding properties to a Date object. [Not 2]

Methods

- **getDate()**—Returns the day of the month for the current Date object as an integer from 1 to 31.
- **getDay()**—Returns the day of the week for the current Date object as an integer from 0 to 6 (where 0 is Sunday, 1 is Monday, and so on).
- **getHours()**—Returns the hour from the time in the current Date object as an integer from 0 to 23.
- **getMinutes()**—Returns the minutes from the time in the current Date object as an integer from 0 to 59.
- **getMonth()**—Returns the month for the current Date object as an integer from 0 to 11 (where 0 is January, 1 is February, and so on).
- **getSeconds()**—Returns the seconds from the time in the current Date object as an integer from 0 to 59.
- **getTime()**—Returns the time of the current Date object as an integer representing the number of milliseconds since 1 January 1970 at 00:00:00.
- **getTimezoneOffset()**—Returns the difference between the local time and GMT as an integer representing the number of minutes.
- **getYear()**—Returns the year of the week for the current Date object as a two-digit integer representing the year minus 1900.
- **parse(*dateString*)**—Returns the number of milliseconds between January 1, 1970 at 00:00:00 and the date specified in *dateString*. *dateString* should take the format [Not I]

  Day, DD Mon YYYY HH:MM:SS TZN

  Mon DD, YYYY

- **setDate(*dateValue*)**—Sets the day of the month for the current Date object. *dateValue* is an integer from 1 to 31.
- **setHours(*hoursValue*)**—Sets the hours for the time for the current Date object. *hoursValue* is an integer from 0 to 23.
- **setMinutes(*minutesValue*)**—Sets the minutes for the time for the current Date object. *minutesValue* is an integer from 0 to 59.

- **setMonth(*monthValue*)**—Sets the month for the current Date object. *monthValue* is an integer from 0 to 11 (where 0 is January, 1 is February, and so on).
- **setSeconds(*secondsValue*)**—Sets the seconds for the time for the current Date object. *secondsValue* is an integer from 0 to 59.
- **setTime(*timeValue*)**—Sets the value for the current Date object. *timeValue* is an integer representing the number of milliseconds since January 1, 1970 at 00:00:00.
- **setYear(*yearValue*)**—Sets the year for the current Date object. *yearValue* is an integer greater than 1900.
- **toGMTString()**—Returns the value of the current Date object in GMT as a string using Internet conventions in the form

    Day, DD Mon YYYY HH:MM:SS GMT

- **toLocaleString()**—Returns the value of the current Date object in the local time using local conventions.
- ***UTC(yearValue, monthValue, dateValue, hoursValue, minutesValue, secondsValue)***—Returns the number of milliseconds since January 1, 1970 at 00:00:00 GMT. *yearValue* is an integer greater than 1900. *monthValue* is an integer from 0 to 11. *dateValue* is an integer from 1 to 31. *hoursValue* is an integer from 0 to 23. *minutesValue* and *secondsValue* are integers from 0 to 59. *hoursValue*, *minutesValue*, and *secondsValue* are optional. [Not I]

The document Object [C | 2 | 3 | I]

The document object reflects attributes of an HTML document in JavaScript.

Properties

- **alinkColor**—The color of active links as a string or a hexadecimal triplet.
- **anchors**—Array of anchor objects in the order they appear in the HTML document. Use anchors.length to get the number of anchors in a document.
- **applets**—Array of applet objects in the order they appear in the HTML document. Use applets.length to get the number of applets in a document. [Not 2]
- **bgColor**—The color of the document's background.
- **cookie**—A string value containing cookie values for the current document.
- **embeds**—Array of plugin objects in the order they appear in the HTML document. Use embeds.length to get the number of plug-ins in a document. [Not 2|I]
- **fgColor**—The color of the document's foreground.
- **forms**—Array of form objects in the order the forms appear in the HTML file. Use forms.length to get the number of forms in a document.

- ■ **images**—Array of image objects in the order they appear in the HTML document. Use images.length to get the number of images in a document. [Not 2|I]
- ■ **lastModified**—String value containing the last date of modification of the document.
- ■ **linkColor**—The color of links as a string or a hexadecimal triplet.
- ■ **links**—Array of link objects in the order the hypertext links appear in the HTML document. Use links.length to get the number of links in a document.
- ■ **location**—A string containing the URL of the current document. Use document.URL instead of document.location. This property is expected to disappear in a future release.
- ■ **referrer**—A string value containing the URL of the calling document when the user follows a link.
- ■ **title**—A string containing the title of the current document.
- ■ **URL**—A string reflecting the URL of the current document. Use instead of document.location. [Not I]
- ■ **vlinkColor**—The color of followed links as a string or a hexadecimal triplet.

Methods

- ■ **clear()**—Clears the document window. [Not I]
- ■ **close()**—Closes the current output stream.
- ■ **open(*mimeType*)**—Opens a stream that allows write() and writeln() methods to write to the document window. *mimeType* is an optional string that specifies a document type supported by Navigator or a plug-in (text/html, image/gif, and so on).
- ■ **write()**—Writes text and HTML to the specified document.
- ■ **writeln()**—Writes text and HTML to the specified document, followed by a newline character.

The File Object [S]

The File object provides mechanisms for a server application to work with files on the server. A file object can be created with the syntax *filePointer* = new File(*filename*).

Methods

- ■ **byteToString(*number*)**—Returns *number* as a string. *number* should be a single byte.
- ■ **clearError()**—Clears the error status for the object.
- ■ **close()**—Closes the file.
- ■ **eof()**—Returns a Boolean value indicating if the current file pointer is positioned past the end of the file.

■ **error()**—Returns the current error status for the object.

■ **exists()**—Returns a Boolean value indicating whether or not the file exists.

■ **flush()**—Writes the content of the buffer to the file.

■ **getLength()**—Returns the length of the file in bytes.

■ **getPosition()**—Returns the current position of the pointer in the file.

■ **open(*mode*)**—Opens the file with the specified *mode*.

■ **read(*number*)**—Reads *number* characters from the file.

■ **readByte()**—Reads one byte from the file.

■ **readln()**—Reads the current line from the file.

■ **setPosition(*position*, *reference*)**—Positions the pointer at *position* relative to *reference*. Possible references are 0 (beginning of file), 1 (current position), 2 (end of file), and unspecified (beginning of file).

■ **stringToByte(*string*)**—Converts the first character of *string* to a byte.

■ **write(*string*)**—Writes *string* to the file.

■ **writeByte(*number*)**—Writes the *byte* number to the file.

■ **writeln(*string*)**—Writes *string* to the file followed by a new line character.

The `FileUpload` Object [C | 3]

The `FileUpload` object reflects a file upload element in an HTML form.

Properties

■ **name**—A string value reflecting the name of the file upload element.

■ **value**—A string value reflecting the file upload element's field.

The `form` Object [C | 2 | 3 | I]

The `form` object reflects an HTML form in JavaScript. Each HTML form in a document is reflected by a distinct instance of the `form` object.

Properties

■ **action**—A string value specifying the URL to which the form data is submitted.

■ **elements**—Array of objects for each form element in the order in which they appear in the form.

■ **encoding**—String containing the MIME encoding of the form as specified in the ENCTYPE attribute.

- **method**—A string value containing the method of submission of form data to the server.
- **target**—A string value containing the name of the window to which responses to form submissions are directed.

Methods

- **reset()**—Resets the form. [Not 2|I]
- **submit()**—Submits the form.

Event Handlers

- **onReset**—Specifies JavaScript code to execute when the form is reset. [Not 2|I]
- **onSubmit**—Specifies JavaScript code to execute when the form is submitted. The code should return a `true` value to allow the form to be submitted. A `false` value prevents the form from being submitted.

The `frame` Object [C | 2 | 3 | I]

The `frame` object reflects a frame window in JavaScript.

Properties

- **frames**—An array of objects for each frame in a window. Frames appear in the array in the order in which they appear in the HTML source code.
- **onblur**—A string reflecting the `onBlur` event handler for the frame. New values can be assigned to this property to change the event handler. [Not 2]
- **onfocus**—A string reflecting the `onFocus` event handler for the frame. New values can be assigned to this property to change the event handler. [Not 2]
- **parent**—A string indicating the name of the window containing the frameset.
- **self**—A alternative for the name of the current window.
- **top**—An alternative for the name of the top-most window.
- **window**—An alternative for the name of the current window.

Methods

- **alert(*message*)**—Displays *message* in a dialog box.
- **blur()**—Removes focus from the frame. [Not 2]
- **close()**—Closes the window.

■ **confirm(*message*)**—Displays *message* in a dialog box with OK and CANCEL buttons. Returns true or false based on the button clicked by the user.

■ **focus()**—Gives focus to the frame. [Not 2]

■ **open(*url,name,features*)**—Opens *url* in a window named *name*. If *name* doesn't exist, a new window is created with that name. *features* is an optional string argument containing a list of features for the new window. The feature list contains any of the following name-value pairs separated by commas and without additional spaces:

`toolbar=[yes,no,1,0]`	Indicates if the window should have a toolbar
`location=[yes,no,1,0]`	Indicates if the window should have a location field
`directories=[yes,no,1,0]`	Indicates is the window should have directory buttons
`status=[yes,no,1,0]`	Indicates if the window should have a status bar
`menubar=[yes,no,1,0]`	Indicates if the window should have menus
`scrollbars=[yes,no,1,0]`	Indicates if the window should have scrollbars
`resizable=[yes,no,1,0]`	Indicates if the window should be resizable
`width=`*pixels*	Indicates the width of the window in pixels
`height=`*pixels*	Indicates the height of the window in pixels

■ **prompt(*message,response*)**—Displays *message* in a dialog box with a text entry field with the default value of *response*. The user's response in the text entry field is returned as a string.

■ **setTimeout(*expression,time*)**—Evaluates *expression* after *time*, where *time* is a value in milliseconds. The time-out can be named with the following structure:

name = setTimeOut(*expression,time*)

■ **clearTimeout(*name*)**—Cancels the time-out with the name *name*.

Event Handlers

■ **onBlur**—Specifies JavaScript code to execute when focus is removed from a frame. [Not 2]

■ **onFocus**—Specifies JavaScript code to execute when focus is applied from a frame. [Not 2]

The Function Object [C | 3]

The Function object provides a mechanism for indicating JavaScript code to compile as a function. The syntax to use the Function object is: *functionName* = new Function(*arg1*, *arg2*, *arg3*, ..., *functionCode*). This is similar to

```
function functionName(arg1, arg2, arg3, ...) {
   functionCode
}
```

except that in the former, *functionName* is a variable with a reference to the function and the function is evaluated each time it is used rather than being compiled once.

Properties

- ■ `arguments`—An integer reflecting the number of arguments in a function.
- ■ `prototype`—Provides a mechanism for adding properties to a `Function` object.

The hidden Object [C | 2 | 3 | I]

The `hidden` object reflects a hidden field from an HTML form in JavaScript.

Properties

- ■ `name`—A string value containing the name of the hidden element.
- ■ `type`—A string value reflecting the TYPE property of the INPUT tag. [Not 2|I]
- ■ `value`—A string value containing the value of the hidden text element.

The history Object [C | 2 | 3 | I]

The `history` object allows a script to work with the Navigator browser's history list in JavaScript. For security and privacy reasons, the actual content of the list isn't reflected into JavaScript.

Properties

- ■ `length`—An integer representing the number of items on the history list. [Not I]

Methods

- ■ `back()`—Goes back to the previous document in the history list. [Not I]
- ■ `forward()`—Goes forward to the next document in the history list. [Not I]
- ■ `go(location)`—Goes to the document in the history list specified by *location*. *location* can be a string or integer value. If it's a string, it represents all or part of a URL in the history list. If it's an integer, *location* represents the relative position of the document on the history list. As an integer, *location* can be positive or negative. [Not I]

The `Image` Object [C | 3]

The `Image` object reflects an image included in an HTML document.

Properties

- **`border`**—An integer value reflecting the width of the image's border in pixels.
- **`complete`**—A Boolean value indicating if the image has finished loading.
- **`height`**—An integer value reflecting the height of an image in pixels.
- **`hspace`**—An integer value reflecting the `HSPACE` attribute of the `IMG` tag.
- **`lowsrc`**—A string value containing the URL of the low-resolution version of the image to load.
- **`name`**—A string value indicating the name of the `Image` object.
- **`prototype`**—Provides a mechanism for adding properties to an `Image` object.
- **`src`**—A string value indicating the URL of the image.
- **`vspace`**—An integer value reflecting the `VSPACE` attribute of the `IMG` tag.
- **`width`**—An integer value indicating the width of an image in pixels.

Event Handlers

- **`onAbort`**—Specifies JavaScript code to execute if the attempt to load the image is aborted. [Not 2]
- **`onError`**—Specifies JavaScript code to execute if there is an error while loading the image. Setting this event handler to `null` suppresses error messages if an error does occur while loading. [Not 2]
- **`onLoad`**—Specifies JavaScript code to execute when the image finished loading. [Not 2]

The `link` Object [C | 2 | 3 | I]

The `link` object reflects a hypertext link in the body of a document.

Properties

- **`hash`**—A string value containing the anchor name in the URL.
- **`host`**—A string value containing the hostname and port number from the URL.
- **`hostname`**—A string value containing the domain name (or numerical IP address) from the URL.

- **href**—A string value containing the entire URL.
- **pathname**—A string value specifying the path portion of the URL.
- **port**—A string value containing the port number from the URL.
- **protocol**—A string value containing the protocol from the URL (including the colon, but not the slashes).
- **search**—A string value containing any information passed to a GET CGI-BIN call (any information after the question mark).
- **target**—A string value containing the name of the window or frame specified in the TARGET attribute.

Event Handlers

- **moveMouse**—Specifies JavaScript code to execute when the mouse pointer moves over the link. [Not 2|3]
- **onClick**—Specifies JavaScript code to execute when the link is clicked.
- **onMouseOver**—Specifies JavaScript code to execute when the mouse pointer moves over the hypertext link.

The location Object [C | 2 | 3 | I]

The location object reflects information about the current URL.

Properties

- **hash**—A string value containing the anchor name in the URL.
- **host**—A string value containing the hostname and port number from the URL.
- **hostname**—A string value containing the domain name (or numerical IP address) from the URL.
- **href**—A string value containing the entire URL.
- **pathname**—A string value specifying the path portion of the URL.
- **port**—A string value containing the port number from the URL.
- **protocol**—A string value containing the protocol from the URL (including the colon, but not the slashes).
- **search**—A string value containing any information passed to a GET CGI-BIN call (any information after the question mark).

Methods

- ■ `reload()`—Reloads the current document. [Not 2|I]
- ■ `replace(url)`—Loads *url* over the current entry in the history list, making it impossible to navigate back to the previous URL with the back button. [Not 2|I]

The Math Object [C | S | 2 | 3 | I]

The Math object provides properties and methods for advanced mathematical calculations.

Properties

- ■ `E`—The value of Euler's constant (roughly 2.718) used as the base for natural logarithms.
- ■ `LN10`—The value of the natural logarithm of 10 (roughly 2.302).
- ■ `LN2`—The value of the natural logarithm of 2 (roughly 0.693).
- ■ `LOG10E`—The value of the base 10 logarithm of E (roughly 0.434). [Not 2|3|I]
- ■ `LOG2E`—The value of the base 2 logarithm of E (roughly 1.442). [Not 2|3|I]
- ■ `PI`—The value of PI—used in calculating the circumference and area of circles (roughly 3.1415).
- ■ `SQRT1_2`—The value of the square root of one-half (roughly 0.707).
- ■ `SQRT2`—The value of the square root of two (roughly 1.414).

Methods

- ■ `abs(number)`—Returns the absolute value of *number*. The absolute value is the value of a number with its sign ignored, so `abs(4)` and `abs(-4)` both return 4.
- ■ `acos(number)`—Returns the arc cosine of *number* in radians.
- ■ `asin(number)`—Returns the arc sine of *number* in radians.
- ■ `atan(number)`—Returns the arc tangent of *number* in radians.
- ■ `atan2(number1,number2)`—Returns the angle of the polar coordinate corresponding to the cartesian coordinate (*number1,number2*). [Not I]
- ■ `ceil(number)`—Returns the next integer greater than *number*—in other words, rounds up to the next integer.
- ■ `cos(number)`—Returns the cosine of *number* where *number* represents an angle in radians.
- ■ `exp(number)`—Returns the value of E to the power of *number*.

- **floor(*number*)**—Returns the next integer less than *number*—in other words, rounds down to the nearest integer.
- **log(*number*)**—Returns the natural logarithm of *number*.
- **max(*number1*,*number2*)**—Returns the greater of *number1* and *number2*.
- **min(*number1*,*number2*)**—Returns the smaller of *number1* and *number2*.
- **pow(*number1*,*number2*)**—Returns the value of *number1* to the power of *number2*.
- **random()**—Returns a random number between zero and one (at press time, this method was only available on UNIX versions of Navigator 2.0).
- **round(*number*)**—Returns the closest integer to *number*—in other words rounds to the closest integer.
- **sin(*number*)**—Returns the sine of *number* where *number* represents an angle in radians.
- **sqrt(*number*)**—Returns the square root of *number*.
- **tan(*number*)**—Returns the tangent of *number* where *number* represents an angle in radians.

The mimeType Object [C | 3]

The mimeType object reflects a Mime type supported by the client browser.

Properties

- **type**—A string value reflecting the Mime type.
- **description**—A string containing a description of the Mime type.
- **enabledPlugin**—A reference to plugin object for the plug-in supporting the Mime type.
- **suffixes**—A string containing a comma-separated list of file suffixes for the Mime type.

The navigator Object [C | 2 | 3 | I]

The navigator object reflects information about the version of Navigator being used.

Properties

- **appCodeName**—A string value containing the code name of the client (in other words, "Mozilla" for Netscape Navigator).
- **appName**—A string value containing the name of the client (in other words, "Netscape" for Netscape Navigator).

- **appVersion**—A string value containing the version information for the client in the form

versionNumber (platform; country)

For instance, Navigator 2.0, beta 6 for Windows 95 (international version), would have an appVersion property with the value "2.0b6 (Win32; I)."

- **mimeTypes**—An array of mimeType objects reflecting the Mime types supported by the client browser. [Not 2|I]
- **plugins**—An array of plugin objects reflecting the plug-ins in a document in the order of their appearance in the HTML document. [Not 2|I]
- **userAgent**—A string containing the complete value of the user-agent header sent in the HTTP request. This contains all the information in appCodeName and appVersion: Mozilla/2.0b6 (Win32; I).

Methods

- **javaEnabled()**—Returns a Boolean value indicating if Java is enabled in the browser. [Not 2|I]

The Option Object [C | 3]

The Option object is used to create entries in a select list using this syntax:

optionName = new Option(*optionText, optionValue, defaultSelected, selected*)

and then

selectName.options[*index*] = *optionName*

Properties

- **defaultSelected**—A Boolean value specifying if the option is selected by default.
- **index**—An integer value specifying the option's index in the select list.
- **prototype**—Provides a mechanism to add properties to an Option object.
- **selected**—A Boolean value indicating if the option is currently selected.
- **text**—A string value reflecting the text displayed for the option.
- **value**—A string value indicating the value submitted to the server when the form is

submitted.

The password Object [C | 2 | 3 | I]

The password object reflects a password text field from an HTML form in JavaScript.

Properties

- ■ **defaultValue**—A string value containing the default value of the password element (the value of the VALUE attribute).
- ■ **enabled**—A Boolean value indicating if the password field is enabled. [Not 2|3]
- ■ **form**—A reference to the form object containing the password field. [Not 2|3]
- ■ **name**—A string value containing the name of the password element.
- ■ **value**—A string value containing the value of the password element.

Methods

- ■ **focus()**—Emulates the action of focusing in the password field.
- ■ **blur()**—Emulates the action of removing focus from the password field.
- ■ **select()**—Emulates the action of selecting the text in the password field.

Event Handlers

- ■ **onBlur**—Specifies JavaScript code to execute when the password field loses focus. [Not 2|3]
- ■ **onFocus**—Specifies JavaScript code to execute when the password field receives focus. [Not 2|3]

The plugin Object

The plugin object reflects a plug-in supported by the browser.

Properties

- ■ **name**—A string value reflecting the name of the plug-in.
- ■ **filename**—A string value reflecting the file name of the plug-in on the system's disk.

■ `description`—A string value containing the description supplied by the plug-in.

The `project` Object [S]

The `project` object provides a means to track global information for a server-based application.

Methods

■ `lock()`—Locks the `project` object so that other clients can't modify its properties.

■ `unlock()`—Unlocks the object, enabling other clients to make changes.

The `radio` Object [C | 2 | 3 | I]

The `radio` object reflects a set of radio buttons from an HTML form in JavaScript. To access individual radio buttons, use numeric indexes starting at zero. For instance, individual buttons in a set of radio buttons named `testRadio` could be referenced by `testRadio[0]`, `testRadio[1]`, and so on.

Properties

■ `checked`—A Boolean value indicating if a specific button is checked. Can be used to select or deselect a button.

■ `defaultChecked`—A Boolean value indicating if a specific button was checked by default (reflects the CHECKED attribute). [Not I]

■ `enabled`—A Boolean value indicating if the radio button is enabled. [Not 2|3]

■ `form`—A reference to the `form` object containing the radio button. [Not 2|3]

■ `length`—An integer value indicating the number of radio buttons in the set. [Not I]

■ `name`—A string value containing the name of the set of radio buttons.

■ `value`—A string value containing the value a specific radio button in a set (reflecting the VALUE attribute).

Methods

■ `click()`—Emulates the action of clicking a radio button.

■ `focus()`—Gives focus to the radio button. [Not 2|3]

Event Handlers

■ `onClick`—Specifies JavaScript code to execute when a radio button is clicked.

■ `onFocus`—Specifies JavaScript code to execute when a radio button receives focus. [Not 2|3]

The request Object [S]

The request object provides data about the current request from the client.

Properties

- **agent**—A string value containing the name and value of the client browser for the current request.
- **ip**—A string value containing the IP address of the current client.
- **method**—A string value reflecting the request method. Possible values are GET, POST, or HEAD.
- **protocol**—A string value reflecting the protocol and protocol level used by the client.

The reset Object [C | 2 | 3 | I]

The reset object reflects a reset button from an HTML form in JavaScript.

Properties

- **enabled**—A Boolean value indicating if the reset button is enabled. [Not 2|3]
- **form**—A reference to the form object containing the reset button. [Not 2|3]
- **name**—A string value containing the name of the reset element.
- **value**—A string value containing the value of the reset element.

Methods

- **click()**—Emulates the action of clicking on the reset button.
- **focus()**—Specifies JavaScript code to execute when the reset button receives focus. [Not 2|3]

Event Handlers

- **onClick**—Specifies JavaScript code to execute when the reset button is clicked.
- **onFocus**—Specifies JavaScript code to execute when the reset button receives focus. [Not 2|3]

The `select` Object [C | 2 | 3]

The `select` object reflects a selection list from an HTML form in JavaScript.

Properties

- **`length`**—An integer value containing the number of options in the selection list.
- **`name`**—A string value containing the name of the selection list.
- **`options`**—An array reflecting each of the options in the selection list in the order they appear. The `options` property has its own properties:

`defaultSelected`	A Boolean value indicating if an option was selected by default (reflecting the `SELECTED` attribute).
`index`	An integer value reflecting the index of an option.
`length`	An integer value reflecting the number of options in the selection list.
`name`	A string value containing the name of the selection list.
`selected`	A Boolean value indicating if the option is selected. Can be used to select or deselect an option.
`selectedIndex`	An integer value containing the index of the currently selected option.
`text`	A string value containing the text displayed in the selection list for a particular option.
`value`	A string value indicating the value for the specified option (reflecting the `VALUE` attribute).

- **`selectedIndex`**—Reflects the index of the currently selected option in the selection list.

Methods

- **`blur()`**—Removes focus from the select list. [Not 2|3]
- **`focus()`**—Gives focus to the select list. [Not 2|3]

Event Handlers

- **`onBlur`**—Specifies JavaScript code to execute when the selection list loses focus.
- **`onFocus`**—Specifies JavaScript code to execute when focus is given to the selection list.
- **`onChange`**—Specifies JavaScript code to execute when the selected option in the list changes.

The server Object [S]

The server object provides global information about the server.

Properties

- **hostname**—A string value containing the full host of the server, including port number.
- **host**—A string value reflecting the host and domain name of the server without the port number.
- **protocol**—A string value containing the protocol being used, including the trailing colon.
- **port**—A string value reflecting the port number the server watches for incoming requests.

Methods

- **lock()**—Locks the server object so that other clients can't modify its properties.
- **unlock()**—Unlocks the object, enabling other clients to make changes.

The String Object [C | S | 2 | 3 | I]

The String object provides properties and methods for working with string literals and variables.

Properties

- **length**—An integer value containing the length of the string expressed as the number of characters in the string.
- **prototype**—Provides a mechanism for adding properties to a String object. [Not 2]

Methods

- **anchor(*name*)**—Returns a string containing the value of the String object surrounded by an A container tag with the NAME attribute set to *name*.
- **big()**—Returns a string containing the value of the String object surrounded by a BIG container tag.
- **blink()**—Returns a string containing the value of the String object surrounded by a BLINK container tag.

- **bold()**—Returns a string containing the value of the String object surrounded by a B container tag.
- **charAt(*index*)**—Returns the character at the location specified by *index*.
- **fixed()**—Returns a string containing the value of the String object surrounded by a FIXED container tag.
- **fontColor(*color*)**—Returns a string containing the value of the String object surrounded by a FONT container tag with the COLOR attribute set to *color* where *color* is a color name or an RGB triplet. [Not I]
- **fontSize(*size*)**—Returns a string containing the value of the String object surrounded by a FONTSIZE container tag with the size set to *size*. [Not I]
- **indexOf(*findString,startingIndex*)**—Returns the index of the first occurrence of *findString*, starting the search at *startingIndex* where *startingIndex* is optional—if it isn't provided, the search starts at the start of the string.
- **italics()**—Returns a string containing the value of the String object surrounded by an I container tag.
- **lastIndexOf(*findString,startingIndex*)**—Returns the index of the last occurrence of *findString*. This is done by searching backwards from *startingIndex*. *startingIndex* is optional and is assumed to be the last character in the string if no value is provided.
- **link(*href*)**—Returns a string containing the value of the String object surrounded by an A container tag with the HREF attribute set to *href*.
- **small()**—Returns a string containing the value of the String object surrounded by a SMALL container tag.
- **split(*separator*)**—Returns an array of strings created by splitting the string at every occurrence of *separator*. [Not S|2|I]
- **strike()**—Returns a string containing the value of the String object surrounded by a STRIKE container tag.
- **sub()**—Returns a string containing the value of the String object surrounded by a SUB container tag.
- **substring(*firstIndex,lastIndex*)**—Returns a string equivalent to the substring starting at *firstIndex* and ending at the character before *lastIndex*. If *firstIndex* is greater than *lastIndex*, the string starts at *lastIndex* and ends at the character before *firstIndex*.
- **sup()**—Returns a string containing the value of the String object surrounded by a SUP container tag.
- **toLowerCase()**—Returns a string containing the value of the String object with all characters converted to lowercase.
- **toUpperCase()**—Returns a string containing the value of the String object with all characters converted to uppercase.

The `submit` Object [C | 2 | 3 | I]

The `submit` object reflects a submit button from an HTML form in JavaScript.

Properties

- ■ **`enabled`**—A Boolean value indicating if the submit button is enabled. [Not 2|3]
- ■ **`form`**—A reference to the `form` object containing the submit button. [Not 2|3]
- ■ **`name`**—A string value containing the name of the submit button element.
- ■ **`type`**—A string value reflecting the TYPE attribute of the INPUT tag. [Not 2|I]
- ■ **`value`**—A string value containing the value of the submit button element.

Methods

- ■ **`click()`**—Emulates the action of clicking on the submit button.
- ■ **`focus()`**—Gives focus to the submit button. [Not 2|3]

Event Handlers

- ■ **`onClick`**—Specifies JavaScript code to execute when the submit button is clicked.
- ■ **`onFocus`**—Specifies JavaScript code to execute when the submit button receives focus. [Not 2|3]

The `text` Object [C | 2 | 3 | I]

The `text` object reflects a text field from an HTML form in JavaScript.

Properties

- ■ **`defaultValue`**—A string value containing the default value of the text element (in other words, the value of the VALUE attribute).
- ■ **`enabled`**—A Boolean value indicating if the text field is enabled. [Not 2|3]
- ■ **`form`**—A reference to the `form` object containing the text field. [Not 2|3]
- ■ **`name`**—A string value containing the name of the text element.
- ■ **`type`**—A string value reflecting the TYPE attribute of the INPUT tag. [Not 2|I]
- ■ **`value`**—A string value containing the value of the text element.

Methods

- **focus()**—Emulates the action of focusing in the text field.
- **blur()**—Emulates the action of removing focus from the text field.
- **select()**—Emulates the action of selecting the text in the text field.

Event Handlers

- **onBlur**—Specifies JavaScript code to execute when focus is removed from the field.
- **onChange**—Specifies JavaScript code to execute when the content of the field is changed.
- **onFocus**—Specifies JavaScript code to execute when focus is given to the field.
- **onSelect**—Specifies JavaScript code to execute when the user selects some or all of the text in the field.

The textarea Object [C | 2 | 3 | I]

The textarea object reflects a multi-line text field from an HTML form in JavaScript.

Properties

- **defaultValue**—A string value containing the default value of the textarea element (the value of the VALUE attribute).
- **enabled**—A Boolean value indicating if the textarea field is enabled. [Not 2|3]
- **form**—A reference to the form object containing the textarea field. [Not 2|3]
- **name**—A string value containing the name of the textarea element.
- **type**—A string value reflecting the type of the textarea object. [Not 2|I]
- **value**—A string value containing the value of the textarea element.

Methods

- **focus()**—Emulates the action of focusing in the textarea field.
- **blur()**—Emulates the action of removing focus from the textarea field.
- **select()**—Emulates the action of selecting the text in the textarea field.

Event Handlers

- **onBlur**—Specifies JavaScript code to execute when focus is removed from the field.
- **onChange**—Specifies JavaScript code to execute when the content of the field is changed.

- **onFocus**—Specifies JavaScript code to execute when focus is given to the field.
- **onSelect**—Specifies JavaScript code to execute when the user selects some or all of the text in the field.

The window **Object [C | 2 | 3 | I]**

The window object is the top-level object for each window or frame and is the parent object for the document, location, and history objects.

Properties

- **defaultStatus**—A string value containing the default value displayed in the status bar.
- **frames**—An array of objects for each frame in a window. Frames appear in the array in the order in which they appear in the HTML source code.
- **length**—An integer value indicating the number of frames in a parent window. [Not I]
- **name**—A string value containing the name of the window or frame.
- **opener**—A reference to the window object containing the open() method used to open the current window. [Not 2|I]
- **parent**—A string indicating the name of the window containing the frameset.
- **self**—An alternative for the name of the current window.
- **status**—Used to display a message in the status bar—this is done by assigning values to this property.
- **top**—An alternative for the name of the top-most window.
- **window**—An alternative for the name of the current window.

Methods

- **alert(*message*)**—Displays *message* in a dialog box.
- **blur()**—Removes focus from the window. On many systems, this sends the window to the background. [Not 2|I]
- **close()**—Closes the window. [Not I]
- **confirm(*message*)**—Displays *message* in a dialog box with OK and CANCEL buttons. Returns true or false based on the button clicked by the user.
- **focus()**—Gives focus to the window. On many systems, this brings the window to the front. [Not 2|I]
- **navigator(*url*)**—Loads *url* in the window. [Not 2|3]

■ **open(*url,name,features*)**—Opens *url* in a window named *name*. If *name* doesn't exist, a new window is created with that name. *features* is an optional string argument containing a list of features for the new window. The feature list contains any of the following name-value pairs separated by commas and without additional spaces: [Not I]

`toolbar=[yes,no,1,0]`	Indicates if the window should have a toolbar
`location=[yes,no,1,0]`	Indicates if the window should have a location field
`directories=[yes,no,1,0]`	Indicates if the window should have directory buttons
`status=[yes,no,1,0]`	Indicates if the window should have a status bar
`menubar=[yes,no,1,0]`	Indicates if the window should have menus
`scrollbars=[yes,no,1,0]`	Indicates if the window should have scroll bars
`resizable=[yes,no,1,0]`	Indicates if the window should be resizable
`width=pixels`	Indicates the width of the window in pixels
`height=pixels`	Indicates the height of the window in pixels

■ **prompt(*message,response*)**—Displays *message* in a dialog box with a text entry field with the default value of *response*. The user's response in the text entry field is returned as a string.

■ **setTimeout(*expression,time*)**—Evaluates *expression* after *time* where *time* is a value in milliseconds. The time-out can be named with the structure

`name = setTimeOut(expression,time)`

■ **scroll(*x,y*)**—Scrolls the window to the coordinate *x,y*. [Not 2|I]

■ **clearTimeout(*name*)**—Cancels the time-out with the name *name*.

Event Handlers

■ **onBlur**—Specifies JavaScript code to execute when focus is removed from a window. [Not 2|I]

■ **onError**—Specifies JavaScript code to execute when a JavaScript error occurs while loading a document. This can be used to intercept JavaScript errors. Setting this event handler to `null` effectively prevents JavaScript errors from being displayed to the user. [Not 2|I]

■ **onFocus**—Specifies JavaScript code to execute when the window receives focus. [Not 2|I]

■ **onLoad**—Specifies JavaScript code to execute when the window or frame finishes loading.

■ **onUnload**—Specifies JavaScript code to execute when the document in the window or frame is exited.

Independent Functions and Operators

Independent Functions

- **callC(*FunctionName, arguments* ...)**—Calls the external function *FunctionName* and passes the *arguments* to it. [S]

- **debug(*expression*)**—Displays the result of *expression* to the trace window or frame. [S]

- **escape(*character*)**—Returns a string containing the ASCII encoding of *character* in the form %xx where xx is the numeric encoding of the character. [C|2|3|I]

- **eval(*expression*)**—Returns the result of evaluating *expression* where *expression* is an arithmetic expression. [C|S|2|3|I]

- **flush()**—Displays buffered data from previous write() function calls. [S]

- **isNaN(*value*)**—Evaluates *value* to see if it is NaN. Returns a Boolean value. [C|S|2|3|I] [On UNIX platforms, Not 2]

- **parseFloat(*string*)**—Converts *string* to a floating point number and returns the value. It continues to convert until it hits a non-numeric character and then returns the result. If the first character can't be converted to a number, the function returns "NaN" (zero on Windows platforms). [C|S|2|3|I]

- **parseInt(*string,base*)**—Converts *string* to an integer of base *base* and returns the value. It continues to convert until it hits a non-numeric character and then returns the result. If the first character can't be converted to a number, the function returns "NaN" (zero on Windows platforms). [C|S|2|3|I]

- **redirect(*url*)**—Redirects the client to *url*. [S]

- **registerCFunction(*FunctionName, library, externalName*)**—Registers the external function *externalName* in the library specified by *library* and assigns it the internal name *FunctionName*. [S]

- **taint(*propertyName*)**—Adds tainting to *propertyName*. [C|3]

- **toString()**—This is a method of all objects. It returns the object as a string or returns "[object *type*]" if no string representation exists for the object. [C|2|3]

- **unescape(*string*)**—Returns a character based on the ASCII encoding contained in *string*. The ASCII encoding should take the form "%integer" or "hexadecimalValue". [C|2|3|I]

- **untaint(*propertyName*)**—Removes tainting from *propertyName*. [C|3]

Operators

■ Assignment operators—Table C.1 shows assignment operators in JavaScript. [C|2|3|I]

Table C.1. Assignment operators.

Operator	Description
=	Assigns value of right operand to the left operand.
+=	Adds the left and right operands and assigns the result to the left operand.
-=	Subtracts the right operand from the left operand and assigns the result to the left operand.
*=	Multiplies the two operands and assigns the result to the left operand.
/=	Divides the left operand by the right operand and assigns the value to the left operand.
%=	Divides the left operand by the right operand and assigns the remainder to the left operand.

■ Arithmetic operators—Table C.2 shows arithmetic operators in JavaScript. [C|2|3|I]

Table C.2. Arithmetic operators.

Operator	Description
+	Adds the left and right operands.
-	Subtracts the right operand from the left operand.
*	Multiplies the two operands.
/	Divides the left operand by the right operand.
%	Divides the left operand by the right operand and evaluates to the remainder.
++	Increments the operand by one (can be used before or after the operand).
—	Decreases the operand by one (can be used before or after the operand).
-	Changes the sign of the operand.

■ Bitwise operators—Bitwise operators deal with their operands as binary numbers but return JavaScript numerical values (see Table C.3). [C|2|3|I]

Table C.3. Bitwise operators.

Operator	Description
AND (or &)	Converts operands to integers with 32 bits, pairs the corresponding bits, and returns one for each pair of ones. Returns zero for any other combination.
OR (or ¦)	Converts operands to integers with 32 bits, pairs the corresponding bits and returns one for each pair where one of the two bits is one. Returns zero if both bits are zero.
XOR (or ^)	Converts operands to integers with 32 bits, pairs the corresponding bits, and returns one for each pair where only one bit is one. Returns zero for any other combination.
<<	Converts the left operand to an integer with 32 bits and shifts bits to the left of the number of bits indicated by the right operand—bits shifted off to the left are discarded and zeros are shifted in from the right.
>>>	Converts the left operand to an integer with 32 bits and shifts bits to the right of the number of bits indicated by the right operand—bits shifted off to the right are discarded and zeros are shifted in from the left.
>>	Converts the left operand to an integer with 32 bits and shifts bits to the right of the number of bits indicated by the right operand—bits shifted off to the right are discarded and copies of the left-most bit are shifted in from the left.

■ Logical operators—Table C.4 shows logical operators in JavaScript. [C|2|3|I]

Table C.4. Logical operators.

Operator	Description
&&	Logical and—returns `true` when both operands are true, otherwise it returns `false`.
¦¦	Logical or—returns `true` if either operand is true. It only returns `false` when both operands are false.
!	Logical not—returns `true` if the operand is false and `false` if the operand is true. This is a unary operator and precedes the operand.

■ Comparison operators—Table C.5 shows comparison operators in JavaScript. [C|2|3|I]

Table C.5. Logical (comparison) operators.

Operator	Description
==	Returns true if the operands are equal.
!=	Returns true if the operands are not equal.
>	Returns true if the left operand is greater than the right operand.
<	Returns true if the left operand is less than the right operand.
>=	Returns true if the left operand is greater than or equal to the right operand.
<=	Returns true if the left operand is less than or equal to the right operand.

■ Conditional operators—Conditional expressions take one form:

```
(condition) ? val1 : val2
```

If `condition` is true, the expression evaluates to `val1`, otherwise it evaluates to `val2`. [C|2|3|I]

■ String operators—The concatenation operators (+) is one of two string operators. It evaluates to a string combining the left and right operands. The concatenation assignment operator (+=) is also available. [C|2|3|I]

■ The **typeof** operator—The typeof operator returns the type of its single operand. Possible types are `object`, `string`, `number`, `boolean`, `function`, and `undefined`. [C|3|I]

■ The **void** operator—The void operator takes an expression as an operand but returns no value. [C|3]

■ Operator precedence—JavaScript applies the rules of operator precedence as follows (from lowest to highest precedence):

comma (,)
assignment operators (= += -= *= /= %=)
conditional (? :)
logical or (¦¦)
logical and (&&)
bitwise or (¦)
bitwise xor (^)
bitwise and (&)
equality (== !=)
relational (< <= > >=)

shift (<< >> >>>)
addition/subtraction (+ -)
multiply/divide/modulus (* / %)
negation/increment (! - ++ --)
call, member (() [])

JavaScript Statements

- **break**—Terminates the current loop. [C|S|2|3|I]

- **continue**—Jumps to the start of the next iteration of the current loop. [C|S|2|3|I]

- **for(*initial, condition, increment*)**—Creates a loop that counts from *intial* by the steps specified by *increment* until *condition* is true. [C|S|2|3|I]

- **for(*variable* in *object*)**—Loop iterates through each property of *object* and reflects them in *variable* inside the loop. [C|S|2|3|I]

- **function**—Defines a function. [C|S|2|3|I]

- **if (*condition*) *JavaScriptCode* else *OtherCode***—If *condition* is true, *JavaScriptCode* is executed; otherwise *OtherCode* is executed. [C|S|2|3|I]

- **new**—Creates an instance of an object. [C|S|2|3|I]

- **return**—Returns a value from a function. [C|S|2|3|I]

- **this**—A reference to the current object. [C|S|2|3|I]

- **var**—Declares a variable. [C|S|2|3|I]

- **while (*condition*)**—A loop that iterates as long as *condition* is true.

- **with (*object*) *JavaScriptCode***—Sets *object* as the default object for *JavaScriptCode*.

D

Character Entities

by Wes Tatters

Table D.1 contains the possible numeric and character entities for the ISO-Latin-1 (ISO8859-1) character set. Where possible, the character is shown.

Table D.1. ISO-Latin-1 character set.

Character	Numeric Entity	Hex Value	Character Entity (if any)	Description
	&#00;-&#08;	00-08		Unused
	&#09;	09		Horizontal tab
	&#10;	0A		Line feed
	&#11;-&#31;	0B-1F		Unused
	&#32;	20		Space
!	&#33;	21		Exclamation mark
"	&#34;	22	&quot;	Quotation mark
#	&#35;	23		Number sign
$	&#36;	24		Dollar sign
%	&#37;	25		Percent sign
&	&#38;	26	&amp;	Ampersand
'	&#39;	27		Apostrophe
(	&#40;	28		Left parenthesis
)	&#41;	29		Right parenthesis
*	&#42;	2A		Asterisk
+	&#43;	2B		Plus sign
,	&#44;	2C		Comma
-	&#45;	2D		Hyphen
.	&#46;	2E		Period (fullstop)
/	&#47;	2F		Solidus (slash)

Character	Numeric Entity	Hex Value	Character Entity (if any)	Description
0-9	0 - 9	30-39		Digits 0-9
:	&#58;	3A		Colon
;	&#59;	3B		Semicolon
<	&#60;	3C	&lt;	Less than
=	&#61;	3D		Equals sign
>	&#62;	3E	&gt;	Greater than
?	&#63;	3F		Question mark
@	&#64;	40		Commercial at
A-Z	A-Z	41-5A		Letters A-Z
[	&#91;	5B		Left square bracket
\	&#92;	5C		Reverse solidus (backslash)
]	&#93;	5D		Right square bracket
^	&#94;	5E		Caret
—	&#95;	5F		Horizontal bar
`	&#96;	60		Grave accent
a-z	a-z	61-7A		Letters a-z
{	&#123;	7B		Left curly brace
|	|	7C		Vertical bar
}	&#125;	7D		Right curly brace
~	&#126;	7E		Tilde
	&#127;-	;7F-A0		Unused
¡	&#161;	A1		Inverted exclamation
¢	&#162;	A2		Cent sign
£	&#163;	A3		Pound sterling
¤	&#164;	A4		General currency sign
¥	&#165;	A5		Yen sign
¦	&#166;	A6		Broken vertical bar

continues

Table D.1. continued

Character	Numeric Entity	Hex Value	Character Entity (if any)	Description
§	&#167;	A7		Section sign
¨	&#168;	A8		Umlaut (dieresis)
©	&#169;	A9	© (NHTML)	Copyright
ª	&#170;	AA		Feminine ordinal
‹	&#171;	AB		Left angle quote, guillemotleft
¬	&#172;	AC		Not sign
-	&#173;	AD		Soft hyphen
®	&#174;	AE	® (HHTM)	Registered trademark
¯	&#175;	AF		Macron accent
°	&#176;	B0		Degree sign
±	&#177;	B1		Plus or minus
²	&#178;	B2		Superscript two
³	&#179;	B3		Superscript three
´	&#180;	B4		Acute accent
µ	&#181;	B5		Micro sign
¶	&#182;	B6		Paragraph sign
·	&#183;	B7		Middle dot
ç	&#184;	B8		Cedilla
¹	&#185;	B9		Superscript one
º	&#186;	BA		Masculine ordinal
›	&#187;	BB		Right angle quote, guillemotright
¼	&#188;	BC		Fraction one-fourth
½	&#189;	BD		Fraction one-half
¾	&#190;	BE		Fraction three-fourths
¿	&#191;	BF		Inverted question mark
À	&#192;	C0	&Agrave;	Capital A,

Character	Numeric Entity	Hex Value	Character Entity (if any)	Description
				grave accent
Á	&#193;	C1	&Aacute;	Capital A, acute accent
Â	&#194;	C2	&Acirc;	Capital A, circumflex accent
Ã	&#195;	C3	&Atilde;	Capital A, tilde
Ä	&#196;	C4	&Auml;	Capital A, dieresis or umlaut mark
Å	&#197;	C5	&Aring;	Capital A, ring
Æ	&#198;	C6	&AElig;	Capital AE dipthong (ligature)
Ç	&#199;	C7	&Ccedil;	Capital C, cedilla
È	&#200;	C8	&Egrave;	Capital E, grave accent
É	&#201;	C9	&Eacute;	Capital E, acute accent
Ê	&#202;	CA	&Ecirc;	Capital E, circumflex accent
Ë	&#203;	CB	&Euml;	Capital E, dieresis or umlaut mark
Ì	&#204;	CC	&Igrave;	Capital I, grave accent
Í	&#205;	CD	&Iacute;	Capital I, acute accent
Î	&#206;	CE	&Icirc;	Capital I, circumflex accent
Ï	&#207;	CF	&Iuml;	Capital I, dieresis or umlaut mark
Ð	&#208;	D0	&ETH;	Capital Eth, Icelandic

continues

Table D.1. continued

Character	Numeric Entity	Hex Value	Character Entity (if any)	Description
Ñ	Ñ	D1	Ñ	Capital N, tilde
Ò	Ò	D2	Ò	Capital O, grave accent
Ó	Ó	D3	Ó	Capital O, acute accent
Ô	Ô	D4	Ô	Capital O, circumflex accent
Õ	Õ	D5	Õ	Capital O, tilde
Ö	Ö	D6	Ö	Capital O, dieresis or umlaut mark
×	×	D7		Multiply sign
Ø	Ø	D8	Ø	Capital O, slash
Ù	Ù	D9	Ù	Capital U, grave accent
Ú	Ú	DA	Ú	Capital U, acute accent
Û	Û	DB	Û	Capital U, circumflex accent
Ü	Ü	DC	Ü	Capital U, dieresis or umlaut mark
Ý	Ý	DD	Ý	Capital Y, acute accent
	Þ	DE	Þ	Capital THORN, Icelandic
	ß	DF	ß	Small sharp s, German (sz ligature)
à	à	E0	à	Small a, grave accent
á	á	E1	á	Small a, acute accent
â	â	E2	â	Small a,

Character	Numeric Entity	Hex Value	Character Entity (if any)	Description
				circumflex accent
ã	&#227;	E3	&atilde;	Small a, tilde
ä	&#228;	E4	&aauml;	Small a, dieresis or umlaut mark
å	&#229;	E5	&aring;	Small a, ring
æ	&#230;	E6	&aelig;	Small ae dipthong (ligature)
ç	&#231;	E7	&ccedil;	Small c, cedilla
è	&#232;	E8	&egrave;	Small e, grave accent
é	&#233;	E9	&eacute;	Small e, acute accent
ê	&#234;	EA	&ecirc;	Small e, circumflex accent
ë	&#235;	EB	&euml;	Small e, dieresis or umlaut mark
ì	&#236;	EC	&igrave;	Small i, grave accent
í	&#237;	ED	&iacute;	Small i, acute accent
î	&#238;	EE	&icirc;	Small i, circumflex accent
ï	&#239;	EF	&iuml;	Small i, dieresis or umlaut mark
ð	&#240;	F0	&eth;	Small eth, Icelandic
ñ	&#241;	F1	&ntilde;	Small n, tilde
ò	&#242;	F2	&ograve;	Small o, grave accent
ó	&#243;	F3	&oacute;	Small o,

continues

Table D.1. continued

Character	Numeric Entity	Hex Value	Character Entity (if any)	Description
				acute accent
ô	`&#244;`	F4	`&ocirc;`	Small o, circumflex accent
õ	`&#245;`	F5	`&otilde;`	Small o, tilde
ö	`&#246;`	F6	`&ouml;`	Small o, dieresis or umlaut mark
÷	`&#247;`	F7		Division sign
ø	`&#248;`	F8	`&oslash;`	Small o, slash
ù	`&#249;`	F9	`&ugrave;`	Small u, grave accent
ú	`&#250;`	FA	`&uacute;`	Small u, acute accent
û	`&#251;`	FB	`&ucirc;`	Small u, circumflex accent
ü	`&#252;`	FC	`&uuml;`	Small u, dieresis or umlaut mark
ý	`&#253;`	FD	`&yacute;`	Small y, acute accent
	`&#254;`	FE	`&thorn;`	Small thorn, Icelandic
ÿ	`&#255;`	FF	`&yuml;`	Small y, dieresis or umlaut mark

E

Colors by Name and Hex Value

by Wes Tatters

Table E.1 contains a list of all the color names recognized by Navigator 2.0. It also includes their corresponding HEX triplet values. To see all these colors correctly, you need to have a 256 color or better video card and the appropriate video drivers installed. Also, depending on the operating system and computer platform you are running, some colors may not appear exactly as you expect.

NOTE

All the color names on the following list are single words or multiple words combined into one long word. All color words used in Navigator 2 and 3 are one word, without spaces or punctuation.

Table E.1. Color values and HEX triplet equivalents.

Color Name	HEX Triplet
ALICE@(UE	#A0CE00
ANTIQUEWHITE	#FAEBD7
AQUA	#00FFFF
AQUAMARINE	#7FFFD4
AZURE	#F0FFFF
BEIGE	#F5F5DC
BISQUE	#FFE4C4
BLACK	#000000
BLANCHEDALMOND	#FFEBCD
BLUE	#0000FF
BLUEVIOLET	#8A2BE2
BROWN	#A52A2A
BURLYWOOD	#DEB887
CADETBLUE	#5F9EA0
CHARTREUSE	#7FFF00
CHOCOLATE	#D2691E
CORAL	#FF7F50
CORNFLOWERBLUE	#6495ED
CORNSILK	#FFF8DC
CRIMSON	#DC143C

Color Name	HEX Triplet
CYAN	#00FFFF
DARKBLUE	#00008B
DARKCYAN	#008B8B
DARKGOLDENROD	#B8860B
DARKGRAY	#A9A9A9
DARKGREEN	#006400
DARKKHAKI	#BDB76B
DARKMAGENTA	#8B008B
DARKOLIVEGREEN	#556B2F
DARKORANGE	#FF8C00
DARKORCHID	#9932CC
DARKRED	#8B0000
DARKSALMON	#E9967A
DARKSEAGREEN	#8FBC8F
DARKSLATEBLUE	#483D8B
DARKSLATEGRAY	#2F4F4F
DARKTURQUOISE	#00CED1
DARKVIOLET	#9400D3
DEEPPINK	#FF1493
DEEPSKYBLUE	#00BFFF
DIMGRAY	#696969
DODGERBLUE	#1E90FF
FIREBRICK	#B22222
FLORALWHITE	#FFFAF0
FORESTGREEN	#228B22
FUCHSIA	#FF00FF
GAINSBORO	#DCDCDC
GHOSTWHITE	#F8F8FF
GOLD	#FFD700
GOLDENROD	#DAA520
GRAY	#808080
GREEN	#008000

continues

Table E.1. continued

Color Name	HEX Triplet
GREENYELLOW	#ADFF2F
HONEYDEW	#F0FFF0
HOTPINK	#FF69B4
INDIANRED	#CD5C5C
INDIGO	#4B0082
IVORY	#FFFFF0
KHAKI	#F0E68C
LAVENDER	#E6E6FA
LAVENDERBLUSH	#FFF0F5
LEMONCHIFFON	#FFFACD
LIGHTBLUE	#ADD8E6
LIGHTCORAL	#F08080
LIGHTCYAN	#E0FFFF
LIGHTGOLDENRODYELLOW	#FAFAD2
LIGHTGREEN	#90EE90
LIGHTGREY	#D3D3D3
LIGHTPINK	#FFB6C1
LIGHTSALMON	#FFA07A
LIGHTSEAGREEN	#20B2AA
LIGHTSKYBLUE	#87CEFA
LIGHTSLATEGRAY	#778899
LIGHTSTEELBLUE	#B0C4DE
LIGHTYELLOW	#FFFFE0
LIME	#00FF00
LIMEGREEN	#32CD32
LINEN	#FAF0E6
MAGENTA	#FF00FF
MAROON	#800000
MEDIUMAQUAMARINE	#66CDAA
MEDIUMBLUE	#0000CD
MEDIUMORCHID	#BA55D3
MEDIUMPURPLE	#9370DB

Color Name	HEX Triplet
MEDIUMSEAGREEN	#3CB371
MEDIUMSLATEBLUE	#7B68EE
MEDIUMSPRINGGREEN	#00FA9A
MEDIUMTURQUOISE	#48D1CC
MEDIUMVIOLETRED	#C71585
MIDNIGHTBLUE	#191970
MINTCREAM	#F5FFFA
MISTYROSE	#FFE4E1
NAVAJOWHITE	#FFDEAD
NAVY	#000080
OLDLACE	#FDF5E6
OLIVE	#808000
OLIVEDRAB	#6B8E23
ORANGE	#FFA500
ORANGERED	#FF4500
ORCHID	#DA70D6
PALEGOLDENROD	#EEE8AA
PALEGREEN	#98FB98
PALETURQUOISE	#AFEEEE
PALEVIOLETRED	#DB7093
PAPAYAWHIP	#FFEFD5
PEACHPUFF	#FFDAB9
PERU	#CD853F
PINK	#FFC0CB
PLUM	#DDA0DD
POWDERBLUE	#B0E0E6
PURPLE	#800080
RED	#FF0000
ROSYBROWN	#BC8F8F
ROYALBLUE	#4169E1
SADDLEBROWN	#8B4513
SALMON	#FA8072

continues

Table E.1. continued

Color Name	HEX Triplet
SANDYBROWN	#F4A460
SEAGREEN	#2E8B57
SEASHELL	#FFF5EE
SIENNA	#A0522D
SILVER	#C0C0C0
SKYBLUE	#87CEEB
SLATEBLUE	#6A5ACD
SLATEGRAY	#708090
SNOW	#FFFAFA
SPRINGGREEN	#00FF7F
STEELBLUE	#4682B4
TAN	#D2B48C
TEAL	#008080
THISTLE	#D8BFD8
TOMATO	#FF6347
TURQUOISE	#40E0D0
VIOLET	#EE82EE
WHEAT	#F5DEB3
WHITE	#FFFFFF
WHITESMOKE	#F5F5F5
YELLOW	#FFFF00
YELLOWGREEN	#9ACD32

Several Web sites provide mechanisms for testing color combinations. These include:

- **Knack Imaging's Webcolor Picker**—http://www.teleport.com/~knack/next/color/index.html.
- **ColorCenter from hIdaho Design**—http://www.hidaho.com/colorcenter/. This color picker also is an excellent example of using JavaScript to create a sophisticated interactive application.
- **Thalia's Guide: The Color Page**—http://www.sci.kun.nl/thalia/guide/color/. Offers color databases and an interactive color picking engine.

■ **Clickable Palette**—`http://www.bga.com/~rlp/dwp/palette/palette.html`. Provides a single image map palette. By clicking on a given color, the user is presented with the RGB hexadecimal triplet for the color.

■ **ColorServe Pro**—`http://www.biola.edu/cgi-bin/colorpro/`. Provides an interactive color picker based on color wheels similar to the color palettes found in many Windows-based graphics applications.

■ **DynaColor**—`http://www.nedesign.com/COLOR/`.

■ **HTML Background Color Selector**—`http://www.imagitek.com/bcs.html`.

■ **Invented Worlds Color Background Browser**—`http://www.enterprise.net/iw/cbrowser.html`.

F

Reference Resources

by Arman Danesh

The following is a list of selected JavaScript reference resources, as well as a few resources on related topics such as plug-ins and Java.

- Netscape's JavaScript Reference Guide: `http://home.netscape.com/eng/mozilla/3.0/handbook/javascript/index.html`.

- Netscape's LiveConnect/Plug-in Developer's Guide: `http://home.netscape.com/eng/mozilla/3.0/handbook/plugins/index.html`.

- Java Home Page—Sun's official Java presence on the Web: `http://www.javasoft.com/`.

- Gamelan—A leading repository of Java applets, which also includes a JavaScript section: `http://www.gamelan.com/`.

- The JavaScript Index—A comprehensive index of JavaScript-related pages, including sites using JavaScript, teaching JavaScript, and offering consulting and development services: `http://www.c2.net/~andreww/javascript/`.

- Introduction to JavaScript by Stefan Koch—An excellent introductory JavaScript tutorial: `http://rummelplatz.uni-mannheim.de/~skoch/js/index.htm`.

- JavaScript Tips and Tricks from *Windows Magazine*: `http://www.winmag.com/web/tips/jscript.htm`.

- Morphic Molecules—A collection of information and mini-tutorials about different aspects of JavaScript: `http://www.txdirect.net/users/everett/`.

- DryRoast JavaScript Index—A collection of links to JavaScript-related pages: `http://dryroast.randomc.com/javascript/`.

- Darren Jefford's Java and JavaScript Page—Includes a tutorial and a source code library: `http://www.geocities.com/SiliconValley/8698/java.html`.

- JavaScript Library—A growing library of JavaScript source code: `http://www.c2.net/~andreww/javascript/lib/`.

- The JavaScript Archive—A small but useful collection of JavaScript source code examples: `http://acwww.bloomu.edu/~mpscho/jsarchive/`.

- LiveSoftware's JavaScript Developer's Group: `news://news.livesoftware.com/livesoftware.javascript.developer`.

- LiveSoftware's JavaScript Examples Group: `news://news.livesoftware.com/livesoftware.javascript.examples`.

- Usenet Group: `comp.lang.javascript`: `news:comp.lang.javascript`.

- JavaScript Talk Mailing List: `http://www.farhorizons.com/jstalk/jstalk.html` (or send an e-mail to `majordomo@listserv.bridge.net` and include "subscribe javascript-talk" in the body of the message).

- JavaScript Mailing List: `http://www.obscure.org/` (or send an e-mail to `majordomo@obscure.org` and include "subscribe javascript" in the body of the message).

G

Navigator Plug-ins

by Arman Danesh

This chapter contains a selected list of Navigator plug-ins offered by a variety of third-party vendors. A more complete list of plug-ins is available from Netscape's home page at `http://home.netscape.com/comprod/mirror/navcomponents_download.html`.

Selected Navigator Plug-ins

AboutPeople

Vendor: Now Software

URL: `http://www.nowsoft.com/plugins/plugin_download.html`

Description: A viewer for address books created with Now Software products

AboutTime

Vendor: Now Software

URL: `http://www.nowsoft.com/plugins/plugin_download.html`

Description: A viewer for calendars created with Now Software products

Acrobat Reader

Vendor: Adobe

URL: `http://www.adobe.com/acrobat/3beta/main.html`

Description: A viewer for Public Document Format (PDF) files

Action

Vendor: Open2u

URL: `http://www.arasmith.com/action/action.html`

Description: A viewer for embedded MPEG videos with synchronized sound

ActiveX

Vendor: Ncompass

URL: `http://www.ncompasslabs.com/binaries/download_plugin_pro.html`

Description: Allows Navigator to use ActiveX controls

Bubbleviewer

Vendor: Omniview

URL: http://www.omniview.com/plugin.htm

Description: A viewer for complete 360 degree images

Carbon Copy/Net

Vendor: Microcom

URL: http://www.microcom.com/cc/ccdnload.htm

Description: Remote control software for the Internet (see Figure G.1)

FIGURE G.1.
With the Carbon Copy/Net plug-in, it's possible to take control of another PC from inside Navigator.

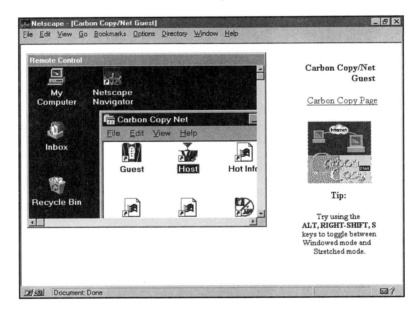

Cineweb

Vendor: Digigami

URL: http://www.digigami.com/PlugIns.html

Description: A viewer for real-time streamed audio and video from standard AVI, MOV, and MPG files

CMX Viewer

Vendor: Corel

URL: http://www.corel.com/corelcmx

Description: A viewer for Corel's vector graphic format (see Figure G.2)

FIGURE G.2.
With the CMX Viewer from Corel, CorelDRAW! vector graphics can be displayed by Navigator.

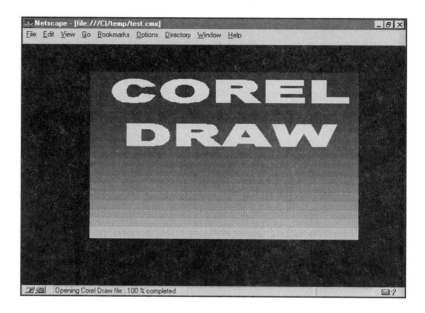

Corel Visual CADD

Vendor: Corel

URL: http://www.corel.com/products/cad/visualCADD/plug-ins.htm

Description: A computer-aided design program designed for the Internet

Cosmo Player

Vendor: Silicon graphics

URL: http://vrml.sgi.com/cosmoplayer

Description: A VRML 2.0 viewer

Crescendo

Vendor: Liveupdate

URL: `http://www.liveupdate.com/midi.html`

Description: A player for stereo MIDI music

Cyberage Raider

Vendor: Cyberage Communications

URL: `http://www.miint.net/cyberage/download.htm`

Description: A sophisticated front end to multiple search engines

EarthTime

Vendor: Starfish Software

URL: `http://www.starfishsoftware.com/getearth.html`

Description: A world clock which displays the time in eight user-selected locations

Echospeech

Vendor: Echo Speech

URL: `http://www.echospeech.com/plugin.htm`

Description: A player of compressed speech

FIGleaf Inline

Vendor: Carberry Technology

URL: `http://www.ct.ebt.com/figinline/download.html`

Description: A viewer for numerous graphics formats including CGM, GIF, JPEG, TIFF, BMP, WMF, and WPS that supports zooming, rotation, and multipage files (see Figure G.3)

Formula One/Net

Vendor: Visual Components

URL: `http://www.visualcomp.com/f1net/download.htm`

Description: An Excel-compatible spreadsheet

FIGURE G.3.

Carberry Technology makes it possible to view and zoom numerous file formats, including TIFF images, using the FIGleaf Inline plug-in.

KEYview

Vendor: FTP Software

URL: http://www.ftp.com/mkt_info/evals/choice.html

Description: A viewer of graphic and non-graphic files including Word, WordPerfect, Excel, PCX, and EPS files that supports cutting, pasting, and conversion between formats

Live3D

Vendor: Netscape

URL: http://home.netscape.com/comprod/products/navigator/live3d/download_live3d.html

Description: A VRML viewer with support for Java-based multi-user VRML applications

MacZilla

Vendor: Knowledge Engineering

URL: http://maczilla.com

Description: A player for QuickTime, MIDI, WAV, AU, AIFF, MPEG, and AVI files

PointCast Network

Vendor: PointCast Incorporated

URL: http://www.pointcast.com

Description: PointCast provides up-to-the-minute news streamed over the Internet

PointPlus

Vendor: Net-Scene

URL: http://www.net-scene.com/down2.htm

Description: A viewer that plays specially prepared PowerPoint files over the Internet

PowerPoint Animation Player & Publisher

Vendor: Microsoft

URL: http://www.microsoft.com/mspowerpoint/internet/player/installing1.htm

Description: A PowerPoint player from Microsoft

Quick View Plus

Vendor: INSO Corporation

URL: http://www.inso.com/consumer/qvp/demo.htm

Description: A viewer for more than 200 word processor, spreadsheet, database, and graphics formats

RealAudio

Vendor: Progressive Networks

URL: http://www.realaudio.com/products/player.html

Description: A player of real-time, on-demand streamed audio

Shockwave for Authorware

Vendor: Macromedia

URL: http://www.macromedia.com/Tools/Shockwave/Plugin/plugin.cgi

Description: A player for Authorware courses

Shockwave for Director

Vendor: Macromedia

URL: `http://www.macromedia.com/shockwave/`

Description: A player for Director presentations

Shockwave for FreeHand

Vendor: Macromedia

URL: `http://www.macromedia.com/Tools/Shockwave/Plugin/plugin.cgi`

Description: A viewer for FreeHand files that enables users to pan and zoom images

ToolVox

Vendor: VoxWare

URL: `http://www.voxware.com/download.htm`

Description: A compressed speech player

Webxpresso

Vendor: Dataviews

URL: `http://www.dvcorp.com/webxpresso/download.html`

Description: Displays 2D and 3D drawings, graphs, and controls (see Figure G.4)

FIGURE G.4.

Webxpresso can display a variety of graphs and charts.

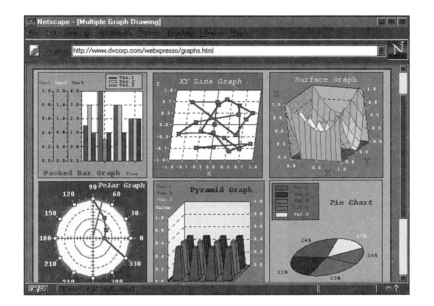

H

Java Applets

by Arman Danesh

This appendix contains a selected list of Java Applets offered by a variety of authors and vendors. A more complete list of Java Applets can be found in the Gamelan index at `http://www.gamelan.com/`.

Selected Navigator Plug-ins

Abacus

Author: Luis Fernandes

URL: `http://www.ee.ryerson.ca:8080/~elf/abacus.html`

Description: An online abacus with a tutorial

FIGURE H.1.
Luis Fernandes' Abacus Applet enables users to learn to use an abacus.

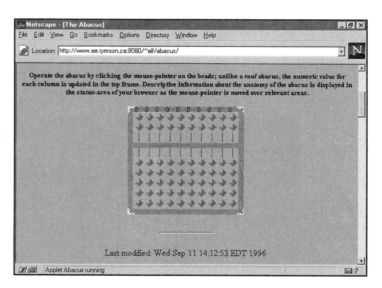

Alien Invasion

Author: Ben Librojo

URL: `http://www.tardis.ed.ac.uk/~benl/invasion/inv_intro.html`

Description: An arcade-style game

Bay Area Rapid Transit Simulation

URL: `http://www-itg.lbl.gov/vbart`

Description: A simulation of San Francisco's subway system

Chernobyl Reactor

Author: Henrik Eriksson

URL: `http://www.ida.liu.se/~her/npp/demo.html`

Description: Simulation of a nuclear power plant that enables the user to control the plant

Curtain

Author: Peter Parnes

URL: `http://www.cdt.luth.se/~peppar/Curtain_java.html`

Description: Opens a curtain to display an image

Electro Magnetic Poetry

Author: Maria Winslow

URL: `http://prominence.com/java/poetry/`

Description: Create poetry by dragging words around on the screen

Equation Renderer

URL: `http://www.geom.umn.edu/~rminer/jmath/`

Description: Displays equations defined in HTML 3

Fireworks

Author: Erik Wistrand

URL: `http://www.ivee.com/~wistrand/fireworks/`

Description: Adds fireworks to a page

FontViewer

Author: Paton Lewis

URL: `http://www.cs.brown.edu/people/pjl/fontviewer.html`

Description: Enables users to view Java fonts and character codes

The Frog Pond

Authors: The SEP Group at Stanford

URL: `http://sepwww.stanford.edu/pub/sep/krl/FrogPond/FrogPond.html`

Description: Simulates the waves generated by a frog jumping in a pond

FIGURE H.2.
Learn about waves with the Frog Pond applet from the SEP Group at Stanford.

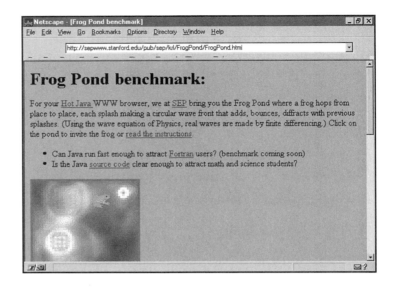

GifSlider

Author: Rich Barrette

URL: `http://www.ohiou.edu/~rbarrett/java/rich/gifslider/`

Description: Slides an image across the page

The Impressionist!

Author: Paul Haeberli

URL: `http://reality.sgi.com/grafica/impression/`

Description: Creates abstract renditions of GIF images

JavaEyes

Author: Mirko Bulaja

URL: `http://student.math.hr/~mbuly/jsrc/ochi.html`

Description: Displays a pair of eyes that follow the mouse pointer as long as it's inside the applet's area

Juggling

Author: Chris Seguin

URL: `http://www.acm.uiuc.edu/webmonkeys/juggling/`

Description: A juggling tutorial

FIGURE H.3.
Learn to juggle with Chris Seguin's juggling applet.

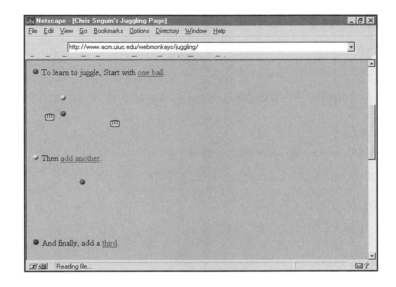

Master Fwap AI: a Conversational Applet

URL: `http://www.himalaya.com/`

Description: Holds conversations with the user about a range of topics, including Buddhism

Orbit Simulator

Author: Kelly Jo Brown

URL: `http://observe.ivv.nasa.gov/observe/exhibit/reference/module/orbits/`
`➥orbit_sim.html`

Description: An interactive satellite orbit simulator

Sideways Stars

Author: Richard Sexton

URL: `http://vvv.com/m2/public_html/m2java.html`

Description: Displays an animated starfield

Slide Projector with Audio

Author: Suresh Srinivasan

URL: `http://www.thomtech.com/~suresh/java/beta/`

Description: A slide projector with audio support

Sun Clock

Author: Mark Tacchi

URL: http://www.europa.com/~mlt/sunclock.html

Description: Shows where the sun is shining on a map in real time

Telnet

URL: http://w3.gwis.com/~thorn/telnet/

Description: A Telnet client with ANSI emulation

Terminal Emulator

URL: http://www.unige.ch/hotjava/HotSIBIL.html

Description: An IBM 3270 Terminal Emulator

A Waving Flag

Author: Zilun Gong

URL: http://java.science.yorku.ca/~zilun/3D/cflag.html

Description: A flying Canadian flag

FIGURE H.4.

The Canadian flag can wave on a Web page using Zilun Gong's Waving flag applet.

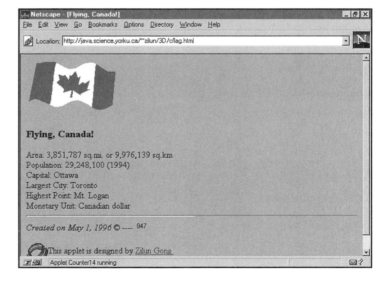

WebDraw Applet

Author: Mark Sherman

URL: `http://www.microsurf.com/WebDraw`

Description: Enables two users on the Net to draw together on a shared page

Weight

Author: Patrick Amato

URL: `http://www.it.hq.nasa.gov/~amato/Work/Java/Amato/Weights/Weight.html`

Description: Users can calculate their weight on other planets

I

On the *JavaScript 1.1 Developer's Guide* CD-ROM, you will find all the sample files that have been presented in this book, as well as a wealth of other applications and utilities.

> **NOTE**
>
> Please refer to the readme.wri file on the CD-ROM (Windows) or the Guide to the CD-ROM (Macintosh) for the latest listing of software.

Windows Software

Java

- Sun's Java Developer's Kit for Windows 95/NT, version 1.0.2
- Sample Java Applets
- Sample JavaScripts
- JFactory Java IDE
- Jpad Java IDE
- JPad Pro Java IDE
- Jamba!
- Javelin
- JDesignerPro 1.0
- Kawa Java IDE
- Studio J++

ActiveX

- Microsoft ActiveX Control Pad and HTML Layout Control

Explorer

- Microsoft Internet Explorer 3.01 for Windows 95 and NT 4

HTML Tools

- Microsoft Internet Assistants for Access, Excel, PowerPoint, Schedule+, and Word
- W3e HTML Editor

- CSE 3310 HTML Validator
- Hot Dog 32-bit HTML editor
- HoTMeTaL HTML editor
- HTMLed HTML editor
- HTML Assistant for Windows
- Spider 1.2
- Web Analyzer
- WebEdit Pro HTML editor
- Web Weaver HTML editor
- ImageGen

Graphics, Video, and Sound Applications

- Goldwave sound editor, player, and recorder
- MapThis imagemap utility
- Paint Shop Pro 3.12 graphics editor and graphic file format converter for Windows
- SnagIt screen capture utility
- ThumbsPlus image viewer and browser

Utilities

- Microsoft Viewers for Excel, PowerPoint, and Word
- Adobe Acrobat viewer
- Microsoft PowerPoint Animation Player & Publisher
- WinZip for Windows NT/95
- WinZip Self-Extractor is a utility program that creates native Windows self-extracting ZIP files

Macintosh Software

Java

- Sun's Java Developer's Kit for Macintosh version 1.0.2
- Sample Applets
- Sample JavaScripts

HTML

- BBEdit 3.5.1 freeware
- BBEdit 4.0 Demo
- HTML edit 1.7
- HTML Editor 1.1.1
- HTML Web Weaver
- HTML Markup 2.0.1
- WebMap 2.0b9
- Web Painter

Graphics

- Graphic Converter 2.4.4
- GIFConverter version 2.3.7

Utilities

- Adobe Acrobat reader
- Fast Player 1.1
- SnagIt Pro 5.13
- SoundApp version 1.5.1
- Sparkle 2.4.5
- ZipIt 1.3.5 for Macintosh

About Shareware

Shareware is not free. Please read all documentation associated with a third-party product (usually contained with files named readme.txt or license.txt) and follow all guidelines.

Index

Teach Yourself JavaScript in a Week, Second Edition

Arman Danesh

Teach Yourself JavaScript in a Week, Second Edition, has been revised and updated for the latest version of JavaScript from Netscape and includes detailed coverage of new features, such as how to work with Java applets with LiveConnect, writing JavaScript for Microsoft's Internet Explorer, and more!

CD-ROM includes full version of Netscape Navigator Gold, additional tools, and ready-to-use sample scripts.

Price: $39.99 USA/$56.95 CDN
ISBN #: 1-57521-195-5   *600 pp.*

JavaScript Unleashed

Richard Wagner, et al.

Programming JavaScript is much simpler than programming for Java, because JavaScript code can be embedded directly into an HTML document. *JavaScript Unleashed* unveils the mysteries of this new code, enabling programmers to exploit its full potential in their Web applications.

Covers Netscape LiveWire server system, Netscape Navigator Gold, and more.

Readers learn to use JavaScript for dynamic Web page creation.

CD-ROM includes source code from the book, sample applications, and third-party utilities.

Price: $49.99 USA/$70.95 CDN
ISBN #: 1-57521-118-1   *900 pp.*

Laura Lemay's Web Workshop: JavaScript

Laura Lemay and Michael Morrison

Readers will explore various aspects of Web publishing, from CGI scripting and interactivity and graphics design to Netscape Gold in greater depth than the *Teach Yourself* books.

CD-ROM includes the complete book in HTML format, publishing tools, templates, graphics, backgrounds, and more.

Provides a clear, hands-on guide to creating sophisticated Web pages.

Price: $39.99 USA/$56.95 CDN
ISBN #: 1-57521-141-6   *400 pp.*

Teach Yourself Java in 21 Days, Professional Reference Edition

Laura Lemay and Charles L. Perkins

Introducing the first, best, and most detailed guide to developing applications with the hot new Java language from Sun Microsystems.

Provides detailed coverage of the hottest new technology on the World Wide Web. Shows readers how to develop applications using the Java language. Includes coverage of browsing Java applications with Netscape and other popular Web browsers.

CD-ROM includes the Java Developer's Kit.

Price: $59.99 USA/$84.95 CDN
ISBN #: 1-57521-183-1   *900 pp.*

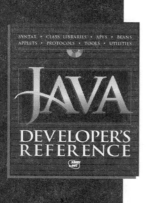

Java Developer's Reference

Mike Cohn, et al.

This is the information- and resource-packed development package for professional developers. It explains the components of the Java Developer's Kit (JDK) and the Java programming language. Everything needed to program Java is included within this comprehensive reference, making it the tool developers will turn to over and over again for timely, accurate information on Java and the JDK.

CD-ROM contains source code from the book and powerful utilities. Includes tips and tricks for getting the most from Java and your Java programs. Contains complete descriptions of all the package classes and their individual methods.

Price: $59.99 USA/$84.95 CDN
ISBN #: 1-57521-129-7   *1,200 pp.*

Teach Yourself ActiveX Programming in 21 Days

Kaufman and Perkins

This 21-day tutorial teaches readers the fundamentals of Microsoft's new Internet technologies, code-named "ActiveX." Coverage includes everything from Active Movie and Active VRML to Active Documents and Network services. After reading this book, programmers will be able to add activity to their applications, Web pages, and documents.

Discusses ActiveX controls that help increase functionality on the Internet. Teaches how to use the controls included with the Internet Control Pack, and how to create new controls. CD-ROM includes the Microsoft ActiveX Developer's Kit and source code from the book.

Price: $39.99 USA/$56.95 CDN
ISBN #: 1-57521-163-7   *800 pp.*

Web Programming with Visual Basic

Craig Eddy and Brad Haasch

This book is a reference that quickly and efficiently shows the experienced developer how to create Web applications using the 32-bit power of Visual Basic 4. It includes an introduction and overview of Web programming, then quickly delves into the specifics, teaching readers how to incorporate animation, sound, and more into their Web applications. CD-ROM contains all the examples from the book, plus additional Visual Basic programs.

Includes coverage of Netscape Navigator and how to create CGI applications with Visual Basic. Discusses spiders, agents, crawlers, and other Internet aids.

Price: $39.99 USA/$56.95 CDN
ISBN #: 1-57521-106-8   *400 pp.*

Teach Yourself VBScript in 21 Days

Keith Brophy and Tim Koets

Readers learn how to use VBScript to create living, interactive Web pages. This unique scripting language from Microsoft is taught with clarity and precision, providing the reader with the best and latest information on this popular language.

CD-ROM contains all the source code from the book and examples of third-party software. Teaches advanced OLE object techniques. Explores VBScript's animation, interaction, and mathematical capabilities.

Price: $39.99 USA/$56.95 CDN
ISBN #: 1-57521-120-3   *720 pp.*

Add to Your Sams.net Library Today
with the Best Books for Internet Technologies

ISBN	Quantity	Description of Item	Unit Cost	Total Cost
1-57521-195-5		Teach Yourself JavaScript in a Week, Second Edition (Book/CD-ROM)	$39.99	
1-57521-118-1		JavaScript Unleashed (Book/CD-ROM)	$49.99	
1-57521-141-6		Laura Lemay's Web Workshop: JavaScript (Book/CD-ROM)	$39.99	
1-57521-183-1		Teach Yourself Java in 21 Days Professional Reference Edition (Book/CD-ROM)	$59.99	
1-57521-129-7		Java Developer's Reference (Book/CD-ROM)	$59.99	
1-57521-163-7		Teach Yourself ActiveX Programming in 21 Days (Book/CD-ROM)	$39.99	
1-57521-106-8		Web Programming with Visual Basic (Book/CD-ROM)	$39.99	
1-57521-102-3		Web Programming with Java (Book/CD-ROM)	$39.99	
		Shipping and Handling: See information below.		
		TOTAL		

Shipping and Handling: $4.00 for the first book, and $1.75 for each additional book. If you need to have it NOW, we can ship product to you in 24 hours for an additional charge of approximately $18.00, and you will receive your item overnight or in two days. Overseas shipping and handling adds $2.00. Prices subject to change. Call between 9:00 a.m. and 5:00 p.m. EST for availability and pricing information on latest editions.

201 W. 103rd Street, Indianapolis, Indiana 46290

1-800-428-5331 — Orders   1-800-835-3202 — FAX   1-800-858-7674 — Customer Service

Book ISBN 1-57521-084-3

Installing the CD-ROM

The companion CD-ROM contains all the source code and project files developed by the authors, plus an assortment of evaluation versions of third-party products. To install, please follow these steps:

Windows 95 / NT 4 Installation Instructions

1. Insert the CD-ROM into your CD-ROM drive.
2. From the Windows 95 / NT 4 desktop, double-click the My Computer icon.
3. Double-click the icon representing your CD-ROM drive.
4. Double-click the setup.exe icon to run the CD-ROM installation program.

Windows 3.1 and NT 3.51 Installation Instructions

1. Insert the CD-ROM into your CD-ROM drive.
2. From File Manager or Program Manager, choose Run from the File menu.
3. Type *drive*\setup and press Enter, where *drive* corresponds to the drive letter of your CD-ROM. For example, if your CD-ROM is drive D:, type D:\SETUP and press Enter.

Follow the on-screen instructions.

NOTE

Windows 3.1 and NT 3.51 users will be unable to access the \WIN95NT4 directory because it was left in its original long filename state with a combination of upper- and lowercases. This was done to enable Windows 95 and Windows NT 4 users direct access to those files on the CD. All other directories were translated in compliance with the Windows 3.1 operating system and may be accessed without trouble. (Attempting to access the \WIN95NT4 directory will cause no harm; you simply will not be able to read the contents.)

Macintosh Installation Instructions

1. Insert the CD-ROM into your CD-ROM drive.
2. When an icon for the CD appears on your desktop, open the disc by double-clicking its icon.
3. Double-click the icon named Guide to the CD-ROM, and follow the directions that are displayed.